UPLIFTING THE RACE

KEVIN K. GAINES

UPLIFTING

THE RACE

BLACK LEADERSHIP,

POLITICS, AND CULTURE

IN THE TWENTIETH CENTURY

(((

THE UNIVERSITY OF NORTH CAROLINA PRESS

CHAPEL HILL AND LONDON

The paper in this book meets the guidelines for permanence
and durability of the Committee on Production Guidelines for
Book Longevity of the Council on Library Resources.

Library of Congress Cataloging-in-Publication Data

Gaines, Kevin Kelly.
Uplifting the race: Black leadership, politics, and culture
in the twentieth century / Kevin K. Gaines.
p.   cm.
Based on the author's thesis (Ph.D.)—Brown University, 1991.
Includes bibliographical references (p.) and index.
ISBN 0-8078-2239-6 (cloth: alk. paper).
—ISBN 0-8078-4543-4 (pbk.: alk. paper)
1. Afro-Americans—Cultural assimilation—History—20th century.
2. Afro-American leadership—History—20th century.
3. Afro-Americans—Politics and government. I. Title.
E185.86.G35   1995
973'.0496073—dc20   95-7956
CIP

00 99 98 97 96   5 4 3 2 1

An earlier version of part of Chapter 7 appeared as "Assimilationist
Minstrelsy as Racial Uplift Ideology: James D. Corrothers's
Literary Quest for Black Leadership," *American Quarterly* 45,
no. 3 (September 1993): 341–69.

For my parents,
Melvin and Marilyn Gaines

CONTENTS

《 《 《

ILLUSTRATIONS

《 《 《

The Intersections of Racial Liberalism

and Racial Uplift Ideology

(((

In the period between his departure from the Nation of Islam in March of 1964 and his assassination on February 21, 1965, Malcolm X broadened the terms of identity and the tactics of struggle for African Americans. "We need to expand the civil-rights struggle to a higher level—to the level of human rights," he argued. Malcolm declared that African Americans should circumvent a federal government reluctant to protect black lives and political rights in the South and bring their grievances to the United Nations as a human rights issue: "Civil rights means your asking Uncle Sam to treat you right. Human rights are something you were born with. Human rights are your God-given rights. . . . And anytime anyone violates your human rights, you can take them to the world court."[1]

Malcolm voiced the growing disenchantment within the black freedom movement with federal reluctance to protect black and white demonstrators against segregationists' state-sanctioned terror. Civil rights legislation did not protect African Americans in the South from such abuses. Nor did these reforms address the poverty and discrimination suffered by blacks in urban ghettoes. Central to Malcolm's critique of civil rights was a changing black consciousness and politics joining struggles for racial and social justice. Malcolm questioned the Cold War liberalism that held sway over the civil rights consensus, with its injunctions that black leadership attend solely to formal equality before the law and remain silent on economic issues and U.S. foreign policy. Reframing black Americans' struggles within the international context of African liberation movements, Malcolm asserted the citizenship and humanity of African Americans as unassailable first principles.

Malcolm's critique is a sobering reminder that the civil rights movement fell short of its promise of racial justice in the courts and might have gone on to address disparities in the distribution of wealth and power. Through the post–civil rights, neoliberal ideology of color blindness, race continues to defer political mobilization against social inequalities. Ironically, as neoliber-als deny the existence of racism, they nonetheless exploit racial anxieties with coded (or visual) racist references to crime, drugs, and welfare in public dis-course. According to Linda Gordon and Nancy Fraser, the trope of welfare dependency has animated attacks on civil rights and the welfare state in the postindustrial United States. And as John Hope Franklin has noted, federal nonenforcement of post-Brown reforms, as seen, for example, in the Reagan administration's removal of the ban on tax exemptions for racially discrimina-tory private schools, belies claims of a color-blind society.[2]

Today we face the paradoxes of persistent racism amidst claims of color blindness. The expansion of the black middle class amidst deepening poverty and social disintegration in black communities is equally unsettling, as many black citizens continue to bear the brunt of joblessness, recession, and inade-quate schools. Nostalgic mass-media narratives of civil rights try to deflect these crises by dwelling on images of a charismatic, messianic leader, invari-ably male, and usually martyred. In the meantime, since the 1980s, conserva-tive black leadership has assisted the federal assault on civil rights reforms, maintaining for some the illusion of color-blind fairness. No wonder that many middle-class African American media spokespersons respond with ap-parent nostalgia for the era of segregation, interring the memory of Mal-colm's critique of civil rights. By this shortsighted racial reckoning, in which black ideals of self-help respond to and reinforce the majority society's hos-tility to federal enforcement of civil rights, integration, antipoverty programs, and the expansion of the black middle class have produced a culture of pov-erty, ending a golden age of supposedly healthy black communities during the era of de jure segregation.

There is a clear relationship between post–civil rights neoliberal claims of a color-blind society and the enlistment by the federal government of black conservatives, aided by the confused responses of mounting black anger and disaffection with civil rights and of nostalgia for segregation and self-help. Documentary media remembrances of the civil rights era recycle the dream of a charismatic leader as if to avoid confrontation with the enduring night-mares of racism, joblessness, and social misery. For many blacks, this master narrative of civil rights signals a sense of malaise, exemplified in the mass-media lament over the disappearance of role models. Such mythologizing re-presses the democratic, anti-imperialist agenda that Malcolm X and Martin Luther King were evolving when they were slain, and which W. E. B. Du Bois and Paul Robeson had pursued until they were branded nonpersons at the height of the repression of civil rights and civil liberties during the Cold War.

This book examines the historical circumstances that have led us to the post–civil rights media spectacle of posthumous black messianic leadership. The search for the origins of racial liberalism, civil rights, the myth of color blindness, and the reactive black messianism that circumscribes black struggle and distorts its history leads us back to the turn of the century. Even the most seemingly principled expressions of liberalism from that period were not immune to racism. In his dissent to *Plessy v. Ferguson*, the 1896 Supreme Court decision that established "separate but equal" as the legal basis for segregation, Justice John Marshall Harlan found the ruling as objectionable and pernicious as the Dred Scott case. At the same time, however, his dissent shared with the majority opinion a fundamental distinction between political and social equality as they pertained to the American racial landscape:

> The white race deems itself to be the dominant race in this country. And so it is in prestige, in achievements, in education, in wealth, and in power. So, I doubt not that it will continue to be for all time, if it remains true to its great heritage and holds fast to the principles of constitutional liberty. But in view of the Constitution, in the eye of the law, there is in this country no superior, dominant, ruling class of citizens. There is no caste here. Our Constitution is color-blind, and neither knows, nor tolerates classes among citizens. In respect of civil rights, all citizens are equal before the law.[3]

While claiming the Constitution as the color-blind, classless guarantor of formal equality before the law, Harlan regarded white dominance as axiomatic and eternal. Without evident irony, he believed that white supremacy would be upheld by "principles of constitutional liberty," a profound, if unintended, indictment of the original intentions of the framers, for whom African slavery was evidently essential to liberty for white men. In both the theory and practice of federalism, civil rights and racial (and social) inequality went hand-in-hand, as southern legislatures would eventually repeal black male suffrage and the provisions of the equal protection clause of the Fourteenth Amendment with race-neutral (i.e., color-blind) amendments to state constitutions. Formal equality was not enough to protect southern blacks from political terror, and under the rubric of states' rights, local courts facilitated the exploitation of black and white agricultural labor. Harlan's dissent, defining equality in form but not substance, affirmed that federalism protected the interests of racists and landowners more than those of impoverished blacks and whites.

Although prompted by an inquiry into the sedimented, and often unconscious, racial assumptions driving much U.S. political discourse, this study concentrates on black elites' responses and challenges to white supremacy since the turn of the century. Since then, how have African American spokespersons answered the widespread charge that people of African descent were noncitizens, less than fully human? A sustained reflection on their contradictory position as both an aspiring social class and a racially subordi-nated caste denied all political rights and protections, struggling to define themselves within a society founded on white dominance, offers a profound understanding of the historical nexus of race, class, national and sectional politics, and black leadership in our society.

The self-help ideology of racial uplift describes the response of educated African Americans, who, according to Alfred Moss, numbered roughly 2 per-cent of the black population in the 1890s, to de jure, or legal, segregation.[4] Against the post-Reconstruction assault on black citizenship and humanity, black ministers, intellectuals, journalists, and reformers sought to refute the view that African Americans were biologically inferior and unassimilable by incorporating "the race" into ostensibly universal but deeply racialized ideo-logical categories of Western progress and civilization. Generally, black elites claimed class distinctions, indeed, the very existence of a "better class" of blacks, as evidence of what they called race progress. Believing that the im-provement of African Americans' material and moral condition through self-help would diminish white racism, they sought to rehabilitate the race's im-age by embodying respectability, enacted through an ethos of service to the masses.

Through racial uplift ideology, elite blacks sought the cooperation of white political and business elites in the pursuit of race progress. Their social vision of blacks within American society was largely determined by those powerful whites who reasserted control over black and white labor by disfranchising blacks and poor whites after the democratic experiment of Reconstruction. In other words, racial uplift ideology cannot be regarded as an independent black perspective. Black middle-class ideology cannot be isolated from domi-nant modes of knowledge and power relations structured by race and racism. While black elites' oppositional claims of self-help may have symbolized their desire for independence and self-determination, this self-image obscured the extent to which self-help also functioned as an accommodation to blacks' noncitizenship status.

Besides the limitations of self-help ideology (as opposed to more practical self-help efforts), black elites' class-bound argument for black humanity was deeply contradictory. The attempt to rehabilitate the image of black people through class distinctions trafficked in claims of racial and gender hierarchy. In light of Malcolm's claim, it is noteworthy that the appeal implicit in racial uplift ideology for the recognition of black elites' capacity for citizenship— indeed, humanity—had overshadowed postemancipation arguments by blacks and whites that posited inalienable rights as the basis for black male citizen-ship, economic rights, equal protection, and group empowerment.

Two interrelated objectives guide this study. The first is to elucidate the contested meanings of uplift among African Americans, and how this contestation informed discussions of rights and the relation between black leadership, consciousness, and political behavior. There was a historical tension between two general connotations of uplift. On the one hand, a broader vision of uplift signifying collective social aspiration, advancement, and struggle had been the legacy of the emancipation era. On the other hand, black elites made uplift the basis for a racialized elite identity claiming Negro improvement through class stratification as race progress, which entailed an attenuated conception of bourgeois qualifications for rights and citizenship. This tension between elite racial and popular social images of uplift within black leadership and culture leads to my second objective, namely, historicizing the concept of race in the United States since the turn of the century. The limitations of black elites' defensive appropriation of dominant racial theories for the purpose of erecting a supposedly positive black identity resulted from their desperate situation. Ultimately, this says more about power, black vulnerability, and the centrality of race in the nation's political and cultural institutions than it does about the motives or complicity of black elites.

Historicizing Race

"Race" is a historical phenomenon. It is not, as commonly assumed, a natural, fixed biological essence, or a physical fact. While late-nineteenth-century social scientists and commentators produced a great deal of writing on race, presuming their expertise, it is important to realize the extent to which forms of knowing besides "right reason"—feelings, fears, desires, and other nonrational processes—have invaded intellectual and cultural expressions regarding race, and ultimately, how these cultural narratives about race reflect power relations.[5]

Historicizing the cultural narratives structured by ideologies of racial difference requires subtler ways of thinking about race. First, we must acknowledge that there were, and are, many degrees and varieties of racial discourse, indeed, of racism. Secondly, the varieties of racism, in word, image, and deed, are shaped and reshaped by historical processes and trends, including industrialization, immigration, internal migrations, urbanization, empire building, and social contestation, particularly in debates over national identity and cultural authority. Finally, the embeddedness of race in these sociohistorical contexts and its material consequences for blacks and whites require us to treat it as more than mere illusion. Indeed, the way we discuss race in the contemporary political climate of "color blindness" is of utmost importance. Such intellectual work should be guided, as Cornel West has argued, by the spirit of "critical negation, wise preservation and insurgent transformation."[6]

Building on the contributions of critical race theory and cultural studies, my analysis of race and racism pays close attention to the production of knowledge about race, and how that knowledge is institutionalized and contested.[7] Ideologies of race promiscuously bundled together intellectual and popular expressions. Moreover, gendered and sexualized meanings lent murderous terror and thus material reality to negrophobic cultural attitudes. Inseparable from issues of reproductive sexuality, the many-headed beast of U.S. racism fed upon an irrational amalgam of fear, desire, and even guilt, despite rhetorical professions of scholarly expertise and rationality. Antiblack racism might well be regarded as a theodicy of whiteness, making permissible and seemingly natural the hatred, oppression, and degradation of black people by any means necessary, however contrary such acts were to the moral and political ideals of the Republic. Regardless of what African Americans did or felt, whites' claims about the category of blackness were reproduced in a variety of media besides the printed page, including such commodified forms and forums as mass-produced illustrations, toys and material objects and ephemera, public performance rituals, and, finally, in the darkness of often-segregated movie houses. Mass-media technologies and industries provided new, more powerful ways of telling the same old stories of black deviance and pathology, confounding claims for a rational basis for the tangled meanings attributed to race. It should be noted, however, that at the same time mass-culture industries provided opportunities for black cultural production, the construction, or reconstruction, of black consciousness, and further struggle and contestation over representations of race.

It should be clear that this approach questions the validity of knowledge about race produced by intellectuals, white and black alike. This is not to say that intellectuals were in any way united in purpose. Nor do I wish to devalue the antiracist words and deeds of black and white intellectuals. Nevertheless, the majority of writers and intellectuals inescapably drew on deeply problematic varieties of knowledge about race. Although there were exceptions, discussions of race and class by blacks and whites, albeit contested, remained separate and unequal, reinforcing racial essentialism. Dominant discourses on race were fraught with a biological determinism that naturalized and upheld existing relations of power and knowledge in regard to political economy, gender, sexuality, citizenship, and American politics and conceptions of nationhood.

The first three chapters sketch the sociopolitical and cultural contexts of racial uplift ideology. Chapter 1 discusses the changing meaning of uplift, amidst the demise of black political power after Reconstruction, from a collective sense of social advancement to an evolutionary racial ideology. Chapter 2 examines some of the humiliations of the Jim Crow social order in the South for African Americans and revolves around an instance of white supremacy at its most lethal—the Atlanta riot of 1906. Chapter 3 explores black elites' deeply conflicted racial visions of uplift, self-help, group consciousness, and political protest, all as reactions to popular minstrelsy and racist social science, amid the changing sociopolitical contexts and crises of labor insurgency, mob violence, urban migration, disfranchisement, and U.S. imperialism.

The first three chapters, which sketch the social origins, problems, and concerns of racial uplift ideology, lay the groundwork for the several biographical chapters that follow. These chapters, 4 through 9, are both chronological and thematic in design, charting the emergence of an increasingly dominant academic sociological discourse of uplift in response to black migration, a trend opposed by the post–World War I development of radical anticolonial and black nationalist critiques of black elites' traditional support of Republican politics. The biographical chapters show their ambivalent subjects struggling to reconcile racial uplift ideology's ideals with changing social realities, the end result all too often being their personal and political disillusionment. The major themes addressed, all interrelated, are black nationalism, gender tensions, and the intersections of black and mainstream racial discourses. These themes give rise to the central problem racial uplift ideology addressed: black elites' quest for the authentic, or "positive," black middle-class subject. These biographical chapters survey the writings of representative figures, not to rehearse simplistic messianic, or dichotomous, constructions of black leadership (e.g., accommodation vs. resistance), but to document the ideological and social diversity of the black intelligentsia, and the conflicts inherent in its members' assimilationist visions of black respectability and leadership. Some of these writers, including W. E. B. Du Bois, Paul Laurence Dunbar, and Anna Julia Cooper, are familiar; others, such as William Ferris, James Corrothers, and Hubert H. Harrison, more obscure. The writings and activities of this group of intellectuals and race leaders, representative, yet marginal by definition, reflect the various genres in which black middle-class discourse was formulated and contested, including autobiography, fiction, essays, journalism, and sociological writing. Above all, they illustrate the complexity and contingency of black middle-class subjectivities, complicating the quest for a stable, unitary vision of respectability and race progress.

Chapters 4 and 9 illustrate the intersections of black nationalism with racial uplift ideology. Although usually understood as a political discourse, black nationalism, like dominant Anglo-American nationalism, was intensely concerned with gender issues and illustrates the affinity between black and white anxieties surrounding racial purity, intermarriage, paternity, and the reproductive sexuality of black and white women. During the period covered by this study, black nationalism, like uplift, was a contested concept. While some black nationalists based their sense of cultural authority on ethno-centric conceptions of an African continent in need of redemption, or on biological fictions of race purity, for others, such as Hubert H. Harrison, an anti-imperialist pan-African consciousness opposed affinities with racial-ized thought, or with what he otherwise identified as an oppressive white civilization.

In considering the question of black nationalism at the turn of the century, we should not be driven by presentist assumptions, nor by the expectation that there exists a normative black nationalism to be apprehended historically as a usable past. Then, as today, "black nationalists" reflected on the meaning of African Americans' relation to peoples of African descent in the diaspora and on the African continent, past and present. American-born black nation-alist intellectuals' visions of the African past often expressed contemporary yearnings. Diaspora visions of blackness at the turn of the century contended with black nationalist preoccupations with the vexed question of gender rela-tions. For example, the concept of Africa (as opposed to a more direct knowl-edge of the continent's cultural diversity) was commonly invoked as a symbol of the normative patriarchal gender relations associated with race progress. The quest for the race's supposed authentic origins in Africa thus came at the expense of black women intellectuals' claims to equal status, although the pressures of patriarchal U.S. political culture also had much to do with the situation. Such leading black women intellectuals as Anna Julia Cooper and Ida B. Wells found themselves marginalized within black bourgeois and na-tionalist ideologies that equated race progress with male dominance and Victorian ideals of sexual difference in both political and domestic life. Barraged with sexual and racial stereotypes, black women, like black elites in general, campaigned for moral authority, and for a position of respectability from which to speak publicly.

Chapter 7 concerns the writings of Paul Laurence Dunbar and James Corrothers, and literary production and mass culture as sites at which the struggle for the representative black middle-class subject was further waged. This was a complex modern moment of collision between cultures, literary and vernacular, and between those of African Americans and nonblack immi-grants, resulting from the urbanization of black culture and the nation. The moment also saw the rise of mass cultural industries based on blackness as a contested commodity, and the search by some black writers for distinctive black expression against the popular stereotypes and racial formulas white au-diences had come to expect. On the one hand, African American writers and artists who stood for uplift and respectability employed an assimilationist cul-tural aesthetic, hoping to refine Negro folk materials into a universalistic ex-pression of high culture. On the other hand, those black writers less beholden to "positive" images and racial vindication played with white stereotypes of "authentic" blackness, manipulating minstrelsy, Negro folklore and dialect, and black vernacular forms in search of new forms of black cultural expression, including Negro humor.

Such subversive literary appropriations of black vernacular humor were risky, given that for many middle-class blacks, the political necessity of defending the race was no laughing matter. Chapter 6 concerns a more characteristically earnest expression of the black intelligentsia: the links between racial uplift ideology and academic and journalistic sociological writing on urban blacks. Ambivalence, marked by the tension between racialized and social, environmentalist perspectives, describes Du Bois's sociological tour de force, *The Philadelphia Negro*. Although Du Bois's pathbreaking study documented the discrimination faced by blacks in Philadelphia, it also flirted with dominant racial visions of urban pathology that viewed the presence of poor blacks in the city, and particularly that of single black women, as a moral peril.

Normative assumptions about elite blacks and racial uplift were shackled, so to speak, to the sociological images of urban pathology and, ultimately, to the racist constructions of blackness that uplift ideology purported to transcend. Racial uplift ideology answered, without dispelling, the negrophobic minstrel images and journalistic claims asserting ineradicable black difference, immorality, disease, and mortality. Consciously or not, these racial assumptions influenced Du Bois's and subsequent sociologists and journalists in their propensity to view segregated, impoverished urban blacks through the distorted ideological lens of family disorganization. Racialized sociological claims of pathology were essential to claims for the existence of respectable blacks, those proverbial credits to the race, exceptions to the rule.

Reflecting their precarious social position, as well as internal divisions across lines of class, color, culture, region, and gender, African American elites disagreed amongst themselves on a number of issues, despite white elites' penchant for viewing Booker T. Washington as the Moses of his people and the guarantor of interracial consensus. The racial crisis at the turn of the century saw perpetual arguments over the meaning of education for blacks, over the advisability of participation in imperialist and foreign wars, and over questions of citizenship rights, gender relations, and the meaning of black culture. Black intellectuals presented within the apparent unity of uplift ideology—for who was opposed to the advancement of the race?—a diversity of views that belied such social fictions as a monolithic, messianic black leadership, even as elite blacks themselves sought recognition from influential whites in those very terms.

Given that racial uplift ideology constituted a complicated, contested appropriation of dominant racial discourses, some readers will no doubt wonder what precisely is the difference between black middle-class ideology and that of Anglo-American elites. To be sure, I will argue that there were similarities, the crucial one being that both black and white elites spoke the same dominant language of race in defining their middle-class status. At the same time, obviously, there were crucial divergences. The unequal social positions and thus disparate experiences of blacks and whites made all the difference. To fully comprehend this, we must examine not only black intellectuals' struggles to define themselves against the dominant society's refusal to recognize their humanity. Beyond this, we must also consider the psychosocial perceptions of those who defined themselves as white, as well as the extent to which political institutions and the public sphere, including department stores, businesses, public accommodations, labor unions, and the courts, to name just a few sites, reinforced whiteness as a preferred status by excluding blacks. Because of its preferential status, whiteness meant that its subscribers would never in their right minds want to live their lives as African Americans. Small wonder that those African Americans able to "pass" for white would claim for themselves the opportunities and freedoms denied to the race, sparking anxiety in many whites, and in some African Americans as well. The bottom line was that black elites, like all black people, were demonized and terrorized by white supremacists of all social strata, and were especially vulnerable to attack when claiming full equality. However much black elites sought interracial cooperation and searched for an ideological common ground with whites, the violence of the era, as commonplace as it was explosive, exposed the limits of black accommodation. Under these circumstances, it would be profoundly erroneous to equate a racialized black middle-class ideology with an antiblack white racism that, far from being aberrant or extreme, existed at the center of American politics and culture.

Thus, to consider historically what it has meant to be black in America is ultimately to pose a different, yet related, question: What has it meant to be white?[8] Furthermore, if all this talk about a color-blind society were really true, how would this alter our way of conceptualizing rights, citizenship, justice, and democracy? In a society rigidly stratified by interlocking systems of race and class dominance during the late nineteenth century, and undergoing unsettling changes of industrialization, immigration, and urbanization, progressive reformers sought social control by defining citizenship as a bourgeois privilege. In accordance with class-bound restrictions on suffrage, race, gender, and empire were becoming the ideological ingredients of bourgeois status; to be middle class was to claim a normative, often unenunciated whiteness, synonymous with bourgeois morality.

A central concern throughout will be the ambiguous intersection between racist and antiracist discourses, even as they exist in apparent opposition to one another, each echoing and reinforcing the other, particularly on biological notions of race, gender, and sexuality. In the introduction, I will discuss the social and psychic barriers to a secure middle-class status for African Americans at the turn of the century. The bitter contradiction between lofty personal ambitions and uplift ideals and the suffocating realities facing black elites made racial uplift ideology a faulty construction that offered little protection during a difficult period.

A NOTE ON USAGE

❨ ❨ ❨

The reader will note that the terms "black," "African American," and "Afro-American" are used interchangeably in this study. Although I have used "African American" a great deal, there are places in which I chose not to use the designation precisely because the usage seems anachronistic and inappropriate when applied to certain figures whose relationship with Africa was ambivalent at best. I have rejected the outmoded terms "Negro" and "colored" to refer to black Americans, but I continue to alternate among "African American," "black," and "Afro-American" partly because I wish to preserve a contextual option for using all three terms. After all, anyone who remembers the decisive and seemingly permanent historical shift from "Negro" to "black" around 1966 will doubtless hold a measure of skepticism toward recent claims that there is a single, normative usage. I have chosen not to capitalize "black" because I prefer not to reify color as a basis for group identity, the logic of which would also seem to require that I capitalize "white." Thus, for quite personal reasons, among them the realization that it is far easier to agree on incorrect designations for group identity than on a single "correct" one, throughout the book I will alternate primarily between "African American" and "black."

ACKNOWLEDGMENTS

❨ ❨ ❨

It is a pleasure to acknowledge my debt to the many friends, faculty, colleagues, archivists, students, and staff who helped me in writing this book. Elizabeth Coogan and the staff in the interlibrary loan section at the John D. Rockefeller Library at Brown University could not have been more helpful. The same can be said of Esmé Bhan, the archivist at the Moorland-Spingarn Research Center at Howard University. I am also indebted to the staff of the Schomburg Center for the Study of Black Culture at the New York Public Library. The book could not have been done without the support of the Dorothy Danforth Compton Foundation and Dean Bernard Bruce of Brown University. As a visiting scholar at Yale University, I spent a most productive semester working my way through the James Weldon Johnson Collection at the Beineke Rare Book Library, and I thank the staff there for its cheerful efficiency. Princeton's University Committee on Research in the Humanities and Social Sciences was most generous in providing funds for additional research and travel during the revision of the manuscript. The completion of the book was greatly assisted by the resources provided by the Christian Gauss Memorial Preceptorship at Princeton.

Over the years I have received assistance, support, and friendship from Sisa Sternback-Scott, Sybil Mazor, Ibrahima Camara, Abdoul Doumbia, Harry McKinley Williams, Roseanne Camacho, Barbara Walzer, Dan McKee, Gail Bederman, Robin D. G. Kelley, Suzanne Kolm, Ray Rickman, Richard Newman, Tricia Rose, Todd Gernes, Linda Grasso, Bob McMichael, Nancy Rosenblum, Jessica Shubow, Lyde Cullen-Sizer, Mari Jo Buhle, Paul Buhle, Bruce Rosenberg, David Bullwinkle, Chaela Pastore, Amanda Lewis, Beth Parkhurst, Lauri Umansky and Nan Boyd. Matt Jacobson and Oscar Campomanes provided stimulating company and conversation while carpooling between Providence and New Haven.

Among the many colleagues and friends whose fellowship and conversation enriched my work and helped make Princeton a more livable place, I wish to thank Jeremy Adelman, Steven Aron, James Belk, Nicholas Bromell, Miguel Centeno, Laura Doyle, Natalie Davis, Steven Feierman, Signithia Fordham, Don Gibson, Eddie Glaude, Amy Green, Sherrill Cohen, Arcadio Diaz-Quiñones, Barbara Gershon, Michele Lamont, Paul DiMaggio, Gary

Gerstle, Judith Herrin, Loreé Jones, Felicia Kornbluh, Sheldon Garon, Susan Kent, Charles Ponce de Leon, Eric Lowery, Jennifer Delton, Michael Jímenez, Walter Johnson, Bill Jordan, James McPherson, Kenneth Mills, Eric Mumford, John Murrin, Steve Kotkin, Jerald Podair, Arno Mayer, Karen Merrill, Philip Nord, Deborah Nord, Gayle Pemberton, Pamela Groves, Dr. Gerald Groves, Mona Zaki, Laura Engelstein, Elizabeth Lunbeck, Gyan Prakash, Dean Robinson, Joan Wallach Scott, Robert Shell, Howard Taylor, Richard Sobel, Marla Stone, Laura DeLuca, Robert and Marian Tignor, Becky Thompson, Devora Tulcensky, Judith Jackson-Fossett, Jack Washington, Patricia Schechter, and Deborah Gray White.

Hazel Carby, Thadious Davis, Robin Kilson, Evelyn Brooks Higginbotham, Amy Kaplan, Donald Pease, Gary Kulik, Nancy Robertson, and David Scobey all provided most helpful readings of parts of my work. James Siegal, Paul Kramer, Joe Cattolico, Eddie Olivera, Michay Brown, Janine Pisani, Maureen Witt, and Nsenga Lee did invaluable research. More than once, Ruth Simmons exercised a much needed calming influence with her sage advice and guidance. Dan Rodgers was both a generous critic and a wise mentor. Arnold Rampersad offered support and encouragement from the project's inception. I am grateful to have had the benefit of readings of all or part of the manuscript from Penny Von Eschen, Wahneema Lubiano, Paula Giddings, Dirk Hartog, Christine Stansell, Sean Wilentz, Cornel West, Toni Morrison, Gwen Bergner, Nichole Rustin, Colin Palmer, and Cheryl Hicks. I am especially privileged to have had the benefit of Nell Irvin Painter's warm friendship, and I thank her for her meticulous reading of the manuscript.

Charles Nichols, Stuart Clarke, William McLoughlin, and Ann duCille all provided indispensable criticism when it was most needed. Anani Dzidzienyo encouraged me to bring a broader, pan-African perspective to my project, a suggestion I hope to truly make good on in my next book. Early on, James Patterson encouraged me to situate racial uplift ideology within the context of U.S. progressive reform movements. It is difficult to imagine this book existing without the guidance and support of Wilson Moses and his inexhaustible willingness to discuss and share ideas. Although I scarcely realized it at the time, the idea for the book emerged in large part from a conversation of ours, in which he called attention to the theme of uplift in black thought and culture.

The most heartfelt thanks are due to family and loved ones. My grandfather, Rev. Ernest W. Stevens, shared with me his recollections from the early twentieth century spanning rural Florida to the east side of Cleveland. My parents, Marilyn and Melvin Gaines, to whom this book is dedicated, provided the love and encouragement necessary to imagine the completion of such a project in the middle of those inevitable dark nights of the soul, and I thank my father for offering nothing but kind words for some very rough early drafts. I am grateful to my brother, Skip, and his wonderful family, not only for their unfailing support but also for being the most persistent in demanding that I get this book out. Finally, my most profound gratitude is reserved for my companion and colleague Louise Newman, who contributed to this work in more ways than I can enumerate, as a patient reader, generous critic, and expert editor of countless drafts, and as a constant source of love, inspiration, and encouragement.

UPLIFTING THE RACE

INTRODUCTION

Uplift, Dissemblance, Double-Consciousness,

and the Ideological Dimensions of Class

It is a peculiar sensation, this double-consciousness, this sense of always looking at one's self through the eyes of others, of measuring one's soul by the tape of a world that looks on in amused contempt and pity.

W. E. B. DU BOIS, THE SOULS OF BLACK FOLK

I had learned my Jim Crow lessons so thoroughly that . . . I learned to lie, steal, to dissemble. I learned to play that dual role which every Negro must play if he wants to eat and live.

RICHARD WRIGHT, "THE ETHICS OF LIVING JIM CROW:
AN AUTOBIOGRAPHICAL SKETCH"

I remember the sickening thrill with which I heard a . . . black boy arraign the mulatto teachers for always giving the choice parts in plays, the choice chores, the cleanest books to mulatto children. He called the teachers "color struck," a phrase that was new to me, and "sons-of-bitches," a phrase that was not. He was put out of school. Many black children were put out of school, or not encouraged to continue.

J. SAUNDERS REDDING, NO DAY OF TRIUMPH

❨ ❨ ❨

Since the late nineteenth century, and throughout the era of segregation, the term "uplift" has held mixed meanings for African Americans. One popular understanding of uplift, dating from the antislavery folk religion of the slaves, speaks of a personal or collective spiritual—and potentially social—transcendence of worldly oppression and misery. Describing a group struggle for freedom and social advancement, uplift also suggests that African Americans have, with an almost religious fervor, regarded education as the key to liberation. This sense of uplift as a liberation theology flourished after emancipation and during the democratic reforms of Reconstruction. Ideals of group advancement would be kept alive by generations of blacks in the singing of "Lift Every Voice and Sing," its lyrics written by James Weldon Johnson at the turn of the century. Sung by school assemblies and church congregations since the days when black communities celebrated each new year as the anniversary of emancipation, the optimism of this secular hymn (widely considered the Negro national anthem) was rooted in the memory of past horrors: "Sing a song full of the faith that the dark past has taught us / Sing a song full of the hope that the present has brought us."

Another, quite different connotation of uplift, strongly associated in the minds of many African Americans with the legacy of group struggle, is difficult to isolate. Reflecting both their desire for social mobility and the economic and racial barriers to it, African Americans have described themselves since the post-Reconstruction era as middle class through their ideals of racial uplift, espousing a vision of racial solidarity uniting black elites with the masses. For many black elites, uplift came to mean an emphasis on self-help, racial solidarity, temperance, thrift, chastity, social purity, patriarchal authority, and the accumulation of wealth. Its unifying claims aside, this emphasis on class differentiation as race progress often involved struggling with the culturally dominant construction of "the Negro problem." Amidst legal and extralegal repression, many black elites sought status, moral authority, and recognition of their humanity by distinguishing themselves, as bourgeois agents of civilization, from the presumably undeveloped black majority; hence the phrase, so purposeful and earnest, yet so often of ambiguous significance, "uplifting the race."

Contestation surrounds the idea of uplift, which embraces elite and popular meanings and encompasses the tension between narrow, racial claims of progress and more democratic visions of social advancement. In another sense, uplift, as African Americans of all social positions have known it, marks the point where history falls silent and memory takes over. Collective memory recognizes the service of countless parents, teachers, ministers, musicians, and librarians as community builders. Although amateur historians have recorded such efforts at the transmission of group consciousness and history, historians have generally framed black thought and leadership narrowly, stressing the opposition between self-help and civil rights agitation, as embodied by Booker T. Washington and W. E. B. Du Bois, respectively. Civil rights liberalism remains the focus of such dichotomous—and masculinist— constructions of black leadership, to the exclusion of more democratic conceptions of uplift.

Popular meanings of uplift, rooted in public education, economic rights, group resistance and struggle, and democracy tend to be absent in those records in which black elites espoused bourgeois values of race progress in several settings: in the pulpit, at academic "Negro" conferences held at black colleges such as Atlanta University and Hampton Institute, at annual meetings of the Negro Business League, and at the meetings of black clubwomen. Didactic expressions of racial uplift ideals were on display as well in a spate of entrepreneurial books, and in black newspapers and periodicals. Although the racial uplift ideology of the black intelligentsia involved intensive soul-searching, ambivalence, and dissension on the objectives of black leadership and on the meaning of black progress, black opinion leaders deemed the promotion of bourgeois morality, patriarchal authority, and a culture of self-improvement, both among blacks and outward, to the white world, as necessary to their recognition, enfranchisement, and survival as a class.

Although blacks believed they were opposing racism by emphasizing class differences, uplift ideology had as much to do with race as class. African Americans' middle-class ideology, like the majority society's ideals of social mobility, remained trapped within that which it has denied, or tried to forget: that historically, the conditions for social mobility and class formation among all Americans, blacks, immigrant groups, and other racially marked groups, including whites, have been circumscribed by race and color, and implicated within the legacy of slavery, segregation, and white supremacy. Elite African Americans were replicating, even as they contested, the uniquely American racial fictions upon which liberal conceptions of social reality and "equality" were founded.

It is crucial to realize that uplift ideology was not simply a matter of educated African Americans' wanting to be white, as E. Franklin Frazier's polemic attacking a materialistic, status-addicted black bourgeoisie suggested.[1] On the contrary, uplift, among its other connotations, also represented the struggle for a positive black identity in a deeply racist society, turning the pejorative designation of race into a source of dignity and self-affirmation through an ideology of class differentiation, self-help, and interdependence. What was problematic about this was not African Americans' quite understandable desire for dignity, security, and social mobility. Rather, the difficulty stemmed from the construction of class differences through racial and cultural hierarchies that had little to do with the material conditions of African Americans, and less to do with the discrimination they faced in a racially stratified southern labor market, with the active complicity of the state and opinion-making apparatuses of civil society.

Racial uplift ideals were offered as a form of cultural politics, in the hope that unsympathetic whites would relent and recognize the humanity of middle-class African Americans, and their potential for the citizenship rights black men had possessed during Reconstruction. Elite blacks believed they were replacing the racist notion of fixed biological racial differences with an evolutionary view of cultural assimilation, measured primarily by the status of the

family and civilization. Cultural differences, then, rather than biological notions of racial inferiority, were said to be more salient in explaining the lower
social status of African Americans. And a middle-class consciousness stressing
racial solidarity and self-help, uniting blacks across class lines, promised a
more legitimate basis for social differentiation than color.

But uplift ideology's argument for black humanity was not an argument for
equality. Indeed, the shift from race to culture, stressing self-help and seemingly progressive in its contention that blacks, like immigrants, were assimil-
able into the American body politic, represented a limited, conditional claim
to equality, citizenship, and human rights for African Americans. Black elites
espoused a value system of bourgeois morality whose deeply embedded assumptions of racial difference were often invisible to them. It was precisely as
an argument for black humanity through evolutionary class differentiation
that the black intelligentsia replicated the dehumanizing logic of racism. Still,
however problematic, the bourgeois cultural values that came to stand for intraracial class differences—social purity, thrift, chastity, and the patriarchal
family—affirmed their sense of status and entitlement to citizenship.

Racism and its demeaning logic have made the articulation of a positive
racial identity for African Americans a divisive struggle whose contradictions
often went unnoticed in favor of the unifying, uplifting rhetoric of self-help
and solidarity. Reflecting the clash between blacks' communal quest for social
justice and individualistic imperatives of survival, uplift ideology was forged
in the fire of U.S. racism, emerging through peonage, disfranchisement, Jim
Crow, the terrorism of lynching and rape, and the ubiquitous contempt for
persons of African ancestry. Although uplift ideology was by no means incompatible with social protest against racism, its orientation toward self-help
implicitly faulted African Americans for their lowly status, echoing judgmental dominant characterizations of "the Negro problem."

Rooted in inequality, uplift ideology struggled to contain tensions and contradictions. It was comprised of several currents, reflecting popular and elite
tensions: black folk religion and group aspirations for emancipation, land-
ownership, literacy, legal marriage, equal rights, federal protection, and the
suffrage contended with an elite, missionary culture of Christian evolutionism, whose rhetoric gained authority in the context of U.S. imperialism.
There were other strains as well; the nationalist theories of Alexander Crummell, Martin Delany, and others equated black progress and humanity with
territorial nation building, civilization, and patriarchal authority. Not surprisingly, there were gender tensions. During the early 1890s, black women
journalists, intellectuals, novelists, and reformers were contributing their
own visions of racial uplift, calling for women's leadership as vital to race
progress, a view that clashed with a male-dominated vision of race progress
within a patriarchal political culture. Thus, while the African American intel-

ligentsia spoke universally of the race's advancement, there was vigorous disagreement on precisely how this was to be achieved. There were bitter debates among African American elites over issues of education, citizenship, equal rights, gender relations, and cultural identity.

Dissemblance, the Romance of Family, and Internalized Racism

The historian Darlene Clark Hine, referring specifically to the social vulnerability and powerlessness of black women, has described their "culture of dissemblance," which "involved creating the appearance of disclosure, or openness about themselves and their feelings, while actually remaining an enigma to whites." This tactic, she argues, enabled their survival within a suffocatingly oppressive situation. Powerlessness required black women and men to know, and indeed master, their white employers, if they possibly could. Dissemblance, however, describes more than a guarded demeanor. It must also be understood as part of the majority American culture's silence, evasion, or outright distortion on matters of race. In short, African American men and women dissemble to survive in a racialized world not of their own making.

More positively, dissemblance might be seen as a weapon, indeed, a source of strength for African Americans. It may well be viewed as the psychic armor enabling the survival of the powerless. But this self-protective withholding of one's true feelings from more powerful others might also work too well, sundering African Americans from a history of group oppression and struggle. One may survive, even prosper, while leaving oneself vulnerable to any number of self-lacerating racial falsifications. In short, desperation, ambition, and the imperatives of survival might produce an ostensibly positive black identity in simplistic, reductive terms that replicate the racist and sexist cultural codes of the oppressive society.[2]

Dissemblance describes African Americans' defensive response to the gendered dimension of racial oppression. Oppression kept African Americans from fulfilling the majority society's normative gender conventions, and racist discourses portrayed society's denial of the authoritative moral status of the patriarchal family as a racial stigma, a lack of morality, and thus, a badge of inferiority. For educated blacks, the family, and patriarchal gender relations, became crucial signifiers of respectability. Bitter, divisive memories of the violence and humiliations of slavery and segregation were and remain at the heart of uplift ideology's romance of the patriarchal family, expressed by black men and women's too-often-frustrated aspirations to protect and be protected. Claiming respectability often meant denouncing nonconformity to patriarchal gender conventions and bourgeois morality. A sense of shame might also compel silences or revisions, producing a secretive family lore on any number of sensitive matters of parentage, disease, transgressive sexuality, or other behaviors or occurrences to which a real or imagined racial stigma might be attached.

The problem with *racial* uplift ideology is thus one of unconscious internalized racism. The racist and antiracist preoccupation with the status of the patriarchal family among blacks and the notion of self-help among blacks as building black homes and promoting family stability came to displace a broader vision of uplift as group struggle for citizenship and material advancement. At worst, this misplaced equation of race progress with the status of the family blamed black men and women for "failing" to measure up to the dominant society's bourgeois gender morality, and seemed to forget that it was the state and the constant threat of violence, not some innate racial trait, that prevented the realization of black homes and families. Racial uplift ideology's gender politics led African American elites to mistake the effects of oppression for causes, influencing theories of oppression and liberation that, echoing racist social science arguments, frequently faulted blacks for supposed weaknesses branded into the race's moral fiber by slavery.

The displacement from societal oppression to the moral, behavioral realm of the family was not the only outcome of dissemblance. From yet another angle, dissemblance might be viewed as part of an open, ongoing struggle for autonomous self-consciousness, and a black identity less susceptible to racist untruths. The violence and other crises calling out for protest ruptured patterns of dissemblance that kept one's deepest feelings, including rage, hidden away. For example, the increased racial violence in the South during the Spanish-Cuban-American War was met with outraged protests by black spokespersons, journalists, and soldiers. Nevertheless, the concept of dissemblance, along with the self-censorship mandated by a repressive social order in the South (and North) that was intolerant of freedom of thought and expression, raises troubling questions about the very "truth" or intentionality of much of black middle-class uplift ideology. Given the threat of force, elite blacks' accommodations to segregation and violence made a virtue of self-preservation. For many educated black men and women, uplift ideology often meant repressing anger toward whites, their struggles to make themselves and the race acceptable potentially leaving a psychic residue of self-doubt and shame. An elite self-image that might overcome powerlessness and racial stigmas perhaps required the displacement of feelings of anger and shame onto other powerless blacks, or perhaps rival elites, even in the name of racial uplift.

The romance of the family exerted, and continues to exert, an enormously powerful, yet ambiguous, role in crystallizing black aspirations for freedom and security, serving as a smoke screen for oppressive sociocultural forces. Despite elite or rising African Americans' tendency to regard theirs as a natural familial relationship to the group in terms of support and interdependence, one cannot help but detect a half-concealed alienation in this desire to represent "the race" as a family. Occasionally, critical reflections on what it means to describe one's self as a member of the black middle class address the grim internal dynamics of oppression, often unspoken, underlying that self-image.

The African American essayist and literary critic J. Saunders Redding reflected on the injuries of race, color, sex, and class repressed by the unifying rhetoric of uplift. In his autobiography, published in 1942, Redding recalled his youth in Wilmington, Delaware, and the impact of black migration after World War I. He described an oratorical contest before a full school assembly of parents in which he competed with a dark youth, one Tom Cephus, impressive of voice and self-possession. Intimidated, Redding, "from sheer fright and nervous exhaustion burst into uncontrollable tears," but still managed to finish his oration. "I was certain that I had lost." Cephus, for his part, was "superb." He was the clear favorite of the audience, which Redding described as "row after increasingly dark row of black faces and beaming eyes." More than a school contest to them, "it was a class and caste struggle." After the audience's "deafening and vindicative" applause, one of the judges "icily" announced Redding the winner, with Cephus taking second. "Stunned beyond expression and feeling, the back rows filed out." The front rows, filled with light-complexioned families partial to Redding, cheered. A disconsolate Redding could not face Cephus and avoided school for a week. The incident was even more disastrous for Cephus, who, later that year, dropped out of school.[3]

Redding's memory of his high school years was a confession, indeed, exorcism, of his complicity with internalized racism among blacks. For young women, such color prejudices were compounded by sexist stereotypes. Redding, who claimed to be "only lightly color-struck," recalled, as a high school senior, being warned by Edwina Kruse, the "near white" school principal, to end his friendship with Viny, a dark youth who worked as a servant girl to Kruse. Kruse did not mince words. "'Let her alone! . . . [W]hat would you look like married to a girl like that?' she said bitingly. 'No friends, no future. You might as well be dead!'" As Redding recalled their conversation, Kruse predicted a dire future for Redding, delivering ice or cleaning outdoor privies. "Don't you know girls like her haven't any shame, haven't any decency? She'll get you in trouble." According to Redding, after Viny quit and moved away, he received letters from her once a year. Haunted by the question of what became of "those I came to know in 1919," Redding reported that many, including Cephus, were dead.

At Brown University during the 1920s, Redding shared little with the only other black student except a preoccupation with the gaze of unsympathetic whites and a strenuous avoidance of the appearance of clannishness: "We never ate together." This fellow student left school, unable to abide such isolation, and further distressed, as Redding told it, at the prospect of having impregnated a young black woman, also a student, from Philadelphia. While the fate of the young woman remained obscure, as for his black classmate, "I never saw him again," Redding recalled, "for in the late spring he killed himself in the bathroom of his parents' home in Cleveland." According to Redding, this was the first of five suicides in their circle of fifteen black New England collegians.[4]

Redding's candor amounts to a sort of black middle-class survivor's guilt, disclosing the alienation of black pioneers within elite white social settings, anxieties over bourgeois sexual mores that doubtless weighed more heavily on already stigmatized black Americans, and overall, the internal tensions of class, gender, sexuality, and color seldom mentioned by privileged African Americans. When one acknowledged, as did Redding, the inconsistencies between black bourgeois ideals and conduct, claims of race solidarity could not withstand the devastating realities of segregation and poverty.

Educated African Americans' struggle to define uplift and realize their aspirations for freedom was complicated by a dissemblance that often unconsciously evaded the most painful aspects of an oppressive past and present, and the shame of being at the mercy of whites, body and soul, and perhaps also, a burden of guilt for having internalized codes of white supremacy.

Dissemblance and disclosure might go hand-in-hand in some meditations on race, class, and uplift ideology. Born in South Carolina and raised in Boston and Queens, Celia Delaney was brought up by aunts after her mother and an uncle had "died in a fight with some white men who were bent on raping my mother." She recalled that her aunts never spoke of her mother, but constantly dwelled on the memory of the uncle. "My aunts taught me," remembered Delaney, a schoolteacher interviewed by an anthropologist in the 1970s, "that the better-class-of-colored people had a responsibility to lead the less fortunate of our race." Although it was understood that the "less fortunate" included darker-complexioned blacks, at the same time, she was taught that dark skin and other black physical traits were "handicaps" that might be "overlooked" if the persons "had money or behavior." Revealingly, she confessed to being snobbish, or "sedidy" (demonstrating that the African American lexicon had developed a vocabulary for intraracial class tension and snobbery), adding, "I was properly finished at Spelman and Radcliffe" colleges. Still, she believed that African Americans "have no choice about sticking together," and that "for all our color hang-ups, we are a great deal saner than white people about it. We don't kill each other about our color." Even the most candid recollections by elite African Americans, revealing racial uplift ideology at its most defensive and ambivalent on matters of intraracial color hierarchy and its compensatory noblesse oblige, banished from speech and memory the more painful, gendered aspects of black oppression, specifically the rape of black women by white men.[5]

Double-Consciousness and the Quest for Black Identity

Within the historical tension between collective, social, and elite racial meanings of uplift is the constant struggle for an independent black identity and the social and political implications of this struggle. Although he did not explicitly acknowledge its middle-class character, and what is more, spoke only in masculine terms, W. E. B. Du Bois's formulation of the "double-consciousness" of educated blacks, by which the latter often viewed themselves (and other blacks) through the judgmental gaze of whites, even while struggling to break free of falsified white images of blackness into self-consciousness, captures the inner conflicts of black middle-class ideology.[6] Double-consciousness captures the tragic difficulty of *racial* uplift ideology: its continuing struggle against an *intellectual* dependence on dominant ideologies of whiteness and white constructions of blackness.[7]

Through double-consciousness, Du Bois described the alienation of persons of African descent in America: "One ever feels his twoness,—an American, a Negro; two souls, two thoughts, two unreconciled strivings; two warring ideals in one dark body, whose dogged strength alone keeps it from being torn asunder." Double-consciousness describes Du Bois's struggle, and that of other black elites, to transform a pejorative concept of race into an affirming vision of cultural distinctiveness. The national destiny hinged on what Du Bois called blacks' pursuit of "self-conscious manhood," which he represented as a synthesis of American and African identities: "He would not Africanize America, for America has too much to teach the world and Africa. He would not bleach his Negro soul in a flood of white Americanism, for he knows that Negro blood has a message for the world. He simply wishes to make it possible for a man to be both a Negro and an American, without being cursed and spit on by his fellows, without having the doors of Opportunity closed roughly in his face."[8]

However influenced by the racial mysticism of his day, Du Bois's analysis of African Americans' ambivalent quest for self-consciousness captured the imagination of literate blacks, reflecting more than their desire for a hybrid of American and Negro identities. Sharing nothing but alienation from their cultural origins, with virtually all memory of the land and language of their ancestors lost to them, and furthermore, laboring under ethnocentric dismissals of "the dark continent," elite blacks confronted abuses on American soil that only intensified their desire for a true homeland, even one of the imagination. Du Bois had thus articulated yearnings that had long existed among literate African Americans, yearnings that had oscillated between the indefinite, unrealized poles of African and American identity. A sense of Du Bois's impact on his audience, however impressionistic, emerges in the remarks one optimistic reader jotted in a 1907 edition of Du Bois's text, autographed by the author in 1909. In the margin, next to Du Bois's words, "He would not bleach his Negro soul . . . Negro blood has a message for the world," this reader was moved to write: "This simple ambition is slowly but surely lifting the colored American into the ranks of achievement all along the line." Du Bois's lyrical meditations on the messianic gift of African Americans to American civilization and democracy attacked the dominant formulation of "the Negro problem" and promised the resolution of the struggles of double-consciousness. *The Souls of Black Folk* provided a vehicle for an incipient black middle-class cultural sensibility, instilling in generations of race women and men a sense of collective historical destiny. Whatever the intellectual or philosophical constraints of racial uplift ideology, black middle-class consciousness was multifaceted and contingent, representing a myriad of responses under changing historical circumstances to the fundamental ambivalence of being black in America.[9]

Along with Hine's concept of dissemblance, Du Bois's concept helps explain a great deal of public discourse by African Americans. The struggle for black identity was subject to historical forces. Black elites responded to changing relations of capitalist production, including urban migration and the consequent economic competition between blacks and whites in cities, defining themselves and their social function with terms for labor organization set largely by white elites. Despite the state's hand in maintaining forced labor in the South, many black elites seconded the plantation legend that held that African Americans were better off in the rural South as an agricultural peasant class than in cities as industrial wage workers. Black elites' earliest images of the growing urban black working class relied heavily on minstrel stereotypes of urban black idleness and immorality. Moreover, postReconstruction nostalgia for the plantation legend fueled concomitant myths of black urban pathology and immorality, which, among other things, discredited blacks' political participation in Reconstruction and fueled the movement to disfranchise black voters. Focusing on the supposed innate capacity and behavior of African Americans, and paying scant attention to those elements of the state and civil society that combined to control black labor, uplift ideology, like white supremacy, was ultimately subject to the logic of market values and minstrel representations prescribing the subordinate social place of African Americans.

But if some elite spokespersons tended to see black farm workers as white planters, philanthropists, and journalists perceived them, impoverished blacks

in the rural South were less beholden to these stereotypes. Through migration, they rejected the sharecropping system and its abuses, first gradually,
throughout the 1890s, then by the millions during World War I. Despite
the opposition of some black elites to the movement cityward, many African
Americans sought freedom, jobs, education, leisure, and citizenship in the
North. Thus, while these developments hinted at new possibilities for black
consciousness and a social expression of uplift, black elites responded with the
sociological discourse that sought empirical demonstrations of racial uplift
ideology's standard of social differentiation, or its absence, in urban settings.
Throughout, the general pattern was that black elites seized upon the status of
the family and moral and cultural distinctions (with their inevitable racial overtones) between themselves and the black masses to affirm the class differences
among African Americans that racist whites were loathe to acknowledge.

The wartime mass migration of blacks from the U.S. South, joined by migrants from the West Indies, created the conditions for a militant, black diasporic "New Negro" race consciousness that challenged uplift ideology's accommodation to the racial and economic status quo. Among New Negro
militants and a younger black intelligentsia of artists and writers critical of established black leadership and given to satirizing professional race uplifters, the
evolutionary rhetoric of class stratification rang hollow. New Negro militancy
ranged from the socialist, anti-imperialist internationalism fusing race and class
consciousness embodied by Hubert Harrison, to the popular nationalism of
Marcus Garvey's Universal Negro Improvement Association, to the NAACP's
liberal program of antilynching agitation and a judicial struggle against segregation that, following the assumptions of uplift, relied on class distinctions to
claim both legal standing and evidence of discrimination or injury.

Finally, uplift's representation of class through evolutionary cultural differences based on patriarchal family norms and bourgeois values informed a liberal social science discourse after World War II that explained poverty and
ghettoization as pathologies of family disorganization rather than as the result of systemic factors such as exclusion from the labor market and housing
discrimination. Recent and contemporary popular culture and journalistic
and academic commentaries on the "underclass" reinforce this cultural essentialism. African American opinion leaders' class-bound articulations of a
separate-but-equal social function of self-help, linked to pathological conceptions of impoverished blacks, thus reinforce widespread misconceptions that
poverty, misrepresented as an African American problem, is fundamentally
the responsibility of the black middle class, not a matter of broader social
concern. African Americans' self-image and analysis of social reality thus remains the captive of double-consciousness and the oppressive logic of racial
hierarchy.

Dissemblance, Double-Consciousness, and Gender Tensions

To restore moral authority and promote bourgeois selfhood among black men and women, advocates of racial uplift, as we have seen, seized upon the status of home and family, and upon the respectability supposedly conferred by patriarchal gender conventions. What made uplift compelling for many African Americans was its vision of black freedom and security in the image of the home and the patriarchal family. As political options were foreclosed, the home and family remained as the crucial site of race building. Moreover, insofar as the minstrel stereotypes that comprised whites' commonsense knowledge of blacks defined the deviation from patriarchal norms and sexual immorality as racial traits, many African American elites responded in kind, making conformity to patriarchal family ideals the criterion of respectability. Since race progress was conventionally defined as male dominance and distinction not only within the family but also within such masculine domains as politics, the market, and the military, black women's public activities, independence, and leadership were controversial within uplift ideology insofar as they departed from the only legitimate realm for black women's activity, their reproductive capacity within patriarchal black families.

Just because elite African Americans projected repressive Victorian sexual mores, emphasizing respectable reproductive sexuality within the safe confines of marriage, did not mean that they were silent on, or blithely unconcerned about, sexuality. On the contrary, uplift ideology was deeply concerned with sexuality, which was inseparable from the most violent aspects of domination. Late in his life, W. E. B. Du Bois recalled that in his days as a student at Fisk University and a schoolteacher in rural Tennessee, "murder, killing and maiming Negroes, raping Negro women—in the '80s and in the southern South, this was not even news; it got no publicity; it caused no arrests; and punishment for such transgression was so unusual that the fact was telegraphed North." [10] Du Bois's recollection of southern antiblack violence illustrates the struggle of black elites to achieve middle-class status, defined not only materially, but more importantly, in the gendered terms of male protection and protected femininity that were so important to black spokespersons.

Gender tensions within uplift ideology reflect the extent to which blacks were and continue to be haunted by racist and sexist ideologies and the painful legacy of oppression, specifically, the legal tolerance of the rape of black women in the South, fueled and justified by sexual stereotypes of black women's promiscuity. The myth of the black male rapist led to white mob rituals of lynching and mutilation (though it is important to remember that black women were lynched as well). Black spokespersons were often at pains to rebut the white supremacist mindset that mandated segregation, disfranchisement, and lynching as safeguards against "social equality," the white South's hysterical coded term for the miscegenation taboo.

The male-dominated gender politics of uplift posed difficulties for black women as race leaders. The defensive preoccupation with conformity to Victorian patriarchal conventions, as a reaction to minstrel, journalistic, and social science slanders of black families, militated, for example, against the political protest waged by black women leaders in the interests of black people—opposition to Ida B. Wells's antilynching campaign among black ministers is the most notable example. Furthermore, dissension on gender questions has long been perceived as divisive, as airing the "dirty laundry" of "family" conflicts. Black women are thus placed in the subordinate position of sacrificing gender consciousness and their reproductive self-determination in the name of race unity. In other ways, this male orientation affected how black oppression was theorized, emphasizing the victimization of black men through lynching or economic exclusion and silencing the particular victimizations of black women. The consequence of this dissemblance, this interpretation of the history of black oppression and liberation focusing on the private, depoliticized space of family and emphasizing cultural or behavioral explanations for black poverty, was a self-lacerating middle-class ideology that often pitted black men and women against each other, internalizing prevailing antiblack and misogynist attitudes.

The Racial Content of Class

This study surveys the black intelligentsia's response to racism and its contribution to national discussions of race since the turn of the century. I am less concerned with documenting the black elite's existence as an objective social group than I am in unpacking that group's ideology, and the extent to which that "group" was itself socially and ideologically fragmented. Following Raymond Williams, ideology, in the broadest sense of the term, consists of a system of beliefs characteristic of a particular class or group, and the societal processes by which meanings and ideas are produced.[11] Accordingly, I examine the internal content and tensions of uplift ideology, its external influences, namely, the ideologies and social forces that shaped its concerns and the process by which it, in turn, shaped and continues to reshape dominant perspectives on race, black leadership, and social theory and public policy toward African Americans. I discuss uplift ideology largely through the perspectives and words of African Americans themselves in order to demonstrate that their perspective was not insignificant, or peripheral, but, on the contrary, influential. Since the post-Reconstruction period, uplift ideology has worked to maintain (and sometimes challenge) relations of power and dominance, and subsequent articulations of racial uplift and self-help discourse continue to do so.

As my use of the recollections of Delaney and Redding indicate, this study is concerned less with the material aspects of class formation than with the cultural or ideological dimensions of status that figured in representations of class, which, for whites as well as blacks at the turn of the century (and in the present as well), derived as much meaning from racial and gender categories as from economic or material realities. Although I am somewhat interested in the material conditions of what might very loosely be termed a black middle class, I am more interested in how the black intelligentsia sought to promote itself as a "better class" in a society that relentlessly denied black Americans both the material and ideological markers of bourgeois status. What were the historical implications of their expressions of black middle-class identity? My purpose here is not to contribute yet another study of a pioneering, persevering black middle class. Nor do I approach my subject as a social historian, political scientist, or an economist might, using statistical and other empirical maneuvers to demonstrate the existence of a black middle class, its income, and its occupational structure. Nor do I want to reinforce the wishful but wrongheaded assumption that heralds the arrival of the black middle class as fanfare for America's entry into an era of color blindness and social harmony.

"Uplift" is thus meant to describe a black middle-class ideology, rather than an actual black middle class. Occupations within the black community widely perceived by historians as middle-class, including that of teacher, minister, federal officeholder, businessman, and professional, cannot be regarded as equivalent with the business, managerial, and craft labor occupations among whites from which blacks were largely excluded. The same applies to the occupations that blacks held to service white clienteles throughout the late nineteenth century in the urban North and South, such as barbering, catering, and other personal service and domestic jobs. Calling these service occupations middle-class introduces a false universal standard for class formation that ignores the extent to which the very notion of the black middle class—indeed, of class itself—is built on shifting ideological sands.

This book addresses the tension between black elites' *perception* of themselves as middle class and the social and cultural forces that relentlessly denied that status. It is more accurate to speak of the struggles of African Americans to overcome their marginality and achieve the security, protection, respectability, and recognition withheld by the nation's industries and political and civic institutions (churches, schools, the military, labor organizations and political parties, the courts, journalism and the mass media). In short, uplift ideology describes African Americans' struggles against culturally dominant views of national identity and social order positing the United States as "a white man's country."

Upon closer scrutiny, the category of the "black middle class" obscures the extent to which the social position of blacks is irretrievably mired in racial and class inequalities, with the two fused together in a manner that grants neither one primacy. The enduring significance of race within changing social relations, and the subordinate "place" of blacks within them, is illustrated in the case of black service workers. One instance of a postemancipation *racial economy of class* is found in the social relation between black domestic workers, and Pullman porters, and the whites they toiled for. Jack Santino argues in his study of oral histories of Pullman porters that the crucial element of the Pullman company's luxury overnight train service to its customers was provided by black porters, "whose job [was] one of total personal attention to the passenger." During the 1870s, Pullman hired former slaves as porters, whose duties, according to Santino, "were several and servile." The porter came to symbolize to white travelers the company's service and luxury, as well as its institutionalization of black subordination, reinforcing white passengers' assumptions of class privilege and authority. For the porters, low wages, harsh working conditions, and constant confrontations with Jim Crow customs and patronizing, if not abusive, passengers made the job all too reminiscent of slavery.[12]

Its demeaning aspects aside, however, to work for Pullman conferred status within the black community, since the job paid better than the few, mostly menial jobs then available to black men. The Pullman company offered travel, enabled social mobility for many of the children of porters, and promised black men deliverance from the drudgery of field labor. Eventually, the job attracted better-educated men and yielded some leisure for study and self-improvement, as the Jamaican historian J. A. Rogers suggested. An educated railroad porter was the protagonist of Rogers's novel *From Superman to Man*, in which the porter gets the best of a white supremacist U.S. senator from the South in a debate on contemporary race relations during an overnight journey.[13]

For all its apparent benefits, however, the job epitomized the tragically stunted aspirations of black men within a racist social formation. "Being out here on the road, seeing the things that go on, I have sat here and cried a many a night because I did not . . . finish college," remarked Homer Glenn, who went on to insist, "I do like the job. . . . I had no alternative—no other alternative. So when I found out I had no alternative, I liked the job."[14] Glenn's attitude toward being a porter reveals the lack of any meaningful options for black men except difficult, painful ones.

Also not exactly middle-class were the domestic jobs black women accepted in cities and towns at the turn of the century. Although such jobs promised economic independence, they also exacted a prohibitive cost in drudgery, dependence, and the risk of sexual exploitation by white male employers. In 1912, an anonymous domestic worker in the South, writing in the *Independent*, detailed an endless series of responsibilities, including child care, gardening, housecleaning, and cooking. "I don't know what it is to go to church," she wrote, noting the loss of a rare public outlet for the recognition of dignity and respect; lectures and entertainments were equally impossible. "I live a treadmill life and I see my children only when they happen to see me on the streets when I am out with the children, or when my children come to the 'yard' to see me," which wasn't often "because my white folks" forbade such visits. Paid ten dollars a month, and having to rely on "the service pan" of her employer's leftovers to feed her own children, she observed that "'tho today we are enjoying nominal freedom, we are literally slaves." This was clearly an educated woman, trapped in an exploitative system and enduring material and spiritual impoverishment. Her life could not have been further removed from the leisure associated with white middle-class ladyhood. Still, it is clear that many of these women and men, domestics and porters, passed their aspirations for a better life on to their children, in whom they inculcated ambition through education. Before being supplanted by black teachers and other professionals, porters and domestics serving the most affluent whites occupied a privileged position within the black class structure. But they were far from the social and economic equals of the whites they worked for, or even those whites at the bottom of the class structure. Indeed, Gerald Jaynes notes that at the turn of the century, black domestic workers made from five to ten dollars per month, or about half of what working-class white women made in textile mills.[15]

It would be useful, then, to discard our generally color-blind notion of middle-class status, whose effect is to mask race and class inequalities through a reified category of the black middle class. Pullman porters' and domestic workers' status as exploited workers confirms the impact of race on the class structure. When we examine the experience of those who, at the turn of the century, sought recognition as being, as they would have put it, a "better class," we find that a restricted labor market, segregation, the lack of legal protection and full citizenship status, and threats of violence or sexual abuse all fly in the face of conventional notions of bourgeois status. After all, to be bourgeois was to be free and protected by the law, as African Americans had nominally been under Reconstruction governments in the South. Through uplift ideology, elite and less-privileged African Americans were striving for bourgeois respectability in the absence of rights or freedom. Their hope was that rights and freedom would accrue to those who had achieved the status of respectability. And although marital status, the possession of a home or education, or the wish to acquire these, are considered markers of middle-class status, the material condition of many blacks with these aspirations was often indistinguishable from that of impoverished people of any color. Conse-

who didn't have
similar aspirations.

quently, through uplift ideology, elite blacks also devised a *moral economy* of class privilege, distinction, and even domination *within the race*, often drawing on patriarchal gender conventions as a sign of elite status and "race progress."

The conflation of race and class undermined the assimilationist assertion that class stratification would eradicate antiblack racism. In the minds of some black contemporaries, attributes of cultural assimilation, demonstrated by "white" appearance and behavior and figured by regional criteria such as northern origins (not completely distinguished from behavioral or color standards), were often associated with elite status. Thus, in light of their tragic plight within a racist social formation, it is more accurate to say that many blacks, or whites, for that matter, were not middle class in any truly material or economic sense, but rather, represented themselves as such, in a complex variety of ways. At the same time, however, many of these "representative" blacks lived out the very contradictions of uplift ideology, and they and subsequent generations of the black intelligentsia, in the realm of literature, art, and culture, would come to question and challenge many of its cultural and moral tenets.[16]

To approach the subject of black middle-class ideology and leadership is to raise searching moral questions about the American past. Only through a recognition of those ways in which black middle-class ideology, as a product of the most nightmarish aspects of our history, has affected African Americans for the worse can black elites and intellectuals redefine uplift not just in those narrow, racial, masculinist, and class-specific terms, but as an ongoing project of social emancipation—self-help in the truest sense. But while acknowledging uplift's contradictions, one must also recognize the potential within uplift ideals for democratic visions, including one rooted in an ethos of social kinship, perpetuating the collective memory of emancipation, whose ideals of struggle and aspiration countered the social and psychic effects of racism, discrimination, and brutality.

1

FROM FREEDOM TO SLAVERY

Uplift and the Decline of Black Politics

One of the unmistakable signs of growth is this increasing tendency towards class distinctions among the colored people. . . . There is, it is true, some caste feeling among the colored people that is based upon very trivial considerations, . . . superficial appearances, irrespective of personal worth or intellectual qualifications. But these classifications are false and will disappear. . . .

The depression in farm products and prices . . . are driv[ing] large numbers of the drifting population from the country to the city, where, in too many cases, want and misery and crime await them. The reclaiming of this element is a matter for much thought among the editors, preachers and leaders of the race.

SOUTHERN WORKMAN, 1899

(((

When General O. O. Howard, head of the Freedmen's Bureau, and later, founder of Howard University, visited the Walton Springs School for freedpersons in Atlanta during the 1860s, he asked the class what message he might convey to the children of the North. The youthful Richard R. Wright is said to have exclaimed, "Tell them, General, we're rising." Wright's response to Howard epitomized African Americans' group aspirations for freedom, literacy, and political and economic independence. Wright's distinguished career bore out his childhood prediction; he was valedictorian of the first graduating class of Atlanta University. In 1889 Wright founded the Georgia State Industrial College for Colored Youth, in Savannah, and served as its president. In 1921, Wright embarked on a new career as founder of the Citizens and Southern Bank and Trust Company in Philadelphia. In "Black Boy of Atlanta," the abolitionist poet John Greenleaf Whittier helped immortalize Wright's statement, inspiring a generation of abolitionists and reformers, black and white. Years afterward, the journalist Ray Stannard Baker observed that "We Are Rising" had become a folk motto among Georgia blacks.[1]

But this optimistic vision of group advancement was hard pressed to withstand a social and cultural order committed to reasserting control over the labor and lives of African Americans. In 1901, with the departure of George H. White of North Carolina, African Americans lost their last representative in Congress. His final speech praised the achievements of African Americans despite antiblack sentiment. "This, Mr. Chairman," declared White, "is perhaps the Negro's temporary farewell to the American Congress; but let me say, Phoenix-like, he will rise up some day. . . . These parting words are in behalf of an outraged, heart-broken, bruised and bleeding, but God-fearing people, . . . [a] rising people—full of potential force." White's terms in Congress coincided with the decline of black political representation from the peak years in the 1870s, when sixteen blacks served in the Congress, and many more were elected to state legislatures during Reconstruction. Elected to the House of Representatives in 1896 by a coalition of Republicans and Populists, White, as the only black member of that body, could do little more than protest the assault on black life, voting rights, and status. In 1901, White introduced the first bill that sought to make lynching a federal crime. The measure was defeated. After his term, White moved to Philadelphia, where he practiced law. In 1903 he founded an all-black town, Whitesboro, New Jersey.[2]

White's valedictory captured both the dismal outlook for African Americans in the post-Reconstruction era and the optimistic sense of uplift that elite blacks struggled to maintain. During a devastating period that historian Rayford Logan has called the nadir of African American history, with disfranchisement and the rout of blacks from electoral and third-party politics and the federal government's appeasement of the forces of reaction in the South, "uplift" was a hotly contested term. For many black cultural elites, uplift described an ideology of self-help articulated mainly in racial and middle-class specific, rather than in broader, egalitarian social terms, as the epigraph that heads this chapter suggests. Black elites who spoke of uplift opposed racism by calling attention to class distinctions among African Americans as a sign of evolutionary race progress.[3]

This understanding of uplift, shaped by the imperatives of Jim Crow terror and New South economic development, departed from the liberation theology of the emancipation era: generally, amidst social changes wrought by industrialism, immigration, migration, and antiblack repression, post-Reconstruction advocates of uplift transformed the race's collective historical struggles against the slave system and the planter class into a self-appointed personal duty to reform the character and manage the behavior of blacks themselves. In the antebellum period, uplift had often signified both the process of group struggle and its object, freedom. But with the advent of Jim Crow regimes, the self-help component of uplift increasingly bore the stamp of evolutionary racial theories positing the civilization of elites against the moral degradation of the masses. The shift to bourgeois evolutionism not only obscured the social inequities resulting from racial and class subordination but also marked a retreat from the earlier, unconditional claims black and white abolitionists made for emancipation, citizenship, and education based on Christian and Enlightenment ethics. It signaled the move from antislavery appeals for inalienable human rights to more limited claims for black citizenship that required that the race demonstrate its preparedness to exercise those rights.

Although it obtains heuristically, this transformation was never absolute. Indeed, dim echoes of Reconstruction-era social democracy persisted within the new conservatism of uplift. On the one hand, ironically, Booker T. Washington's economic self-help ideology and his calls for property ownership were popular among many ambitious former slaves because it evoked their collective hopes for land redistribution and economic self-sufficiency. And on the other hand, the egalitarian Radical Republicanism of Frances Ellen Watkins Harper, the prolific antislavery lecturer and poet, was informed by conservative civilizationist, self-help ideologies that, by the 1890s, endorsed educational and property qualifications for citizenship. But Harper, teacher of the freedpeople, temperance reformer, and novelist, expressed the postemancipation ideals of evangelical reform, speaking for those elites who directed their energies toward the social uplift of emancipated blacks. In an 1875 speech before a northern audience, she called the work of uplift a "glorious opportunity" for the youth of the race, and hoped that social advantages would not "repel" black women and men "from helping the weaker and less favored." She concluded, "Oh, it is better to feel that the weaker and feebler our race the closer we will cling to them, than it is to isolate ourselves from them in selfish, or careless unconcern." In this context, uplift signified the aspiring black elite's awareness that its destiny was inseparable from that of the masses. Harper's exhortations reflected the optimism of a postemancipation reform culture that regarded education as crucial to group advancement. Later, with black political leadership in retreat, elite blacks' use of uplift ideology to forge a sense of personal worth and dignity in an antiblack society pointed to intraracial division along class lines virtually as an end in itself, as a sign of race progress.[4]

An overview of the Reconstruction era and its demise—its political and social advances for blacks, the ultimate disappointment of African Americans' social aspirations, and the decline of black politics—is necessary for an understanding that does not merely naturalize the era's racial ideologies and concomitant ideologies of self-help. The loss of black political power, and the economic and political repression of the Jim Crow order, including peonage, the convict lease system, lynching, and the surge in violence and racist utterances accompanying U.S. imperialism were the harsh conditions shaping black political thought. Although, as August Meier has argued, there is no essential incompatibility between ideologies of equal rights, on one hand, and self-help and racial solidarity, on the other, the conflict between these two options within a southern Jim Crow order hostile to independent black politics was by no means inconsequential. Viewed in this light, the period describes a general shift in black leadership and discourse from a sense of the complementary relation between economic and political rights to an accommodationist notion that asserted the incompatibility of political rights and "self-help."

As George White's farewell to Congress attested, political power and opportunities for advancement were short lived for blacks in the South. Economic competition in the impoverished South fueled smouldering racial resentments, and mob terror was constant throughout the postemancipation period. The disappointment of popular black hopes for land redistribution, the lack of labor opportunities in cities, and a series of draconian "black codes" forced many former slaves back onto the plantations as field hands in a condition of perpetual peonage. Democratic Reconstruction reforms— public education and suffrage—clashed with the dominant laissez-faire vision of economic development espoused by New South industrialists and their spokesmen. The violent repression of black politics and labor organizing, including lynching, exerted a chilling effect on black leadership. In the midst of domestic violence, the national debate on expansion found black leadership divided, protesting white supremacy in the South yet appropriating the racial rhetoric of civilization to articulate elite aspirations at the expense of earlier, unconditional claims for equal rights and citizenship.[5]

Reconstruction's failed economic agenda dealt a cruel blow to the freedpeople's hopes for economic independence. The Freedmen's Bank failed in 1874, as the life savings of many hopeful blacks was squandered in a saturnalia of overspeculation and incompetence by the bank's white directors, including General Howard. Southern landowners, aided by the withdrawal of federal troops as part of the presidential election compromise of 1877, consolidated their control over the black labor force. Although federal troops were called in to put down labor unrest, during, for example, the railroad strike of 1877, they were seldom deployed to quell racial violence against blacks throughout the South. The inaction of the new president, Rutherford B. Hayes, created a political vacuum, as violence and fraud ensured the Republican Party's defeat throughout the South in 1878.[6]

Postemancipation competition between emancipated blacks and white workers, whose social identity was predicated on racial slavery, intensified with the Panic of 1873, and persisted in the economically depressed South. Gerald Jaynes notes the development of a quota system guaranteeing whites one-half of the jobs in seaboard ports throughout the South. Indeed, the emerging racial hierarchy in the labor market paralleled that of fusion politics, which allocated political offices and patronage to whites despite black political majorities. Senator W. B. Roberts pointed to Bolivar County, in his home state of Mississippi, where black voters held a sixteen-to-one majority over whites as an example of the effectiveness of fusion politics. There, fusion allowed "the Negroes to have some of the offices, and the whites of course [to have] the best ones." Even this state of affairs proved intolerable to whites, as Democratic "redeemers" throughout the South made good on their promise to displace blacks, particularly black Republicans, from preferred jobs.[7]

By 1890, blacks were largely excluded from industrial jobs in the South. Eighty-six percent of black workers toiled on farms or as domestic servants. As for those fledgling New South mining and mineral industries that employed blacks, their owners' need for northern investment and cheap labor was considerable, since mining demanded of workers a costly level of skill and training. In the 1870s, black workers increasingly took their skills to the mines of the North and West, whether recruited as strikebreakers or attracted by higher wages. This led southern newspapers to complain of an "exodus" of skilled black workers. The solution to high costs and a vanishing labor supply was the convict-lease system, which depressed wages industry-wide. Severe prison sentences, often for misdemeanors and other trivial offenses, yielded an abundant supply of convict workers to be leased to contractors by the state. Working conditions were wretched, with what C. Vann Woodward called an appalling death rate, but the system was profitable enough to squelch objections from virtually all quarters. In 1866, the Mississippi Central Railroad Company paid twenty dollars a month and board for each convict worker. Twenty years later, it leased convicts from the state at a cost of four dollars a month plus board. Well into the twentieth century, mining, railroad, and turpentine industries thrived on the pact between northern investors and southern economic and political elites over the use of convict labor.[8]

Fleeing coerced labor and intimidation, many southern blacks migrated westward in 1879, animated by the Old Testament Exodus story that had informed antislavery struggles. Their actions, as the historian Nell Painter has shown, represented a spontaneous opposition to southern tyranny independent of the moral prescriptions of black leadership. Mass politics was also an option. Although black men could exercise the suffrage, fusion with third-party movements was a bulwark against white supremacy. Such coalitions also

Convict labor gang, North Carolina, ca. 1910.

provided blacks room for independent political agitation. In Richmond, according to Peter Rachleff, a convention of black labor leaders passed resolutions calling for racial organization and threatening white elites with migration, "provided our condition is not bettered." Short-lived political coalitions with whites such as the Readjuster Party in Virginia helped obtain for blacks more schools and an end to exclusion from juries.[9]

Some black elites denounced the concentrated power of the planter class and condemned the New South order with the language of working-class politics. The Florida-born journalist T. Thomas Fortune and the South Carolina lawyer D. Augustus Straker (both of whom would join the out-migration of professional blacks in the post-Reconstruction period) criticized the New South and its land and railroad monopolies, the region's widespread illiteracy, and the exploitation and intimidation of black and white labor. Fortune noted that the condition of the South's workers had deteriorated to that of workers in Europe, where centuries of usurpation and tyranny had "reduced the proletariat class to the verge of starvation and desperation." Voicing his skepticism that "a black skin has anything to do with the tyranny of capital," Fortune called for an interracial labor alliance and "the more equitable distribution of the products of labor and capital."[10]

Straker, writing in 1888, rejected accusations of the thriftless indolence of blacks. Although black labor had helped double cotton production since the war, "poor wages, bad laws and race prejudice" had kept "the laboring blacks and poor whites . . . in a constant state of peonage." Straker detailed the abuses of the crop-lien system, which advanced farming supplies, tools, and subsistence necessities at exorbitant interest rates to black and white tenant farmers: "The poor laborer's political will is yet manacled by his employer, the capitalist, and he is asked to bow or starve." Unequal justice in the South was rooted in economic conditions "like unto the feudal times of the lord and the peasant." Medieval conditions notwithstanding, Straker maintained that blacks had made substantial progress in property ownership. Both he and Fortune called for full citizenship rights, and their analysis of poverty and land monopoly owed a great deal to the reformer Henry George, and to the producer ethos that was central to the era's labor ideology.[11]

In the rural South, African Americans were only nominally free, and third-party, working-class politics had been a viable option for many. But by the time Straker and Fortune argued for the inseparability of economic and political rights for African Americans, black leaders of the Reconstruction era were channeling labor protests against New South planters and industrialists into mainstream political parties, a pattern that would persist well into the next century, and to this day. As white vigilantes and state militias crushed black labor and populist politics, and as the gradual repeal of black voting rights throughout the South ended an already moribund tradition of radical Republicanism, the tacit cooperation of some black leaders with this state of affairs was secured by federal political appointments to "Negro jobs" and patronage. Southern intolerance of even this limited tokenism was illustrated in 1898, when Frazier B. Baker of Lake City, South Carolina, was lynched by a local mob after being appointed postmaster. Here, again, by failing to intervene, federal authorities permitted the subversion of this spoils system for blacks.[12]

White violence had been a constant throughout the period of Reconstruction. Lynching was increasingly employed against blacks in the late 1880s; 1889 was the first year in which more blacks were lynched than whites. Between 1893 and 1904, more than one hundred blacks on the average were lynched each year, compared to an average of twenty-nine whites. Lynching became a ritual of white power in the South, encouraged tacitly in the name of home protection by influential temperance reformers such as Frances Willard, or in more brazen fashion by race-baiting politicians and newspaper editors. Senator Benjamin Tillman from South Carolina, nicknamed Pitchfork Ben, invoked the standard justification for lynching when he declared "to hell with the Constitution" and due process if it prevented mob violence against suspected black rapists. The myth of the black rapist made the most gruesome acts of mutilation and torture, sometimes carried out with families and children in tow, the stuff of popular entertainment throughout the South. But blacks were lynched mainly to terrorize them into silence and submission.

Lynching, Paris, Texas, ca. 1890. The inscription on the scaffold reads "Justice."

In 1918, Mary Turner, a pregnant woman close to term, was hanged and burned in Georgia after threatening to divulge the names of her husband's killers.[13]

State force would be used in a variety of antilabor actions, but never to protect black lives and property in the South. Indeed, legal and extralegal restraints on black labor and politics were extensive. Even as black troops joined the U.S. Army in its intervention in the conflict between colonial Spain and Cuban nationalist rebels, they encountered discrimination in a Jim Crow army and harassment from white citizens. In an example of what Joel Kovel has termed "metaracism," in which "non-racists"—African Americans, in this case—participate in the racist practices of the state, blacks served among the army regulars who were used throughout the period to subdue Indians on the frontier, as in the massacre of the Sioux at Wounded Knee, South Dakota, in 1890. In addition to those the Indians called Buffalo soldiers, black soldiers joined U.S. forces in the imperialist wars against Spain in 1898 and against the rebellion in the Philippines in 1899.

Despite the racially charged debates on imperialism, within which the non-white Filipinos were widely considered incapable of self-government, military service was seen by many African Americans as a golden opportunity. The uniform promised status, citizenship, and full partnership in the nation's destiny. Although domestic racism and the denial of constitutional protection led some angry black dissidents to oppose expansion and black soldiers' participation, others argued that patriotic service to the American nation would earn recognition of and respect for the race's manhood. The soldiers and many in their communities hoped their patriotism would have an antiracist influence, as many black men who have shouldered arms for the United States have since believed.

But the highly racialized context of these wars, combined with antiblack violence and Jim Crow in the South, complicated matters. It was difficult for many blacks to muster support for expansion, unless one were able to subordinate racial identity to a sense of the nation's destiny. One black soldier reported that while the Filipinos constantly reminded African American troops that "there is no difference between them and us[,] . . . we only laugh, for we are U.S. soldiers, and all the enemies of the U.S. government look alike to us, hence we go along with the killing." But such imperialist adventures, including the gunboat diplomacy that sent the marines to Panama in 1903 and to Nicaragua in 1909 (which occurred during James Weldon Johnson's tenure with the U.S. consulate there), represented a higher national priority than the protection of blacks at home.

Blacks' ambivalence surrounding the group's participation in foreign wars did not alter the fact that since the Civil War, displays of military prowess and national loyalty among blacks had constituted a significant tradition within uplift ideology, providing black men with a rare outlet for the assertion of strong, courageous masculinity. Many black politicians and editors whose newspapers were subsidized by the expansionist Republican Party invested the race's patriotic service in racist foreign wars with the same emancipatory aura that surrounded black soldiers in the Grand Army of the Republic. Although the wisdom of black participation in subsequent foreign wars would be intensely debated among blacks in light of the denial of equal protection at home, the race's military service throughout U.S. history would remain a sacred tenet for many, if not all. In 1926 William Pickens, as field officer of the National Association for the Advancement of Colored People (NAACP), urged authors of history textbooks to record that Crispus Attucks, a slave, was the first man killed in the Boston Massacre in 1770, and that 5,000 blacks fought in the Revolutionary War, 250,000 in the Civil War, and 400,000 had enlisted for World War I.[14]

If many blacks thrilled to the image of the race's manhood in uniform, many whites remained unmoved, if not angered, by such displays. Black soldiers encountered hostile white mobs while stationed in the South during the Spanish-American War. On the domestic front, black soldiers were the target of racist propaganda that contrasted them harshly with the faithful, innocent Old Negro of the plantation legend. The soldiers were slandered as disorderly, brutish sexual predators against white women, embodying the menace that served as a justification for lynching.[15] Bombarded with such views, elite blacks agonized over the race's participation in imperialist wars as the white South remained undeterred in its repressive tactics. In addition, black soldiers and newspaper editors felt betrayed anew by the army's refusal to commission black officers. Yet even as African Americans reaped few tangible gains, military service was also inspiring to black communities, as armed black soldiers, including many from the North, were unwilling to tolerate southern bigotry and quite willing to defend themselves against hostile individuals or mobs.

But African Americans' yearning for inclusion was complicated by the tortuous justifications among some whites that sought to downplay the use of force. "White supremacy is not oppressive tyrannical supremacy," argued Rep. William Langford of Georgia, "but is compassionate, God-like supremacy exercised for the good of our nation, the happiness of the human race, and the civilization of the world." Alluding to the violence lurking beneath the nostrums of missionary benevolence, one black anti-imperialist wryly suggested, "maybe the Filipinos have caught wind of how the Indians and the Negroes have been Christianized and civilized" in America.[16]

To Langford and many others, the attributes of citizenship and gender conventions of respectable manhood and womanhood did not apply to black Americans in the South, or anywhere else for that matter. Negrophobic southerners boldly drew the color line on matters of citizenship. "I am just as much opposed to Booker Washington as a voter, with all his Anglo-Saxon reinforcements," frothed James Vardaman, governor of Mississippi, "as I am to the cocoanut-headed, chocolate-colored, typical little coon . . . who blacks my shoes every morning. Neither is fit to perform the supreme function of citizenship."[17]

Vardaman's outburst may have shocked more moderate voices, but heading into the new century, calls for disfranchisement became less rabid and more commonplace. Legal racism and state repression increasingly reflected the new national consensus against rights for blacks since 1883, when the Supreme Court declared Congress's Civil Rights Act of 1875 unconstitutional. After that ruling, state militiamen were summoned to put down rebellions by outraged blacks in Texas. Booker T. Washington's triumphant address at the Atlanta Exposition of 1895 capitalized on the trend toward segregation. "In all things that are purely social," Washington proclaimed, "we can be as separate as the fingers, yet one as the hand in all things essential to mutual progress." Washington seized upon an image of social harmony and cooperation that seemed to exorcise the recent memory of populist and labor struggles against concentrated wealth and power in the South, and promised a truce between the once-warring sections.[18]

Segregation was firmly established by 1896 with the Court's *Plessy v. Ferguson* decision, which invoked natural law and the belief in fundamental

Black soldiers of the Twenty-fourth Infantry in Cuba.

race differences in upholding the principle of "separate but equal" in public accommodations: "Legislation is powerless to eradicate racial instincts or abolish distinctions based on physical differences, and the attempt to do so can only result in accentuating the difficulties of the present situation." The strangeness of the case was compounded by the fact that Homer Plessy, the plaintiff, was to all appearances a white man, and had never admitted to having any "Negro blood." His counsel, the white liberal Albion Tourgee, filed a brief stating that Plessy had one-eighth African blood, with no discernable black features, and was thus entitled to the legal privileges of a white person. Tourgee never brought up the issue of equal accommodations, and neither did the Court. Drawing on precedents for segregation that held racial antipathies as natural, eternal, and ironically enough, outside the legal process, the Court rejected Plessy's challenge.[19]

Widespread opposition to social and political equality was heard in the belligerent cries of "Negro domination" that fueled the white supremacy movement that secured the repeal of black voting rights throughout the South during the 1890s. The Afro-American Council, founded by a group of dissidе black leaders earlier that decade, including Fortune and Ida B. Wells, journalist, clubwoman, and antilynching activist, convened in Chicago in 1899 to protest lynching, segregation, and disfranchisement, and to encourage black migration and economic boycotts as mass protests against these abuses. But by this time the perception of self-help as a preferred alternative to political agitation had prevailed, embodied by Booker T. Washington's National Negro Business League, which, not coincidentally, held its first convention in Chicago while the anti-Bookerite radicals were meeting across town. By this time, with black leadership fractured and sundered from a popular base of support, African Americans existed wholly outside the protection of federal law, denied due process throughout the South.[20]

As Plessy's case indicates, it is impossible to understand racism in the South as simply a matter of instinctual white antipathy toward the color of African Americans. To be sure, many blacks experienced Jim Crow along visible differences of color, but this was hardly the whole story. Racial dominance accompanied, and was aggravated by, the bitter class conflicts sparked by New South industrialization. Jim Crow was the white South's, and the nation's, solution to the social advancement of a rising class of African Americans that threatened a polity founded on white supremacy. The absolute separation of the races that southern elites insisted on, as well as black disfranchisement, prevented coalitions among black and white workers that might have challenged the landowning class's political and economic stranglehold. Agrarian populist movements responded to these economic dislocations, as poor farmers and small landholders resisted the shift toward large-scale cotton production. The Populist Party sought government ownership of railroads and telephone and telegraph companies, and openly recruited black farm workers alongside whites. Although such white Populist leaders as Thomas Watson of Georgia had encouraged interracial cooperation, the movement's opponents disingenuously identified it with the alleged abuses of Reconstruction. "Negro domination" became the rallying cry of white supremacists, including a transformed, race-baiting Watson. White supremacy, backed by violence, hastened the decline of Populist influence in southern and national politics, and ensured the hegemony of wealthy landowners, railroad magnates, merchant bankers, and industrialists. Southern states' disfranchisement strategies of poll tax and literacy requirements (with the exception of the "Grandfather clause," which after 1898 banished from the polls all those whose *ancestors* had been slaves in Louisiana) ultimately disqualified not only many blacks but also thousands of poor whites. As one historian put it, "The real question was *which whites* should be supreme." Although some black leaders, including Washington, petitioned state legislatures to defeat the measures, such appeals were to no avail. Beginning with Mississippi in 1890, the southern states embarked on the expulsion of black men from the polls.[21]

To dilute popular threats to the planters' hegemony, blacks became the scapegoat of southern society. Racism provided the terms by which elites secured the consent of poor whites to the New South industrial order that kept their own wages well below the national averages in their industries. However well-intentioned, those black elites in the 1890s who called for self-help and Negro improvement tacitly confirmed the commonplace view that the impoverished status of blacks was a matter of moral and cultural deficiency, not coercion and economic exploitation.

Antebellum Origins of Uplift

Although constrained by the bleak conditions of the era, racial uplift ideology was by no means confined to that moment. Since the antebellum period and long afterward, when African Americans were a quasi-free, stateless people, their efforts at self-help constituted the major political response to oppression and inequality. Uplift's origins were in antislavery efforts among enslaved blacks, as well as in the network of institutions for group elevation established within antebellum free black communities. Barred from white churches, schools, and public and social facilities, free blacks in the North, including Canada, and the urban South, formed their own institutions, providing for themselves a space for fellowship, solidarity, mutual aid, and political activism. Churches, political conventions, newspapers, debate, literary and library societies provided forums for antislavery agitation, education, and self-improvement. Many historians have shown that the small but influential class of free blacks was widely feared by proslavery forces as a potential source of insurrection, and that their anomalous presence threatened the institution of slavery.

In antebellum days, uplift, rising, elevation, and advancement described the passage of blacks from slavery to freedom, stressed the importance of group education, and based black claims for suffrage, leadership, and jury service on natural-rights arguments. The independent black church was prominent in championing this perspective, through educational, moral, and antislavery activities. Black abolitionists affirmed enlightenment ideals of inalienable rights and human progress by insisting on freedom not merely as a reward for upright, cultured behavior, but instead, in the spirit of the Declaration of Independence, as a moral right ordained by God. Although some black clergymen and editors espoused a view of moral uplift as a political necessity to prove the race's fitness for citizenship, throughout the crisis of the 1850s, black leaders' words and actions were generally uncompromising on this question. Abolitionists, black and white, vigorously denounced segregation in the North, the kidnapping of free and fugitive blacks by "slave catchers," and the 1857 Dred Scott decision by invoking the natural-rights, egalitarian vision of the Declaration of Independence.[22]

As the nineteenth century concluded, some black intellectuals sought to keep the memory of antebellum struggles and achievements alive. Anxious to dispel widespread and enduring myths of slave docility and black depravity, these proponents of uplift commemorated the past literary, oratorical, and antislavery activities of free blacks. These black historians, including the versatile black politician, scholar, and adventurer George Washington Williams, and the Virginia reconstruction politician, newspaperman, and teacher John Wesley Cromwell, glorified the egalitarian tradition of emancipation and radical Reconstruction as crucial precedents for the race's continued activism and progress. For these and countless other men and women, including such community builders as teachers, librarians, music teachers, reformers, and entrepreneurs, education remained the touchstone of advancement.[23]

Freedmen's Education

Among black elites, there was no disputing the value of education. Nevertheless, uplift encompassed the tension between competing philosophies of black education orchestrated by the vision of economic development and racial accommodation advanced by white industrialists, reformers, and philanthropists. As James Anderson has shown, the democratic aspirations of the freedpersons for universal education for citizenship, political leadership, and social advancement were challenged by the program and philosophy of normal school education established at Hampton Institute by its founder, Samuel C. Armstrong, a missionary who, with his wife, had worked in Hawaii and among Native Americans. In the late nineteenth century, the education of former slaves was seen by philanthropists, educators, and the American Missionary Association as congruent with efforts to bring Christianity and civilization to Native Americans, Hawaiians, and foreign "races" abroad, in Africa, India, China, and Japan. Already a school for African Americans, Hampton entered the business of Native American assimilation and dispossession when it took on federal prisoners of war captured in an Indian uprising in 1878. Hampton personnel constantly worried that Indian alumni would "go back to the blanket," regressing from the institution's deculturation upon their return to the reservation.[24] This concern was especially pronounced during the Ghost Dance revival of 1890. Before that, Armstrong's star pupil, Booker T. Washington, had served briefly in 1880 as housefather of the Indian boys' dormitory. Favored Native American students and graduates of Hampton gratified their teachers by contributing autobiographical

sketches to the *Southern Workman* of how they "learned of the noble work being done by the white people for the lower races of mankind." The standard
account of how "I determined to be one of those workers for the uplifting of
my people" fired the imaginations of African American students as well. At
Hampton, whether Native American or African American, the students
seemed to absorb the institution's missionary rhetoric of service in a manner
that seemed to shield them from the brutal realities of conquest and political
subordination.[25]

Anderson contends that before the rise of Washington and the form of ideological education he came to embody, blacks had their own objectives for education: "The prevailing philosophies of black education and the subjects
taught in black schools were not geared to reproduce the caste distinctions or
the racially segmented labor force desired by . . . postbellum white industrialists." Black intellectuals and educators such as R. R. Wright, Anna J. Cooper,
Ida B. Wells, and countless others received the New England classical liberal
curriculum, transplanted to southern black elementary, normal, and colle-
giate institutions. According to Anderson, such an education, while assimilationist, was not necessarily hostile to the ethnic identity and pride of black
students. For example, Wright's classical training led him to conclude that
"these differences of race, so called, are a mere matter of color and not of
brain." Nevertheless, students trained in the schools established by the
Freedmen's aid societies generally imbibed the missionary, service-oriented
ideals of their liberal New England teachers. The bourgeois morality of their
cultural mentors was drummed into black students: piety, thrift, self-control,
temperance, and the work ethic—all deemed crucial for economic independence and citizenship.

Still, this was a complex encounter across classes and cultures, one that
might have egalitarian implications. The Mississippi-born Ida B. Wells recalled, "All my teachers had been the consecrated white men and women
from the North who came into the South to teach immediately after the end
of the war. It was they who brought us the light of knowledge and their splendid example of Christian courage." Wells's tribute reflected the egalitarian
racial attitudes of many of the white teachers who embraced the cause of
freedmen's education. Since then, the belief in education as an indispensable
means of social advance for African Americans has remained a central tenet of
black middle-class aspiration and ideology. "Educate! Educate! Educate! Get
all the knowledge within reach," advised the Atlanta journalist J. Max Barber
in 1905, adding, "then use it for the good of the race."[26]

The Hampton-Tuskegee philosophy clashed with the freedpeople's emancipatory vision of education. But it also clashed with the views of unrecon-
structed southerners who feared that any sort of education, however minim '

was instilling in African Americans a desire for social equality. Consequently, to appease southern opponents and northern philanthropists and industrialists, the ideological thrust of industrial education, as originated by Armstrong at Hampton, opposed blacks' involvement in politics, situated the black labor force at the bottom of the southern economy and acquiesced in the separation of the races. Advertised as a missionary program of uplift (indeed, the American Missionary Association had a hand in Hampton's founding in 1868), the institution and its philosophy were represented by the *Southern Workman*, which printed letters from graduates who had returned to their towns or reservations to spread the gospel of service, piety, and thrift. Tuskegee Institute was founded along similar lines in 1881, and under Washington, it emphasized manual training, sought to inculcate the dignity of labor, taught a curriculum of rudimentary education, and was intended to produce common-school teachers who would, to the benefit of southern black farmers and their families, inculcate habits of industry, thrift, and morality. Industrial education would produce the class distinctions necessary for the tutelage and uplift of a race of thrifty agricultural toilers who had little use for organized labor or political activity.

By the turn of the century, those blacks who challenged the vogue of industrial education among philanthropists and reformers tried to capture these terms for their own ends by stressing the social utility and paternalism of higher education: Kelly Miller, a Howard University professor and advocate of liberal arts training, noted that "higher education tends to develop superior individuals who may be expected to exercise a controlling influence over the multitude." Unabated racial violence and attacks on black citizenship would make the accommodation and paternalism embodied by Hampton and Tuskegee intolerable to black intellectuals sympathetic to rival liberal arts institutions. In 1906, W. E. B. Du Bois of Atlanta University would shock a gathering at Hampton by calling the institution the center of "educational heresy" in its pursuit of a "false distinction" between industrial and higher education.[27]

The Inegalitarian Racial Assumptions of Civilizationism

In the post-Reconstruction era, egalitarian assumptions were further eroded as theories of racial hierarchy extended their authority within U.S. political culture. These theories provided the intellectual and ideological foundations of racial uplift ideology. Despite political and tactical differences among black politicians and intellectuals, they all shared roots in the missionary culture of evangelical reform, and in its rhetoric conflating moral and social uplift. Elite blacks' vision of self-help regarded bourgeois values of self-control and

Victorian sexual morality as a crucial part of the race's education and progress. Through these efforts, black leaders and intellectuals sought to demonstrate to potential white sympathizers African Americans' capacity for assimilation and citizenship. By the turn of the century, theories of racial hierarchy
were understood in evolutionary terms, and African Americans argued along
these civilizationist lines for the race's development and potential. Although
today this logic would strike us as inegalitarian, if not racist, in its day, the
false universalism of civilization reigned for those innocent of our hard-won
skepticism toward civilization and its legacy of enslavement, conquest, carnage, and genocide. For those who remained innocent of, or silent on, or un-
abashedly approving of the brutality in their midst (and here we must acknowledge the rank inadequacy of the defense by apologists that the racism
of so-called progressive elites revealed them as the product of their times, as
if there were no indignant dissenters on the planet at that time), the concept
of civilization represented progressive, humanitarian thinking on race questions. Moreover, it was deemed by black elites a significant advance over the
view that blacks were biologically inferior and unassimilable. Given the objections of southern extremists that black education was a futile, if not risky,
endeavor, education of the freedpeople was often tied to moral evolution and
industrial training rather than citizenship and political independence. In a
period in which many elite blacks, including those supposed antagonists
W. E. B. Du Bois and Booker T. Washington, were largely in agreement on
endorsing restrictions on citizenship, education was a hotly contested issue
among black leadership.

The sociopolitical impact of racial hierarchies inscribed in evolutionary
theory kept pace with their widespread appeal. According to Herbert
Hovenkamp, blacks faced a tradition of prejudice in the courts that distinguished political equality from social equality. Indeed, it was this narrow,
"whites only" view of equality that the abolitionists had opposed. Although
the Fourteenth Amendment was widely perceived by the courts not to pertain
to social segregation, in 1887, Ida B. Wells castigated blacks for retreating
from principles of full equality. By taking segregated excursions, and accepting segregated public facilities, blacks gave whites further justification for
drawing ever more rigid social barriers. "Consciously or unconsciously,"
Wells argued, "we do as much to widen the breach already existing and to
keep prejudice alive as the other race." There seemed to be a class component
to Wells's criticism, as black elites in pulpit and press periodically scorned the
masses' penchant for segregated excursions. They may also have been object-
ing to what they perceived as the embarrassing public displays of uninhibited
leisure at such occasions, which, to them, were injurious to the race's image.
But the central issue of segregated public facilities was particularly urgent
for Wells, because three years earlier she had successfully sued a Tennessee

railroad company after three of its employees physically tried to remove her to the train's Jim Crow car. To Wells's dismay, the decision was reversed in April of 1887 by the state supreme court. Whatever the accuracy of Wells's claim that acquiescence to the de facto segregation of public facilities in the 1880s made de jure segregation possible, the principle of equality seemed to her to be losing force among the black masses, and black leadership as well.[28]

Evolutionary Alternatives: Domination or Uplift

Amidst national debates over the recent American past, the African American intelligentsia disputed the meaning of slavery and Reconstruction within American culture. At the heart of these conflicting interpretations of recent history, epitomized by the conflicting positions on slavery and Reconstruction taken by Frances Harper and Booker T. Washington, were questions of the capacity of blacks for education, citizenship, and leadership. Black writers' commentaries on the meaning of racial uplift and the role of black leadership in pursuing it were often shaded by social Darwinian conceptions of racial struggle, specifically, the view that two distinct races on the same land mass could never coexist, as the dominant race would inevitably annihilate the subordinated one.

In her 1892 novel set during slavery and emancipation, *Iola Leroy, Or Shadows Uplifted*, Frances Harper described blacks' current plight by portraying social relations between "stronger and weaker races." Her analysis informed by popular Darwinian notions of the "survival of the fittest," Harper posed a choice between two possibilities: domination or uplift. She dramatized this set of options in a debate between Dr. Gresham, a northern white doctor, and Iola, Harper's black (though white in appearance) female protagonist. To Gresham's claim that blacks "learn to struggle, labor and achieve" against a "proud, domineering, aggressive" Anglo-Saxon race "impatient of a rival, and . . . [with] more capacity for dragging down a race than uplifting it," Iola countered that blacks would one day assume a higher level of civilization than that of "you Anglo-Saxons," who "will prove unworthy of your high vantage ground if you only use your superior ability to victimize feebler races and minister to a selfish greed of gold and a love of domination."[29]

By placing the reunion of family members separated by slavery at the center of the novel's action, Harper reinforced her theme of a natural, organic relationship between black elites and masses, figuring the race as a family transcending class, cultural, and color differences. Interestingly, the family reunions depicted by Harper are conspicuously matriarchal, as characters invariably search for their mothers, displaying no evident sense of loss at the sence of fathers. Through her novel, an intervention against reactionary antiblack trends nationwide (including lynching), Harper sought to promote a moral vision of racial uplift ideology that might revive the abolitionist, Radical Republican legacy of the Reconstruction era. Her depiction of slavery's cruelty, remanding Iola into slavery despite her education, refinement, and white appearance and tearing apart black families, debunked the popular plantation legend of the Old South. Harper also meant to strengthen the resolve of educated blacks to devote themselves to service to their race, and to rekindle the sympathies of whites who might have strayed from the cause of blacks. Although the novel ends on an uplifting note of romantic love and marriage, Iola has, on behalf of black women, insisted on her right to economic independence as a clerical worker, a position from which black women were excluded. For Harper and subsequent generations of blacks, uplift would be epitomized by the quest of blacks for literacy, higher education, power, and self-reliance.

As Harper's writing suggests, in addition to its roots in reform traditions, uplift ideology felt the cultural impress of the conservative, social Darwinist thought of the times. The desire among northern and southern industrialists for national reunion led religious and secular guardians of social stability and economic expansion to espouse a Darwinian view of social evolution and economic growth. In addressing problems of class conflict, the writings of influential social theorists such as Herbert Spencer, Benjamin Kidd, and William Graham Sumner ascribed a moral imperative to capitalist accumulation and deemphasized social conflict in favor of a conciliatory, organic notion of social "equilibration." Social reforms were regarded by Spencerian social Darwinists as meddlesome in light of the social principle of "the survival of the fittest," elevating government laissez-faire and business prosperity to the status of moral necessity. In addition, racial separation was said to be embedded in human nature and thus impossible to legislate away. Booker T. Washington, the prominent black educator and spokesman, was adapting uplift ideology along the contours of Gilded Age conservatism when he declared in 1900 that black Americans would receive citizenship "through no process of artificial forcing, but through the natural law of evolution."[30]

The Rise of Booker T. Washington

Reflecting national antiblack trends, Washington appropriated the evangelical reform spirit in a manner that eclipsed the Radical Republican tradition exemplified by Harper. In his popular 1901 autobiography *Up From Slavery*, Washington captured the spirit of uplift ideology, transforming freedmen's education into his program of industrial training. But his was a more conservative version of uplift in tune with the times, one that portrayed enslavement less harshly than did Harper, and one that depended for its content not only on evangelical missionary crusades but also on a none-too-subtle language of empire. Notwithstanding what he called the "cruelty and moral wrong" of enslavement, Washington asserted that American blacks who "went through the school of American slavery" were "materially, intellectually, morally and religiously" the most advanced "black people in any other portion of the globe." Pressing his point, Washington noted that those assimilated graduates of "the school of slavery are constantly returning to Africa as missionaries to enlighten those who remained in the fatherland." Washington's ideological bid for the status of an agent of civilization had more to do with the status aspirations of African American elites like himself than the material advancement of African Americans. Rooted in assumptions of evolutionary racial hierarchy, Washington's comments contributed to the view that the African American people of the South were incapable of self-government. Such evolutionary thinking lent credibility to the fallacy that peoples of color were culturally undeveloped, rather than at the mercy of political and economic subordination, in the U.S. South as well as in Cuba and the Philippines.

Along with his skillful use of the success myth, Washington manipulated civilizationist ideology and uplift ideals of self-help. He saw no contradiction in his self-help philosophy and his success in monopolizing the philanthropy of the business classes. He portrayed his message as a beacon of enlightenment among benighted southern blacks. Washington pathologized blacks' pursuit of higher education and politics, those false idols of the Reconstruction period, putting these errors down to "generations in slavery, and before that, generations in the darkest heathenism." Throughout *Up From Slavery*, Washington (who as a member of the Knights of Labor had been burned by antilabor repression as a young man) spoke of black opposition—strikes or independent black voting—as the archaic, almost minstrel-like behavior of the undeveloped "Old Negro," who was "largely disappearing" to make way for a more responsible black leadership committed to a vision of uplift that, as Washington would have it, served the interests of all races and classes. Washington carried forward the habit of Tuskegee supporters, philanthropists, and reformers, products of those laissez-faire times, of referring to rights and duties as mutually exclusive categories. Political rights, it was held, were the subject of unproductive agitation when they would more certainly accrue to those who had demonstrated their fitness for them through property ownership and dutiful service to the community through self-help.[31] It is of no small import that such sentiments, embodied by a southern black man and former slave, helped legitimize a settlement that might well have otherwise been regarded as morally suspect.

Much of Washington's popularity and power stemmed from his talent for speaking simultaneously to differently situated audiences. He became, after the death of Frederick Douglass in 1895, the most powerful black leader. A trusted political advisor to President Theodore Roosevelt, the "Wizard" was able to appease the more rabid elements in the white South, secure political patronage for reliable black allies, and drive a wedge in black opposition by skillfully dispensing political favors and punishments.[32] Washington's use of civilizationist rhetoric was as compelling to blacks as it was to whites, because it coincided with an avid missionary interest in Africa among elite black Americans, dating since the antebellum period. Indeed, it was at the 1895 Atlanta Exposition, where Washington made the speech that catapulted him to national prominence, that black American missionaries, including Alexander Crummell, took part in the "Congress on Africa." Although Crummell's belief in higher education led him to oppose Washington, his role in the congress matched the period's prevailing view of Africa as a "dark continent" of heathenism and backwardness.

Crummell's writings, like Washington's, indicate that blacks' adoption of this image of African heathenism was a source of status for African Americans. Since the antebellum period, the missionary enterprise, with its image of a "pagan" Africa awaiting "regeneration" by its elite progeny, was central to some black Americans' self-image and attempts to demonstrate black progress in a racist society that barred conventional routes to power and professional status. According to a black historian of the 1880s, "A morning star of Hope for the millions in Africa who have yet learned nothing of Christianity, nor taken the first lessons of civilization, shines over the lowly cabins of their brothers in America." By the 1890s, the analogous function posited by elite blacks' responsibility for the uplift of black Americans would serve a similar mission. The imagined uplift of African peoples from their presumed degraded condition offered elite African Americans an affirming sense of purposefulness. It represented an early version of the so-called Progressive Era's modern cultural construction of Western bourgeois identity through an understanding of its relation to "primitive" peoples.[33]

African Americans' interest in Africa, whether missionary or emigrationist in intent, fused evangelical ideals of self-help with the political, nation-building aspirations that Crummell and other elites projected onto the "dark continent" in lieu of political influence and social opportunities at home. For Washington had often proclaimed—in tandem with northern white philanthropists, religious and civic leaders, and southern politicians and planter elites—that blacks forsake politics for an indefinite period of time. He discredited the political and educational gains of Reconstruction as "mistakes," their reforms "artificial and forced." Perhaps the gravest of these errors was "the desire to hold office" among blacks; he described his own "temptations to enter political life" as if he had weathered a struggle against sin and damnation.[34] Washington's use of the myths of black political immaturity and corruption within the repressive New South social and economic order of disfranchisement, political terror, debt slavery, and gerrymandering had grave consequences for black leadership and a black population whose only recourse in those days was to leave the South, often at considerable risk from local white elites.

Black spokespersons believed universally in uplift and education. The sticking point of debate was over precisely what sort of education would be made available to blacks. W. E. B. Du Bois's Atlanta University study, *The College-Bred Negro*, defended higher education for blacks. Such a stand had become necessary with Washington's frequent assertions, in print and in platform lectures, that blacks sought the useless "abstract knowledge" of higher education to escape what he, and many white elites perceived, as their true calling as farm workers. While Washington had carried on the Reconstruction tradition of southern black leaders' demands of economic opportunity for the race and had celebrated the freedpeople's thirst for literacy, he broke with tradition by disparaging higher education as unnatural. Washington, a tireless and effective fundraiser for Tuskegee, seldom lost opportunities to recite anecdotes about overeducated ministers working in poverty and squalor because they had been taught useless luxuries like theology and Greek syntax, instead of "the dignity of labor and practical farming." Moreover, Washington believed that "a large proportion took up teaching and preaching as an easy way to make a living," rather than as a means of practical service and uplift. By conjuring the specter of indolent, immoral, urban blacks, Washington exploited and legitimized the racial fears of his time, for like white elites, he realized that educated blacks might threaten the social order. With good reason, his black opponents saw his rhetoric as an attack on educated blacks. For his part, Washington summoned the aura of religious authority then common to black leadership, also placing slavery within a divine scheme of uplift. "God, for 250 years," he proposed, "was preparing the way for the redemption of the Negro through industrial development." As late as 1912, Washington reassured concerned whites that "we are trying to instil into the Negro mind that if education does not make the Negro humble, simple, and of service to the community, then it will no longer be encouraged."[35]

By portraying educated blacks as suspect, unproductive, and potentially criminal, Washington echoed the general hostility toward black elites and higher education. In suggesting that education for blacks achieved the opposite from its intended purpose of producing a black leadership class, Washington blurred the social distinction that many educated blacks maintain between themselves and the black majority, a distinction defining and legitimizing their role as race leaders. With the three so ignominiously declassed, cast down into the urban slum underworld, it must have seemed to many educated blacks that they had no alternative, really, but to insist on their moral superiority to the black masses, both urban and rural. Whether or not they endorsed Washington's program, many blacks took an avid interest in reforming and controlling the behavior of poor blacks. "Something must be done," said a participant in the Hampton Negro Conference, referring to the moral shortcomings of the black masses, "or these people will drag us down." Such a view reflected prevailing middle-class anxieties about the poor as a threatening source of moral and social disorder.[36]

Self-Help and Uplift as Critique: Rising above Politics

As Washington's rhetoric indicates, the post-Reconstruction South was notable for its hostility to black involvement in politics and higher education. While black radicals like William Monroe Trotter, Fortune, and Wells denounced disfranchisement, white reformers and philanthropists incessantly advised blacks to forsake politics for the sake of social peace in the South.[37] Following Washington's example (and coerced by rampant violence), many black elites withdrew from political agitation and stressed self-help.

While Washington made much of the view that blacks and politics did not mix, others, noting the hopelessness of the situation, shaped uplift ideology into a critique of racial accommodation, denouncing the venality of politicians who betrayed the race's interests. Corrupt office-seeking politicians gave the occupation—and the race—a bad name. In one of his regular diatribes against such men, John E. Bruce denounced these "perennial office holders and professional Negroes" as "foul niggers" and "white darkies." Color, for Bruce and others like him, symbolized a bitter struggle among blacks for possession of the few opportunities for leadership positions. Among many upwardly mobile blacks shut off from political power or its trappings, those men who managed to secure appointments were "time-serving demagogues" who reaped the unjust benefits of a combination of white ancestry and of political spoils controlled by Washington and his black Republican allies, among them, William Lewis in Boston and Charles Anderson in New York.[38]

For many intellectuals, reformers, and journalists, the alternative to office seeking and influence peddling was a vision of uplift that asserted mutuality of interest between leaders and masses. The black intelligentsia cultivated the

disinterested Christian ideals of sacrifice and service against the grasping ambition and materialism of the times. Intellectual integrity, and a true commitment to social uplift, particularly through higher education, were the core
principles of these dissenting views. The writer and educator Anna Julia
Cooper denounced what she saw as the selfish opportunism of black "demagogues and politicians" and regarded the race's true leaders to be "men of intellect . . . to whom the elevation of their people means more than personal
ambition and sordid gain." Du Bois counseled an assembly of black high
school graduates in Washington, D.C., that they would do well to model
their lives after St. Francis of Assisi, who renounced wealth and status for a
life of service and hardship. In *The Souls of Black Folk*, which contained an attack on Washington, Du Bois noted the betrayal of higher ideals implicit in
limiting the training of blacks to industrial education. "In the Black World,"
he wrote, "the Preacher and Teacher" embodied the race's strivings toward
freedom, enlightened religion, and knowledge. Such ideals were endangered
by "a question of cash and a lust for gold." Du Bois depicted Atlanta University, with its liberal arts curriculum and integrated faculty, as a pastoral refuge
from that city's factories, and feared that blacks' historical quest for the "fair
flower of Freedom" would be trampled as the "Mammonism of the re-born
South" was "reinforced by the budding Mammonism of its half-wakened
black millions." Du Bois's was a romantic, antimaterialist defense of higher
education.[39]

Similarly, in Washington, D.C., black intellectuals of the American Negro
Academy believed that Washington's advocacy of manual training threatened
higher education for blacks. Alexander Crummell saw civilization as a "primal need," providing the spiritual and idealistic alternative to those men,
black and white, who stressed "material ideas . . . as the master need of the
race, and as the surest way to success." Rather than from property or money,
"the greatness of a people springs from their ability to grasp the grand conceptions of being." Crummell visualized black intellectuals as philosopher-
kings, as only "trained and scholarly men," he believed, could sufficiently
bring their expertise, knowledge, and culture down to the "crude masses."
According to Crummell, who served as an intellectual mentor for Du Bois,
Cromwell, Bruce, Cooper, and many others, true leadership and independent
thought were impossible for those mired in the fray of political rivalries, ig-
noring the fact that his organization had been founded in part as a counter-
offensive against Washington's conservatism.[40]

Black women joined the chorus denouncing those who exploited the ideals
of uplift for personal power and gain. While they also urged an altruistic vision of uplift against self-serving black leadership, their remarks on the subject challenged the male authority generally assumed within such uplift institutions as churches, schools, and hospitals. Barred from white women's clubs,

socially active black women participated in their own club movement partly out of the conviction that their contributions were also not respected by black male elites. To Anna Julia Cooper, the emphasis on individual achievement in the professions and politics as evidence of the race's progress was a fallacy. It obscured the vital role of black women, who were "the fundamental agency under God in the regeneration, the re-training of the race," and the "starting point of its progress upward." Cooper also criticized what she regarded as black male leaders' reluctance to speak out boldly against racism. Liberal whites such as Albion Tourgee, in her opinion, were more forthright. "Not many colored men," she observed, "would have attempted Tourgee's brave defense of Reconstruction" or "would have dared, fearlessly as he did," to seek reparations for blacks for their unpaid labor as slaves.[41]

Cooper was hardly alone in such views. The Chicago clubwoman Fannie Barrier Williams hailed the antilynching efforts of Ida B. Wells, which were supported by the National Association of Colored Women. She remarked that "at the very time when race interest seems at such a low ebb, when our race leaders seem tongue-tied and stupidly inactive in the presence of unchecked lawlessness and violent resistance to Negro advancement, it is especially fortunate and reassuring to see and feel the rallying spirit of our women." Sharing the era's belief in woman's moral superiority, Williams regarded the unholy machinations of politics as particularly inappropriate within the clubwomen's movement, which claimed to serve the highest ideals of uplift. In one of her several jeremiads against the colored women's clubs, Williams felt that the most able black women were "unwilling to enter into an unseemly contention for office," so put off were they by the "vanity and compromising ambitions" that too often characterized club leadership.[42]

The barrier to politics was absolute for educated, ambitious black women, leaving a void for a wide range of literary, journalistic, protest, and social reform activities, including the temperance movement for northern black women like Harper and Wells. Yet however much black elites disclaimed politics for the self-help, social purity activities of uplift, it would be inaccurate to see their views and actions as inhabiting a realm altogether distinct from politics. On the contrary, the range of uplift endeavors provided the context for hotly contested debates over black politics, the role of the federal government, the quality of leadership, gender roles, and the true meaning of progress—of uplift itself.[43]

Black Leadership in the North

There was a regional cast to the political and ideological factions of black leadership, which, along with personal and gendered differences and divisions, placed the phantom of a unified black middle-class male subject imagined by racial uplift ideology even further out of reach. Yet as we have seen, racial uplift ideals might provide the terms for political dissent among black elites, who challenged Booker T. Washington's legitimacy as "the Moses of his race." Nowhere was this the case more than among northern blacks, who enjoyed a relative measure of freedom and political power through the suffrage, and who certainly enjoyed more freedom of expression than leaders in the South. This is not to say, however, that northern blacks knew nothing of economic discrimination and segregation, as they were denied white collar jobs and equal access to hotels, restaurants, and theaters. Then again, they, too, labored under the same popular journalistic attacks on their morals and aspirations to bourgeois selfhood. In an attempt to counter the biases of the white press on matters of sexual morality, one black muckraker from Philadelphia published a luridly detailed exposé of news accounts of white rape, incest, and gang rape in the North, seeking to affirm that white men were the worst offenders when it came to "the unmentionable crime." This approach would have been dangerous in the South. Members of the small, relatively prosperous black professional class, which included the Boston journalist Trotter, the physician Nathan Mossell of Philadelphia, and the antilynching crusader Wells, from Chicago, opposed Washington's leadership. Northern blacks were freer to criticize the deplorable conditions in the South. On one notable occasion, they forcefully did so in Washington's presence. In 1903, Trotter, a man devoted to the principle of equal rights but possessed of the discretion of a runaway locomotive, was jailed briefly for his role in what became known as the "Boston riot," after he and several others, including the Yale-educated intellectual William Ferris, disrupted a Washington lecture in that city.[44]

Northerners shared with southern black elites a bitter awareness of the difficulty of making a decent living through work commensurate with their education and status aspirations. Pauline Hopkins, the Boston-based journalist and author of several novels that addressed politics and uplift at the turn of the century, observed in her best known work, *Contending Forces*, that educated black women were barred from office work in Boston. Drawing on her own experience as a stenographer, Hopkins noted the tension between apparent freedom and restricted economic opportunities: "Here in the North we are allowed every privilege. There seems to be no prejudice until we seek employment; then every door is closed against us." Along with the unpredictability of discrimination or hostility, northern blacks were excluded from skilled trades, and their traditional hold on such service jobs as caterers, barbers, and headwaiters was slipping. The northern press shared the common contempt for the higher aspirations of black Americans. "Let the Negro learn," the *New York Times* admonished in 1900 in the wake of a race riot in that city in which blacks were assaulted for two days by white mobs and po-

lice, "to clean stables, care for horses, feed and harness and drive them, r
lawn mowers, and also keep engagements."[45]

When it became impossible to ignore the challenge posed by northern
blacks, conservative blacks wielded self-help as a weapon against protest. An
editorial in the Tuskegee-controlled *Colored American Magazine* attacked the
Niagara movement, which demanded civil and political rights for blacks. "It
is much easier to make an abusive speech 'cussing out' [presidents] Roosevelt
and Taft, than it is to go South and teach a school or pastor a church, or give
a lecture that will be uplifting and helpful to our people in that section who
need help." In rural southern districts, where public schooling was neglected
by the state, it had become common for black student teachers to fill the void
during their summers away from college. These teachers were compensated,
housed, and fed by the black community, practicing the best ideals of self-
help.[46] Such criticism, however, reflected a tendency among conservative
black leaders to condemn dissenters—a kill-the-messenger mentality that
fetishized the pragmatism of self-help (or, at least, paid lip service to self-help
ideals) over insisting on equal rights. During the nadir, such pronouncements were hardly persuasive to those many blacks, including Du Bois,
Charles Chesnutt, Ida B. Wells, and many others, who had already worked
in the South as teachers or had fled repression and a lack of opportunities
there.[47]

As we will see in chapter 3, uplift ideologues borrowed heavily from popular minstrel, journalistic, and social science assumptions about race in their
response to urban migration. Black reformers and opinion makers embraced
the home and family as sites of racial progress and respectability, and it is not
surprising that the home was so idealized, given the potential horrors that
awaited African Americans in public life. At the same time, however, black
elites' claims of class differentiation were self-serving in accepting oppressive
constructions equating racial difference with pathology and placing a moral
stigma on poverty. In this view, disease and mortality were hereditary liabilities passed down to offspring by sexually licentious parents. Sexual deviance
explained illness and poverty for many black reformers who sought immediate solutions to the social ills of blacks in southern cities and towns, as well as
a rhetorical basis for social differentiation. But as they sought to establish
their own moral authority as elites, they seemed unaware of the contradiction
posed by their deterministic view of biologically inherited disease and immorality and the agency promised by uplift's environmental project of home
training.

The uplift preoccupation with self-help and respectability, tied to racial
stereotypes that demonized the race, revealed the defensive position of aspiring black elites. Accordingly, black ministers, reformers, and educators, increasingly dependent on white philanthropists, generally sided with economic

and political elites against organized labor and the unemployed poor. Their construction of class differences relied more heavily on cultural ideologies rooted in white supremacy than on economic realities. But although the magnitude of antiblack violence qualified black elites' support for the status quo, particularly around such hotly contested issues as lynching and imperialism, the sense of agency, respectability, and moral authority promised by uplift ideology made it no less compelling for many African American elites, who were ultimately as powerless as those disfranchised populations they sought to dissociate themselves from.

2

LIVING JIM CROW

The Atlanta Riot and Unmasking "Social Equality"

I know many souls . . . but none . . . intrigue me more than the
Souls of White Folk. . . . I know their thoughts and they know
that I know. This knowledge makes them now embarrassed,
now furious! . . . The discovery of personal whiteness among
the world's peoples is a very modern thing,—a nineteenth and
twentieth century matter, indeed. The ancient world would
have laughed at such a distinction. The Middle Age regarded
skin color with mild curiosity. . . . Today, we have changed all
that, and the world, in a sudden, emotional conversion has discovered that it is white and by that token, wonderful!

W. E. B. DU BOIS, *DARKWATER*

(((

A theme common to much African American autobiographical writing is the
telling of the moment, usually during childhood, at which the author learns
the drama of "social equality," or, as James Weldon Johnson put it, "the brutal impact of race and . . . how race prejudice permeate[s] the whole American
social organism." In these accounts the autobiographical memory of the
youthful trauma of racial rejection is inevitably shaped by mature reflections
on what Johnson implied was a pathological "American social organism."
These narratives of racial (and gendered) initiation describe the painful so-
cialization of young African American males and females into a negrophobic,
Victorian social order. At another level, while these autobiographical narratives subtly protest the sexual dimension of racism, they also convey the ambivalence of racial uplift ideology's desire for the recognition of whites.
Clearly, the desire for recognition of one's humanity is a natural impulse in
a childhood world innocent of race. But the remembered pain of rejection
by white peers or schoolmates produces a retelling that not only renounces
that desire for recognition, but more importantly, begins to question the

pathological whiteness that, in its own fearful renunciation of desire, deludes itself about its own humanity.

W. E. B. Du Bois waxed poetic in recalling a lost innocence: "I remember well when the shadow swept across me," he wrote of his Massachusetts boyhood, and the day his schoolmates exchanged visiting cards. "The exchange was merry, till one girl, a tall newcomer, refused my card. . . . Then it dawned on me that I was different from the others . . . shut out from their world by a vast veil." Du Bois claimed that the experience left him with no desire "to tear down that veil," but instead, had bred in him contempt for those beyond it. He sought revenge by outperforming his classmates, and occasionally, "beat[ing] their stringy heads." Mary Church Terrell winced at the memory of the day when she joined several of her white schoolmates, a group of young girls posing before a mirror, "joking about their charms." When Terrell, joining their game, asked, "Haven't I got a pretty face, too?" she heard, "You've got a pretty black face" and was hurt by the girls' derisive shrieks. Gathering her wits, Terrell insisted she "wanted her face nice and dark just like it is." Marcus Garvey recalled that his playmates in Jamaica included white children: "To me, . . . there was no difference between White and Black." Of his friendship with "the little White girl whom I liked most," Garvey noted, "We were two innocent fools who never dreamed of a race feeling and a problem." When Garvey was fourteen, the girl's parents ended the friendship by banishing her to Scotland. "I did not care about the separation," Garvey claimed, because he never thought that his white playmates were better than him; to the contrary, "they used to look up to me. So I simply had no regrets."[1]

These autobiographical narratives are concerned with more than unanticipated racial rejection and the disturbing first awareness of one's despised, racialized self. But when Du Bois, Garvey, or Terrell highlight their contempt for the rejecting other, they also raise the question what it has meant to be white.

Such an inquiry emerges in Walter White's account of his youthful coming to terms with his racial identity during the Atlanta riot of 1906, a terrifying moment of racial violence in which mobs of whites attacked the city's black neighborhoods. To call White's story unique is an understatement—"white" in appearance, White's case, however uncommon, reveals the sociological dimension of race. "I am a Negro," his autobiography begins. "My skin is white, my eyes are blue, my hair is blond," observed the executive secretary of the NAACP. Not surprisingly, White's claim of black identity invited skepticism from all quarters. In the first chapter of his autobiography, entitled "I Learn What I Am," White explains the moment "in which I discovered what it meant to be a Negro," and concomitantly, the true meaning of white identity predicated on the attitude of white supremacy. As he told it, this occurred in Atlanta, in September of 1906, when he was thirteen years old. At the time, he was aiming a pistol to defend his home and family from an advancing white mob.[2]

White's account is more revealing of the adult autobiographer's awareness of race than it is of the youthful Walter. "I had read the inflammatory headlines in the *Atlanta News* . . . which reported alleged rapes and other crimes committed by Negroes," White recalled, but these were so commonplace that they made little impression on him. Perhaps this was because White's family, all of whose members he described as phenotypically Caucasian, lived on the border between black and white sections. Walter usually accompanied his father, a mail collector, on his route, and on this day, his father told him that "ominous rumors of a race riot were sweeping the town." The occasion for these rumors, and the sensationalist headlines, was the gubernatorial election between Hoke Smith, the negrophobic reform candidate, and Clark Howell, editor of the *Atlanta Constitution* and the candidate backed by the state Democratic Party. Smith, with his ally Tom Watson, in White's words, "stumped the state screaming, 'Nigger, nigger, nigger!'" White quoted an editorial in the *Atlanta Journal* echoing the campaign oratory of Smith and Watson calling for Negro disfranchisement: "Political equality being preached to the negro in the ring papers and on the stump, what wonder that he makes no distinction between political and social equality? He grows more bumptious on the street, more impudent in his dealings with white men, and then, when he cannot achieve social equality as he wishes, with the instinct of the barbarian to destroy what he cannot attain to, he lies in wait, as that dastardly brute did yesterday near this city, and assaults the fair young girlhood of the south."[3]

Demonstrating the power of racism as a commodity within the press, the Atlanta *News* entered the fray with its "eight-column streamers of the raping of white women by Negroes." Its circulation rose, and only later would it become known that these stories were fabricated. "Atlanta became a tinderbox," as White put it, and "fuel was added to the fire" by a local theater performance of Thomas Dixon's novel *The Clansman*, deplored as "incendiary and cruel" by Ray Stannard Baker. On Saturday, September 22, as White accompanied his father on his route, they witnessed "a lame Negro bootblack from Herndon's barber shop pathetically trying to outrun a mob of whites." Less than a hundred yards away, "the chase ended. We saw clubs and fists descending to the accompaniment of savage shouting and cursing." On spotting another unlucky black man, the mob left its victim. "The body with the withered foot lay dead in a pool of blood on the street." After five days of violence, at least ten blacks and one white were killed, with scores injured, and much devastation of property in black residential areas.[4]

Although protected by their white appearance, Walter and his father were glad to complete the route, and they left the post office at eleven that evening.

On the way home, their wagon nearly collided with another fleeing a white mob, three blacks desperately holding on to its sides. The wagon's driver, a white man, found his whip useful in alternately lashing the horses and cracking it in the faces of men in the mob giving chase. Taking an alternate route they believed would be safer, the Whites encountered another mob closing in on a black woman who cooked for one of the downtown white hotels. Handing Walter the reins, his father, "though he was of slight stature," reached down and lifted the woman up into their cart to safety.

Sunday afternoon White's father was warned by friends of a plan among whites to gather that night on Peachtree Street and invade "Darktown," the black residential section three blocks below, "to clean out the niggers." With the lights turned out, and White's mother and sisters crouched in the rear of the house, Walter and his father waited at the front windows of the parlor with guns. As the mob approached, some bearing torches, White recalled that they heard a familiar voice yell, "That's where that nigger mail carrier lives! Let's burn it down! It's too nice for a nigger to live in." Softly, the elder White said, "Son, don't shoot until the first man puts his foot on the lawn and then—don't you miss!"

As White recalled it, "I knew then who I was. I was a Negro, a human being with an invisible pigmentation which marked me as a person to be hunted, hanged, abused, discriminated against, kept in poverty and ignorance," all so that those with white skin would have proof of their superiority, a proof "accessible to the moron and the idiot as well as to the wise man and the genius." The lowest whites could claim superiority to the two-thirds of the world's population that was not white. The threat posed by the rioters to White's family was an example of the "one-drop rule," namely, the legal and social classification in the South of persons with known black ancestry—the proverbial single drop of "black blood"—as Negroes, despite their nonblack appearance. This was a legal attempt to maintain absolute racial boundaries despite the long and continued history of miscegenation in the South. White's recollection of the riot echoed one of the central grievances of uplift ideology, the dominant group's refusal to acknowledge class differences among blacks: "It made no difference how intelligent or talented my millions of brothers and I were, or how virtuously we lived. . . . There were white men who said Negroes had no souls, and who proved it by the Bible. Some of these were now approaching us, intent on burning our house." Despite what must have been a tense situation, "the inexplicable thing" was evidently not lost on Walter—"that my skin was as white as the skin of those who were coming at me."

Suddenly, as the mob edged closer, and as Walter wondered how it would feel to kill a man, there was a volley of shots. The mob halted. Some friends of White's father had barricaded themselves nearby and had fired on the mob. They fired again, and the mob retreated. The tension lingered long after the danger had passed, but White recalled feeling that he knew who he was and was glad of it. He was "sick with loathing" for the hatred of the mob, "glad I was not one of those whose story is in the history of the world, a record of bloodshed, rapine and pillage." Perhaps the riot had led White to such an understanding of race. We can be more certain, however, that an accretion of subsequent experiences, including work as an undercover investigator of lynchings for the NAACP, as well as his frequent confrontation with the indeterminacy of his racial affiliation, and even ideological disputes among the NAACP's leadership, animated White's search for the origin of his racial identity, and the intensity of his desire to dissociate himself from whiteness.[5]

Whatever impact it had on the formation of White's racial and middle-class subjectivity, and his commitment to racial justice, the Atlanta riot marked the collapse of what had appeared to be a harmonious period of interracial cooperation, with moderate white elites joining with civic-minded black leadership in the birthplace of Booker T. Washington's 1895 Atlanta Compromise address. The *Outlook* called the riot "An American Kishniev," after the site of a pogrom against Jews in Russia in 1903.[6] From the perspective of J. Max Barber, editor of the Atlanta periodical *Voice of the Negro*, and other contributors to the journal after its relocation in Chicago, the Atlanta riot was the culmination of a series of antiblack incidents, including the racist gubernatorial campaign, the staging of Dixon's *Clansman*, and the so-called Brownsville Affray, in which President Theodore Roosevelt discharged 170 black soldiers after a violent dispute with local whites in that Texas town. These incidents resulted from the white South's obsession with "social equality," the miscegenation taboo, and ongoing efforts to suppress free speech among black editors in that region.[7] Although it would provide the catalyst for black and interracial political opposition that would eventually result in the founding of the NAACP, the riot was the most extreme manifestation of a system of daily humiliations that blacks endured under Jim Crow.

Struggles against Jim Crow

Jim Crow in Atlanta, and throughout the South, beset African Americans with substandard public facilities, forbade blacks and whites to interact in public and private life as equals, as human beings, and menaced blacks' attempts at social advancement. Under Jim Crow's reign of terror, whites coveted the property and possessions of successful blacks and raised the constant threat of psychic and physical violence and humiliation. African Americans struggled in a variety of ways to define themselves, maintain self-respect, and insulate themselves and their families against this systematic brutality.

In their daily lives and public utterances, African Americans insisted on their respectable status, a concern often articulated in terms of gender conventions. As part of the "high destiny" of black people in America, Du Bois noted the "development of strong manhood and pure womanhood," as a crucial part of a "race ideal" that would serve "the uplifting of the Negro people." The frequent references to "manhood" as a signifier for citizenship, militancy, humanity (as opposed to the stereotype of animalism), and the protection of black women, were all rooted in the nineteenth-century political culture that held bourgeois rights and the realm of politics as a masculine domain.

 The preoccupation with manhood as a response to the racial and gendered restrictions on citizenship also illustrated the powerlessness of southern blacks, facing bigotry ranging from daily encounters with whites to matters of life and death. The refusal of many white hospitals to admit blacks for treatment, and the substandard resources and care of segregated black facilities plagued all African Americans. In 1931, Walter White's elderly father was hit by a car and taken to Atlanta's white hospital, only to be shifted across the street to the Negro ward when his Negro identity became known. As he lingered on for days afterward, Walter and his brother kept a vigil, trying not to notice the "dinginess, misery and poverty" of the crowded ward. There were numerous private hospitals managed by churches, but none admitted blacks, leaving Atlanta's ninety thousand African Americans to those limited, squalid facilities set aside for them. White wrote, "When death had come, he had been ushered out of life in the meanest circumstances an implacable color line had decreed for all Negroes, whatever their character or circumstances might be." Among all southern blacks, such conditions were painfully familiar. Although historians debate whether segregated medical facilities and delayed treatment caused the deaths of such prominent blacks as the singer Bessie Smith and Dr. Charles R. Drew, African Americans and the black press usually suspected the worst. When Juliette Dericotte, a dean at Fisk, died after an automobile accident in Georgia, after being denied treatment at a whites-only hospital, E. Franklin Frazier, then on the faculty at that institution, organized campus and community protests. Such discriminatory conditions, in addition to poverty, contributed to a fear and distrust of hospitalization among many blacks of southern origin.[8]

Stories of life under Jim Crow abound in the lore of countless African American families. African Americans might encounter the whims of white supremacy just by going out in public. Richard Wright wrote a chilling autobiographical essay on growing up under Jim Crow, in which he recounted

how the threat of constant violence forced blacks to adapt, feigning and performing the role of submissive Negroes in order to survive. Needless to say,
the system of segregation was equally effective in producing hostile whites.
To paraphrase Simone de Beauvoir, white supremacists under Jim Crow were
not born—they were made. This is illustrated by a story told within my own
family. In Birmingham, Alabama, during the 1930s, while window shopping,
a black woman felt a blow to her leg. More shocked than injured, she saw that
a child, a small white boy of five or six years, had kicked her, without so much
as a word. As the child's mother appeared and made a show of reprimanding
the boy, the woman calmly told her that she, as the child's parent, not the
child, was to blame.

A more lethal form of violence was practically lying in wait for black men
whose dignified public appearance and demeanor defied white expectations
of deference. Arna Bontemps recalled the confrontation that sparked his father's decision to move his family out of Louisiana, to California. Bontemps's
father, a prosperous builder, was generally well-dressed, a breach of Jim
Crow expectations of black subordination. One night, "two white men wa-
vered out of a saloon," blocking his path; "one of them muttered, 'Let's walk
over the big nigger.'" Although "capable of fury," Bontemps's father "calmly
stepped aside," as local custom dictated. To do otherwise would have given
his tormentors license to shoot him out of hand. The trouble began, ironically enough, when a black man tried to make himself respectable in appearance and conduct, upsetting even the poorest whites' expectations of privilege. To publicly present one's self, as the elder Bontemps did, not as a field
hand, but as successful, dignified, and neatly attired, constituted a transgressive refusal to occupy the subordinate status prescribed for African American
men and women.[9]

Perhaps middle-class sanctuaries like black college campuses shielded blacks
from such crude encounters with white supremacy. But even there, it was no
guarantee that rotten personalities could be kept out. More than one hundred
students at Talladega College in Alabama went on strike in January of 1906 following the appointment of a new superintendent of the school's agricultural
department. Accounts of the dispute noted that this superintendent "began to
move among the students with an air of superiority, to address them by their
first names," and that he refused to share a residence with students because he
was opposed to "social equality." The Atlanta journalist J. Max Barber commented that "conditions are such in the South, generally, and the average
white man of this section is so arrogant and presumptious, that the young
Negro of intelligence and self-respect does not care to have contact with him."
Barber held that the students were justified in their action.[10]

The lack of career options was a common complaint for college-trained
blacks in both sections, but the South's assault on relations between black

men and women kindled the resentment of those who struggled to meet pre-vailing standards of bourgeois selfhood. Sutton E. Griggs, a Memphis minis-ter, testified to the material difficulties of blacks in the South. Griggs pointed out the extent to which free speech and political assertiveness were incompat-ible with the pursuit of a livelihood, harming black men and their ability to support families. In *Imperium In Imperio*, a popular novel published in 1899, Griggs, who supported both Tuskegee and the Niagara movement, imagined a conspiracy among blacks to establish a separate black nation. Griggs de-scribed the undoing of his hero, Belton Piedmont, which pushed him toward his fateful course. Belton, a brilliant teacher and journalist, lost his teaching appointment when he editorialized against election fraud in Richmond. Dismissed from a lowly clerical patronage job in the post office for refusing to support a Republican Party candidate he knew to be a racist, Belton found that although "he possessed a first class college education" and "there were positions around by the thousands which he could fill . . . his color debarred him." In contemplating this situation, which "precluded his earning a liveli-hood" for his new bride, Belton found "scores of young men in just his predicament." Teaching positions were all taken, and the situation was wors-ened as "colleges were rushing class after class forth with his kind of educa-tion, and there was no employment for them." In Griggs's narrative, the dark-complexioned Belton's marriage ends after his new bride gives birth to a pale "white" baby, a shocking development meant to illustrate the worst fate that could befall black men who were unable to support, and thus protect, their wives. While the implication Griggs drew cast black women in a negative light as race betrayers, the episode conveyed the powerlessness of black men to establish, let alone protect, their families in accordance with patriarchal norms.[11]

Corroborating Griggs's scenario, W. E. B. Du Bois's Atlanta University study of *The College-Bred Negro* recorded a threefold increase from 1880 to 1899 of black college graduates, and seemed chagrined to note that "they are not rushing into matrimony and its responsibilities without forethought." As career prospects did not always fulfill the expectations raised by education, the problem of "getting a living," as Du Bois termed it, remained a deep con-cern of educated blacks, North and South. "How many times," recalled the southern-born scholar and minister Benjamin Brawley, "have I seen respon-sible Negro men detached from something stable and uncertain as to the way to turn! The higher they are, the more difficult is the problem. Some never seem to find the way again." Though Brawley's lament came during the Depression, it illustrates not only the precarious status of educated blacks but also, for black men, the violence this situation did to their sense of identity as men. Clearly, the material difficulties faced by black men and women, whose unprotected lives, bodies, and property could be instantly taken and seized without redress, had an enormous impact on gender relations and on the quality and concerns of uplift ideology.[12]

Insofar as Jim Crow mores had spread above the Mason-Dixon line, blacks in the North were no less vulnerable on matters of gender identity. In her biography of her mother, Margaret Lawrence, a pioneer African American psychoanalyst, Sara Lawrence Lightfoot discusses the impact of racism on her mother, who recalled meeting her supervisor for a summer job with the department of public health in Jackson, Mississippi, while in medical school at Cornell. The year was 1938. "As she entered his office, his greeting made her feel like she had been hit in the stomach." In Dr. Lawrence's words, "He immediately called me 'Margaret.' . . . He made it clear that as a Negro, despite the fact that I was [in] medical school, I had no title. . . . He knew who I was, 'Miss Margaret Morgan.' . . . But he needed to demean me. I was greatly offended." Margaret Morgan and her future husband Charles Lawrence were from the South, but when she told him of what happened, as she remembered it, "Charles was infuriated. . . . He was so angry, he was destroyed." Through tears, Dr. Lawrence explained to her daughter—her biographer—Charles Lawrence's devastation (reading her present marital status back into the period of their engagement): "To have reached his manhood, to have married . . . to have his wife not respected. . . . In this place he was rendered helpless as a man. . . . He could not protect his wife from indignity." The memory of that incident brought back another, in which Margaret Lawrence had arranged for her mother to have kidney surgery in a New York hospital. Reviewing correspondence to her New York colleagues from her mother's doctor in Vicksburg, Dr. Lawrence was shocked to discover that he referred to his patient throughout as "Mary." "He spoke so disrespectfully, calling her 'Mary,'" Dr. Lawrence angrily recalled, "as if this was someone who was working on his plantation!"[13]

Sara Lightfoot, a sociologist, concluded that her mother's response "reflects the long shadow of black folks' tireless attempts to gain status as full-fledged human beings. . . . In the first-name address, Negroes heard the old contempt, the brutal infantilization" of slavery. Besides infantilization, the first-name address of black women by white men signaled a stolen intimacy, a falsely claimed familiarity, hardly mutual. In the context of institutionalized sexual exploitation of black women, this verbal violation of privacy was tantamount to the physical act of rape. In this light, we can better understand Charles Lawrence's rage and sense of helplessness at being unable to protect his fiancée. African Americans steeled themselves against such displays of power by whites, which perversely masqueraded as social niceties.

According to Lightfoot, generations after slavery, in the Deep South, blacks found ingenious methods of avoiding the humiliating first-name address. It was not uncommon for black parents to name their sons President,

Mister, Deacon, or even Royal, or to name their daughters Queen or Princess, so that whites would be compelled to address them using a respectful title. An alternative open to both men and women was to maintain circumspect silence on one's first name and to go by one's initials, as Charles Lawrence's mother did. White paternalism could also be subverted by naming children, usually male, after popular political or military leaders, such as Roosevelt (as in Franklin), or somewhat earlier, Maceo, the latter after Antonio Maceo, the black general of the Cuban rebellion widely admired among southern blacks in the 1890s and afterward. Of course, southern whites could escalate this psychological warfare, insisting on the black man's subordinate place by addressing him as "boy," or by otherwise calling black men and women, and indeed, the race, "out of their names," as blacks referred to it. The everyday prevalence of such racist practices informed an internal moral code among blacks governing interpersonal relations and demanding mutual respect, especially for those elders who had survived the worst aspects of the past.[14]

In the South, white landlords exercised their absolute power over their black tenants through the system of concubinage, reserving an unrestricted right to sexual relations with women on the plantation. Concubinage was not just assumed by whites to be an integral part of peonage, for it was widely practiced in urban settings by white employers of domestic workers, and by others, as well. Black men and women who refused to comply, or who challenged the system—and there were many—invariably faced violent retribution, especially men. It should be mentioned that many African Americans raised families under these conditions of terror. Some black women, however, exploited the system by becoming prostitutes, but it is difficult, and indeed misleading, to regard the actions of black women as freely chosen and consensual under a system of legalized rape, maintained by anti-intermarriage laws. African Americans of all classes struggled against concubinage to protect their female relatives. Among privileged blacks, it was commonly believed that daughters would be safer away at schools, where the pietistic missionary culture would afford a measure of protection. In a fictionalized magazine sketch, one commentator described concubinage as the essence of Jim Crow, recounting a tragic case of the separation of a young girl from her long-suffering mother, an urban washerwoman.[15] Black men bitterly resented the system but were largely powerless to oppose it. If their repressed rage could be vented, it might come at the expense of black women themselves, or target rival black male suitors. Such rage could be directed against those white males who preyed on black women only indirectly. The white anthropologist Hortense Powdermaker told of a prank several black youths played on white male visitors inquiring after black women. The boys directed the men to the best white residential section. "The youth of the boys and the satisfaction in the prank were equally telling," observed Powdermaker.[16]

Black commentators, particularly those intent on projecting an image of re-spectability, were understandably reticent about concubinage. Silence about sexual domination might be partly overcome by dissemblance, or by displace-ment through historical analogy. One writer situated his denunciation of concubinage in an account of French aristocrats' "droit de Seigneur," by which "every bride was his for the asking." He warned that such crimes would drive southern blacks to revolt against their oppressors as surely as French peasants had done in the eighteenth century. For elite blacks, concu-binage was generally a class issue, and despite their concern for the chastity of their daughters, many were prone to equate concubinage with prostitution or the supposed sexual indiscretions of lower-class women. For many, re-spectability meant condemning the morals of black women caught within the system as much as they condemned the system itself. But in those times all black women were vulnerable to such accusations. Black women were no doubt devastated to hear that such murmurings had originated among blacks. As a young woman, Ida B. Wells confronted a minister who had spread the rumor that her dismissal from a teaching position in Memphis on political grounds was actually punishment for a breach in moral conduct. Having se-cured his public retraction of the accusations, Wells saw a larger significance in her action: "I felt I had vindicated the honor of the many southern girls who had been traduced by lying tongues."[17]

Public-spirited black women were equally zealous about defending their names and image against the verbal slanders and physical outrages of racist whites. Invariably their bylines appeared in the black press with the title "Mrs.," displaying to the world their respectable status. Moreover, there was the need for the protection that was not forthcoming in the courts. This pre-occupation with morals, status, and conformity to bourgeois gender norms among educated blacks may have been repressive and indicative of a misogy-nistic distrust of single black women in certain contexts, but it also reflects African Americans' outrage at abuses such as concubinage. The widespread concern for family stability among blacks has to be attributed to the sheer magnitude of racist domination that threatened to humiliate, segregate, and dispossess, if not murder and rape, black men and women regardless of social status.[18]

Social Equality and the Miscegenation Taboo

Amidst widespread portrayals of disorderly black sexuality, there was little mention that black women and men were largely the prey of state-sanctioned

white aggression, as victims of rape and violently homoerotic lynchings culminating in castration and mutilation. Two words—"social equality"—were
sufficient to unleash such explosions of mob fury and terror. As the corner-
stone of white supremacist ideology, the slogan, signifying black rape and the
miscegenation taboo, was routinely invoked in southern newspapers, many of
which often took pains to report the so-called orderliness and self-control exercised by lynch mobs.

In addition, genteel magazines and journals of wider circulation did their
part, transmitting fearful images of sexual racism to white middle-class readers nationwide. When black men were not being depicted as butts of racist
humor, they were portrayed as sexual predators needing to be controlled at
all costs. In 1904, *McClure's* magazine brought out Thomas Nelson Page's series of articles defending the southern method of handling the black population. He deemed lynching a useful defense against rape by black men and
concurred with the view that Reconstruction was a "national blunder" and
that blacks lacked the maturity and intelligence necessary for responsible citizenship, an idea given national prominence, oddly enough, by Washington's
Up From Slavery. Popular racism was made respectable by men like Booker T.
Washington, Page, and countless others, and endlessly exploited by race-
baiting politicians. At the turn of the century, the racist perception that black
people embodied what was then widely termed the "Negro problem" was so
pervasive in American society—a sentiment shared by both southern extremists and "moderates"—that black spokespersons were obliged to enter this
debate on these disadvantageous terms.[19]

Miscegenation was regarded by the white South as the rape of white
women by black men. Consensual sexual relations between white women and
black men remained inadmissible and unspeakable within the reigning terms
of black criminality and pure, passionless white womanhood, as the bolder
black journalists who contested this myth periodically discovered. White
males' criminal acts—rapes of black women—also remained unspoken, or
were explained away by images of black women as wanton seductresses. The
law reinforced this sexual domination, as anti-intermarriage statutes denied
black women legal redress against white attackers. Lynching, often on the
pretext of rape, upheld and enforced this regime, punishing black men who
attempted to protect black women from whites' assaults.[20]

For the black South, miscegenation was synonymous with the rape of black
women by white men. Among educated circles, theories influenced by scientific racism and eugenics positing the immorality and degeneracy of mulattoes also provided an additional basis for arguments against intermarriage.
Drawing on such theories, but also in an assertion of race pride, black elites
with nationalist leanings challenged the views supporting miscegenation espoused by men like Frederick Douglass, T. Thomas Fortune, and the Wash-

ington, D.C., bibliophile Daniel Murray (all of whom had nonblack ancestry). Against the dominant view of mulatto degeneracy, these men had argued that progress through biological "race assimilation" was inevitable, accompanied by an eventual fading of racial differences. But this tendency to look favorably on "amalgamation," shared by the most radical of the abolitionists, was hardly universal among blacks. The tightening coils of white supremacy, along with the perception of the snobbery and opportunism of mulatto elites and the persistent white conviction that black progress and achievement were the result of white parentage, led a growing number of blacks, drawn mainly from the rising ranks of journalists, educators, professionals, and self-made men to reject such arguments. In the first place, arguments positing race mixing as a precondition for black progress presupposed black inferiority. And the race mixing that had occurred during and after slavery was a sign of moral degradation, not progress. Finally, such "assimilation" as had already occurred had failed to reduce white antipathy.[21]

No matter how much blacks spoke of race integrity, white opinion would not be dissuaded from its hypocritical, sexualized obsession with racial purity and social equality. Central to the justification of lynching as a deterrent to rape, the maintenance of the Jim Crow social order founded on involuntary servitude through debt peonage, convict labor, and elaborate customs, protocols, and rituals of racial deference—was white intolerance of interracial contact. Blacks and whites, particularly black men and white women, were forbidden to meet publicly as equals. For the white South, civilization also seemed to rest on preventing black men from interfering with clandestine or criminal sexual contact between white men and black women. In short, "social equality" was a sexualized diversion from and justification for political and social inequality, a slogan mobilized frequently, but most effectively at election time, herding white workers into the Democratic Party with appeals for the disfranchisement of blacks. Explaining local custom to a national audience, and in the process seeming to lend southern extremism a veneer of reasonableness, Thomas Nelson Page observed that the white South held "universal and furious hostility to even the least suggestion of social equality." Most blacks opposed lynching on grounds of its violation of due-process rights. But white extremists disingenuously equated antilynching protests with support for social equality, or worse, the condoning of rape, and many blacks defensively tried to divest their claims for social equality of their sexual implications (by opposing intermarriage) or insisted on the necessity of literacy and property qualifications for suffrage to eliminate poor blacks (and whites) from the inequitable social equation.[22]

The tragic irony of such accommodationist rhetoric was a stunning revelation to William Crogman in the aftermath of the Atlanta riot. Crogman, who would soon assume the presidency of Clark College in Georgia through

T. Washington's influence, noted as he recovered from injuries sus-
_ in the violence, that "here we have worked and prayed and tried to
make good men and women of our colored population, and at our very door-
step the whites kill these good men. But the lawless element in our population, the element we have condemned fights back, and it is [to] these people
that we owe our lives." Crogman was referring to the residents of Darktown
who had fought off an invading white mob. The Atlanta crisis forced men like
Crogman to see the transparency of the moral distinctions claimed by some
advocates of uplift ideology. Crogman was not the only victim; Rev. J. W. E.
Bowen, president of Atlanta's Gammon Theological Seminary, was beaten
with a rifle butt by a policeman. That elite blacks were not immune to the riot's
violence suggested the ultimate futility of moralistic repudiations of the behavior of the urban black population in the name of progress and civilization.[23]

J. Max Barber and Black Leadership in Atlanta

During the brief period before the riot that he edited the *Voice of the Negro*,
Jesse Max Barber's editorials vigorously protested race prejudice in Atlanta's
civic affairs and in national politics, and encouraged interracial cooperation.
Barber's journal was the voice of Atlanta's black leadership. Its editorial board
had included J. W. E. Bowen of Gammon Theological Seminary and Henry
Hugh Proctor, the influential pastor of the biracial First Congregational
Church. Proctor was deeply involved in local moral reform efforts, including
a protracted, unsuccessful struggle to eliminate Atlanta's vice and entertainment district, though in 1902 he succeeded in closing several dance halls. The
year before Proctor had helped defeat a measure that would have disfranchised blacks in Georgia. Black and white reformers had managed to block a
persistent movement for disfranchisement in Georgia since the late 1890s.
Bowen and Proctor were joined on the *Voice* staff by Emmett J. Scott, Booker
T. Washington's personal secretary and confidant. W. E. B. Du Bois contributed articles from Atlanta University. Pauline Hopkins joined as a regular
contributor after losing her position as contributing editor to the *Colored
American Magazine* in Boston.[24]

The circulation of the *Voice* ranged from three thousand at its first appearance to fifteen thousand in 1906. The magazine was available through sub-
scription and distributed nationwide by agents. It ran advertisements for local
black businesses and promoted its own publishing ventures, generally books
of didactic and success literature aimed at African Americans and promoting
uplift ideals. Frequently, the "vivid interpretation to the current history of
the day" found in its pages was reprinted and excerpted by "the press of both
races," sometimes, to Barber's displeasure, without attribution.[25]

Initially, the magazine's editorial and political content reflected prevailing black bourgeois sentiment on politics and cultural affairs, much of it promoting images of success and achievement. There were the usual features boosting black business enterprise and the constructive role in race progress played by Washington's Negro Business League.[26] The editors opposed segregation in public facilities and praised successful economic boycotts of streetcar companies that practiced Jim Crow, but they took issue with the older, integrationist claim that opposed separate black institutions such as hospitals, schools, and YMCAs on principle as "drawing the color line" or practicing self-segregation. The journal's position on labor relations echoed the usual New South argument by black elites that blacks comprised the most loyal and effective labor force in the region and were thus preferable to other immigrant groups. Contributors called for an end to the exclusion of blacks from northern industries and labor unions. Editors and contributors opposed black disfranchisement, insisting that literacy, not color, be the criterion for exercising the suffrage, so that elite blacks might be able to hold onto the vote against the tide of disfranchisement.[27] The magazine promoted ideals of black beauty and moral perfection through idealized, wholesome images of the race's manhood and womanhood in the visual arts and literature.[28] It published the occasional short story, and a great deal of poetry, some of it appearing in the dialect verse of such lesser-known southern black bards as Daniel Webster Davis and Silas X. Floyd. The journal decried the racial exclusion practiced by the officials of the Louisiana Purchase Exposition in St. Louis in 1904, and supported the Roosevelt administration's expansionist policy, though by 1906, the lofty praise Roosevelt received from such black Republicans as William Scarborough during the previous national campaign would give way to angry disillusionment over his handling of domestic racial politics.[29] The magazine opened its pages to black women contributors, such as Fannie Barrier Williams, Mary Church Terrell, and Josephine Silone Yates, and brought out a "Negro Women's Number" in 1904 that publicized the activities of the National Association of Colored Women. There were numerous publicity features on black cultural, self-help, and reform institutions.[30] Throughout the life of the journal, there were frequent occasions for condemnations of lynchings and the complicity of southern courts and newspaper editors with mob tyranny.[31]

What distinguished the journal was the maverick presence of Barber, whose editorials were often sharply worded protests against the abuses of southern society. Born to poor former slaves in Blackstock, South Carolina, Barber received his bachelor's degree from Virginia Union University in Richmond. Barber waged constant war on southern shibboleths, whether uttered by blacks or whites. Of the conservative race leader who asserts "I do not believe in social equality," Barber maintained that "men make their social spheres and men do believe in social equality." The magazine's support of black business was by no means incompatible with protest, a position many Bookerites were in the habit of asserting. John Mitchell, the Richmond journalist turned banker, drew Barber's wrath for telling a national banking conference in New York that "Negro loafers are the only block to our advance. . . . There is no fight between the intelligent white man and the intelligent Negro." Barber reminded Mitchell that many southern whites "do not like to see the Negro advance materially," quoting an item from a northern newspaper on a prosperous black minister and his family from Clay County, Mississippi, run out of town by "an envious mob." Barber called for "more discriminating language" on the part of black spokespersons: "What these men say is caught upon the wings of the wind and heralded to all parts of the country," sowing disinformation and self-delusion among whites on race questions.[32]

Barber used his editorials to provide a timely rebuttal to the numbingly commonplace negrophobic pronouncements in the southern press and pulpit. He delighted in debunking the self-righteous assumptions of white supremacists. To a white newspaper's demagogic broadside against black vagrancy, Barber countered that "particularly obnoxious and dangerous is the white tramp," who, according to Barber, "in many instances . . . paint their faces black, and, thereby, throw the police off their tracks." Casting doubt on the media furor over the Negro vagrant, Barber insisted that "this is one question where surely there can be no race discrimination." In the same number, he printed an account of the lynching of whites, including "the burning of a little white child . . . by his playmates" in West Virginia. According to Barber, "Saturn is devouring his own children," and "in the parlance of the man in the street, 'chickens are coming home to roost.'" Barber supported Fannie Barrier Williams's defense of the Frederick Douglass Center, an interracial reform organization founded in Chicago in 1904, from the assertion that it promoted "social equality." Indeed, this epithet was commonly hurled at antiracist efforts at interracial cooperation. Barber accepted the southern designation of the militant, "insolent Negro" as a badge of honor, calling for justice in the courts, on the railroads and electric cars, and at the polls: "[The insolent Negro] retorts that 'Grandfather clauses' and 'understanding clauses' belong to the days of feudalism and are the irrational and inhuman prerogatives of Monarchies and Oligarchies; that Democracy means 'the people' and that there are no grandsons in a Democratic government." In 1906, Barber used the pages of his journal to publicize the militant Niagara movement, in which he was actively involved. Members of the movement, a forerunner of the NAACP founded at Niagara Falls the previous year, challenged statements by such influential northerners as Lyman Abbott favoring disfranchisement, opposed the stage adaptation of Thomas Dixon's Clansman, and celebrated the memory of John Brown in hopes of strengthening ties between white liberals and black militants. Barber ran Du Bois's charge that an anonymous black leader (Booker T. Washington) subsidized five black newspapers with "$3,000 of hush money." Washington's supporters, including Oswald Garrison Villard, demanded conclusive proof from Du Bois. Although Villard remained unpersuaded, according to Louis Harlan, Washington employed "espionage and repression" in an attempt to derail the Niagara movement.[33]

Not surprisingly, such outspoken editorial content did not endear Barber to those civic leaders in Atlanta who regarded such statements outside the bounds of permissible speech. Barber was apparently made aware of this not long after his journal appeared, noting that "neither freedom of speech nor freedom of the press has ever been tolerated in the South." As evidence, Barber cited the dismissal of two white college professors for speaking out against the mistreatment of blacks in that section, adding that "it is far worse for the Negro." One of Barber's agents was harassed in Louisiana, forbidden to sell the periodical because "it was a political number and colored people were not allowed to discuss politics in those parts." Barber reprinted an editorial responding to his criticism of a white newspaper, which stated that "Negroes of this temper ought not to be allowed in these troubled times to hold positions in which they can threaten or disturb the peace of society." The editorial went on to say that if the law could not "suppress a pestilent nuisance like this," then "the usual result" was likely to befall "this insolent coon." Barber concluded with an appeal to "the better classes of white people" for the protection of freedom of speech and for blacks "to seek by right living to secure the confidence of the better element of the white people." Barber's reflections on free speech were a portent of what was to come when, as the gubernatorial campaign wore on in 1906, he attacked the candidates' descent into racist demagoguery. Though Barber's militancy, and the threats it elicited, suggested otherwise, white moderates committed to interracial cooperation could be found in Atlanta, and nationwide, and Barber sought their assistance as energetically as anyone else, including Washington. Washington had visited Atlanta a month before the riot to give the keynote address at a gathering of the National Negro Business League. Hoping to calm what had become an increasingly incendiary atmosphere, Washington found his speech reported in the press as primarily a denunciation of black crime.[34]

That August, another crisis, this one involving the black soldiers of the Twenty-Fifth Infantry stationed in Brownsville, Texas, would discredit Washington's leadership among blacks. Local white citizens protested the soldiers' presence to their congressman and repeatedly complained to officers about "uppity" black troops. The troops were accused of not giving way on the sidewalk to whites (a breach of Jim Crow custom), and when a white woman told of being thrown on the ground by a black soldier, all army passes for black troops were canceled. There was a search of the barracks for a black soldier who was alleged to have assaulted a white woman in her home. The allegation further angered the black soldiers, who considered the charge a fabrication designed to harass them, and insisted on their innocence. On the evening of August 13, nine to fifteen black soldiers reportedly entered the town and fired their weapons, killing a bartender and wounding the chief of police. They returned to the base and rejoined the regiment. When an investigation failed to reveal the persons involved, the soldiers again claimed innocence. Abandoning, in the eyes of black critics, the square deal, President Roosevelt dismissed the entire regiment of approximately 170 men without a trial, disqualifying them from further military support or employment. W. E. B. Du Bois called Roosevelt's action impulsive and stubborn, and found himself at a loss in wondering what Roosevelt had ever done on behalf of black Americans. Roosevelt brushed aside Washington's private entreaties on behalf of the soldiers, and the black educator was compelled to abide by the decision, losing whatever credibility he still had with the Talented Tenth. Noting white officers' defense of the discharge, Mary Church Terrell regretted that "this everlasting social equality question must be injected into everything." As if to prove her point, Roosevelt declared before Congress at the end of 1906, "The greatest existing cause of lynching is the perpetration, especially by black men, of the hideous crime of rape." He urged respectable blacks not to harbor criminals, and regarded industrial education as the best remedy for lynching. Barber strongly condemned Roosevelt's message, and protests against the president's handling of the Brownsville Affray wore on for months, including a mass meeting in New York organized by white sympathizers under the aegis of John Milholland's Constitution League, which sought to breathe life into the civil rights amendments. Eventually, partly through the efforts of Senator Joseph Foraker of Ohio, those of the soldiers found to be innocent were reinstated.[35]

Barber published his account of the riot from Chicago, explaining the causes of the lawlessness, and the circumstances of his abrupt departure from Atlanta in the riot's aftermath. He denounced "the wholesale arrest and disarming of colored people" as whites armed themselves. In the days after the bloody weekend, martial law was instituted, and militia, police, and armed citizens "became agents for Negro intimidation." Barber estimated that five thousand black citizens had quit the city, and he called the riot the inevitable result of an antiblack campaign orchestrated by unscrupulous politicians and newspaper editors. Barber cited the performance of Thomas Dixon's *Clansman* the previous winter, with its attack on Reconstruction, the Ku Klux Klan's heroic role in the redemption of the South, and the rescue of white women threatened by lustful black politicians as the first incitement to the mob spirit. Next was the eighteen long months of Hoke Smith's "vituperation" during the gubernatorial campaign. Barber attributed Smith's victory to his abusive rhetoric and calls for black disfranchisement. Barber charged that the editor of the *Atlanta News*, "the open champion of mob law," had "deliberately fomented and precipitated the riot." Once again, Barber confronted the hypocritical charge of social equality, noting that it was black women who were in real danger of rape. He reported the mysterious circumstances surrounding an assault on two white women that August, just before the white primary. A member of the investigating posse disclosed to Barber that the bloodhounds led them to the door of a white man, at which point the search was given up. Barber's source surmised that a white man in blackface had committed the crime. Barber found this a likely scenario, as "white men with blacked faces have been killed in South Carolina, Kentucky and Texas and one is now in jail in the District of Columbia for playing Negro while committing crime." Barber concluded that blacks had no monopoly on rape, and that many accusations were pure fabrications. Some cases involved whites disguised as blacks, others were cases of "mutual consent." In addition, Barber rejected the idea that the mob was comprised of "hoodlums": "Tho[ugh] launched by the rabble, the creative force of this mob was the upper class." Finally, the mob's orchestrated wrath was not directed at black criminals, indeed, it claimed among its victims a black woman, and had driven many enfranchised blacks out of town. " 'Humiliate the progressive Negro' was the command to the mob." [36]

Barber had telegraphed his account of the riot, with the assertion that white men in blackface were behind the "Negro rapes," to the *New York World*, in answer to John Temple Graves's charge that the riot was retribution for "a carnival of rapes" in Atlanta. He went further, accusing those men in blackface of being emissaries of Hoke Smith.[37] Barber signed his dispatch "A Colored Citizen." With that, Barber had transgressed the permissible limits of free expression. Barber's claims were circumstantial, but plausible, compared with the routine disinformation practiced by white editors. His cause was not helped by the anonymity of his sources, who faced similar punishment if they became known. Summoned by a tribunal of civic leaders headed by James English, president of the Fourth National Bank of Atlanta, Barber was accused of penning the offending letter, and told to get out of town or face a criminal trial. Not caring "to be made a slave on a Georgia chain gang," Barber departed for the North.[38]

Barber's account of the causes and aftermath of the riot went to the heart of antiblack southern (and national) ideology and, at the same time, challenged those aspects of racial uplift ideology that operated as rhetorical accommodations to the status quo. Even before the riot, Barber's editorial and political actions foreshadowed the emerging militancy of black leadership, a state of affairs that put Washington on the defensive. He typified those

African Americans of all social strata, race women and men, who were not as uncommon in the South as those northerners who fancied themselves culturally superior would have thought, and who went down fighting, or loudly protesting, that they knew their rights. Barber praised the "mighty hegira of Negroes from the country to the cities," attributing the migration to "the new slavery, peonage," and lynching.[39] He continued publishing the journal from Chicago for just one more year, until its final number appeared in October 1907.

Barber remained politically active, taking part in a number of fledgling black and interracial protest organizations in the first decade of the century. He attended the National Negro Conference in 1909, which led to the founding of the NAACP. The interracial conference was called after a race riot in Springfield, Illinois, the birthplace of Abraham Lincoln. The disturbance was touched off by an accusation of rape, and when a lynch mob was frustrated in its attempt to storm the jail, it vented its fury on two innocent black men and burned black homes and property. At the conference, Barber urged that full citizenship, the suffrage, and jury service were imperative necessities for African Americans. Barber moved to Philadelphia not long afterward and enrolled in dental school (at Temple University), beginning his practice there in 1912. He served in the Philadelphia branch of the NAACP (with the former North Carolina congressman George White) and joined the National Board of Directors of that organization after 1920. He was married and widowed twice, and died in 1949. Although he remained involved in civic affairs, he had left his mark as editor of the *Voice of the Negro* while still in his twenties.[40]

W. E. B. Du Bois was absent from Atlanta during the riot. While returning on the train he composed an angry poem, "Litany of Atlanta," which attempted to come to terms with the catastrophe: "Surely, Thou too art not White, O Lord, a pale, bloodless, heartless thing?"[41] The riot was a massive evil that mocked belief in a benevolent deity. Du Bois bitterly imagined Atlanta's black community as the sport of a racist white God. "Social equality" and the lynching for rape scenario functioned similarly as a popular justification for the evils of white supremacy in an avowed Christian republic. The combined abuses of disfranchisement, which was finally adopted in Georgia in 1908, the Brownsville dismissals, the Atlanta riot, and lynching merely required what many might regard a morally sufficient reason to justify them. Social equality and the myth of the black rapist provided persuasive justifications and incitements to legal and extralegal domination. In this period, and for a considerable time afterward in the South, social equality, the polarizing slogan of sexual racism, served the purposes of such state and national politicians as Hoke Smith and Roosevelt as effectively as a blackface disguise.

3

FIGURING CLASS WITH RACE

Uplift, Minstrelsy, Migration, and "the Negro Problem"

> The American people have fallen in with the bad idea that this
> is a Negro problem, a question of the character of the Negro
> and not a question of the nation. It is still more surprising that
> the colored press of the country and some of our colored or-
> ators, have made the same mistake and still insist upon calling
> it a "Negro problem," or a race problem. . . . Now, there is
> nothing the matter with the Negro whatever; he is all right.
> Learned or ignorant, he is all right.
>
> FREDERICK DOUGLASS, 1895

((((((

Uplift ideology protested the disfranchisement, segregation, and violence
wielded against black Americans, but it was also a reaction to the cultural dimension of white supremacy—the minstrel stereotypes that saturated American journalism and popular culture throughout the period. These demeaning
white images of blackness informed the popular understanding of racial issues
by social commentators as "the Negro problem," an assumption challenged
by Frederick Douglass and others. Since antebellum days, minstrelsy demeaned
blacks and effectively equated bourgeois morality—indeed, humanity—with
whiteness. Perhaps the most insidious aspect of minstrelsy, well into the
twentieth century, was its mockery of African Americans' aspirations to equal
status, its accusation that such aspiration meant a futile desire to be white.

But minstrelsy had more to do with white fears—and desires—than it had
to do with African Americans. Minstrel performance rituals, both in public
and at home, freed whites to entertain otherwise forbidden and dangerous
ideas about sexuality, assuaged their guilt, and enabled them to maintain a
sense of moral and racial superiority. Pretending that racial barriers were
nonexistent in society, many whites used the popular culture of minstrelsy to
assert blacks' immorality and nonconformity to patriarchal gender norms (a
crucial marker of civilized status). Douglass's perception of the tendency to

associate "the Negro problem" with the bodies of black men and women identified the terms by which racists, moderates, and even antiracists, black and white, reproduced the logic of bigotry. But for black elites, the constant threat of violence, or national controversies such as imperialism or foreign wars, might compel a reordering of priorities toward a militant perspective, yielding an identity that surpassed self-help ideology.[1]

African Americans struggled against the self-loathing of a narrowly racialized identity by attacking the ubiquitous and seemingly indestructible anti-black stereotypes found in popular literature, newspapers, Progressive Era magazines, advertisements, toys, and various forms of printed ephemera. The new mass-communications technologies of recorded sound, radio, and motion pictures would soon lend minstrelsy further social veracity through the reproduction of "real" photographic and audio images.

The elaborate nature of minstrel images was hardly arbitrary, linking narratives of antebellum blackface minstrelsy and slavery with the postbellum plantation legend calling for the control of black labor and obsessed with maintaining African Americans in their subordinate place. Through mass-produced photographs or illustrations circulated nationwide at the turn of the century, blacks were represented in rural scenes conforming to these expectations centering on labor and leisure. Often, blacks were depicted as farm workers, usually content with this status, or pictured in more leisurely pastimes. Such images of tattered, but carefree, banjo-playing, watermelon-eating blacks convinced whites that although blacks' simple joys made them virtually unexploitable, they needed to be protected from their natural inclination to indolence. Through these images, and within the coon songs that were so popular in the 1890s, minstrel narratives represented the desire to discipline black labor and discredit urban migration and the aspirations of black people to escape exploitation as field hands.[2] Feeling thus merged imperceptibly into thought, as the interdependence of the plantation legend and coon song themes of urban pathology inhabited much respectable commentary on race and social relations.[3]

It was difficult for African Americans to ignore minstrelsy, a major obstacle to the assertion of bourgeois black selfhood. Because photography was crucial in transmitting stereotypes, African Americans found the medium well suited for trying to refute negrophobic caricatures. In addition, black painters, illustrators, and sculptors, along with writers of fiction, produced antiracist narratives and iconography featuring ideal types of bourgeois black manhood and womanhood. At a broader, grass-roots level, there is an extensive photographic record of African Americans' concern to infuse the black image with dignity, and to embody the "representative" Negro by which the race might more accurately be judged. Studio portraits of uplift and respectability—depicting black families with attributes of cleanliness, leisure, and literacy—

Portrait of mother and children, ca. 1920s. This James Van Der Zee portrait,
taken in Harlem, enshrines the ideals of motherhood and domesticity.
(Courtesy of Donna Van Der Zee)

found expression in the sitters' posture, demeanor, dress, and setting. In most
portraits, whether of individuals, of wedding portraits, or of groups, one sees
an intense concern with projecting a serious, dignified image. And these still
portraits of refinement sprang to life in performance rituals, often based in
the church, of elocution, preaching, and in the jubilee and quartette singing
of Negro spirituals. Anything less than stylized elegance would betray the
ideals of race advancement and, indeed, hold the race back, as did the pro-
fusion of commodified, demeaning portraits taken of unsuspecting, often
youthful, and destitute African Americans.[4]

Many whites, however, remained unmoved by African Americans' attempts
at respectful self-representation. If images of black respectability were not
omitted from the white press altogether, they were relentlessly mocked and
parodied through minstrelsy. Minstrelsy's influence on ostensibly reasonable
public commentaries on race among social scientists, muckrakers, politicians,
jurists, and reformers must be acknowledged. Minstrelsy mocked the elite aspirations of African Americans, expressed, for example, through a missionary
interest in African nationhood, as "putting on airs." Its objective was often to
undermine transgressive images of black power and equality, as when Theodore Roosevelt, soon to be elected governor of New York, resorted to a comic
portrayal suggesting black soldiers' cowardice in the Spanish-American War

for Cuban independence after it had been widely reported that black troops had contributed significantly to the defeat of Spain.

Minstrel stereotypes encompassed a range of racist perceptions that laid the intellectual and emotional foundation for the assumption by social scientists, clergy, and jurists that African Americans were biologically inferior, disorderly, appetitive at the expense of reason, and, finally, unassimilable. In 1900, Nathaniel S. Shaler, the Harvard biologist, observed in the *Atlantic Monthly* that "coons will get wild when there was [*sic*] a racket going on, but all they will need is the firm hand of the master race." Having once criticized disfranchisement and lynching, the New York Presbyterian minister Charles H. Parkhurst voiced a change of heart. Claiming that "niggers" were unqualified for citizenship (he used the epithet "because that is what they call themselves"), he judged that "they never, never, never will contribute, in any part, toward forming the national type of the Americans of the future." Physical and biological differences proved that blacks were unassimilable. "They grow blacker and blacker every day. Their color forms a physical barrier, which even time, the great leveler, cannot sweep away."[5]

The Plantation Legend and Urban Pathology

Besides trivializing black power and aspirations to citizenship and equality, minstrelsy also sought to assuage white guilt. The plantation legend of popular literature reflected many whites' nostalgic desire that blacks remain the good-natured, humble creatures that they knew and loved in slavery days. Such nostalgia reflected the belief that blacks were contented, and did not need to be coerced and controlled as workers, although in fact they were policed through legal and extralegal means. And the mammy stereotype not only stirred fond memories of plantation life, it also provided whites with a forgiving image of maternal black womanhood that released them from a guilty awareness of black women as victims of rape by white men. In other words, these variations on the plantation legend, with their fictions of harmonious interpersonal master-slave relations, enabled whites to persist in the denial of the more brutal and systemic aspects of white supremacy.

Minstrelsy functioned as a theodicy that provided the state and civil society moral arguments for the necessity of racist beliefs, institutions, policies, and practices, much as the quasi-religious ideology of the civilizing mission functioned to justify imperial conquest. In this light, its importance in American culture pointed to a complex tangle of conflicting emotions, including guilt over antiblack violence, a vague sense of the betrayal of Christian and democratic principles, and yet, all the while, a continued desire for ownership and

Advertising trade card, ca. 1880s. (Courtesy of Louise Newman)

control of black male and female bodies mediated through fantasies of black forgiveness and submission, resided at the core of the plantation legend. Transported by the memory of her "dear good old Mammy," a southern woman writer hoped to correct the "misrepresentations" of those, carping so unfairly on "blood-curdling" accounts of lynching in the South, "who know nothing of the feeling which existed between slaves and their owners." While claiming to oppose slavery and to welcome its abolition, she insisted that "most of the colored people were far happier and better cared for as they were than as they are now." She averred that "the very happiest days of my life are connected with slavery, and I have always felt the joy of heaven would be incomplete were my dear old Mammy's face absent from the group that came to welcome me."[6]

Such nostalgia for pastoral scenes of the gallant old South provided only a momentary refuge from present fears. The plantation imagery also registered anxiety over urbanizing trends among African Americans. The nostalgia of the plantation legend, sparked by its antithesis in the menacing, sex-crazed, and peripatetic black brute of negrophobic literature, represented anxiety over the preservation of institutionalized white dominance predicated on racial purity. Fears of urban black men and miscegenation were further stoked by the image of the rootless, underemployed "worthless Negro" of southern towns, a monstrous image that was central to the journalistic and social science representations of urban pathology and mulatto degeneracy. The darkest white fantasies crept into presumably evenhanded journalistic writing about blacks. With reproductive sexuality as the linchpin for a Jim Crow social order predicated on racial purity, apologists for the white South's violent practice of lynching invoked their sense of the ultimate evil, of a fate worse than death.

Journalistic and Social Science Fears of Mulatto Degeneracy

The equation of miscegenation with the Negro rapist constituted a pornographic theodicy that provided a moral justification for lynching, which otherwise might have seemed to many reasonable people a patently evil practice. Against black and white critics, white southerners insisted that lynching, however barbaric, was necessary to protect white women from marauding black rapists and thus maintain racial purity. This visceral fear found calmer, more genteel expression in the fear of mulatto degeneracy, particularly the fear that mulatto men constituted a depraved, morally and physically diseased, threat to racial purity. Such fears had an enormous impact on public policy, as they were central to legal justifications for segregation in public accommodations.

Another daughter of the South, while denouncing "the atrocious conduct of an "inhuman" lynch mob, promised "facts" in defense of such behavior. Southern white women, she insisted, were constantly at risk of assault by "a savage brute" who "is nearly always a mulatto." With enough white blood to replace native humility with Caucasian audacity, this creature was above average intelligence and "sure to be a bastard." In this hereditary theory of debased racial nature, religion was powerless to halt an epidemic of illegitimacy among blacks; indeed, "the most prominent women in their religious enthusiasms are oftenest public prostitutes." As evidence, she cited the spectacle of a streetcorner female evangelist whose "ethics were high, while her gestures were lewd and blasphemous." From this "cesspool of vice" emerges a hideous monster with "the savage nature of and the murderous instincts of the wild beast, plus the cunning and lust of a fiend." Education was only increasing the likelihood of evil; little wonder that North Carolina, Mississippi, and Louisiana had already disfranchised blacks. The writer's language grew more agitated as she contemplated the threat: "For years the South has been a smouldering volcano, the dark of its quivering nights lighted here and there with the incendiary's torch or pierced through by the cry of some outraged woman. The days are feverish with suppressed excitement." Consequently, "these Negro men never can, nor ever could, have been received at the same fireside with white women." Although she seemed to hint at a forbidden sexual desire, repression won out as the writer warned antilynching advocates that they were excusing the crimes of brutes, and confessed that she was moved to speak on the issue "on account of a real anxiety."[7]

Leaving aside further speculation on the sources of this writer's anxiety, we would do well to note that men of state were no less susceptible to extreme utterance and action in projecting sexual anxieties onto black bodies. In 1909, Senator William H. Milton of Florida introduced a bill to ban intermarriage, providing evidence that fused scientific racism with minstrel caricatures. By a narrow margin, the Senate approved a motion introduced by Joseph Foraker of Ohio to table the bill.[8]

The desired effect of such respectable racism was to placate white fears and anxieties surrounding black freedom and social advancement. But this was hardly possible, requiring the power of the state to enforce the containment of African Americans. Herbert Hovenkamp, writing on the history of segregation, notes that although the legal profession is responsible for institutionalized racism, "the law is not autonomous . . . particularly in areas of explicit public policy making." Legal arguments in segregation cases were often influenced by the racist social science of the day and the "background" of race prejudices that were simply part of the cultural atmosphere. In *Berea College v. Kentucky* (1908), the Supreme Court relied on social science data to uphold a Kentucky statute mandating school segregation. Berea had been an anomaly as a racially integrated coeducational school in the South established by abolitionists. Postbellum fears of amalgamation, or race mixing, culminated in the Kentucky statute establishing segregation in that state. Berea challenged the constitutionality of the law, claiming that its religious freedom and rights to freedom of association were being violated. Hovenkamp cites a brief filed on behalf of Kentucky which included a scientific text that claimed to prove natural, fixed, and God-given black mental inferiority. This work of scientific racism was central to the state's justification for denying African Americans higher education at Berea and keeping the races apart. Belief in racial differences was so deeply entrenched in the late nineteenth century that "separate but equal" had been an accepted legal basis for segregation well before the 1896 *Plessy* decision. Popular and social science fears of intermarriage and mulatto degeneracy motivated what Hovenkamp called "the ultimate anti-amalgamation statute," namely, Baltimore's 1910 ordinance establishing residential segregation.[9]

Legal challenges to segregation by and on behalf of African Americans were sporadic, as federal and state courts were of no disposition to permit social equality, so closely tied was it in racist minds to miscegenation and the loss of white privilege. The courts would not become a major site of struggle until after the founding of the NAACP, in 1910.

In the meantime, the black intelligentsia struggled to turn public opinion in their favor. Adopting the racialized terms of bourgeois morality, elite blacks' intellectual response to popular and scientific racism was to affirm their humanity through the evolutionary idea of progress, assuming the authoritative role of agents of civilization and uplift in relation to the black majority. Black intellectuals and elites would guide blacks' assimilation into American society. Whether uplift endeavors meant the service of black ministers and teachers to the rural and urban black masses in the United States, the participation of black soldiers in imperialist wars in Cuba and the Philippines, or the evangelical errand of black church missionaries in Africa, black elites hoped that their support for the spread of civilization and the interests of the American nation would topple racial barriers and bolster their claims to humanity, citizenship, and respectability.

But even as elite blacks championed the respectability of uplift against embarrassing minstrel portrayals of ne'er-do-well blacks, they did not necessarily contradict the minstrel stereotypes confining them to field labor in the rural South. Indeed, black opinion makers occasionally embraced minstrel representations stressing culturally backward, or morally suspect blacks as evidence of their own class superiority. Uplift ideology thus revealed the contradictions of a black bourgeois ideology whose assimilationist claim to equality was limited, and like normative whiteness, itself indelibly tarred by race and gender inequality. While the ideology of a "better class" of blacks challenged dehumanizing stereotypes, it also exploited them, and could never fully escape them—this elite version of uplift ideology assented to the racist formulation of "the Negro problem" by projecting onto other blacks dominant images of racialized pathology.

Blacks' use of uplift rhetoric could be empowering in certain contexts, and did not automatically entail a belief in black inferiority. Nevertheless, the middle-class character of the emphasis on positive representations of educated, assimilated blacks of sterling character was interdependent on the image of the so-called primitive, morally deficient lower classes. This was a departure from earlier, Reconstruction-era notions of uplift based on inalienable rights and the legal protections associated with citizenship. Whether or not its exponents took cognizance of the fact, uplift ideology's vision of race progress thus remained trapped in a repressive, demeaning binary logic of race that was predicated on class and gender inequality and imposed by the defeat of working-class politics and social democracy in the South. In response, black elites tried to gain recognition of *their* humanity by ranking themselves at the top of an evolutionary hierarchy within the race based on bourgeois morality. That many African Americans had internalized these hierarchies testifies to their hegemonic character in a society so deeply racist that few were able to escape its impress. In short, through uplift's bourgeois evolutionism, black elites tried to alchemize elite status out of cultural narratives whose *prima material* was, and remained, ideologies of race.

At another level, elite African Americans responded with a flurry of literary and intellectual activity, including social work efforts and institution-building which sprang from this ideology of service, reform, and professionalization. Throughout the 1890s, and continuing through the first decade of the new century, altruistic uplift efforts among blacks coincided with the urban progressives' similar efforts to alleviate class and cultural divisions through the Americanization of immigrants within such moral reform crusades as temperance, the settlement-house movement, and other forms of social and charity work. In response to industrialism, many middle-class Americans embraced voluntaristic efforts, filling the void created by government inaction.

Whatever the goals of these civic-minded African Americans—to defend "the race" against its enemies, to bolster their own precarious status, or to accomplish both simultaneously—these intellectuals and spokespersons, as an extension of their duties as educators, ministers, reformers, clubwomen, or journalists produced a vast output of essays, sermons, instruction manuals, inspirational success literature, novels, historical works, and autobiographical writings on "the Negro problem" and formed organizations committed to promoting thought and culture, group self-help through education and self-improvement, and, at times, political protest on behalf of black Americans. As the Negro problem was increasingly understood as an urban problem, the self-styled black elite defined itself in public-spirited terms of a social mission of commitment and service to the masses.[10]

The Assimilationist Cultural Aesthetic of Uplift

Black elites' assimilationist cultural aesthetic was one of cultural vindication, in response to pejorative minstrel-based constructions of blackness. At the turn of the century, elite cultural values were crucial in discerning that which migration, in hurling southern rural black greenhorns in close contact with old settler northern black elites, had thrown into question: the ideological class boundaries that the latter group labored to maintain as evidence of group progress.

The exaltation of domestic virtue, symbolized by home, family, chastity, and respectability, all infused with an ethic of religious piety, provided the moral criteria for uplift's cultural aesthetic. Although outraged at whites' lucrative expropriations of black culture, virtually all but the most unchurched and bohemian black elites were unable to distinguish the aesthetically ambitious ragtime piano compositions of, for example, Scott Joplin, from coon songs. They would have nothing of the racial content of popular culture, judged guilty by their sinful "low-life" settings and minstrel associations.

Eurocentric images and ideals of respectability were central to elite blacks' aesthetic tastes. Grounded more or less in images of religious piety, only literature that was politically engaged, morally uplifting, and depicted heroic, idealized representatives of the race was worthy of the name. Beauty and physical perfection in literary heroes and heroines, often but not always patterned on European models, countered minstrel caricatures of blackness. Knowledgeable blacks claimed as their own such European writers of African descent as Pushkin and Dumas, against common assumptions of their whiteness. In the visual arts, the painter Henry O. Tanner (son of Philadelphia's AME church bishop Benjamin T. Tanner), who studied and worked in France, and the sculptor Meta Warrick Fuller produced dignified images of blacks, ideal "Negro types," as blacks proudly called them. Ira Aldridge, the African American thespian whose acclaimed performances in Shakespearian tragedies (including *Othello*) during the nineteenth century took place entirely in Europe, was a culture hero to many African Americans.

At the same time, elite black Americans dreamed of a universalizing fusion of black and European forms, in a manner that nonetheless privileged nonblack aesthetic criteria. In music, the model black artist was the West African–British composer and conductor Samuel Coleridge-Taylor, who transcribed and orchestrated Negro spirituals and West African folk melodies for the concert stage. In a preface to the composer's "Twenty-Four Negro Melodies," Booker T. Washington praised Coleridge-Taylor as a "British composer" of "native bent and power." To Washington and many others, black culture was an admissible idea only within the context of elite culture. Washington lauded Coleridge-Taylor's settings of "plantation songs" of the past generation and complained that "the Negro song is in too many minds associated with 'rag' music and the more reprehensible 'coon' song, that the most cultivated musician of his race, a man of the highest aesthetic ideals, should seek to give permanence to the folk-songs of his people by giving them a new interpretation and an added dignity." Washington may also have sought to rehabilitate his own image through association with Coleridge-Taylor, given his own use of minstrelsy in his writings and platform oratory.[11]

Yet the sheer popularity of black musical comedy (derived from minstrelsy), and the success of some of its stars, such as blackface comedian Bert Williams, challenged uplift's refined aesthetic ideals. Williams's fame and material success far overshadowed the achievements of men such as Coleridge-Taylor, who, although celebrated by African diaspora elites, died in relative obscurity in 1912 at the age of thirty-seven. By 1910, Washington seemed to have forgotten Coleridge-Taylor when he praised Williams's resourcefulness in gathering "material for some of those quaint songs and stories in which he reproduces the natural humor and philosophy of the Negro people." While proclaiming his distaste for "tiresome" vaudeville performances, Washington saw in Williams an exemplar of the "peculiar genius . . . of the Negro." The comedian's triumph did not rest wholly on artistic grounds: Washington also noted that he had "never heard him whine or cry about his color, or about any racial discrimination." To Washington, such forbearance made Williams "a tremendous asset of the Negro race . . . because he has succeeded in actually doing something, and because he has succeeded, the fact of his success helps the Negro many times more than he could help the Negro by merely contenting himself to whine and complain about racial difficulties and racial discriminations." Perhaps Washington had come to accept through Williams a pluralist conception of black cultural distinctiveness; as usual, however, he equated individual success and the renunciation of protest with the advancement of the race. His command over black leadership challenged by the recently formed National Association for the Advancement of Colored People (NAACP), Washington invoked Williams to counter the new protest organization. For Washington, the lowly minstrel origins of Williams's art, which carried him to Broadway as the star of the Ziegfeld Follies from 1910 to 1919, were redeemed by his success, which Washington harped on incessantly as if to ward off his own diminishing influence.[12]

The Role of the Home

Successful blacks such as Williams used minstrel formulas to gain access to white audiences. In their desire to counter such stereotypes, black elites based their authoritative status on equally formulaic racialized conceptions of bourgeois morality. Specifically, elite blacks celebrated the home and patriarchal family as institutions that symbolized the freedom, power, and security they aspired to. Through their frequent tributes to home and family life, African Americans laid claim to the respectability and stability withheld by the state and by minstrelsy's slanders. As a measure of evolutionary race progress, the cultivation of Christian homes had been a major tenet of freedman's education. Not altogether dissimilar from the photographic rebuttals by African Americans of racist minstrel images were the domestic scenes pictured in photographic exhibits of moral uplift commissioned by Hampton Institute and the American Missionary Association.[13] Thus, conformity to patriarchal gender conventions of sexual difference, and male protection and protected femininity, were proffered as a rebuke to minstrel stereotypes that denied conventional gender roles to black men and women. Although patriarchal family ideals created tensions between black men and women, they were a popular aspiration of African Americans, central as they were to uplift's vision of respectability.

So thoroughly did disfranchisement and Jim Crow contaminate the public sphere that many black reformers focused on those private areas perceived to be within their control, namely, the domestic realm. This was fundamentally a moral vision of racial uplift, centering on self-help. W. E. B. Du Bois spoke for many educated blacks when he held that "we look most anxiously to the establishment and strengthening of the home among members of the race, because it is the surest combination of real progress." Many regarded the patriarchal family as a sign of the race's triumph over the ruinous impact of slavery, and they wielded home life as a shield against slanders against respectable black men and women.[14]

In a late-Victorian age that restricted respectable sexuality to reproduction within marriage, educated blacks idealized matrimony as a platonic sharing of racial uplift responsibilities. In this view, the very idea of sexual pleasure was illicit. Procreative passion seized on the chaste ideal of "race building." At a more mundane level, marriage promised economic security, often to both partners, beyond its moral and instrumental advantages. Above all, marriage, as a sign of monogamous sexual purity, conferred status on black men and women, especially women, reflecting the extent to which their reputation was under siege. Marriage, so closely associated with moral superiority, could seemingly neutralize all the misogynist insults hurled by the dominant cul-

Negro exhibit, American Missionary Association, Boston, ca. 1905.

ture. Thus, a stable home and family life were often viewed as panaceas for the problems facing the race.

But uplift's paeans to patriarchal family life complicated the position of black women. Even as they sought the protective authority of matrimony, politically active black women like Ida B. Wells and Anna Julia Cooper gave voice to these difficulties. Wells described a tense exchange with Susan B. Anthony, the woman suffrage leader, on the conflict between marriage and public activism. "I noticed the way she would bite out my married name in addressing me," Wells recalled. "Finally I said to her, 'Miss Anthony, don't you believe in women getting married?' She said, 'Oh yes, but not women like you who had a special call for special work. . . . Since you have gotten married, agitation seems practically to have ceased.'" While acknowledging Anthony's "well-merited rebuke from her point of view," Wells "could not tell Miss Anthony that [her marriage] was because I had been unable, like herself, to get the support which was necessary to carry on alone."[15]

For her part, Cooper, in arguing for black women's right to higher education, attacked the myth that it rendered women unmarriageable. Cooper, who never remarried after her husband died in her early twenties, noted that education made women less reliant on "physical support," which, besides, did not always accompany marriage anyway. To Cooper, education expanded women's horizons, adding a range of platonic pursuits to an existence whose sole pleasures might otherwise be centered on "sexual love." But while they challenged expectations of women's subordination within marriage, both Wells and Cooper agreed with the importance of home, family, and marriage among blacks, and for American civilization. They, and other black women elites of the era, contested black bourgeois patriarchy from within its confines.[16]

Moral Reform Applied to Urban Problems

For progressive reformers, black and white, the home and family life epitomized middle-class morality and behavior. The home was a refuge from urban industrial society, with its poverty, disease, mortality, corruption, immorality, and crime. As blacks migrated from rural districts to towns and cities in the South, sensationalized journalistic accounts of crime, vice, and vagrancy associated black mobility with racial morbidity. For many educated blacks, as well as whites, for whom heredity explained both urban problems and influenced much of their vision of reform, social pathologies resulted from ill-considered sexual selection, as well as by prenatal and parental neglect. Among participants in conferences devoted to the study of the race's social problems, tributes to family, motherhood, and fireside training as bulwarks against sexual degradation, disease, and crime approached mystical proportions. This outlook was reinforced by popular science, which lent the participants' religious prescriptions an air of secular expertise.

At the end of the nineteenth century, eugenics, genetics, and heredity served as secular rearticulations of Calvinist notions of original sin and predestination. "While environment is a powerful factor in producing marked modifications of hereditary tendencies," claimed one such expert, "yet the influence of heritage has still greater power in the formation of character." In the laissez-faire spirit of the age, the burden for reform rested squarely on the shoulders of individuals and families. "To give uplift to the vitality of the [N]egro race," another reformer recommended, "the best work needs to be put into the enlightenment of present and prospective parenthood. Criminals," she warned ominously, "are often made years and years before they are sentenced to prison. Alas! too often made criminal before they are born." Anna Julia Cooper expressed a similar, albeit exaggerated, view of congenital immorality: "In order to reform a man, you must begin with his great-grandmother."[17]

To undo the damage of such biological determinism, one commentator called for reform institutions and "industrial grounds," instead of prisons, for the rehabilitation of kleptomaniacs, whose "disease was the intuitive inbred peculiarity of the parent." If strategies varied, the conventional wisdom on heredity and eugenics was highly influential among intellectuals and reformers, including blacks, as seen, for instance, in the scholarship of Thomas N.

Baker, the first African American to receive a doctorate in philosophy from
Yale University in 1903. Baker's dissertation on "The Ethical Significance of
the Connection between Mind and Body" asserted the disastrous physiologi-
cal consequences of impure thoughts and debased ideals, and approvingly
cited the work of Francis Galton, the British founder of eugenics. Besides
Baker, others employed nineteenth-century sciences such as phrenology.
Given that the courts were mining these sources of knowledge as well, it
would be surprising if reform-minded African Americans did otherwise.[18]

The concern for eugenics and heredity presupposed the dissolution of
moral restraints in the urban environment. Consequently, for many blacks,
"home training" represented the blueprint for social mobility and success.
Mrs. A. E. Pride of Lynchburg, Virginia, proclaimed that "The Home is the
seat of power and influence, that must advance and elevate any people."
Indeed, the family symbolized freedom from societal oppression.[19]

As the basis for moral, self-help strategies that located the roots of poverty
and social discord in the absence of patriarchal family life, popular scientific
theories of heredity made intractable problems like disease, crime, and mortality seem more manageable. Social inequality was a matter of careful sexual
selection and home training. But theories of heredity posited a biological determinism that clashed with the environmentalism of uplift's calls for home
training. However well-intentioned, these proponents of moral reform were
deeply conflicted in trying to assert control through racial uplift ideology as a
means of overcoming inbred pathology. Construing oppression as biologically transmitted moral failings offered them the agency and purposiveness
they sought as reformers. But at these public gatherings, this outlook ironically required the absence of the lower orders, the objects of their concern.
Had a representative of that class been in attendance to participate in the discussion, the sense of mission no doubt would have been deflated considerably.

Although much of what then passed for medical and social science would
strike us today as outmoded, such statements, not far removed from the scientific racism of claims of black pathology, represented the peculiar blend of
religious and technocratic impulses within uplift ideology. Strongly influenced by the racial assumptions of elite whites, African American reformers
reinforced dominant racial assumptions and theories. African Americans
were, after all, sexualized beings in dominant minstrel, journalistic, and social
science representations. But the reformers' biologism posed a feeble challenge to racial and sexual stereotypes, remaining imprisoned within an antiblack bourgeois morality.

Within the reform culture of uplift, urban pathology was traced to sexual misconduct. In a study of urban mortality, Eugene Harris, a white professor from Fisk University, linked infant mortality to "enfeebled constitutions
and congenital diseases, inherited from parents suffering from the effects of

sexual immorality and debauchery." After a careful consideration of the facts, Harris concluded, "I do not believe that . . . poverty or [the Negro's] relation to the white people presents any real impediment to his health and physical development." Only "a higher social morality" would conquer disease and mortality, problems aggravated by the frequency of single mother-headed households and "debauched and immoral parentage." In positing moral causes for the sickness and death of poor urban blacks, uplift proponents employed an apocalyptic Darwinian rhetoric of racial extermination; due "to a lack of moral stamina within," blacks might perish "in the environment of a nineteenth century civilization" if proper measures were not taken. The remedy involved a denial of the existence of oppression and a rationalization of poverty as the outcome of "sexual vices." The preoccupation with moral purity distinguished between deserving and undeserving poor, and social services were sometimes extended or withheld on these grounds. The New Orleans Afro-American Woman's Club Visiting Nurses Association organized to provide skilled assistance to the sick, but also took upon itself the duty to report "contagious cases" to health authorities and refused to send nurses to "persons in immoral houses."[20]

Although such punitive benevolence might assert itself within academic uplift institutions like the annual Hampton and Atlanta conferences, not all blacks subscribed to, or invested fully, in this view of uplift as a moral struggle waged within the race. Yet the interpretation of poverty and its attendant social ills as an outgrowth of vice and licentiousness was typical of uplift's emphasis on moral behavior as the basis for class distinctions. To be sure, such a "politics of respectability" might have a redemptive significance, serving the interests of some, particularly, as Evelyn Brooks Higginbotham has argued, working-class African American women held in contempt by U.S. society and culture, in addition to being no strangers to disfavor within the black community. For others, however, moral criteria explained the social difference between success and failure, the former accruing to membership in professional, institutional settings of racial uplift.[21]

The moralism of these conferences was enduring, expressed not only within black educational and religious institutions based on ideals of service but also through the establishment, through philanthropic largesse, of such charity institutions as the Camp Pleasant summer resort near Washington, D.C., for disadvantaged mothers and their children, founded in 1906. With its quasi-military regimentation, the camp's daily activities promised a refuge from urban problems and provided a model of social control. From the "supervised attention to the personal toilet" of the mothers upon rising at 6:00 A.M., to "the general assembly on the pavillion for morning prayer, for flag-raising," and for supervised games, to the sexual segregation of the children and the brief "free-time" when "the social worker gets a chance to

study" the children "under normal and natural conditions," the goal of training better mothers and more obedient children was constantly in evidence.
Each day ended much as it had begun, with "the lowering of the flag, music,
songs, and . . . giving thanks in prayer for the day's benefits received." Since
the camp lacked a bugler, taps was sung by the mothers before bedtime.
Here, and at local community centers under the control of the Board of
Education, as well as the Phyllis Wheatley YWCA in Washington, the goal
was to instill citizenship values and domestic virtues through "sewing, hand-
work, dramatics and music." Christian principles, ideals of social service, and
an interest in the arts were encouraged as providing a "wholesome and
unique method of sublimation." A major concern of the organization, from
this description, was the threat posed by women's sexuality: "There is an effort on the part of the personnel to appreciate, control and direct the human-
nature impulses and desires of the young women." The presumption of sexual immorality echoed the dominant culture's low opinion of black women.
In urging the camp's mothers to renounce sexuality, reformers were not only
guiding them toward Victorian ideals of chastity but also, perhaps less consciously, promoting a eugenic agenda.[22]

Black Social Advancement and Racial Antagonism

Even as elites perceived impoverished urban blacks as an object of reformist
concern, if not embarrassment, the striving and success of some African
Americans elicited the antagonism of many whites. This was particularly the
case in the white South, with its opposition to black education and federal
officeholding, and where Jim Crow laws and customs demanded the deference of all blacks. Indeed, many blacks discovered that their modest gains and
conformity to bourgeois mores had called forth not the anticipated acceptance of whites but, on occasion, even more animosity throughout the South.
Black elites were divided in their response to white antagonism: while some
identified a white backlash against black social progress, others sought to appease white supremacist views by projecting a racial stigma of social disorder
onto the black masses.

W. A. Lewis noted in the *Colored American Magazine* that blacks had made
"rapid progress" since emancipation "under the most trying circumstances,"
until "it was noticed that the Negro race was gaining success along many
lines." Lewis described the violent white response: "Impediments became
more numerous," as whites committed the "blackest crimes" against the race.
This view was endorsed by a number of anonymous college-educated black
contributors to one of W. E. B. Du Bois's Atlanta University social studies, a
view that transcended sectional differences among blacks. These respondents,

while claiming to be "hopeful" for the future of black Americans, saw blacks' advancement itself as socially disruptive: "I sometimes think that it is the progress rather than our lack of progress that is causing the continued friction between the races," reported a northern correspondent. Another found "the South . . . to be growing more antagonistic to [the Negro's] progress and self respect as a citizen." Still another, who noted the tendency of southern white politicians and journalists to inflame race hatred, believed that "the Negro's ignorance, superstition, vice and poverty do not disturb and unnerve his enemies so much as his rapid strides upward and onward." The African American novelist Charles Chesnutt regarded disfranchisement as an attempt to "forestall the development of the wealthy and educated [N]egro, whom the South seems to anticipate as a greater menace than the ignorant ex-slave." Frances Harper voiced through one of her fictional characters the fear that "in some sections, as colored men increase in wealth and intelligence, there will be an increase in race rivalry and jealousy." The vulnerability of black elites confounded those who emphasized intraracial moral and class distinctions, undermining the prevailing sentiment that disreputable elements were holding the race back.[23]

The plight of southern blacks produced several responses. Some concluded, as did the AME church's bishop Henry McNeal Turner, that continued white hostility in the face of black progress meant that the only future for black Americans lay in emigration to Africa. Turner's vehement calls for emigration in the 1890s, a popular movement among aggrieved blacks in the South, had precedents in the mid-nineteenth-century colonizationist, nation-building agenda of elite black nationalists such as Alexander Crummell and Martin Delany. Seeing little future for blacks in America, these leaders had sought opportunities for the uplift and "redemption" of Africa, claiming to open it to commerce and Christianity.[24]

Other respondents to Du Bois's survey, perhaps from the South, claimed that economic self-help—blacks' accumulation of wealth and property— would diminish, rather than exacerbate, white hostility. Still others became ventriloquists for stereotypes of Negro depravity. Indeed, their advocacy of economic self-help sometimes drew on such slanders. "The Negro," said one such respondent, "must rid himself of obnoxious characteristics, save money, acquire property, learn trades and become moral. The leading men among us must have sense enough to denounce the rapist as well as the lynchers." But the line would not stay drawn, as the myth of the Negro rapist besmirched and imperiled even the "representative" Negro. Another respondent believed that "for a long time it will be the task of the intelligent Negro kindly to point out deficiencies of the race and make helpful suggestions. Our country demands a better Negro," which only better homes, schools, and churches could produce. Such arguments reflected notions of bourgeois citizenship linking political rights to property ownership. But given the risks of southern life, black claims to property ownership, insufficient in themselves, could be justified and maintained only in the context of racial accommodation.[25]

Black Leadership Responds to Lynching

The unpopularity of black aspiration and advancement in the Jim Crow South, along with the epidemic of white violence, manifested in lynching, demanded a more militant response from black leadership. The violence posed a challenge for black leaders who had witnessed the gains of Reconstruction. In 1886, Douglass, the stalwart Republican then considered the preeminent race leader, denounced the sudden rise in mob violence against blacks, going so far as to warn whites of the consequences of continued oppression. Douglass insisted that "where justice is denied, where poverty is enforced, where ignorance prevails, and where any one class is made to feel that society is an organized conspiracy to oppress, rob, and degrade them, neither persons nor property will be safe." The anarchy of enslavement and its aftermath, not nature, had "maimed and mutilated" blacks. Still, he could only advise that blacks remain loyal to the Republican Party, "toil and trust, throw away whiskey and tobacco, improve the opportunities that we have, put away all extravagance, [and] learn to live within our means." Although Douglass urged thrift, patience, and temperance among blacks, a stance that reflected the Republican Party's stress on politics and equal rights over economic justice, and the usual injunctions toward the poor to remain in their place, he denounced lynching and refused to take a punitive attitude toward accusations of black criminality.[26]

Near the end of his life in 1895, and in the wake of Ida B. Wells's international antilynching campaign, Douglass again analyzed lynching, this time contesting the view that rape by black men justified mob terror. Douglass argued that older rationalizations for antiblack violence, namely, the threat of antebellum slave insurrections (the memory of which was often revived by white southern editors to discredit strikes or labor organizing) and, later, during Reconstruction, the fears of "Negro domination," lacked credibility in the ascendant "solid South" that was busily disfranchising black voters. Thus the cry of rape provided the latest justification for lynching and had the additional impact of bolstering policies mandating racial segregation.

Throughout the 1890s, Douglass's outspokenness on lynching was matched by the journalists Ida B. Wells and John Edward Bruce. The black press was a vital forum for dissent in this period. Wells had provided the earliest and most thorough analysis of lynching, gaining international fame after 1892 through her antilynching lectures throughout America and England.

Wells emphasized that lynching was used to harass and drive out economic competition from black businessmen. She not only disputed the myth that lynching punished and prevented rape, but argued further that some liaisons involving black men and white women were consensual, or coerced, initiated by white women. Such a candid attack on the myth of pure white womanhood placed her life in jeopardy, and Wells abandoned Memphis for Chicago as a mob destroyed her newspaper, the *Free Speech*. Wells urged that African Americans combat lynching with economic boycotts, out-migration, and self-defense. Giving what she called "self-help" an entirely different meaning by equating it with armed self-defense, Wells remarked that a "Winchester rifle should have a place of honor in every black home," to provide the protection that southern and federal authorities denied to African Americans.[27]

Bruce, like Wells a nationally syndicated journalist in the black press, was also a comfortably situated Republican officeholder in Albany, New York. He, too, believed that blacks should meet mob aggression with violent "organized resistance" of their own. Elsewhere he spoke out against "the systematic slaughter of innocent Negro men, women, and children by white men, who control and direct the social and political affairs of that section of the country." In 1901, Bruce, as Wells had done several years before, pointed out the fallacy of the rape charge as a factor in lynching, observing that out of 117 mob victims accounted for in 1900, only 18 had been formally charged with rape. According to Bruce, northern complicity with this state of affairs was the product of the Republican Party's betrayal of its tradition of social justice for interests and concerns "largely commercial." If Bruce, who at election time was a staunch supporter of the GOP ticket, believed lynching was ultimately linked to the imperatives of industrial expansion, Wells's extensive, earlier investigations of lynchings, which yielded the evidence used by Bruce, Douglass, and others, convinced her that whites' hostility to economic competition from blacks, not Negro criminality, was the root cause of mob violence. The myth of the black rapist was merely "an excuse to get rid of Negroes who were acquiring wealth and property and thus keep the race terrorized and 'keep the nigger down.'" Wells had initiated her exposé of mob violence after the lynching of three close friends of hers, businessmen and leaders of the Memphis black community.[28]

Though other blacks criticized lynching, including northern journalists such as Bruce, the volatile William Monroe Trotter, editor of the *Boston Guardian*, T. Thomas Fortune (until he became dependent on Washington's financial support), and Wells, from exile in Chicago, such candor was rare. Western black journalists were also freer to speak out against lynching and other abuses, joining those white editors who condemned mob atrocities.[29] In the South, such candor was dangerous and few risked such criticism, with the

Ida B. Wells, ca. 1890.

notable exceptions of John Mitchell, in Richmond, and J. Max Barber, whose Atlanta periodical *Voice of the Negro* vehemently denounced southern atrocities until the riot compelled his own flight to safety in Chicago.

Generally, southern journalists phrased their opposition tactfully, if at all. Mitchell, editor of the *Richmond Planet*, denounced the conservatism of black leadership. "The educated colored man," he believed, "will discuss every subject under the sun in meeting assembled, except politics, lynchings and kindred outrages." There were good reasons for such restraint, as outspokenness threatened "to bring ostracism . . . and a gentle hint from some unknown quarter that he is a dangerous Negro and a fit subject for removal either by flight or by the shot-gun route." Mitchell frequently ran gun advertisements and observed, as did Wells, that a Winchester rifle in the house combined with a willingness to use it would earn whites' respect. Yet while espousing armed resistance and self-defense, Mitchell also sent appeasing signals, perhaps to gain support for "polite, affable, progressive" blacks like himself. "On the other hand," he cautioned, "there is much to be done among our own people. The lawless, insulting, disreputable classes must be restrained, and . . . forced to the background." His militancy notwithstanding, Mitchell's reliance on uplift's bourgeois rhetoric of social division suggested the caution that conditions in the South exacted from black commentators. To Mitchell, and many others, it seemed that only respectable blacks could truly be victimized by racism.[30]

Anxious Responses to Urban Migration

Many black professionals, politicians, and artisans were at the vanguard of black migration throughout the post-Reconstruction period, hounded out of the South by Jim Crow, lynching, and economic violence. Carole Marks has noted that among the first to quit the rural South were either black professionals or those able to afford the expense of relocating themselves and their families.[31] In addition, younger blacks of all walks of life sought greater opportunity. Southern authorities denounced migration, blasting those who left the cotton fields with accusations of laziness, criminality, and immorality. The plantation legend, a staple of post-Reconstruction literature and popular minstrelsy, figured prominently in alarmist views of black migration, as older, faithful plantation slaves were contrasted in the southern press with younger, discontented, and migratory "worthless" blacks. Along with the hostility to migration, the growth of urban black sections also elicited anxiety among blacks and whites, an anxiety that only echoed dominant perceptions of those blacks trying to escape their lowly status as a labor reservoir in the South.[32]

What was good for black elites became increasingly worrisome if the masses followed suit. Although numbers of elite blacks had migrated, other black elites opposed migration and resorted to pejorative minstrel representations to describe black migrants to the city. Minstrel images provided an expedient framework for their anxieties toward migration, the new urban black communities, and their mass entertainments. To such critics, particularly in the North, urban migration posed a threat to their own status and represented the antithesis of black progress and respectability. Although some touched on shortages of jobs or housing, or cited labor unrest and bitter competition with white workers over industrial jobs, many treated black migration to cities as fundamentally a moral problem. To such alarmists, the image of urban blacks and their forms of leisure portended the doom of racial uplift ideals of service and upright moral conduct. According to this outlook, blacks belonged in the rural South, not in cities, where, it was feared, they would fare badly under the storm and stress of an advanced urban industrial civilization.

Despite the discrimination that made the rural South intolerable for increasing numbers of migrants, the response of William Scarborough, the black classicist of Wilberforce University, to migration in 1903, typified minstrelsy's serviceability for representing class distinctions. Before the American Negro Academy, located in Washington, D.C., Scarborough addressed "the growing problems of our northern cities" and the need to "separate poverty from viciousness and encourage the people to better morals and industrious, clean lives." Too many young urban blacks lacked ambition and a sense of purpose. "We have too many dudes whose ideal does not rise above the possession of a new suit, a cane, a silk hat, patent leather shoes, a cigarette and a good time," Scarborough declared. "Too many in every sense the 'sport of the gods.'" Scarborough alluded to Paul Laurence Dunbar's recent novel, a cautionary tale about the migration of southern blacks to New York City, with its gaudy temptations of cabaret life and the musical comedy stage. Scarborough noted the limited opportunities for blacks in cities, but he also drew on the old minstrel stereotype, updated in coon songs, of the slick, licentious, and criminal urban black dandy. Scarborough, hardly unique among a black leadership class unable to sympathize with destitute or ambitious blacks' flight from misery and repression in the rural South, seemed to play into the hands of mass-media pundits, southern white planters, and northern investors in large-scale agriculture, who, fearing the mass exodus of coerced black farm labor, discouraged migration.[33]

Although the black Methodist minister R. R. Downs was primarily concerned with anti-intellectualism among black ministers, minstrelsy lent him the terms for attacking the "uneducated" minister "who turns the house of God into a low class circus or minstrelsy, telling old stale jokes . . . rolling his eyes . . . and to crown it all by having his church christened a theatre by the young people." At the heart of Downs's vivid denunciation of a less-restrained ministerial style was panic over threats to established religious authority not only from new mass entertainments but also from the new, rival churches that welcomed recent black migrants. Downs conflated minstrel behavior with urban black folk and saw himself engaged in a struggle for leadership over the black masses, a struggle in which he felt hard pressed to compete against charismatic ministers and more participatory styles of worship, let alone the temptations of the stage.[34]

In time, anxiety over the urban black presence would subside, as some black elites acknowledged the benefits of migration for blacks. In 1906, William Pickens recognized that urban blacks had their "baser and uglier traits more than exaggerated" by the southern press, and that inadequate schools and legal protection, along with peonage and vagrancy laws, had launched the exodus to towns and cities. Noting the frequent complaints in the South about labor shortages and the scarcity of domestic servants in the cities, Pickens lauded blacks' increased independence in the trades and professions and commended black parents for sending their teenage daughters to school instead of subjecting them to "the perils" of domestic service, "where, if betrayed, the caste legislation leaves them without a remedy." Pickens noted the educational advantages available to blacks in the North; southern blacks were being robbed of public educational funds. But Pickens, too, used minstrelsy as a demonstration of race progress through class differences—"there is the Negro of the 'coon song,' and of the slum dive"—but argued that "the representative class of city Negroes" was superior to migrants from the backwoods with no chance at civilization. For Pickens, the Yale-educated son of South Carolina sharecroppers who would later become an official with the NAACP, uplift ideology was not a barrier to a sophisticated analysis of the causes of migration and its benefits for blacks, but the old, self-serving habit of associating impoverished urban black migrants with minstrelsy, vice, and criminality persisted.[35]

Evocations of minstrelsy proved useful in Booker T. Washington's promotion of industrial education and his rise to hegemony over black leadership. Washington's criticisms of urban migration lent credence to his rhetorical broadsides against higher education. Higher education seemed to Washington to upset the natural order of things, the devoted black peasant's organic ties to the soil. "The result of this progress," he insinuated, "is that in too many cases the boy thus trained fails to return to his father's farm, but takes up his abode in the city, and falls, in too many cases, into temptation of trying to live by his wits, without honest, productive employment." Thus, higher education did not bring progress but contributed to the ranks of "the large idle class of our people that linger about the sidewalks, barrooms, and dens of

Statue of Booker T. Washington, Tuskegee Institute.

sin and misery of our large cities." In Washington's eyes, educated blacks, having forgotten the virtues and usefulness of slavery and farm labor, bore responsibility for the social disorder associated with urbanization. Washington's use of minstrelsy contributed to his popularity with whites. A youthful Claude G. Bowers, later the author of a popular historical work attacking Reconstruction, marveled in his diary at Washington's platform oratory, which apparently included an inexhaustible store of "darky" jokes.[36]

White politicians and journalists were influenced by such views and in turn contributed to the public apprehension toward migration, which was said to have reaped a misbegotten harvest of vagrant and criminal urban blacks. Contemporary observers could not but regard such migration as a troubling deviation from blacks' appointed function in southern economic and social relations. Taken in by southern journalistic myths, the journalist Ray Stannard Baker attributed the phenomenon of the criminal "worthless

Negro" to the higher wages paid by New South industries, which allowed the "better and more industrious Negroes" to achieve economic independence, leaving behind not only the South, the exploitation of the cotton fields, and the white man's kitchen, but also a growing class of "naturally indolent" rural blacks. Baker, in an attempt to diagnose the causes of the Atlanta riot of 1906, linked "increased Negro idleness" to the recent migration of prosperous blacks. "Many have gone North and West, many have bought farms of their own, thousands, by education have become professional men, teachers, preachers, and even merchants and bankers—always draining away the best and most industrious men of the race and reducing by so much the available supply of common labor." In a manner consonant with contemporary social science attempts to explain the existence of the black "underclass," which claim that black elites had abandoned their historic "uplift" function as "role models" by leaving behind black communities, Baker equated black social mobility with "race problems." In a racially segregated, class-stratified society bent on depressing wages and maintaining blacks as a subservient, reserve labor supply, Baker was unable to credit "industrious" blacks. In describing a "fierce contest between agriculture and industry" for a "limited and dwindling" supply of black labor, Baker felt that blacks were better off as farm laborers "under the discipline of white land owners." However sincere his intentions, Baker's account linked the progress of the few to those " 'worthless' Negroes, perhaps a growing class" that "one finds everywhere." [37]

Perceived through the distorted lens of the plantation legend, black social mobility, in Baker's account, was tainted by the image of the ubiquitous, vagrant Negro male, roaming the southern countryside from town to town. Journalists and philanthropists, professing objectivity, were nonetheless susceptible to this logic. The vagrancy Baker warned of, the product of southern statutes that made it a crime to leave exploitative labor contracts and seek the best price for one's labor, as any free, rational, worker would do, also irked William Baldwin, the New York railroad magnate and trustee of Tuskegee. Baldwin also served on the Southern Educational Board, which dispensed philanthropy for black colleges that emphasized industrial education. Baldwin hoped that education would encourage blacks to "willingly fill the more menial positions, and do the heavy work at less wages." He advised blacks to "avoid social questions; leave politics alone; continue to be patient; live moral lives; live simply; learn to work . . . know that it is a crime for any teacher, white or black, to educate the negro for positions which are not open to him." Some black pundits echoed such skittishness toward migration, and they, too, hoped to reverse the tide of events. Kelly Miller believed that "the 'citification' of the country Negro" as a solution to "the race problem should be accepted . . . with prudent hesitation." The 1901 Hampton Conference committee on resolutions "deplore[d] the rush of our young people to the large Northern cities," where they too often fell "an easy prey to the vices the slums and alleys."[38]

Although many had virtually no economic stake in these matters, being remote from industrial capital and production, southern black clergy, businessmen, and opinion makers with views less extreme than Washington joined the consensus against black migration. Though they reaped little more than moral capital, and perhaps an occasional philanthropic windfall out of their position, black ministers' and small entrepreneurs' views mirrored those of white planter and philanthropic elites, as these black leaders feared losing the congregations and markets upon which they depended for their livelihood. For black intellectuals with even less of a stake in the location of the black population, urban migration constituted a moral and spiritual crisis among younger black migrants, as well as a crisis regarding their own cultural authority. In any case, threatened by their loss of control over the actions of southern blacks, they and other northern black commentators seized on the city as a dangerous place of leisure.

Sharing the dominant culture's general anxieties on the subject of race and urbanization, some elites found fault with the new popular entertainments that served these migrants. Such illicit pleasures, in this view, were seducing southern black men and women away from the forced and ill-paid farm or domestic labor that many—including men of Washington's ilk—characterized as dignified labor and the work ethic. Lest they be confused with newly arrived urban black folk, elite blacks also extolled Victorian and European cultural ideals and looked with disapproval, if not covert and guilty pleasure, upon such emergent black cultural forms as ragtime, blues, jazz, and the social dance styles that animated black vaudeville, minstrel troupes, traveling tent shows, and, later, musical comedy revues. To many genteel blacks, it was bad enough that these urban amusements—saloons, cabarets, and places of gambling and prostitution—were disreputable; still worse was that these black cultural forms were indistinguishable from minstrelsy. Seldom, if ever, did black pundits consider that black cultural expression, while in part contained within the mass cultural industry of minstrelsy, might bear an anterior or independent relationship to it.

Black Leadership on the Labor Question

Black leaders had not always opposed migration, used minstrelsy to characterize urban blacks, or espoused antilabor views. In the 1880s, amidst labor and populist struggles, such men as Fortune and D. A. Straker pursued economic analyses of labor exploitation in the New South. But these men, and other labor advocates such as Henry MacNeal Turner of Georgia and

Robert B. Elliott of South Carolina, were shoved to the wall as a consensus emerged against labor organization and working-class politics, enforced by political violence and reinforced ideologically by laissez-faire appeals to self-help and more efficient agricultural methods. Claiming a harmony of interest between labor and capital, by the 1890s many black spokespersons, including Anna Julia Cooper and Washington, were siding with business elites against organized labor.

For many blacks, besieged from all sides, a bourgeois race consciousness patterned after missionary notions of uplift precluded an understanding of class conflict and the exploitation of workers, black or white. Class survival in a hostile society influenced their thinking on such questions. M. Arnold Morin, a contributor to the *A.M.E. Church Review*, the leading black thought journal of the day, wondered "what has given birth to the numerous trades-unions" and "why . . . the workman, the laborer, [and] mechanic" were "ever ready to follow the advice of the supposed reformer?" Instead, Morin urged "tenacity of purpose . . . these are the qualities . . . of the races that have guided the way to civilization as of those that have led in christianizing the world." To this minister, labor unrest posed a challenge to divine and minis-terial, as well as secular, business authority. Indeed, they were practically one and the same in his analysis.[39]

Morin's remarks on labor agitation also reflected the general antagonism toward organized labor as a source of social disorder at the turn of the century. For African American elites, this conviction was hardened by the dis-criminatory practices of most unions, and the violence that often accompa-nied the use of black strikebreakers by management. The preference of many progressives for moral reform crusades over organized labor was expressed by one black commentator, a temperance advocate, who noted that "strikers, who were, in their sober moments, quiet and inoffensive, have become fren-zied . . . so that they become fiends." In her view, which reflected the anti-labor nativism of the day, intoxicants, the working classes, strikes, and vio-lence were virtually synonymous.[40]

Antilabor sentiment among elite blacks was often an expression of their view that their main antagonist in that era of strained and violent race rela-tions was the white working class, or, in the South, the "poor white." Cer-tainly this rang true enough in the experience of many blacks, North and South. Indeed, black middle-class identity was often defined in relation to the racial prejudice of working-class whites as much as it was constructed in rela-tion to impoverished African Americans. According to Gerald Jaynes, black workers, excluded by white laborers, were "forced to appeal to the 'self inter-est' of profit seeking capitalists for economic salvation." Black spokespersons generally identified with the interests of white business elites and sought an alliance with them against discriminatory white workers. Such antilabor sentiments were often accompanied by nativism, as elite blacks, like their white counterparts, associated unions and radicalism with foreign-born workers. Black opposition to unions was led by Washington and his National Negro Business League, which sought to promote entrepreneurial activity among blacks, somewhat along the lines of Marcus Hanna's National Civic Federation. Washington regularly praised the loyalty of black workers whom he insisted could be trusted not to strike, and who, from his standpoint, constituted "the best free labor in the world," suggesting an altogether different meaning for "free" that reflected the overwhelming advantage of employers. Black elites seldom realized that in their alliance with white elites they were pitting themselves not only against racist white workers, but black workers as well. Indeed, such a position required a refusal to recognize blacks as an economically exploited group, and amnesia on the recent phenomenon of interracial populist politics.[41]

Apart from its opposition to organized labor, the Negro Business League embodied Washington's economic self-help ideology. Within it, racism became a taboo subject. As one of his disciples put it, "We need money. . . . We can't afford to lose time with such things as the so-called color question, especially when there is a dollar in sight. My experience has taught me that the only time my neighbors bothered me about my color was when I became broke." Men of this perspective held much faith in market rationality as a force against antiblack prejudice. Such boosterism ignored not only white intolerance of economic competition from blacks but also the structural impediments to black business. The most viable business enterprises, such as banks or insurance companies, and later, nationally distributed black newspapers such as the *Chicago Defender* (failed newspaper ventures by and for blacks in the urban South were legion) and hair and cosmetics concerns such as the booming trade established by Madame C. J. Walker in 1904, were those that served the specialized needs of the segregated African American market.

Under such strained circumstances, blacks' worship of the gospel of wealth occasionally soured, eliciting less sanguine assessments of "race" enterprises. "Many colored persons in business," remarked one disgruntled commentator who spoke of small shopkeepers, very likely from personal experience, "are lacking in politeness, civility and disposition to please their patrons." Carter G. Woodson located the blame on the other side of the counter, believing that the difficulties of black businesses were aggravated by a lack of race-pride and cooperation among black consumers. While many blacks of the Bookerite persuasion, and later, Garveyite black nationalists, saw the accumulation of wealth as crucial to racial uplift, their analysis of the problems facing black business often remained at the level of castigating blacks for their lack of entrepreneurial spirit, thriftlessness, or their unwillingness to make personal sacrifices, namely, to pay higher prices, to patronize black enterprises. While there was endless discussion of the need to accumulate wealth, commentators on black business seldom addressed disadvantages such as the lack of capital, credit, and business experience, and discriminatory high rents, as well as the difficulties of competing with large-scale enterprises. Such alternatives as consumer cooperatives also remained largely unexplored. The accumulation of wealth was as popular among elite blacks as the embrace of bourgeois morality, but their conflation of moral improvement with the material advancement of the race was often ill equipped to address the systemic barriers to black enterprise.[42]

Black Radicalism and Anti-Imperialism

National controversies such as the Spanish-American War, combined with the ongoing crisis of antiblack violence in the South, represented moments of rupture in which the ideological business of racial uplift ideology was disrupted. The explosive nature of such issues made many black elites reconsider the assumptions of racial uplift. As Willard Gatewood has observed, race and color were crucial in determining national attitudes toward expansion and toward the capacity of the Cuban and Filipino peoples for self-government. Conflicts among African Americans over imperialism reflected the national divisions on the issue, as many Anglo Americans and immigrants, for various reasons, opposed expansion. What enabled a consensus on imperial control over Cuba, and later, in 1899, over the Philippines, was race—specifically, the belief in Anglo-Saxon supremacy. Imperialists argued that the United States would bring progress and civilization to childlike, primitive peoples, preparing them to exercise self-government at some unspecified future date. Black American elites were painfully ambivalent, weighing the avowedly racist justifications for expansion (and for anti-imperialists' arguments as well), escalating antiblack violence in the South, and the mistreatment that black troops faced in a segregated army, over against the fact that the U.S. military and the American nation provided black men with virtually the only opportunity, itself painfully limited, for status, prestige, and advancement.

During the Spanish-American War, black Republican Party regulars serving the party of expansion rallied black support and the enlistment of black troops. They were mortified, perhaps enraged, when black soldiers encamped in the South encountered white hostility, triggered by the sight of armed black men in uniform and the threat of social equality they represented. The black soldier, of necessity on his guard before reaching the actual battlefront, was a controversial figure: to many whites, he threatened assumptions of Anglo-Saxon manliness and dominance; to blacks, he was a glorious example of African Americans' manhood, fitness for equality, and citizenship rights.

During the war, however, blacks were further outraged by the lynching of a black federal postmaster in South Carolina, the bloody massacre of blacks in Wilmington, North Carolina, that had accompanied a political purge of African Americans from that state's politics, and countless other episodes of racial violence. Angered by federal authorities' refusal to protect black lives and property, African Americans generally supported their troops, while expressing less enthusiasm for the war and for expansion. Among blacks, the pragmatic view that the war presented an opportunity to counter racial prejudices through a demonstration of the race's loyalty, patriotism, and courage was enough to turn opposition into ambivalent, qualified support.

There were racial considerations to black support for the war, as well. Many African Americans sympathized with the Cuban cause, claiming a racial kinship with the many Cubans of African descent. Furthermore, African Americans took pride in the widely reported exploits of the black Cuban military commander, Antonio Maceo, who was killed in battle in 1896.[43]

Nevertheless, the black press records a wide-ranging, divided, and often angry debate on the war among blacks. Indeed, the crisis of war and domestic violence helped revitalize a militant equal rights perspective among black commentators. Citing the denial of constitutional rights, the Jim Crow facilities, the mistreatment of black troops by southern white civilians, and the outbreaks of racial violence in the South, a few editors voiced an unconditional opposition to black soldiers' participation. Some editors printed strident attacks against the hypocrisy of expansionists and wished defeat on the United States as retribution for its tolerance of crimes against blacks:

> The American white man's rule in dealing with the American Negro . . . in times of peace and prosperity [relegates] him to the rear, deprives him of his rights as an American citizen, cuts off his opportunities of existence, outrages colored women, burns down his home over his wife and children. . . . More than 500 colored men and women have been murdered by the American white people in the past 25 years and now they have the audacity to talk about the cruelty of Spain toward the Cubans. There is no half-civilized nation on earth that needs a good hard war more than the United States, and it is high time if there is any such being as an omnipotent just God, for Him to rise and show His hand in behalf of the American Negro.[44]

The occasional radical voices of dissent against the forces of imperialism, white supremacy, and plutocracy, and their justification by evolutionary theory, countered the conservative tenor of black thought in this period. Frank Putnam, of Chicago, noted that the "aristocracy of money is enslaving the white masses at the North; is preparing to enslave the patriots of Cuba, Porto

Rico and the Philippines, and is aiding by consent the re-enslavement of the colored men of the Southern states." To this writer, such atrocities were a throwback to the primitive age before Christ, when "survival of the fittest— that law of the jungle, ruled." This commentator, who identified himself as "a laboring man," called for the unification of the forces of labor and democracy. Putnam's analogy between black oppression in the South and U.S. imperial subjugation in the Caribbean and the Philippines was commonly invoked among anti-imperialist black editors and spokespersons; his inclusion of the northern white working class in this analysis, however, was unique. Reverdy C. Ransom, an AME minister and Christian Socialist, also from Chicago, be- lieved that "the Negro will enthusiastically espouse the cause of socialism we cannot doubt." Less concerned with portraying themselves as middle class, Ransom, Putnam, and others resisted the prevailing dogmas branding poor and working people as unfit. From Richmond, John Mitchell contributed to anti-imperialist opinion among black editors, calling attention to troubling developments in the United States. Mitchell, angered by the recent collapse of the Afro-American Council and Ida B. Wells's ouster as chairman of that group's antilynching bureau, equated the "anarchy" of lynching in the South with "slavery in the Philippines."[45]

Although Mitchell was hardly alone among blacks in condemning imperi- alism, others consciously or unconsciously persisted in viewing both domestic and global affairs through the racial lens of developmental paternalism. As for socialism, it did not take hold among many black intellectuals until the post–World War I economic crisis, including antilabor violence against blacks in the South, outbreaks of white mob violence against blacks in several cities across the nation, and the federal government's Red scare.[46]

Imperialism occasioned an angry debate over the abandonment of blacks by the federal government through its denial of equal protection. But the ethos of self-help tacitly discouraged such constitutional concerns. For mar- ginalized black elites, uplift ideology and self-help promised a sense of power and authority, and informed criticism of unscrupulous black politicians. But it held limited effectiveness as an antiracist response. When members of the black intelligentsia anxiously contemplated the urban or rural black masses, their self-help ideology and opposition to urban migration were often indis- tinguishable from the paternalistic views of northern and southern capitalists, moderates, philanthropists, and reformers. Indeed, black elites had appealed directly to the self-interest of the business class. With exceptions, they served mainly as spokesmen, not so much representing blacks as speaking for them, testifying to the loyalty and Americanism of black labor in the South.

A perpetual state of violence, and crises such as the Atlanta riot of 1906, might disabuse black intellectuals and journalists of their dubious conflation of race and class and foster a political consciousness that reasserted an en-

larged vision of civic and political equality. Uplift and its significance fo
black leadership was constantly contested, and there were always those fo.
whom the mere idea of progress could never ward off the dire exigencies of
everyday life or deliver on the promise of social advancement. The precarious
social position of educated African Americans, subjected to humiliation by
the poorest whites and constantly renegotiating their relationship to other
blacks, ensured that racial uplift ideology as a basis for black bourgeois consciousness would be suffused with inherent frustrations and perpetual anxiety.
After all, for racial uplift, understood in these terms, to function properly ultimately depended on the recognition of the other, namely, those often contemptuous whites and insubordinate blacks. And racial uplift ideology seemed
to function best for those of its adherents who had internalized the dominant
language of patriarchal power, as did William H. Ferris and other black nationalists.

The racialized argument for class stratification among blacks represented
the black male intelligentsia's attempt to give uplift to the debased status of
race with the privileged category of masculinity. But the truest spirit of uplift
ideology was marked by a commitment to education, both formal and informal. This meant making the most of limited resources, sharing stories of slavery and freedom, of past and present struggles handed down by elders, and
practicing ideals of kinship in the daily life of the community rather than
merely preaching a sterile public version of it. Images of property ownership,
patriarchal authority, and militarism, striving toward the appearance of national power, marginalized the community's strengths and human resources
and the unsung efforts of community women. In the meantime, through the
rhetoric of uplift, "the better class" sought to rise above minstrelsy and "the
Negro problem." But in opposing migration, elites seemed content to have
destitute, harassed African American men and women remain in their place.

4

THE CRISIS OF NEGRO INTELLECTUALS

William H. Ferris and Black Nationalist Thought

In my mind's eye I see the bronze statue of the college Founder, the cold Father symbol, his hands outstretched in the breath-taking gesture of lifting a veil that flutters in hard, metallic folds above the face of a kneeling slave; and I am . . . unable to decide whether the veil is really being lifted, or lowered more firmly into place; whether I am witnessing a revelation or a more efficient blinding.

RALPH ELLISON, *INVISIBLE MAN*

❨ ❨ ❨

Ralph Ellison's ambiguous reference to the statue of Booker T. Washington, symbolically portraying the founder of Tuskegee as lifting the veil of ignorance from a kneeling former slave, describes the equally ambiguous struggle of William H. Ferris, and generally, black intellectuals of his day, to represent the race's destiny in terms uncontaminated by racism. Educated at Yale and Harvard, and thus poised to be a factor among black leaders, William H. Ferris (1874–1941) drifted through a succession of journalistic jobs, failing "to succeed greatly in any field," as Carter G. Woodson put it. Woodson seemed to attribute Ferris's difficulties to personal flaws, which he may have traced to his assimilationist "mis-education." Woodson could have been more charitable, however, in acknowledging the uphill battle faced by Ferris, and by practically all black intellectuals and journalists. Ordained as an AME minister, Ferris's career included a stint as general literary assistant with that denomination's Book Concern in Philadelphia, from 1917 to 1919. American society had no place for him, and this may well explain his contemporaries' widespread perception that he was an eccentric. After having exhausted the patience of Booker T. Washington, W. E. B. Du Bois, and Monroe Trotter, he finally found his niche within Marcus Garvey's mass movement in the early 1920s.[1]

Apart from his tenure with Garvey from 1919 to 1923 as editor of the *Negro World*, Ferris's most enduring achievement was the publication of his magnum opus, *The African Abroad, or His Evolution in Western Civilization, Tracing His Development under Caucasian Milieu* (1913), an idiosyncratic combination of autobiography, African and African American history, and contemporary analysis of the competing factions within black politics and leadership. Ferris counted himself among the radicals, opposed to Washington's program of industrial education and its apparent acquiescence to black disfranchisement. Written between 1902 and 1913, *The African Abroad* provides a glimpse of the growing opposition to Washington's leadership, an opposition that dated to the founding of the American Negro Academy in 1897 in Washington, D.C., at which Ferris was present. Ferris's ambivalent writings asserted race pride and embodied the quest for a distinctive cultural identity. But his quest for an independent group consciousness, so deeply influenced by Du Bois's paradigmatic statement of the problem of double-consciousness, sunk under the burden of Ferris's negative comparisons of black people to Anglo-Saxon power and civilization. Above all, Ferris's book was a bid for recognition and influence in the realm of ideas. Being a "disfranchised intellectual," to borrow Wilson Moses's apt phrase, in an age of hostility against higher learning for blacks, magnified Ferris's difficulties.[2]

Ferris was born in New Haven, Connecticut, and graduated from Yale in 1899. He had studied under the Darwin-influenced sociologist William Graham Sumner, whose study *What Social Classes Owe to One Another* might be briefly summarized: Nothing. Ferris received his M.A. from Harvard Divinity School in 1900. Little is known about his youth and college days, though while a student at the Divinity School Ferris headed, and perhaps helped draft, a petition read in Congress by the expansionist senator Henry Cabot Lodge of Massachusetts protesting antiblack violence in the South during the Spanish-American War.[3] There are a few scattered letters, his surviving journalistic writings, and finally, the autobiographical passages of *The African Abroad*. In that work, his aspirations and anxieties, and racial uplift's relationship to black nationalism, are on full view. His struggle to wrest personal and group vindication from disappointment was typical enough among untold educated men and women like him, those Pullman porters, barbers, menial workers, and domestics whose lot was to pass their knowledge, ideals, and ambitions on to their children. Ferris, however, was childless and alone when he died in his Harlem apartment. "All that I am or ever hope to be is expressed in this volume," he had written. Ferris's assessment was as accurate as it was candid.[4]

Ferris's writings and career illustrate the intersection of black nationalism and racial uplift ideology, particularly in the equation of race progress and respectability with patriarchal authority. Like many of his contemporaries, Ferris's views were shaped by an oppressive language cluttered with contemptuous stereotypes of black masculinity. Ferris's black nationalism associated civilization with power, mastery, manhood, and the Anglo-Saxon. This might elicit, under differing circumstances or moods, either a grandiose will to power or a debilitating sense of powerlessness. In Ferris, one thus sees an ambivalence seemingly absent in someone as forthright as Garvey, who simply inverted racial hierarchies to assert black civilization, pride, and power. But even the optimism of Garvey's vision of a worldwide majority of African descended peoples, or his slogan "Up you mighty race," might harbor divisive accusations against those blacks perceived as lacking the manly attributes of nation building. The embattled character of black nationalist discourse (like racial uplift ideology), thriving, as Philip Brian Harper has argued, on social division, informed the internecine battles between Garvey's Universal Negro Improvement Association (UNIA) and other race organizations, including W. E. B. Du Bois's NAACP and Cyril Briggs's socialist, black nationalist African Blood Brotherhood.[5]

Garvey was hardly the first—nor the last—to apply popular Darwinian notions of race struggle and "survival of the fittest" to discussions of the destiny of African Americans. C. H. J. Taylor, an Atlanta lawyer and a former minister to Liberia, posed the question starkly: Will he survive? Questions of racial survival were also informed by white social scientists' claims that urban life—indeed, freedom—resulted in social pathology and high mortality rates for blacks. Taylor believed survival possible if blacks bore in mind that "while it is . . . splendid to be a Negro, it is immeasurably better to be a man. To be a man is to act manly, to take part in all that concerns the well-being of society." This meant taking part in government. Taylor warned that "if he refuses" this responsibility, "he cannot survive and he ought not to survive."[6]

Black nationalists' aspiration for power in the all-or-nothing terms of survival and manliness seemed almost to internalize blame for the powerlessness of African Americans. Such exhortations projected the personal anxieties of black spokesmen onto the race. The stakes were incredibly high, as personal weakness or failure might be taken by others, or even one's self, as an indictment against all black people. To Ferris, the race's manhood was on trial against the military, economic, and cultural achievements of European nations, a competition magnified by those nations' colonization of Africa. Such a preoccupation with the race's manhood not only inhibited social analysis and political strategy, but also could lead to attacks on other blacks whose perceived weakness—or lack of manliness—betrayed race ideals. Within this scheme of manliness as black militancy, black women's racial credentials were already rendered suspect.

The Garveyite vision of uplift through the accumulation of wealth was reminiscent of the economic nationalism of Washington's Negro Business League. Indeed, Garvey had hoped to join forces with the Wizard in his dream to establish a college of industrial education in his native Jamaica, only to be swept into New Negro movement politics in Harlem after Washington's death. Soon afterward, Garvey would emerge as the most formidable captain of the race's destiny. Ferris exulted in the symbolic and material power promised by Garvey's Black Star steamship line, which would "send a thrill to the Negroes of two hemispheres and will lift the standing of the race throughout the civilized world." To Ferris, Garvey epitomized the tenacious ambition that the race needed; he was nothing less than "an instrument in the hands of Providence for uplifting the Negro peoples of the world." Recalling the heady, if brief, success of the UNIA after Garvey's death in 1940, just a year before his own passing, Ferris claimed that Garvey "enlarged the Negro's industrial, commercial and political horizon." Also of no small importance to Ferris was the fact that Garvey paid his employees well, and "usually sent them out as gentlemen."[7]

Ferris was an active member of a nationalistic circle of intellectuals that included John E. Bruce, former slave, journalist, and a founder in 1913 of the Negro Society for Historical Research, Pauline Hopkins, Anna Julia Cooper, and American Negro Academy members John Wesley Cromwell, William S. Scarborough, Archibald Grimké, Alexander Crummell, Alain Locke, and W. E. B. Du Bois. Locke, a Rhodes scholar, is best known to us today as the integrationist impresario of the New Negro renaissance during the 1920s in Harlem. But before that, Locke was a close associate of Bruce and Cromwell in Washington, D.C., and dutifully reported to Bruce his findings on ancient Egypt and its artifacts after visiting there in 1923. Ferris was also friendly with the Puerto Rican bibliophile Arthur A. Schomburg. Africans within this network of pan-African intellectuals included Duse Mohammed Alí and the West Indian–born Liberian national Edward W. Blyden. Alí, a Sudanese, was the editor of the *African Times and Orient Review*, a London-based, anti-colonial periodical that welcomed the contributions of African, Asian, Arab, West Indian, and African American writers in the years preceding World War I. Alí contributed a sympathetic review of Ferris's *African Abroad* in that journal, and even helped sell the book from the *Review*'s London office. Ferris was an active member of the American Negro Academy.[8] He shared in the efforts of a pan-African black intelligentsia to bring the scholarly contributions and historical achievements of the African diaspora to light, to promote black organizations, and to support and encourage its members' academic and professional efforts. This extensive diasporic network suggests that black nationalism was a fluid intellectual discourse that held appeal for many within the Talented Tenth. An appreciation of the diversity of black nationalist intellectuals renders pointless the attempts of some students to construct a black nationalist genealogy of singular messianic (and invariably male) leaders in the quasi-biblical, familial sense of who begat whom.[9]

Among those influenced by E. Franklin Frazier, Malcolm X, and black power, there may be some resistance to recognizing Ferris and his bourgeois, Victorian, assimilationist compatriots as black nationalists. But to Ferris, Crummell, and other black nationalists, assimilation connoted an indispensable environmental process of acculturation by which blacks absorbed Western civilizationist ideals and values to achieve the goals of black statehood. In their view, assimilation would reap collective benefits for the race, as blacks mastered for themselves the "Anglo-Saxon" mysteries of military, financial, technological, and economic power. But Ferris, perhaps taking the rhetoric of racial struggle and survival too much to heart, had difficulty distinguishing power from what he understood as Anglo-Saxon racial traits.[10] Furthermore, reflecting uplift's equation of patriarchal family ideals with freedom, Ferris equated worldly power with the respectability of marriage. In addition, Ferris proposed the term "Negrosaxon" as an improvement over what he perceived as the pejorative connotations of "Negro." However idiosyncratic, his thought was steeped in dominant constructions of race, gender, and respectability in a manner typical of much black nationalist discourse. Imagining what might charitably be called a sort of syncretism, Ferris believed that "after the Negrosaxon has been made over into the likeness of the white man he can hope to be made into the image of God."[11]

In addition to suffering from a severe case of double-consciousness, Ferris, like others, stressed class differences as the basis for racial progress. Even in challenging racist appraisals of Reconstruction, Ferris could defend the political performance of blacks only by invoking the nativist snobbery of his mugwump cultural mentors. Whatever the abuses of Reconstruction, to Ferris they were no match for the corruption of "the ignorant foreigners, who make up the rank and file of Tammany Hall." He lamented the white backlash against Reconstruction that meted out "the same kind of treatment to the high Negro that should be meted out to the low." This sort of argument was closer in spirit to the accommodationism of the 1890s than to the militancy of the New Negro movement in Harlem, although the claim that oppression against elite blacks was of greater import than that of the poor would continue to exert influence on both the vision of racial justice and legalistic strategies for achieving it.[12]

As a writer and consumer of racial uplift texts, Ferris preferred the heroic associations of historical romance. He longed for a disinterested black leadership, philosopher-kings in ebony, unfettered by social constraints. Recalling

William H. Ferris, ca. 1910.

Du Bois's highly romanticized sketch of Alexander Crummell in *The Souls of Black Folk*, Ferris praised that evocation of "the pulse-beat of one throbbing Negro soul . . . worth more than all of his pathological studies of Negro criminology, poverty and mortality." In his desire for transcendence, Ferris typified the Victorian sensibility of much of black nationalist thought, and racial uplift ideology, which associated urban poverty with immorality and pathology. If educated blacks like Ferris or Crummell suffered, racial prejudice was the culprit, as indeed it was. As for poor blacks, their lowly condition confirmed their suspect morals and their lack of cultural refinement. The sensibility through which Ferris privileged black elites as the saving element of a fallen race reflected not only a religious outlook, but also, the boundless ambition and idealism of his youthful education. He was convinced that history was made by great men, herculean individuals who made their mark on the ages with the force and lasting imprint of a sledgehammer.

Ferris was occasionally an astute observer of black politics and leadership. Theodore Roosevelt and Booker T. Washington, bound to sham ideals, paled in comparison to prophetic stalwarts like Du Bois. Like Du Bois, Ferris demanded the right of black men to citizenship and higher education and criticized the instrumental perspective that condemned blacks to industrial education and to menial and domestic labor. Ferris predicted that in the twentieth century "the Negro will be regarded as a person and not as a thing." He claimed that the "illiterate, vicious Negro" was less a target for scorn than educated blacks, and he cited the opposition of northern philanthropists to higher education for blacks as proof. Against the tide, enlightened black leaders arose to affirm that "the colored man . . . needs the ballot." The Niagara movement, which, in concert with other black and white "radical" (on race, not economics) organizations, called for citizenship rights, an end to segregation, and demanded federal intervention on behalf of besieged southern blacks.[13]

The ambivalent, emulative character of Ferris's black nationalism certainly frustrates those who look for exemplary, canonical figures within a black nationalist tradition. But it is the quest for the all-powerful black nationalist subject, enacted as an Oedipal craving for the mastery of the white man construed as an omnipotent father, that threatens to alienate black men from the collective strengths of black communities, and that all too often backfires as a blinding, self-destructive rage. When channeled so as not to succumb to the dead end of racial essentialism, black nationalist thought, as espoused later by such figures as Garvey, Hubert H. Harrison, and others, might mature into an anticolonial, internationalist perspective that challenged many of the racial assumptions of civilizationist ideology. Yet at the same time, black nationalism often reflected the social and psychological vulnerability of black men and women in an antiblack culture. Ferris demonstrates several aspects of black nationalist thought at the turn of the century: a teleological, cyclical view of history that hearkens nostalgically for the return of a golden age of black power and cultural achievement in ancient African civilizations; an ambivalent espousal of cultural assimilation tempered by an intellectual search for cultural distinctiveness, or what contemporaries often termed "race ideals"; an anxious desire to enter the world of nations on behalf of African descended peoples within the political and epistemic framework of imperialism; and, finally, a deep anxiety surrounding color differences, sexuality, and miscegenation as they pertained to issues of black leadership and the aspiration to bourgeois stability and respectability. For Ferris and others, underlying and guiding all these concerns was the equation of uplift and power with patriarchal authority and of race integrity with manhood.

As we have seen, the patriarchal family symbolized freedom, security, and power to many black men and women. Indeed, family ideals and bonds have provided African Americans with resources of support and affirmation, taking on for many a collective significance figuring racial solidarity as a form of social kinship. The family thus maintains its importance in black middle-class and popular consciousness, as it has among other upwardly mobile ethnic Americans. But claims of universality submerge the unique heritage of enslavement, and the continued denial to black men of the attributes of power as protectors and providers. Minstrel stereotypes of black male irresponsibility, combined with sociological claims of family disorganization, added insult to injury. At the turn of the century, the frequent calls for citizenship with the slogan "manhood rights" were heard as empowering expressions of black militancy. Historian James Oliver Horton has identified in antebellum free black protest "a pattern of male political visibility" that obscured the indispensable organizational and institutional contributions of black women. The social and cultural norm of the patriarchal family was thus at the heart of blacks' visions of oppression, liberation, and citizenship, and many writers looked to the African past not only to counter antiblack prejudices but also to address their view that black patriarchy required a restorative boost.[14]

For Hortense Spillers, the preoccupation with patriarchal authority among black intellectuals was a product of "the African-American male's peculiar status in a decidedly phallocentric, slaveholding America: for all intents and purposes *banished* (not absent) from their issue, African-American males were compelled to make themselves twice over—once, with regard to female and family, whom they are theoretically obligated to protect, and again, in light of the phallic economies of naming and empowerment by which standard they are measured, *qua* male." Building on Spillers's discussion, enslavement, and in the post-Reconstruction era, Jim Crow and imperialism, all provide insight into the masculinist dimension of black nationalist rhetoric.[15]

Garveyite family portrait by James Van Der Zee, taken in Harlem, ca. 1920s.
(Courtesy of Donna Van Der Zee)

Ancient African Origins as Promise of Future Greatness

The stability of black families was crucial to race-building efforts, and black nationalists continued to focus on the race's problematic paternity since slavery. J. Max Barber bypassed the widespread concern for slavery's disregard for black women's chastity, taking up the question of "The Negro in Ancient History." To Barber, writing sometime after his flight from Atlanta, "the death of African culture is coincident with the rise of slavery in the Western World." Barber located "the golden age of Negro power . . . a thousand years before Christ." Barber was concerned with codifying various myths of racial origins, which, at the turn of the century, usually situated the race's beginnings in ancient Egyptian, or African, civilizations. Against the prevailing assumption that the Egyptians were Aryan, Barber argued that the Egyptians were a mulatto people with Negro ancestry, and also provided information on sub-Saharan African cultures. Barber's re-creation of the "noble past" of the Negro endeavored to prove that "the present is the white man's, but the future belongs, not to the degenerating, morally putrid and cruelly avaricious white man, but to the virile, puissant races in whose hearts there is mercy and justice." Barber was convinced that the world of "the white man" was so decadent that little more than an indifferent shove would be needed to hasten its eventual collapse.

Barber and many other black commentators, including Ferris, invoked a Gibbonesque theory of historical cycles within which civilizations thrive, wither, and topple, with a dash of divine will thrown in for good measure. Before the pendulum had doubled back and clubbed the race into submission, "the Negro in Africa," in Barber's vivid account, "was building cities, carving stone monuments, and making glass when the so-called Anglo-Saxon was living in caves and decorating himself with blue mud." Citing ancient African rulers and other figures of cultural and military distinction, Barber noted of African descended peoples that "they rocked civilization in the cradle." African peoples were culturally advanced while the Anglo-Saxon was worshipping fire, and this affirmed that God "seems to give races turns at the wheel." The upshot of all this for Barber was that "Africa shall be restored . . . to her youth and power, for the prophecy must yet be fulfilled, 'Ethiopia shall stretch forth her hands unto God!'" Along similar lines, Ferris remarked that "the entire cycle of history is replete with instances of a rich, luxurious but effeminate nation falling before a hardier and stronger one." [16]

Barber's was but one of the many contributionist arguments by which black intellectuals attacked the erasure of African descended peoples from world history. Moreover, he invoked the biblical tradition of Ethiopianism, which prophesied black statehood and advancement as the outcome of a divinely preordained teleology. The restoration of African civilizations, queens, and kings to the historical record provided conclusive and inspirational evidence of past and future greatness.

Barber's perspective was shared by the novelist Pauline Hopkins. As Hopkins put it, "Why not allow that the theory of Ethiopia as the mother of science, art and literature is true?" [17] Her 1903 novel *Of One Blood* sounded

A representation of Ethiopianism from the nineteenth century.

pan-African themes then commonplace among black writers who challenged incessant claims of the whiteness of Hellenic civilization. But leaving aside the matter of Eurocentric scholars' falsifications with respect to ancient African cultural and technological achievements and Africa as the site of human origins, Hopkins's genealogical narrative of ancient African greatness was a product of its time, mirroring the equation of race progress with patriarchy. Hopkins, like others, sought to make civilization a racially inclusive, universal concept by calling attention to its origins in ancient African societies. This knowledge would at once be a source of race pride for blacks and a rebuke to racial prejudice. The fantastic plot of Hopkins's novel resolves during an expedition, led by a gadfly British professor, that discovers a lost Ethiopian city, its descendants, and its supernatural technology far advanced beyond that of the West. In a pan-African racial reunion, the brilliant African American (though passing for white) doctor of the expedition, Reuel Briggs, is in turn recognized by the Ethiopians, governed by a female monarch in his absence, as Ergamenes, their king. Accepting the throne, Reuel also reclaims his racial identity, and takes charge of the historical destiny of the race. A fundamental condition of Briggs's ascension is that the Ethiopians exchange their vague spiritualism for Christianity, to which Briggs's Ethiopian advisor and prime minister readily assents on behalf of his people: "O Ergamenes, your belief shall be ours; we have no will but yours. Deign to teach your subjects." As with racial uplift ideology, tensions between authoritarian leadership and democratic consent are explained away. Monarchism takes on the benevolent face of Christianity. The novel became not only an assertion of the racial destiny of what Hopkins called the "modern Ethiopian"; Briggs's restoration to the Ethiopian monarchy carried Hopkins's assumptions of Western cultural superiority. Hopkins also effected a similar restoration of patriarchal authority routinely assumed within uplift ideology and among black leadership. Briggs's subsequent rule in Africa beside the black queen Candace, though clouded by "the advance of mighty nations penetrating the dark, mysterious forests of his native land," constitutes transcendence of the heritage of American slavery, with its horrific legacy of murder, rape, and incest rendered within the domestic American setting of the novel. The novel's content reflected a tradition of amateur scholarly productions by blacks, including Barber's, that sought to Africanize prevailing notions of civilization.[18] Hopkins's fascination with ancient African royalty, civilization, and patriarchal authority reflected a popular African American vision of Africa, and such diasporic yearnings were a central component of black nationalist and racial uplift ideology. Inevitably, however, the attempt to transcend the racialized circumstances of enslavement and Jim Crow through an identification with ancient Africa as the source of the race's origins imposed contemporary needs on its nostalgic vision of the past.

Gender, Imperialism, and Black and Anglo-American Nationalisms

Ferris came of age as Anglo-American elites defined the West's dominant relation to "primitive" lands and their "savage" peoples through imperialism and its rhetoric. Popular imperialist writing, with its overbearing manliness, had most likely conditioned his views. Such literary champions of empire as Rider Haggard and Thomas Hughes were perhaps more influential than they suspected, firing the imaginations of young African Americans and colonials with an outcome about which we can only speculate. In any event, anti-imperialists, black and white, surely contested the exhortation of Rudyard Kipling, the poet laureate of empire, that the West stoically take up the risky, thankless "white man's burden" of civilizing darker, dependant races. Imparting an air of missionary self-sacrifice to the bloody work of imperial subjugation, Kipling's views influenced Theodore Roosevelt's stateside exhortations to patrician yankees of the responsibilities of Anglo-Saxon leaders in a conflict-ridden world. Roosevelt celebrated the "manly virtues" of the "strenuous life." Warning isolationist business leaders lest they succumb to an effete, "over-civilized" life of greedy commercialism and "ignoble ease," he reminded them of "loftier duties" to nation and race. Roosevelt urged his audience to embrace "the life of aspiration, of toil and risk" by supporting military preparedness for American expansionism. Otherwise, "some stronger, manlier power" would perform the task, "and we would have shown ourselves weaklings." Expansionists invoked manhood and gendered imagery to build consensus on that hotly contested issue, alluding ominously, as Roosevelt did, to the perils of hesitation. During the war against Spain, the *Independent* editorialized on the duty of "A Nation's Manhood": "Let our nation, grown to man's estate, take man's duties. Let us not hesitate to join Great Britain . . . in policing the world."[19]

Roosevelt and Kipling, and doubtless many others, were fascinated by the kind of primal strength and mastery that seemed to them to be most readily available at the frontier outposts of "civilization"—elephant hunting on safari, or through the strenuous duty of colonial stewardship. Ferris's version of strenuous masculinity promised to give him an authoritative voice among the civilized colonial subjects of U.S. society. Character, self-control, reason, and strength were traits that yielded success in the masculine domains of politics and the market. Ferris sought to affirm blacks' possession of these qualities by excavating considerable information chronicling the military and political achievements of ancient African societies in the second volume of his study. This was the ancient historical counterpart to the uplift tradition celebrating black manhood through military prowess.[20]

For white nationalists such as Roosevelt, ideologies of sexual difference were crucial to imperialist rhetoric, and, also, to the preservation of race purity as the symbol of social order. Because race as a concept was inseparable from reproductive sexuality, patriarchal notions of motherhood and domesticity complemented Roosevelt's manly militarism. In this scheme, the Anglo-Saxon woman became the guardian and guarantor of race integrity. Roosevelt hoped that white middle-class women would prove equally strenuous in fulfilling their reproductive duties. "The woman . . . must be the wise and fearless mother of many helpful children," Roosevelt had asserted, defining her crucial part in averting what alarmist commentators referred to as race suicide. Advocates of Anglo-Saxon supremacy invoked patriarchal racialism to buttress their expansionist arguments. John R. Dos Passos, a New York corporation lawyer (and sire of his namesake, the radical novelist), called for an alliance between the United States and England, asserting that such a pro-imperialist union would be "as natural as marriage between man and woman. It consummates the purposes of the creation of the race." Fortunately, Dos Passos's vision of Anglo-American rapprochement did not materialize, averting an inevitable dispute over which partner would assume the dominant role of progenitor.[21]

For Ferris and other black nationalists, then, a rhetorical masculinity, so symbolic of ruling power, would be central to the pursuit of an authentic, authoritative, and putatively non-Western cultural identity. Just as Roosevelt's Anglo-Saxonism necessitated control of women's reproductive sexuality, so it was for black nationalists, then and now, that a controlling patriarchal authority was indispensable to racial chauvinism. But among black nationalists, manhood and patriarchal control tended to be symbolic, and compensatory entities, more indicative of the aspiration for power than the actual possession of it. If racial ideologies of whiteness were crucial to the bourgeois aspirations of nonblacks, then gender ideologies of manhood informed African Americans' middle-class ideology of racial uplift. Armed with the nationalistic mystique of race, blood, home, family, and civilization, Western imperialists, explorers, and missionaries and the metropolitan journalists who capitalized on their exploits frequently saw themselves as parental guardians to "childlike" subject peoples and their apparently undifferentiated, collectivist cultures. In the hegemonic parlance on race, virile, northern, civilized Anglo-Saxon nations were destined to subdue effeminate, tropical, savage, and childlike peoples deemed incapable of self-government. Gender differences (presumed to be natural and permanent) were thus invoked to confer a sense of inevitability, naturalness, and necessity upon historically evolving social relations of domination.[22]

Ferris's appropriation of strenuous life masculinity informed his vision of racial uplift. He based his claims for black progress on such male-oriented bourgeois standards as home and property ownership, the growth of a professional class, and the development of intellectual, literary, and journalistic activities. Yet to Ferris, these achievements, although significant, were somehow insufficient. Something more primal and powerful was also needed. "A race," he maintained, "is not only judged by its intellectual acquisitions, but by the quality and fiber of its manhood; by its innate self-respect and inborn desire for freedom." Ferris equated forceful resistance and militancy with manliness. Thus, he augmented his demonstration of the race's growing material prosperity with a history of the heroic exploits of explorers and soldiers. These included the deeds of "revolutionist" slave revolt leaders Nat Turner, Gabriel Prosser, and Denmark Vesey. Ferris's cavalcade of heroes did not fail to recognize the achievements of such women as the white educator Prudence Crandall, branded a criminal for founding a school for black girls in antebellum Connecticut, or the legendary black abolitionists Harriet Tubman and Sojourner Truth. But the race's true "History-Makers" were its military heroes on the battlefields and spokesmen at antislavery meetings, even including white "men of action" such as John Brown, in whom "was incarnated the aggressive courage and humanitarian instinct of the Anglo-Saxons." Such were the examples of stalwart, intrepid masculinity that Ferris sought to appropriate for himself and African Americans.[23]

Ferris was hardly alone in representing the race in masculine terms. Reflecting the gender conventions of much popular literature, the black nationalist novelist Sutton Griggs described one of his black male protagonists, Belton Belgrave, as "a fine specimen of physical manhood" whose "manly appearance always excited interest wherever he was seen." Belton's physique draws the depraved admiration of a white doctor who hopes to dissect Belton if the men who plan to lynch him can refrain from mutilating his body. For Griggs, the murderous, dissecting brutality of white dominance, and the need to protect black homes and families, requires nothing less than the establishment of a separate black nation from which to wage war on the U.S. government. The necessity for black national power is underscored by an episode that dramatizes not only white society's intolerance of black manhood but also the restricted employment options for blacks, not to mention racism's pathological sexual politics. Here, not long after his marriage, a harassed, jobless Belton is forced to go incognito, disguised as a woman, to gain his only chance of securing the only work available to him as a domestic. As if this weren't humiliating enough, he found himself endlessly struggling with white men to retain his "virtue." Griggs suggested that even the strongest black men could be feminized by oppression.[24]

While highly idealized physical attractiveness in heroes (and heroines) was compulsory within the genre of uplift fiction, the preoccupation with manly strength and prowess among black writers like Griggs and Ferris was more than a literary convention. Their sometimes florid descriptions of physical perfection and noble character countered racist stereotypes and symbolized blacks' aspirations to social power and moral authority. They well understood that physical and martial force had been indispensable not only for Western dominance, but also for the emancipation of blacks. What had worked for the Anglo-Saxon, they believed, would make masters out of slaves and realize their goals of "freedom, equality and empire," to quote Sutton Griggs's formulation.[25] Without dwelling on the bourgeois concept of equality fulfilled, ironically, in a vision of empire, at the end of the century, black writers erected literary monuments to the race's respectability with characters who embodied gender conventions of manly strength, character, and chaste virility, and feminine beauty and virtue. These complementary gendered images were deemed crucial for bourgeois ideals of race and nation building.

Segregation dashed his intellectual aspirations, confining Ferris to what he saw as a stifling "colored society." It was painfully clear that "the ostracism of the Anglo-Saxon race" was a direct threat to the intellectual fellowship he sought. "The white idealist, if he desires, can come in intimate and personal association . . . with men of like minds," but the "sacred privilege" of such fellowship "is denied ambitious colored youths." Perhaps even more galling than this isolation was "the lack of sympathy and appreciation" of those relatively well-to-do blacks with whom Ferris and other "colored idealists . . . were forced to associate." Ferris described how a philistine class of elite colored Americans "who only cared for eating and drinking and wearing fine clothes" drove some of his circle of "colored idealists" to "moral suicide" and menial employment.[26]

Ferris's struggles informed his analysis of black leadership. Along with fellow members of the American Negro Academy, Ferris argued that Washington's program of industrial education threatened to consign blacks to inferior status as the unskilled utensils of industrialists. But Ferris also objected to "the fad and craze" of Washington's program of industrial education, because it "discredited the educated Negro." Members of the academy had long insisted that the struggle against racism was first and foremost an intellectual battle, and that the race ought to mobilize its best minds in refuting the popular mythologies of white supremacy. Men and women of Ferris's temper found Washington's leadership baneful because it threatened and belittled their own leadership status as members of the black intelligentsia. Ferris likened the conduct of Washington to the fateful biblical encounter between Samson and Delilah. While Washington and other black leaders, seduced by white patronage, "slept, as Samson slept on the lap of Delilah, they were shorn of their political and civil locks, and awoke one bright morning to find their strength was gone." Figuring Washington's pact with white elites as a symbolic castration, Ferris claimed that blacks would not accept such illegitimate, emasculated leaders who were foisted on the race. "And I would say to our Caucasian friends: 'Please don't extinguish the spark of manliness that is burning faintly in our breasts,'" he wrote, sounding less assertive than he intended.[27]

Personal Struggles and Redemption through Uplift

Ferris was sensitive to the charge that his checkered career betrayed a weak character. Prejudice did not excuse him from the universal test of manly self-reliance. Even for a man of Ferris's liberal training at Yale and the Harvard Divinity School, career prospects were limited to teaching, journalism, or the ministry. Ferris was an ordained AME minister, though it is unlikely that he ever led his own church for more than a brief tenure. He had sought a faculty position at Howard University in 1903, but by then his public opposition to Washington's policies had irreparably harmed his chances.[28] Ferris committed himself to anti-Bookerite protest, justifying his stand as one of independent, self-assertive manhood. Given Ferris's ambitions, the record of his correspondence with Washington is of interest. In a 1902 letter Ferris denounced Washington as a "sychophant [*sic*]" and a "[white man's] nigger. . . . This may sound hard but it is true. . . . Hold your head erect and be a man." But he added in a postscript that "Tuskegee is a monument to your genius & tact & executive ability; but I speak so frankly because I esteem you so highly." Needless to say, Washington found him obnoxious and worked behind the scenes to prevent him from bringing out a third volume of his book.[29]

Ferris expressed sympathy with the militant Niagara movement, but his relations with Du Bois and Trotter eventually soured, dealing a near-fatal blow to his desire to belong to an elite community of race leaders.[30] The brief association with these "radicals" was ultimately a costly decision for Ferris. Besides drawing the everlasting enmity of Washington, he acquired a reputation as an unemployable freeloader, a man whom paternalistic whites and malicious black Bookerites could readily point to as proof of the impracticality of liberal education for blacks. Painfully aware of his reputation, but equally determined to defend higher education for black men, Ferris strove to make *The African Abroad* an act of self-justification.

Ferris hoped to fulfill his mission by molding the minds of black youth. At the time, however, whites held most teaching positions at black colleges, and Washington's sub rosa dealings might exclude black applicants from any remaining positions. To his great disappointment, a college appointment proved elusive. "I had dreamed of teaching colored students in college metaphysics and the philosophy of knowledge, but in this little volume I will teach the Negro race the philosophy of life," Ferris wrote in *The African Abroad*. Obviously, this was hardly a free choice for Ferris. Circumstances forced it upon him, and he tried to redeem himself by embodying the notion of uplift with his book.[31]

Ferris knew that the success myth did not apply to black American males. "The white boy who sweeps out the office may some day become president of the bank," Ferris observed, but "no such vista stretches out before the colored boy. His horizon is limited, his sphere circumscribed. . . . Certain callings are closed to him. . . . In others he can go to a certain point but there must stop, regardless of his ability, aspiration and ambition." Despite his critique of the success myth, Ferris's black nationalism (and Garvey's, for that matter) constantly invoked the ideology of achievement and the self-made man, with the disturbing implication that failure was not just personal, but racial as well.[32]

Ferris's alienation was compounded by his lack of acceptance among the "aristocracy of color," the black leisure class. Ferris probably took this not only as evidence of the latter's contempt for intellect and idealism but also as a sign of the color prejudice of that class against darker-complexioned blacks like himself.[33] This bred within him the peculiar resentment of being spurned by those whose society he yearned for, but to whom he also felt superior, and in his book he took his revenge by portraying his encounter with a feminized "colored society" as an unrequited flirtation of sorts. Jilted by members of an elite world that he more than likely approached as a suitor, Ferris claimed that the "manly" strength and resolve of this class was diluted through race mixture. His contempt for the black bourgeoisie was evident in his descriptions of its frivolous light-complexioned women apparently unimpressed by his lofty ambitions and resolve to fight racism. He dismissed them as blithely lacking "the heroic resolve to overleap the barriers and the wall . . . [of] Anglo-Saxon race prejudice." Ferris suggested that he chose not to pursue these women as unworthy of him; this was preferable to what elsewhere comes across as his sense of outright rejection by "colored society." To Ferris, such women symbolized the racial disloyalty and accommodationism of the generally lighter-hued colored American elite, whose lack of "heroic resolve" betrayed, by implication, a want of manliness. Of one such woman, a once "beautiful quadroon," Ferris noted that the "pace of the high life in New York" had quickly "reduced her . . . from a dazzling beauty to a faded rose." In recounting his decision to spurn these fair-skinned temptresses, Ferris evoked the patriarchal biblical myth of feminine betrayal partially to deflect blame for the stigma of his bachelorhood. After all, such an apparent renunciation of matrimony was in violation of racial uplift dogmas that emphasized procreation and family ideals. Ferris's difficult, but, alas, necessary refusal of the frivolous young daughters of the Afro-American elite in the name of nobler nationalistic race ideals explained his bachelorhood. All this came down to the fact that his own subsistence was not assured, and that the support of a family—that crucial measure of male identity—was beyond his means. He wrote candidly to his friend Arthur Schomburg in 1915 that he needed a steady income "before I lead a fair damsel to the altar."[34]

Ferris's version of his encounter with racially indifferent quadroon socialites indicates his association of militancy and manhood with racial integrity. As his account suggests, issues of color differences, black leadership, and miscegenation were intertwined and steeped in controversy among black commentators at the turn of the century.

Black Nationalism, Leadership, and Mulatto-Bashing

Conflicts among blacks over color differences often took on a bitter tone due to the relatively few political positions of status and privilege available within and beyond the black community at the turn of the century. Members of the small, exclusive, and racially mixed aristocracy that had parlayed its social and cultural advantages in the postbellum era into positions of leadership and prosperity in cities throughout the South, especially the upper South and Washington, D.C., had participated in civil rights activism and social uplift efforts after emancipation. But their protests were directed more against the color line and racial barriers; they tended to be socially exclusive and lukewarm toward the self-help ethos of material advancement that motivated the rise of ambitious, and often darker-complexioned, former slaves and their descendants. Newly prominent blacks whose claims to status were based not on the older credentials of freedom, wealth, or family background, but on education and race-conscious uplift activities, did not take kindly to the elitism of many of these representatives of Afro-American "blue vein" society, that informal designation referring to the visibility of their veins through their light complexions. Like Ferris, John Bruce, the New York journalist, linked white ancestry with political and racial disloyalty. Bruce denounced the "contemptible hypocrisy and snivelling cant" of those he termed "ethnological betweenities," who "whether in politics or outside of it are always ready to sell the race for a mess of pottage." Such mulatto-baiting was habitual for some darker-skinned (with exceptions, of course), nationalistic-minded intellectuals, journalists, and professionals with dim political prospects, who often noted that some light-skinned blacks evaded Jim Crow by passing for white whenever convenient. Alexander Crummell confided to Bruce in 1896 his view that "a fanatical and conceited junto" had arisen, "more malignant than white men, pushing themselves forward as leaders & autocrats of the Race; & at t[he] same time, repudiating t[he] race. And what is the basis for their superiority? Bastardy!" Men like Crummell and Bruce tended to identify the nefarious influence of Booker T. Washington behind that of aristocratic mulatto officehold-ers, with some justification.[35]

While their hostility seems based as much on feeling as fact, the tension nevertheless indicates an equally passionate desire on the part of members of the colored aristocracy to remain apart from those they undoubtedly per-ceived as upstarts. Some members of the older, colored elite voiced this ten-sion through disdain toward those who aspired to middle-class status. "With Afro-Americans," worried Ralph W. Tyler, a member of the Tuskegee ma-chine, "the lines once so tautly drawn are becoming loose." Unimpressed by the civic and social activities of new aspirants to black society, Tyler com-plained that mere membership in churches, or "some charitable or secret so-ciety is too frequently accepted as a prime requisite for social recognition." Any impure woman, or "gambler," "roué," or "degenerate," could enter such organizations. "Real society" for colored Americans, according to Tyler, "is an exclusive affair," the more exclusive the better. Voicing a similar complaint of the lack of deference, Robert Terrell lamented the difficulty of finding African Americans who would work as domestic servants for members of their own race.[36]

As the exchange between Bruce and Crummell suggests, however, the figure of the mulatto, with all its negative moral connotations, loomed large in many discussions of black leadership. Here, as with other questions of race, one finds an area of extreme discursive amalgamation, as a huge compendium of intellectual and popular writings, and folk wisdom on the mulatto fed on itself. Blacks were influenced by popular journalistic, social science, and eth-nological varieties of knowledge on race and the mulatto, which, as we know, was a lightning rod of white anxiety as well. Not only did the mulatto contra-dict ideals of racial purity, he or she was damning evidence that white men themselves were unable to live by them. That Jim Crow society tolerated white men's sexual domination of black women could not make the mulatto man or woman a less controversial figure—he or she embodied the instability of the system of white supremacy. In any case, blacks were hardly unaffected by this national obsession with race and sex, which inflamed ongoing late-Victorian and religious anxieties equating sexuality and women's indepen-dence with transgressive behavior at its most scandalous and sinful.

Apart from questions of sexual politics and power, however, was that of leadership. And here, many blacks and whites perceived a larger proportion of mulattoes among black leadership. Although white ancestry was quite vis-ible in postemancipation black leadership, the situation was complicated by the propensity of whites to refer carelessly to many black leaders as mulat-toes. There were frequent such inaccurate references in the majority press to W. E. B. Du Bois, Ida B. Wells, and Mary Church Terrell as mulattoes. Blacks resented the racist assumption behind such talk that these leaders, and actual mulattoes such as Booker T. Washington and Frederick Douglass, owed their ability and prominence to their non-African ancestry. Against such prejudice, many blacks (sometimes mulattoes themselves) cited as a point of race pride that certain exemplary blacks were "of unadulterated Negro ancestry" (the term "Negro" denoted a complete absence of white ancestry); Sojourner Truth, Toussaint L'Ouverture, Samuel Ringgold Ward, Paul Laurence Dunbar, Phillis Wheatley, Kelly Miller, and Martin Delany, among others, were singled out for praise in this regard.

If some found the image of the mulatto to be suspect, others sought to rehabilitate the mulatto's racial loyalty. As we have seen, Sutton Griggs created a fictional insurrectionary alliance uniting a dark former slave and a free mulatto. Griggs went so far as to explain the saber-rattling rebelliousness of his mulatto protagonist, as compared with the conciliatory stance of the full Negro, as the result of the former's Anglo-Saxon background, it being widely believed that the militant love of liberty was a white racial trait. And the fictions of Pauline Hopkins and Frances Harper featured mulatto characters who were committed race men and women. At the turn of the century, as skin color continued to determine perceptions of racial loyalty and class differences among blacks, many blacks of all colors avowed public commitments to uplift and education as a declaration of racial solidarity transcending color differences. But anxieties surrounding race mixture were not so easily assuaged, as they raised the prospect of race suicide and moral degeneration for blacks and whites alike.

Black Nationalist Ideals of "Racial Conservation"

But African Americans' desire for race purity was qualitatively different from that of whites. For blacks, it meant self-determination and the power to protect themselves against white dominance. Against Darwinian notions of racial extinction, black writers, usually male, elevated "race conservation" to a principle, indeed, a point of race pride, and a vehicle for the assertion of powerful manliness. Blacks employed the term, borrowed from white advocates of racial purity keen on discouraging further white transgressions of the color line during the Progressive Era, to assert black cultural nationalism in prevailing patriarchal terms. In this sense, conservation was understood as a biological matter, holding that black men should eschew intermarriage and thus preserve their distinctive racial character. Related to this was the appeal of racial conservation as a rebuke to scientific racism, specifically the neo-Lamarckianism of social scientists during the Progressive Era who asserted that blacks, as an inferior race, instinctually sought to reproduce with racially superior whites, thus improving the species.[37] Black writers also employed racial conservation to express their skepticism at predictions of cultural or bio-logical absorption. Although biological theories of race provided the context for W. E. B. Du Bois's manifesto "The Conservation of Races," given before the American Negro Academy, Du Bois was clearly searching, if not alto-gether successfully, for a culturalist concept of race. Du Bois urged that "it is our duty to conserve our physical powers, our intellectual endowments, our spiritual ideals." Although T. Thomas Fortune understood Du Bois in bio-logical terms, claiming that his speech confirmed the academy's antimulatto sentiments, Du Bois's primary concern was with the statement of a distinc-tive Negro culture and consciousness. Nathan B. Young exalted "Race ideals," including black standards of beauty, and took encouragement from "the spo-radic evidences of a conserving tendency, gradually returning to the race." Similarly, Ferris employed the Victorian masculine ideals of self-control and sexual restraint to urge against miscegenation. Rhetorically superimposing the male procreative function onto "the race," Ferris believed that the Negro race would die out "if it scatters its energy and attempts to blot out [its] pre-cious traits." Whatever else John Durham of Philadelphia, minister to Haiti, meant when he observed that the Haitian people lacked "the contacts with Teutonic civilization which unman the Negro while they refine him," one hears the equation of racial integrity and manliness.[38]

Discussions of racial conservation were part of the larger intellectual struggle of extracting a positive black identity from pejorative racial theories. This in-tellectual struggle with the malignant language of race, however, was compli-cated, and somewhat limited, by the understanding of race as a natural, bio-logical category, inextricably tied to sensitive questions of gender, sexuality, and reproduction. The many, invariably male, participants in this lively and emotional debate found social Darwinist theories of race struggle and "sur-vival of the fittest" a compelling mode of analysis. Matching the most ardent white supremacist's fetish of racial purity, they might argue, as did William A. Lynch, that the Negro, contrary to popular opinion, did not "desire to mingle his blood with that of the white races." To the contrary, Lynch argued, "there is, though it may seem to some unaccountable, a certain pride of race which leads the Negro to exult in the purity of his blood, and to regard a foreign element in it as not only not desirable, but even objectionable." This, com-bined with "a natural and insuperable repugnance on the part of the white," must keep the races apart, though Lynch insisted that they remain on an "equal footing of freedom." Lynch brought a demographic perspective to the issue, claiming that the black population in the South was growing 20 percent faster than the white population in that section, and he saw this as potential for a future black nation in that area. Dismissing the "rosy" biological theory of assimilation, he reminded his readers that blacks have "a history before them of the noblest and most aggressive character." Whether or not they found direct expression, biological concerns for race survival, and the rhetoric of patriarchal power, were part of the rhetoric of racial conservation, which indicated an aspiration for cultural distinctiveness and in rare cases, a sense that education along civilizationist lines, described as "emasculation," was injurious to ethnic identity and political independence.[39]

Lynch's view was typical of the burgeoning race consciousness and the search for a historical black subject, articulated through the desire for national power, that asserted "racial integrity" along with white social scientists, progressive social gospel reformers, and rabid white supremacists. But it could hardly have been otherwise, as proponents of racial conservation inherited the racialized world view they opposed. Through racial conservation, blacks denied the accusation that black men were universally attracted to white women and challenged the argument made by some blacks and white moderates that amalgamation would eventually eliminate race differences and conflict. Still, racial conservation itself did not succeed in assuaging anxiety over miscegenation among elite blacks. Indeed, among black commentators, the consensus held that intermarriage was an irresponsible act of race suicide.

Monogamous marriage within the race's elite provided blacks a vision of progress that stressed respectability and deliverance from the sexual degradation of slavery and its latter-day counterpart in concubinage. For many, racial purity was thus a crucial signifier of respectability. But internalized shame at whites' sexual domination produced in black elites a profound ambivalence on sex, color, and class. African American women bore the brunt of such anxieties. While black elites defended elite black women against scholarly and journalistic accusations of unchastity, it was also frequently asserted that the race's sexual morality, particularly among peasant black women, had been destroyed by slavery and its aftermath. Miscegenation was a major source of concern, which, for some, placed a judgmental scrutiny on the conduct of black women. The editor Charles Alexander argued that the goal by which "the Negro race" would best "exhibit its full strength" in all forms of activity "is to keep the blood pure." Alexander noted the hypocrisy of white men's cries of social equality given their "wild, insatiable cravings" for black women, but he also seemed to regard black women as complicitous. Thomas Baker allowed that conditions under slavery were horrendous for black women, but in his view, the fact that some slave women insisted on having pure Negro children indicted those women whose "perverted aesthetical sense made them prefer to have mixed blood children." Baker denied that this denoted a laxity in morals, but in effect, he depicted systemic sexual abuse as a matter of black women's consent. He supported his thesis with the dubious assertion that white women's devotion to proper aesthetical ideals made their attraction to men of other races unthinkable. Such tortured logic issued from a guilt-ridden Victorian concept of respectable sexuality confined to reproduction and disclaiming any hint of sexual pleasure. With their own respectability at stake, such commentators banished miscegenation—and black women victimized by concubinage—out into an underworld of sexual depravity. This judgmental posture toward miscegenation in the South illustrated the depoliticized moralism of uplift ideology, which treated systemic sexual oppression as a volitional matter of moral conduct. Many elite blacks, defensive at accusations of sexual immorality, internalized and projected the blame for systemic evils on less privileged others, preaching self-control, instead, it seemed, of the pursuit of justice in the realm of politics and the law.[40]

In the North, where black men and women were perhaps less menaced by lawlessness, miscegenation taboos, and rape, intermarriage still represented among blacks a threat to uplift ideals of family, respectability, and class survival. To one writer, the problem of intermarriage was becoming commonplace in the North, "and this is more prevalent among men than among women." Allowing that marriage across the color line was permissible among social equals, this writer, evidently a black woman, nevertheless believed such parity happened all too rarely, and thus "men entail upon themselves and their children the deadly association of a nature vile, miasmatic and filthy, dealing death to all hope of moral cleanliness." For this writer, the stigma of congenital disease affirmed that the future of the race was guided by natural laws and the hand of science. All this might be endangered without careful sexual selection within—and between—races. This tendency to view intermarriage in disreputable, class-bound eugenic terms was partly explained by dominant bourgeois projections of sexual anxieties onto working-class cultures. And of course, the sordid image of miscegenation in the South contributed its part. Pauline Hopkins explained the villainous nature of one of her northern mulatto characters, an unscrupulous colored politician, by "a mixture of 'cracker' blood of the lowest type on his father's side." In addition, although Hopkins bestowed on her heroine, Sappho Clark, the physical attractiveness then often associated in popular literature with mixed racial ancestry, she pointed out that Sappho's desirability was hardly an advantage. Having moved to Boston to conceal her having borne a child after a white man raped her in the South at fourteen, the tellingly named Sappho had given up all hopes of matrimony: "Men call me beautiful . . . what has beauty been to me but a curse?" For Sappho Clark, there was forgiveness and redemption in love and marriage to a man of the Talented Tenth. To Hopkins and other commentators, the continued vulnerability of black women to rape, and class considerations colored by the miscegenation taboo, influenced what was at best an ambivalent view of intermarriage, which was indefensible unless it involved "the best white blood."[41]

The class and race anxieties surrounding miscegenation characterized the public furor surrounding the controversial black heavyweight champion Jack

Johnson. Incidents of racial violence followed Johnson's victory over Jess Willard for the championship in 1910, and white progressive moral reformers usually blamed Johnson and the disreputable fight game for the riots. Dealing punishing defeats to white challengers was bad enough. Johnson, a man of fierce independence who had begun his career fighting battle royals against other black youths for the amusement of whites in Galveston, openly consorted with white prostitutes and had been married to white women, one of whom committed suicide. Johnson's activities outside the ring provoked intense loathing among many whites. Although he was a hero in many black communities, for some elite blacks (who may nonetheless have secretly admired him), Johnson's affairs with white women, aired in lurid detail in the press, spoiled what might otherwise have been a celebration of his success against white hopes in the ring as a symbol of race advancement. When the federal government arrested Johnson in 1912 for violation of the Mann Act, which targeted prostitution by forbidding the transportation of women across state lines for immoral purposes, southern editorials prescribed lynching, and some prominent blacks condemned Johnson for his involvement with white women. Booker T. Washington denounced Johnson for his self-indulgent style of life, which, he claimed, had injured the race. Ever the counterpuncher, the champion pointed out that unlike Washington, "I never got beat up because I looked in the wrong keyhole." Johnson was referring to the assault on the Tuskegee educator by a white man under mysterious circumstances in New York City.[42]

Johnson's notoriety reinforced the black view that located miscegenation within a seamy underworld of white women prostitutes, white male rapists, and similarly disreputable lower-class black women. Emphatically the wrong sort of interracial cooperation, many believed that such unions were immoral and produced diseased offspring, a commonplace of scientific racism.[43] Perhaps the ultimate literary expression of gendered black ideals of racial purity (although whites were not involved) occurred in Griggs's *Imperium in Imperio*, where Viola Martin, the tortured, beautiful southern heiress and fiancée of Bernard Belgrave, the illegitimate, mulatto son of an aristocratic U.S. senator and his quadroon mistress, chooses suicide over marriage to her beloved Bernard in the belief that the offspring of intermarrying "half-breeds" would be sterile, and that such unions were "slowly but surely exterminating the race." After Viola's ultimate sacrifice to the race, a grieving Bernard swears everlasting loyalty to racial separatism and later joins the black nationalist conspiracy plotted with his boyhood friend, the dark Belton Piedmont. Griggs associated race integrity with a chaste respectability, but he also brought black men's anxious wish to control black women's sexuality to bear on his narrative. A true race woman like Viola, by this logic, would rather kill herself than commit race suicide by having children by the "white" man,

Bernard. By visiting such misfortune on Bernard, who was denied the standard happy ending of romance and marriage, Griggs also challenged the apparent preference for mulatto or light-complexioned protagonists in popular literature for blacks. At any rate, his black nationalist representations of mulattoes, race, and reproduction were influenced by racist social science and popular literature.[44]

Some, such as northerners Ida B. Wells and Reverdy C. Ransom, and former southerners T. Thomas Fortune and Charles Chesnutt, refused to condemn intermarriage on principle. Wells disapproved the snubs Frederick Douglass suffered from blacks after his second marriage in 1884 to Helen Pitts, an English woman, and had defended the couple. There were defensive reasons, as well, for blacks to support intermarriage. In 1907, Fortune condemned a proposal of anti-intermarriage legislation in the House of Representatives, as an attempt to "sanction the legality of concubinage in the District of Columbia." Fortune went on to say that any black who claims he "does not desire for social equality is an unmitigated fool or an outrageous blackguard, who sacrifices what he should know as a primal right to a subservient purpose."[45] Ransom, an AME clergyman, who was said to have married 104 Negroes to white women and 3 white men to colored women, welcomed members of the Manassa Society, an organization of men and women in marriages which crossed the color line, to his church in Chicago. Ransom maintained that white partners in such marriages did not conform to the lower-class stereotype. As these and others understood it, opposing intermarriage gave white supremacists ammunition for their own hypocritical ideals of race purity. Little was resolved by these public discussions, as few legal cases against anti-intermarriage laws were attempted.[46]

Ultimately there were several interrelated reasons for blacks' opposition, or ambivalence toward, intermarriage. Generally, blacks equated intermarriage with the miscegenation that preyed on black women. Echoing whites' obsession with racial degeneration, blacks often described race mixing as mongrelization, or in terms of illicit sexuality and impure, corrupted blood. Moreover, the prevalence of intermarriage involving black men restricted matrimonial options for elite black women, for whom marriage with white men was seldom a possibility. In addition, there was the extremely sensitive matter of color, resulting in some circles in an intraracial color line. Light-complexioned black women were caught in the middle of a dehumanizing system in the South, coveted as sexual servants by white men and sought after by black men for the status they conferred within the race as wives, nationalistic exaltations of "race purity" notwithstanding. Of course, black men never admitted to this, preferring to castigate some black women for their alleged preference for white men.[47] (It should be mentioned here that black women were vulnerable to concubinage and rape in the South regardless of their complexion or social status.) Additionally, the prospect of educated black men marrying outside the race, particularly in the North, fueled blacks' class-specific fears of race suicide. In light of the wrenching issues raised by miscegenation, uplift ideology's ethos of service and education for race advancement offered a loftier standard for bourgeois status, seeking to renegotiate and transcend the significance of color, "amalgamation," and the legacy of slavery in determining class structure among blacks.

Appeals for racial conservation and purity among black nationalists were declarations of race pride, but they also reflected an anxious concern to stabilize racial identity through paternity. To ensure racial integrity and respectability, and to counter widespread accusations of black women's unchastity, black nationalists promoted fidelity to marriage and family ideals. Some held out what they regarded as traditional African gender relations as the virtuous standard to be reclaimed by progressive black Americans. W. E. B. Du Bois lamented the destruction of "the strictly guarded savage home life of Africa" by the slave ship and the urban slum. Thomas Baker countered accusations of black women's promiscuity by citing traditional African cultures' insistence on female chastity, commenting that "in the Soudan and other parts of Africa where girls are subject to infibulation," to prevent "incontinence," no young woman "who is not infibulated can get a husband."[48] Baker was not advocating the practice of infibulation among African American women, but his example nonetheless revealed the extent to which the defense of black women against chastity resulted in a repressive morality associating racial integrity, pan-African cultural nationalism, and respectability with patriarchal control, and by implication, equating deviance or pathology with black female sexuality. It is difficult, in the last analysis, to see the preoccupation with race "conservation" and endogamous marriage entirely in isolation from the southern, and increasingly national, obsession with the policing of black male sexuality. By the "sexual revolution" of the 1960s, black nationalist media celebrities such as Eldridge Cleaver and Melvin Van Peebles would abandon such decorous, chaste self-restraint and resort to phallocentric self-assertion, inverting the stereotypical terms that had trivialized blacks' political rights with the insinuation of "social equality." In this hypermasculinist view, black women existed not as exalted exemplars of female chastity but as sex objects, and in Cleaver's case, as targets of a vengeful misogyny.

Black nationalists' biological notions of race integrity as a sign of respectability echoed dominant injunctions that sought to protect and control white women's sexuality and maintain women as, in effect, men's property. For blacks, however, this quest was rooted in a painful memory linking past and present horrors. As a continuation of the sexual dominance of black women during slavery, concubinage, upheld by violence and the courts, rendered black men virtually powerless. On emotionally charged issues of sexuality, a rhetoric of manhood enjoining the chastity of black women denied the extent to which the sanctity of the home and family for blacks remained menaced by systemic sexual racism.

Ferris's significance, then, and his representativeness, is found in his ambivalence, traced directly to his difficulties in resolving the problematic concept of race. The internalized racialism of black nationalism, modeling black self-determination after Anglo-Saxon manliness, might be relieved by the yearning to reclaim African, or "Negro" cultural identity, to fly back home, so to speak, according to African American folk belief. But without the countervailing influence of a political, historical conception of African or diasporic identity, even the search for authentic racial origins might be troubled by the hidden injuries of race and gender. Ferris seemed aware of the problem of identity when, in a discussion of black literature, he wrote that in adapting to the ideals of Anglo-Saxon civilization, "the Negro went too far in taking his ideas ready-made from the Anglo-Saxon, and in letting his Caucasian brother do his thinking for him." Black writers would be more interesting and effective "when they write as colored men and not as white men." Here, struggling to crack the shell of racial essentialism was a skepticism toward assimilationist hero worship, which warned, however awkwardly, that blacks "must not lose the barbaric splendor of the African imagination." Ferris concluded, "The Negro race must come to a consciousness of itself before it can produce great literature."[49] As Du Bois had with double-consciousness, Ferris keenly grasped the cultural identity crisis confronting black intellectuals: a perennial internal battle between the warring ideals of a pejorative notion of race and an affirming concept of cultural distinctiveness. But new, less racialized, forms of political and cultural consciousness would have to await changing conditions and the efforts of those making history, rather than those cobbling together a self-serving, mythologized version of it. In the meantime, despite the alternatives posed by black women intellectuals such as Anna Julia Cooper, black nationalism and racial uplift ideology would often phrase both the problem and its solution—representing both black oppression and its remedies—as a question of manhood.

5

THE WOMAN AND LABOR QUESTIONS

IN RACIAL UPLIFT IDEOLOGY

Anna Julia Cooper's Voices from the South

I purposely forbear to mention instances of personal violence to colored women travelling in less civilized sections of our country, where women have been forcibly ejected from cars, thrown out of seats, their garments rudely torn, their person wantonly and cruelly injured. America is large and must for some time yet endure its out-of-the-way jungles of barbarism as Africa its uncultivated tracts of marsh and malaria.

ANNA JULIA COOPER, *A VOICE FROM THE SOUTH*

((((((

In her account of the first annual meeting of the American Negro Academy in Washington, D.C., in 1897, Anna Julia Cooper praised the gathering, initiated by the black nationalist cleric and intellectual Alexander Crummell. Noting that the academy was founded to promote intellectual work and higher education among African Americans, to advise "colored people on lines affecting their development and improvement," and to defend the race against vicious assaults, Cooper quoted from the remarks of Crummell and Presbyterian minister Rev. Francis Grimké, another close friend and colleague. Grimké believed that black intellect and reason would sway the American conscience in favor of African Americans "by endeavoring to educate public sentiment to a Christian conception of the Negro as a man." Cooper quoted from Crummell's attack on the vogue of industrial education among white philanthropists, a trend that placed black intellectuals in an even more precarious situation. Instead of manual training, "what the Negro needs is civilization." After all, the object of education for the Negro was "not to make the white man a Croesus, *but to make himself a man*." Calling attention to the limits of this oppositional rhetoric of racial uplift and manhood rights, Cooper remarked of the academy only that "its membership is confined to men." [1]

Cooper's account of the institutional activities of the black intelligentsia of which she had been an active member, yet here found herself relegated to the sidelines, raises questions about the status of the black woman intellectual that cannot be so easily deferred. Although she lived for more than a century, into the civil rights era, Cooper (1858?–1964) made her most significant intellectual contribution to African American intellectual life before 1900. Until her rediscovery in the late 1980s with the reissue of her 1892 volume of essays *A Voice from the South*, Cooper was largely neglected by historians.[2] As Cooper's own words suggest, this neglect had its precedent in the male-dominated character of black leadership and intellectual life at the turn of the century, marked by a middle-class ideology of racial uplift that measured race progress in terms of civilization, manhood, and patriarchal authority.

The initial wave of scholarship on Cooper has understandably addressed the obstacles facing black women intellectuals and has emphasized Cooper's feminist contribution to African American thought.[3] In the following, although I will continue this line of interpretation by surveying Cooper's critique of the male prerogatives encoded within racial uplift ideology, I will also address Cooper's role as a social commentator on a wide array of national questions, which besides gender, included controversies over race, labor, and African American and American cultural identity. The impulse to reclaim Cooper as a black feminist intellectual, although undoubtedly of value within an African American intelligentsia and U.S. political culture still resistant to gender equality, may ultimately impose artificial limits on the critical consideration Cooper warrants. Much of what contemporary readers recognize as "feminist" in Cooper's writing cannot easily be disentangled from her Western ethnocentrism, her staunch religious piety, and a late-Victorian bourgeois sensibility distrustful of social democracy. Of course, these were views she shared with the predominantly male black intelligentsia, complicated, however, by her gender consciousness in such a way as to produce multiple and at times conflicting identities. Out of the multiplicity of her voices emerged that of a southern, nativist apologist for antilabor views.

My intention is not to single her out in this respect, for the middle-class aspirations and agenda of marginal black intellectuals made such accommodationist views commonplace. Rather, it is to suggest that Cooper's thought, particularly her gender consciousness, both contested and reflected the assumptions of the black intelligentsia and black middle-class ideology. Indeed, it is important that we consider racial uplift ideology as a discrete set of values that was understood by educated blacks and yet was at the same time unfinished, provisional, contradictory, and always subject to revision. Cooper thus embodied the contradictions inherent in the avowed status of "representative" Negro leadership: on the one hand, seeking the affirmation and recognition of white elites within the logic of a racist social order while, on the other hand, claiming to represent the political and social aspirations of African Americans.

Cooper, along with fellow members of the black intelligentsia, took for granted that black elites, as "representative Negroes," necessarily spoke for the black majority. Untroubled by the sorts of anxieties of relevance that have preoccupied many black intellectuals since the black power era, Cooper and her cohort of black intellectuals were confident that their writings and reform activities defended the race and, indeed, "uplifted" it. Perhaps the ameliorative, messianic ideals of racial uplift ideology, imposed by an antiblack society, bore a compensatory relation to the devastating indifference, isolation, and hardship black scholars of the day often endured. But for Cooper and other black women intellectuals, including Pauline Hopkins, Ida B. Wells, and others, assumptions of an organic link to the group were eroded by the patriarchal trappings of black intellectual endeavor, racial uplift ideology, and black leadership. Before embarking on a close reading of Cooper's handling of gender and class politics in *A Voice from the South*, and elaborating on their relationship to the ideology of New South economic development, a brief summary of Cooper's life and career is in order.

Cooper was born in Raleigh, North Carolina, to her slave mother and the white man who owned them both. After the Civil War, she attended St. Augustine Normal School in North Carolina, and married Rev. George Cooper in 1877. Widowed two years later, she entered Oberlin College, graduating in 1884. She taught math and science at St. Augustine, then headed the modern languages department at Wilberforce University in Ohio before returning to St. Augustine. In 1887 Cooper received an M.A. degree from Oberlin in mathematics on the strength of her college teaching experience in that subject. This qualified her for an appointment in the Washington, D.C., schools, and she taught mathematics and science at M Street, later known as Paul Laurence Dunbar High School. Cooper never remarried. In 1915, at about age fifty-seven, she adopted five young orphans, the grandchildren of her half-brother.

Cooper was active during a brief period when black leadership enjoyed an ideological diversity that would disappear with the passing of Frederick Douglass and the rise of Booker T. Washington. Cooper embodied that ideological diversity herself, her quest for an authoritative subject position requiring, it would seem—not unlike other black intellectuals—a pragmatic variety of political stances fostered partly by the institutional centers of racial uplift. She was closely associated during the 1890s with Hampton Institute, and her views on education and the organization of labor in the New South were quite similar to those of Washington. It should not be forgotten, however, that the black women's club movement provided a crucial institutional base

Anna Julia Cooper, ca. 1890.

and audience for the work of black women intellectuals and activists within the culture of racial uplift and political activism and protest before the rise of Washington and Du Bois.[4]

Although she supported industrial education during the 1890s, as a teacher of Latin, and later, from 1901 to 1904, principal of the Colored Preparatory School in Washington, D.C., she insisted on the highest standards of academic excellence. Several of her students from the city's only black high school went on to elite universities. Cooper's success may have called forth the resentment and hostility of white officials in the District of Columbia board of education, who dismissed her in 1904, after, it is said, she refused to use racially derogatory textbooks.[5]

Cooper surpassed what could often seem to be the hollow, abstract rhetoric of racial uplift with practical service. Taking in the children was a concrete act of generosity; her commitment to teaching stands out in this regard, too. In addition, Cooper attended a number of conferences devoted to uplift in the 1890s, including the Hampton Negro Conference. She helped organize the Washington, D.C., Colored Woman's League in 1894, which offered domestic training programs for black women. As testimony to both her contemporary prominence, and to the neglect of her peers and subsequent historians, she addressed the first pan-African conference held in London in 1900. Her remarks seem not to have survived. Cooper remained an active teacher and scholar, and an active participant in black Washington's intellectual life. Undoubtedly she was acquainted with such distinguished visitors to the city as the pan-Africanist scholar Edward W. Blyden. Juggling summer research trips to Europe with her teaching duties in the States, Cooper went on to earn a doctorate in French literature from the Sorbonne in 1925, well into her seventh decade. She published articles and essays on an infrequent basis, and after 1930, served for nine years as president of Frelinghuysen University for adult education in Washington. Her efforts revived the institution after a period of decline. In 1929, Cooper had urged W. E. B. Du Bois to answer Claude Bowers's prosouthern, popular history of Reconstruction, *The Tragic Era*; six years later, Du Bois brought out *Black Reconstruction*, a Marxist treatment of the period as a short-lived experiment in interracial social democracy.[6]

A Voice From the South contained Cooper's most sustained treatment of racial uplift ideology. Though she lived for another seven decades, the work marked her only book-length survey of the full landscape of black politics and culture, the women's movement, and American society. The *A.M.E. Church Review* praised the work: "It is the voice of a woman pleading for justice to women and to humanity, and she pleads well." Katherine Davis Tillman observed in the same journal that Cooper "[was] said to have produced the best book written by a Negro on the Negro." The book is divided into two parts, asserting not so much the primacy of gender over race as their inseparability: the first is concerned with the status of black women within racial uplift, and as reformers. In the second part, Cooper addresses a range of national issues, including race relations, the women's movement, labor, the nation's cultural identity, and the decline of religious belief and authority.

Antilabor repression and populist insurgency provided the background for Cooper's writings as much as did segregation, lynching, and the rape of black women. Cooper's views were shaped by the violent class warfare of the late nineteenth century, including the Haymarket Square riot in Chicago in 1886, and the bloody 1892 strike by iron and steel workers against the Carnegie steelworks in Homestead, Pennsylvania. Cooper, like many middle-class commentators on labor issues, blamed workers for the violence, and believed in an essential harmony of interests between capital and labor.[7]

Although Cooper occasionally attacked the greed and materialism of industrializing America, she opposed organized labor as a threat to social peace, national unity, and religious authority. Her position was different from that of a laissez-faire apologist for business, however; Cooper argued elsewhere that the businessman whose "power and greed" prevented his recognition of the rights of labor "was manifestly a robber whether the jailors can catch him or not."[8] But the rights of labor evidently did not include the right to strike. Like many black writers who sought a covenant with white elites, Cooper's antiracism was selective, singling out poor whites and immigrant workers and exonerating southern planters, merchants, and bankers, who personified the "wealth and intelligence" of the region. Yet her bourgeois inclinations met their match in her confrontation with other reformers, such potential allies as black ministers and white women's rights leaders, whose own claims to cultural authority were articulated through sexism and racism, respectively. In other words, Cooper felt betrayed by patriarchy among blacks and by racial prejudice among white women's rights advocates. Yet even as she challenged those aspects of uplift ideology and social reform that invoked and perpetuated race and gender inequalities, she espoused the middle-class, nativist biases of the period, reflecting black elites' indignation at the racism of poor whites and immigrants. Cooper, like most other black writers, was engaged in the contradictory task of using uplift ideology to expose the moral bankruptcy of white supremacy while seeking the recognition and cooperation of white reformers and philanthropic and business elites.

Cooper defended black women from the charges of sexual immorality leveled at them with unnerving frequency. The authoritative style of her learned essays, in which she cited, among others, Emerson, Macaulay, Madame de Stael, and Matthew Arnold, was undoubtedly meant to demolish racial and gender stereotypes. While her appeals to ancient history and assumptions of teleological Christian progress were standard among black intellectuals,

Cooper balked at the usual preoccupation with black manliness. Instead, Cooper broke the silence among many black writers and public leaders on the particular grievances of black women, and the subordinate role that had been reserved for them within conventional views of black progress. Cooper's first essay in the volume called attention to the rape of black women in the South.[9] This sort of candor about oppression was rare amidst the self-congratulatory optimism of the spate of commemorative volumes testifying to black progress. Cooper criticized the tendency to treat the condition of black Americans as "the sole province of the colored man's inheritance and apportionment." She denounced what she regarded a coldly legalistic approach to racial and social conflicts, as well as the penchant among many black writers (male and female) to cite increases in property ownership and professional status as evidence of black progress. She noted the injustice and folly of white "attorneys for the plaintiff . . . and defendant," who "with bungling *gaucherie* have analyzed and dissected, theorized and synthesized with sublime ignorance or pathetic misapprehension of counsel" from black men, and no testimony at all from black women.[10]

In that initial essay, an address delivered before an assembly of Washington, D.C., black ministers, Cooper argued that the rape of black women and girls in the South mocked paeans to black progress. Many black and white reformers exhorted blacks, and black women in particular, to improve their sexual morés. Cooper made it clear that black women were not to be judged for their victimization. Following Alexander Crummell—Cooper alluded to his pamphlet "The Black Woman of the South,"—she urged the ministers to take more of a protective interest in "the Colored Girls of the South . . . so full of promise and possibilities, yet so sure of destruction; often without a father to whom they dare apply the loving term, often without a stronger brother to . . . defend their honor with his life's blood; in the midst of pitfalls and snares, waylaid by the lower classes of white men, with no shelter, no protection nearer than the great blue vault above." In Cooper's view, black women were not immoral, but unprotected. As the daughter of a slave owner, she knew that family ties with such men carried no assurance of protection.[11]

Cooper's impassioned plea for the protection of black women was part of her larger argument that group uplift was impossible without an improvement of their status. It was "absurd to quote statistics showing the Negro's bank account and rent rolls, to point to the hundreds of newspapers edited by colored men and lists of lawyers, doctors, professors . . . etc., while the source from which the life-blood of the race is to flow is subject to taint and corruption in the enemy's camp." Her comparison of the sexual domination of black women with military occupation was a stark indictment of the usual claims for black progress. Furthermore, Cooper objected to the denial of higher education to black women: "Every attempt to elevate the Negro, whether undertaken by himself or through the philanthropy of others, cannot but prove abortive unless so directed as to utilize the indispensable agency of an elevated and trained womanhood." She questioned the habit of black writers to honor "representative" men as beacons of progress, noting that "our present record of eminent men, when placed against the actual status of the race in America to-day, proves that no man can represent the race." According to Cooper, "Only the Black Woman can say 'when and where I enter, in the quiet, undisputed dignity of my womanhood, without violence and without suing or special patronage, then and there the whole Negro race enters with me.'" A broader social recognition of black womanhood represented to Cooper the fundamental criterion for racial progress.[12]

As we have seen, a central rhetorical strategy of racial uplift ideology, as part of its insistence on class differences, was its opposition of racism by invoking conventional gender hierarchies of sexual difference, as this was widely regarded as the behavioral measure of bourgeois civilization. Cooper took this line of argument with her claim that civilizations are measured by the status of women, upon which she based her demand that society recognize the "undisputed dignity" of black womanhood. This, and her appeals to protection, were understandable, given the urgent need to halt the brutality of rape and to challenge the accusations of promiscuity that justified such acts. Cooper went on to dispute the white South's stereotype that black men had a monopoly on rape. Still, Cooper's appeal for protection was indicative of the political disadvantage faced by southern blacks. Calls for male protection seemed to remove the issue from the realm of politics and the courts; the ruffianly element among whites was not the sole source of the sexual abuse of black women; fundamentally, it was a matter of political power in the courts, on juries, and at the polls. Without this political context, calls for protection reduced the issue to self-help and moral conduct. In other words, by this logic, black men were at fault for "failing" to protect, or black women were culpable for "failing" to defend their "virtue." Given that the state denied legal protection to black women, the only meaningful arguments for protection would have been those made by militants, like Ida B. Wells and others, who called for armed resistance and self-defense.

Cooper's call for protection was rooted in gender conventions of respectable manhood and true womanhood. Within racial uplift ideology, however, appropriations of the moral category of "true womanhood" were not always appropriate to the interests of black women. If Cooper and other black women called for black men to fulfill the role of protector, many black men felt most protective in their expectation that black women remain within the sphere of home and family.

Although contemporaries stressed complementary relations between the sexes, the linkage of race progress with male supremacy contradicted uplift's unifying ideals and led to some interesting arguments that spoke to the conflicts at hand. One commentator sought to refute the prejudice against educating black men on grounds that it led to sex across the color line by asserting that because most "women, with a few exceptions, by nature, are inferior in intellectual capacity to men," educated black men would hardly desire association with such inferiors. Voicing anxiety over women's increased public activity as a violation of God and nature, James H. A. Johnson proclaimed in the pages of the *A.M.E. Church Review* that woman's "position was prescribed" as "the 'mother of all living'—made to fill a place peculiar to herself, so that any attempt to change it would be an attempt to change the divine arrangement of society." It was understood that such general pronouncements on the nature and position of "woman" referred to black women. Johnson was especially alarmed at the prospect of black women assuming ministerial authority, one of the few professional careers available to black men, and one already fraught with intense competition. "A true woman, like . . . Amanda Smith," he observed, referring to the extraordinarily popular unordained black woman evangelist, "thinks she is as great in the pew as man is in the pulpit," striving "to satisfy the Lord and not the bubbling ambition of her soul." Though sufficiently deferential, according to Johnson, Smith was, in fact, a threatening presence within the black Methodist church, which refused to ordain her, and which had refused to ordain black women preachers since antebellum times.[13]

Cooper challenged such expectations of women's deference. She pointed out that while "numerous young men have been . . . trained for the ministry by the charities of the Church, the number of indigent females who have been supported, sheltered and trained, is phenomenally small." Gender conflict exposed the contradictions of uplift's vision of progress, a middle-class vision structured in sexual dominance.[14]

Cooper's argument for the education of black women joined an ongoing debate among black writers over the role of black women in racial uplift. In several published testimonials to the black woman's idealized, yet narrowly prescribed role within uplift, bourgeois black women were generally represented, by themselves and others, as being employed in a restricted range of occupations. In addition to the obligatory celebrations of domesticity and motherhood as both a privilege and a duty, black women were praised as race builders through their material labor, which subsidized their children's education and such black institutions as churches and schools. In addition, they were lauded as teachers, writers, journalists, missionaries, elocutionists, musicians, and artists. Membership in such moral reform crusades as the temperance and clubwomen's movements, which projected domestic values into the public realm, were also acceptable badges of status. The *Women's Era*, a Boston journal for African American women, sounded a dissenting note in

1894: "Not all women are intended as mothers. Some of us have not the temperament for family life. Clubs will make women think seriously of their future lives, and not make girls think their only alternative is to marry." But this statement, and Cooper's views, were exceptional. Although black women valued public activism, in keeping with the multivocal, ambiguous character of black middle-class ideology, they usually situated their appeals for women's independence within the rhetoric of female domesticity.[15]

Thus, even the public activities of black women as reformers and journalists reinforced the assumption that their true "power and influence," resided at home and hearthside. Against this, Cooper pointed out that black women were unjustly discouraged by black men from pursuing higher education and social reform: "The colored woman too often finds herself hampered and shamed by a less liberal sentiment and a more conservative attitude on the part of those for whose opinion she cares most." Accordingly, uplift instructed black women on their duties to the race. Seldom were they regarded as intellectual peers on an equal public footing. If allowances were made for the "true type of 'progressive woman' of today," implying the inauthenticity of all others, then by definition, that woman was "modest and womanly, with a reverence for the high and holy duties of wife and mother." Years later, Cooper informed her old friend Francis Grimké that her niece, Annie, had married and left Howard University. That came as "a great and sore disappointment" to Cooper, who had "great hopes on her becoming a teacher to succeed me in the work I am now doing." The deference expected of black women reflected the limited aspirations racial uplift ideology held out for all blacks.[16]

The importance of religious leadership and institutions among blacks contributed to the view that held racial uplift and black leadership synonymous with patriarchal authority. The prospect of extending higher education to black women raised the disturbing possibility of competition with black men for these precious opportunities. It was difficult enough as it was to attract and keep men as church members. Black women's work and economic independence clashed with patriarchal imperatives of male leadership, protection, and support of families. Logic and argument were hardly necessary to discredit such competition between black men and women in the public realm of jobs and status; this was simply at odds with nature.

Such views were not simply a product of restricted occupational and professional opportunities for black men, they also reflected the rising opposition through the 1890s, by women as well as men, to woman suffrage organizations. Antisuffragist views were shared by both misogynists and many of those who claimed to be women's advocates. Cultural anxieties over social change—industrialism, urbanization, immigration, and economic uncertainty—generally settled on fears for the survival of the family, whose health symbolized social harmony and stability. Citizens were men and men only. Reasserting women's sphere as home and family was an effective means of discrediting demands for public activity and citizenship. Thus, antisuffragists feared that enfranchised women would destroy traditional sexual differences, leaving the family, and society, in ruins. Antisuffragist rhetoric and iconography from the turn of the century warned ominously that women voters would wear the pants and henpecked men would be saddled with laundering them. The suffrage, employment, women's education, and other forms of public activity, according to opponents of women's rights, produced unwomanly shrews, and worse, conflicted with women's natural domestic duties. Such logic echoed that employed by white supremacists—the end result of votes for women would not be equality, but domination.[17]

Although opponents to women's suffrage among blacks were few, black elites harbored other assumptions of women's subordination. According to uplift ideals that reflected the status aspirations of black men, black women were to be supported, not independently employed. Cooper broke with convention on such matters, citing an Atlanta University study in 1899 that found that "of 1,137 colored families in that city, 650, or 57.17 per cent. are supported wholly or in part by female heads." She held that "if men cannot or will not help the conditions which force women into the struggle for bread, we have a right to claim at least that she shall have fair play and all the rights of wage-earners in general." Cooper went on to claim similar rights as wage earners for black women's domestic labor in the home, and to criticize Kelly Miller's attribution of "unnatural conditions in our large cities" to the large number of "surplus" unmarried black women. She reminded her readers and critics that "surely the greatest sufferer from the strain and stress attendant upon the economic conditions noted among our people is the colored woman, and she is the one who must meet and conquer the conditions." Cooper insisted that these views were compatible with marriage and family, as black men and women teamed up for race-building: "So, by her . . . calm insight and tact, thrift and frugality . . . the colored woman can prove that a prudent marriage is the very best investment that a working man can make." Concluding her analysis with the sugar-coated homilies of uplift, Cooper argued, as did many of her contemporaries, for the necessity of a black woman's household work as the thrift that stretches the family's wages while extolling her role within marriage and the home as that of an active partner.[18]

The rhetoric of domesticity may have enabled such challenges to assumptions of women's deference, but the expectation that black women maintain home and hearth for the welfare of the race could spark confrontations. Among those black women who, like Cooper, aspired to race leadership, Ida B. Wells clashed on numerous occasions with injunctions of female passivity. She stormed out of a meeting before AME ministers in Philadelphia when they proceeded to debate whether to endorse her antilynching efforts. Outraged that she could not obtain the support of "ministers of my own race," she recalled telling them that she had done the work "that you could not do, if you would, and you would not do if you could." Other black women, who, like Wells, ventured into male-dominated occupations like journalism, and their numbers were more significant than one might suspect, often negotiated their seemingly anomalous public presence by endorsing the gender conventions of the dominant culture, as appropriate for racial uplift. Motherhood and domesticity reigned supreme for the journalist Mrs. Julia Ringwood Cotson, as she insisted that men would marry only "essentially feminine" women who "know naught of women's rights and universal suffrage, . . . are not troubled with the affairs of State, nor are they agents of reform." These "adorable" women entertained "no vicious longing for publicity, no hunger to usurp the sphere of men." Wells was somewhat exceptional, in that her syndicated columns in the black press under the pen name "Iola" covered a wide range of issues, foremost among them, black politics and leadership. In 1892 Wells praised an economic boycott of a streetcar company in Atlanta led by the pastor of one of the largest churches in the city. Wells regarded such boycotts as blacks' most effective protest against segregated public conveyances.[19]

Cooper wrote as the debates over the quality of education to be made available to blacks—higher education, or industrial education based on the Hampton-Tuskegee model that stressed farm and domestic labor—were being duplicated for black women. Among those who debated what sort of education was best for blacks, there were those who feared higher education would unfit its beneficiaries for their perceived station in society as menial workers. Similarly, some held that black women's education was best limited to rudimentary instruction, and that it should emphasize motherhood and domestic and household work. Miller, a faculty member of Howard University and an advocate of higher education for black men, found the "upward ambition and aspiration of colored women . . . encouraging" and urged that "school[s] of domestic service" be established for "every girl of moderate intelligence and ambition. This would indeed be an industrial education that counts." Though Miller's remarks reflected the fact that for most black women, domestic work, dressmaking, marriage, and motherhood were foremost among available respectable occupations, opponents of higher education for black women also reiterated the general arguments against women's education: it would "unsex" women, thus violating norms of sexual difference, and worst of all, make women unfit for marriage.[20]

Among black writers, education was a much discussed matter, as the status of black women within uplift was a constant concern. Thomas Baker, who held a doctorate in philosophy from Yale, warned in 1906 that black women "must not be educated away from being a mother. . . . The race is dependent on her giving her best to her children." Interestingly enough, however, he added that the black woman "be better educated than the man," noting that superior mothers would rear superior men. Baker's fear that educated black women might forsake motherhood was typical of uplift ideology's emphasis on black women's reproductive function, which, it seemed, functioned best with the birth of male infants. Such concerns were rearticulations by blacks of the "race suicide" fears of Anglo-American eugenicists, and also echoed the biological determinism of opponents of women's education.[21]

For Baker, Miller, Cotson, and even Wells, there could be no education for blacks without Christianity, which, among other things, sanctioned patriarchal commands urging marriage and motherhood. Fears of the growing migration of blacks to towns and cities at century's end also spurred concerns that black women were defying nature, as several commentators found the preponderance of single women in towns and cities cause for alarm. Echoing Booker T. Washington's public derision for higher training for blacks, many regarded higher education for black women as impractical, superfluous knowledge that besides making them unmarriageable, raised their aspirations to an unattainable standard of living. Against the humiliating effects of poverty, sexual exploitation, and the public stigma of vice, domestic and family life were so exalted within uplift ideology that some black women endorsed these grounds for limiting their educational opportunities. "Have they been so trained out of sympathy with the plain life," wondered Mrs. S. B. Stevens at the Hampton Negro Conference in 1898, "that they are unwilling to marry and help cheerfully to bear the burdens of life instead of fretting because their homes . . . are not handsomely furnished out of a meagre salary?" Stevens voiced a far more prosaic version of the usual paeans to the so-called powerful influence of black women in homes. However unglamorous and burdensome, black women's unpaid housework, praised as thrift—cooking, laundering, sewing, and child rearing—was part of uplift's master plan, as a vital labor supplement to family incomes considerably below those of middle-class whites. By urging black women to accept domestic labor as their lot, Stevens had also embraced the Hampton-Tuskegee philosophy that similarly assigned subordinate status to black people within the political system, and the industrial order of the New South. The black poet from Richmond, Daniel Webster Davis, voiced similar sentiments in Negro dialect:

Larnin' is a blessed thing
An' good cloze berry fin',
But I likes to see de cullud gal
Dat's been larnt how to 'ine' [iron].[22]

Although Cooper's advocacy of protection and higher education for black women challenged assumptions of male privilege, it is impossible to separate such incipient black feminism from the dominant Hampton-Tuskegee philosophy that prescribed the subordinate and instrumental function of black men and women within the New South labor market. Such feminism (if the term is even appropriate in this context) was tethered to the social and cultural conservatism of uplift. For advocates of industrial education, Native American assimilation, and missionary deculturation of subject peoples, the women of primitive societies might hold strategic influence as agents of civilization, and for the institution of Christian home life, or, in the case of Native Americans, the preference for private property ownership over collective systems of tribal ownership. Hampton materialized its belief in woman as an uplifting and civilizing entity with its curriculum in domestic science, which became the prevailing mode of education available to red and black women in southern institutions. Equating the bravery and devotion of black women in the South to missionary domesticity with that displayed by black soldiers in Cuba, the *Southern Workman* praised its female graduates as "centers of light and civilization in dark communities," and opined that "if every public school in the South could introduce sewing, instead of having all the time devoted to the study of books, much could be accomplished." How often these discursive attempts to police the boundaries of acceptable behavior for black women were contested and subverted in the daily lives of black women, as I will argue in my discussion of the public and private life of Alice Dunbar-Nelson in chapter 8, remains a matter of conjecture. Nevertheless, the rhetoric of female domestic service was perhaps necessary to ensure support in a region where black education in even its most conservative form might provoke violent opposition from white supremacists. Evelyn Brooks Higginbotham has shown that domestic training for black women was vulnerable to such intimidation, as a school in Baton Rouge was accused of "educating the nigger up to think they are the equal of white folks." [23]

Cooper's association with Hampton and its philosophy might be explained by her ideological affinity with its civilizationist philosophy, which conferred status and moral authority on marginalized African American women just as it had for white women, educated Native Americans, and African American men. In any event, Cooper, a graduate of Oberlin College's gentleman's course, saw no conflict between industrial and higher education for blacks, as did many of those who supported Hampton and Tuskegee. Cooper used a rhetorical strategy common to black writers for the purpose of arguing on behalf of black women's education. She appealed to history, marshaling ancient precedents for women's education and independence, including "Sappho, the bright, sweet singer of Lesbos," who wrote "six centuries before Christ"—

Black women's drill team, Wilmington, Delaware, 1905. Military supplies
shown are castoffs from the Civil War and the Spanish-American War.
(Courtesy of Wahneema Lubiano)

she also summoned trends that had yet to be endorsed by middle-class blacks
whose preoccupation with race (understood as masculine) left little room for
women's concerns.[24] Cooper, like other black clubwomen, situated herself
within women's increased social and political presence as reformers. She
linked women's moral influence, which she termed "the sweetening, purify-
ing antidotes for the poisons of man's acquisitiveness," with the essential
progress that could not exist without the black woman. Cooper praised the
work of the Women's Christian Temperance Union and praised women reformers as trenchant critics of a materialistic society that seemed to have
deified economic man over Jesus Christ. Indeed, her claims for the socially
redemptive influence of women resembled the romantic racialism of the antislavery era, which attributed to African Americans the gentle, religious, and
feminine qualities that would somehow temper Anglo-Saxon aggression and
materialism. "In this period," Cooper wrote, "when material prosperity
and well-earned ease are an assured fact from a national standpoint, woman's
work and woman's influence are needed as never before; needed to bring a
heart power into this money getting, dollar worshipping civilization; needed
to bring a moral force into the utilitarian motives and interests of the time;
needed to stand for God and Home and Native Land versus gain and greed
and grasping selfishness." Appropriating the rhetoric of white women reformers, Cooper invoked the Victorian myth of women's moral superiority.[25]

As is apparent from the last quotation, Cooper cannot be fully explained in terms of her gender consciousness. Displaying the anxious moral indignation of the late-Victorian bourgeoisie, Cooper praised the progressive spirit of women reformers as she sought to be counted on the side of right against the forces of disorder, standing for "God and Home and Native Land." Her nativism was evidently a retaliatory response to the racial exclusion practiced by white craft unions. In addition, her marginality within the black community, as well as within the women's reform organizations whose work she otherwise valued so highly, may have made such rhetoric attractive in her bid for authority.[26]

Cooper's Criticism of the (White) Women's Movement

Given her idealized view of women as a force for social betterment, Cooper was deeply disappointed by those women reformers whose social vision was tainted by racist attitudes. In an essay entitled "Woman versus the Indian," Cooper argued that white women reformers had abdicated their moral responsibility in trying to exploit racial prejudice to serve their own interests. She criticized these reform groups, and such leaders as Susan B. Anthony, for their acquiescent silence in allowing white southern women to dictate the increasingly racist character of the national women's suffrage movement. Cooper's title was taken from an address by Rev. Anna Shaw before the National Women's Council in 1891. Shaw's premise was that contemporary debates on the rights of Native Americans came at the expense of what she held to be the more urgent question of women's rights. Cooper opposed Shaw's claim, which paralleled some of the women suffragists' opposition to Negro suffrage, as well as the bigotry that excluded black women from the authoritative public role of women reformers.[27]

Shaw's speech enabled Cooper to analyze the extent to which women reformers, ostensibly concerned with "the broadening, humanizing and civilizing" of American society, actually replicated the oppression they claimed to oppose. To Cooper, these so-called reformers, as women, should have sympathized with the powerless. In a similar vein, Cooper chastised Mary A. Livermore, a white suffragist, temperance advocate and reformer from Massachusetts. Livermore, in an essay describing "the Anglo-Saxon genius for power and his contempt for weakness," waxed prescriptive in a manner that effectively proved Cooper's point. Livermore told of a pack of white children who attacked a Chinese man in San Francisco, throwing his bundle of laundry into a ditch. Because the man did not "teach [the children] a lesson with his two fists," Livermore scoffed, "I didn't much care." An outraged Cooper remarked: "This is said like a man! It grates harshly. It smacks of the worship of the beast." Livermore's statement betrayed Cooper's ideals of women's moral superiority. Racism was the relevant issue here, undermining Cooper's appropriation of white women's universalistic rhetoric of "woman's" moral influence.[28]

To Cooper, such contempt for weakness as shown by Livermore, Shaw, and others was "untrue to the instincts I have ascribed to the thinking woman and to the contribution she is to add to the civilized world." For Cooper, contempt for weakness was a corruption of reform ideals, rooted in Christianity. Their debasement was consummated in a fetish for strength, the "worship of the beast" of power and brutality. Thus, while Cooper generally applauded the efforts of women reformers, she parted with them on the issue of race. For suffragists themselves to engage in acts of discrimination, setting their own rights above those of other powerless groups, demonstrated the narrow, jurisprudential mindset that jealously sought recognition of its privileged status of whiteness before the law. Remember that for Cooper, justice was hardly embodied in the southern legal system, its moral double-standard codified in anti-intermarriage laws and in its denial of equal protection and justice to blacks. In a manner illustrative of prevailing discriminatory conceptions of rights, Cooper vehemently rejected the arguments of white women suffragists that they, as educated, refined white women, were more entitled to the vote than what she sarcastically called "the great burly black man, ignorant and gross and depraved." "Why should woman," she wondered, "become plaintiff in a suit versus the Indian, or the Negro, or any other race or class who have been crushed under the heel of Anglo-Saxon power and selfishness?" In powerful language, Cooper claimed the higher law of Christianity as the final arbiter in such matters. "When the image of God in human form" was fully recognized by society and its laws, and "when race, color, sex, [and] condition are realized to be the accidents, not the substance of life . . . then woman's lesson is taught and woman's cause is won—not the white woman nor the black woman nor the red woman, but the cause of every woman who has writhed silently under a mighty wrong." By representing oppression as rape, in both actual and metaphorical senses, Cooper's analysis of the competition for rights and legal standing between white women and racial minorities put forth a claim for group rights in inclusive terms of justice. White women suffragists who, in their collusion with patriarchal racism, may have considered themselves immune to the problem, would do well to remember that "Woman's cause" was epitomized by the rape of black women. By the same token, rape as a metaphor for the disfranchisement of racial groups struck at the heart of white women's claims to moral, educational, and racial superiority. Through the harrowing image of rape, Cooper alluded to the dominance masked by the category of civilization as a racialized slogan. It followed that polite references to "equality" really entailed

domination and brutality, and that the advancement of white women inevitably claimed a victim. This was a zero-sum, exclusionary conception of
rights and equality, as the historical inertia of a republic for property-owning
white males dictated that one person's rights required another's disfranchisement, whether it involved missionaries seeking to reclaim heathen peoples, a
lynch mob inflicting its murderous will on its victim, or those who inflicted
rape without fear of prosecution.[29]

Cooper's Racial Solution to the Labor Question

Perhaps because racists within the women's movement refused to acknowledge black women's oppression, and had thus betrayed her high expectations
of women as agents of progress, Cooper seemed to vacillate in her designation of which group, women or blacks, was more likely to redeem society.
Still, her faith in the ultimate resolution of social conflict by the messianic intervention of an oppressed group was unshakable. "We would not deprecate
the fact," Cooper wrote, "that America has a Race Problem." The resolution
of racial conflict ensured "the perpetuity and progress" of American institutions, "and the symmetry of her development." Though not much in her experience encouraged her, Cooper believed that "the Negro is appointed to
contribute to that problem," for "his tropical warmth and spontaneous emotionalism may form no unseemly counterpart to the cold and calculating
Anglo-Saxon." Cooper experimented with the period's romantic racialism,
that negritude of the nineteenth century, which sought to turn perceived
racial differences and liabilities into strengths.[30]

Although Cooper waxed sentimental over the moral authority she believed
blacks and women had earned in their respective struggles for inclusion in
American society, significantly, gender did not play a major role in Cooper's
scenario for the resolution of racial and social conflict. Cooper wanted to
affirm a moral advantage held by oppressed blacks, while also seeking the approval of ruling elites. Thus, like most other black exponents of uplift, whose
middle-class aspirations often found expression in attacks on the working
class and organized labor, Cooper was considerably less willing to see any advantages to the bitter and violent class conflicts of her day. Cooper viewed the
confrontations between capital and labor as evidence of foreign subversion;
reflecting black anxieties over immigration, she invoked nativist hostility and
a self-righteous chauvinism to demonstrate the cultural loyalty of African
American farm workers in the South. Her message anticipating that of
Booker T. Washington, Cooper believed that only blacks as a group could
mediate and resolve class antagonism, "prov[ing] indispensable and invaluable elements in a nation menaced as America is by anarchy, socialism, com-

munism and skepticism poured in with all the jail birds from the continents of
Europe and Asia." Cooper appeared untroubled by the extent to which capitalists exploited and exacerbated racial prejudice by pitting black strikebreakers against white workers. She carried her blend of religious piety and anti-
trade unionism well into the twentieth century.[31]

Cooper and other southern black spokespersons feared that southern elites
would make good on their repeated threats to replace black workers with immigrant labor. During the 1890s, there had been widespread efforts throughout the New South to attract European immigrants to work in expanding
cotton mill and railroad industries. According to Charles Flynn, black farm
workers in Georgia protested exploitative conditions after Redemption, and
into the 1880s, resisted the planters' attempts to dictate the terms of labor.
Hysterical press reports characterized union organizing among blacks as im-
pending violent insurrection plots, but it was white violence that invariably
claimed black organizers as victims. Racial hostility and frequent complaints
about insubordinate black labor led to campaigns in the press for immigration, which, it was believed, promised a superior labor force. Immigration
was also proposed to relieve the labor shortage caused by out-migrations of
native-born blacks and whites. The most ardent proponents of immigration
hoped that European immigrants would replace blacks as a labor force. Thus,
black leaders feared that black workers would become superfluous, and they
argued that African Americans held the solution to the threat of class warfare
posed by lawless, violent strikers from southern Europe.[32]

Commenting on the labor question as a black woman for whom the norms
of law and respectability did not then apply, it seems understandable that
Cooper would be drawn to dominant antilabor, nativist arguments. While
she attacked the injustices of racism and patriarchy, Cooper was hardly alone
among southern uplift advocates in taking a conservative, gradualist, deal-
making approach with planters and industrialists. Many black leaders participated in the public ritual of attacking a stigmatized outsider, aligning
themselves with industrialists and against white workers branded "foreign,"
criminal, and, as Cooper described them elsewhere, "ignorant . . . incapable
of sympathy with [the country's] institutions, brewers of anarchy, experts
with dynamite, murderers and terrorizers of honest workers, wholesale dis-
turbers of public comfort and travel, and irresponsible destroyers of the
country's peace and prosperity and safety and freedom."[33]

By comparison, Cooper asserted the loyalty of black workers in servile
terms evocative of the plantation legend—African Americans were "a people
long-suffering and gentle . . . teachable, loyal, loving," and the country was
"demented" not to take advantage of their labor. Cooper's appeal seemed
more concerned with southern blacks as potential laborers than as citizens.
Unhampered by her Christian convictions, Cooper raged against organized

labor, to her personified by atheism, and by racist immigrants who were unworthy of sympathy, forgiveness, and love. Indeed, moral outrage infused her
sense of class conflict. Cooper equated insurgent workers with "crackers" and
"poor whites"—just as she had singled out "the lower classes of white men" as
the main culprits for the sexual abuse of southern black women. In this respect, Cooper's antidemocratic views were analogous to Alexander Crummell's association of democracy with white mob assaults against blacks.
Trusting in the benevolence of a Christlike, disinterested bourgeoisie over
the immoral lust her slaveholder father and poor whites represented, Cooper
singled out "atheistic" white workers and radical foreigners. Her world was
rigidly ordered by the struggle between good and evil, and Cooper struck
what she doubtless believed to be the proper tone of southern, patrician indignation toward the demands of organized labor: "Will you call it narrow-
ness and selfishness, then, that I find it impossible to catch the fire of sympathy and enthusiasm for most of these labor movements at the North?" Her
preference for southern paternalism over northern labor unrest led her to denounce unions as an un-American "body of men who still need an interpreter
to communicate with their employer," and who "threaten to cut the nerve
and paralyze the progress of an industry that gives work to an American-born
citizen, or one which takes measures to instruct any apprentice not supported
by the labor monopoly." Perhaps to placate white southern fears of "Negro
domination" and threats to racial purity, Cooper portrayed organized labor
as a contagion far more threatening to the health of the social organism. Siding with capital against unions, Cooper emphasized class conflict among
whites with the hope of blunting the force of racism. According to Cooper
and others, black labor served a crucial instrumental function within the New
South economic order.[34]

Just as race served—among other things—at the turn of the century as a
distraction from the age's bitter class conflicts, Cooper sought to reverse this
situation, reinscribing the centrality of class polarization, but with blacks
holding the key for restoring order. Though she romanticized blacks and
women as messianic social groups, Cooper finally located virtue and moral
authority in power, as she preached a gospel of accommodation. "Not only
the Christian conscience of the South, but also its enlightened self-interest is
unquestionably on the side of justice and manly dealing with the black man,"
Cooper declared. Directing her argument toward captains of industry, she
adopted the stiff upper lip of the Victorian man of letters, demanding firm
control of recalcitrant workers and espousing feudal New South paternalism.
Cooper offered a clear choice between what she regarded as loyal black
Americans and unassimilated immigrant workers. Compared to the "self-
constituted tribunal of 'recent arrivals,'" as she called unions, "the Negro"
was far more trustworthy by virtue of "his instinct for law and order, his in-

born respect for authority, his inaptitude for rioting and anarchy, his gentle-ness and cheerfulness as a laborer, and his deep-rooted faith in God." Thus spoke Cooper, in a portent of Washington's watershed 1895 Atlanta address, on behalf of the voiceless black masses.[35]

Reflections on Race and the National Culture

Like most blacks educated into a system of Western values, Cooper was of mixed minds on the matter of race, reflecting her shifting, conflicting identi-ties and her ambivalent pragmatism. Indeed, Cooper's place at the vortex of several sites of social conflict—namely, class, gender, race, color, region, reli-gion, and culture, to name those articulated in her essays—made it impossible for her to maintain a consistent ideological position, particularly on the tor-tured question of race. Perhaps as well as anyone else, Cooper demonstrates the impossibility of uplift ideology's project of constructing a unified black subject that might guide the race along the path to progress. Although she could take comfort from romantic racialist stereotypes, Cooper rejected the idea of black cultural differences. She resented the white moderate's belief that blacks preferred segregation, as well as "the intimation that there is a 'black voice,' a black character, easy, irresponsible . . . a black ideal of art and a black barbaric taste in color." To debunk this fallacy, along with the more lurid products of white imaginations, she cited the popular literary stereotype of the mulatto, whose drop of black blood irresistibly summoned forth the atavistic passions of a savage nature. But if whites employed such stereotypes toward racist ends, it seemed, blacks could appropriate them for their own purposes. Thus Cooper was willing elsewhere to exploit the "Uncle Tom" stereotype of black Christian forebearance and what she defined among blacks as a constitutional absence not only of lustful sexual desire, but also, of anger. Noting that most white writers, lacking Harriet Beecher Stowe's re-fined "humility and love," have been unable "to put themselves into the darker man's place," Cooper believed that African Americans served as Stowe's muse for *Uncle Tom's Cabin*. Indeed, she dated the emergence of American literary autonomy from the time the nation's authors took notice of the inno-cence of blacks, "their . . . tropical luxuriance and naive abandon" and the "paroxysms of religious fervor into which this simple-minded, child-like race were thrown by the contemplation of Heaven and rest and freedom." Antici-pating the racial uplift project of refining Negro folklore into high art, Cooper held that America could have no true art that ignored black Ameri-cans. She wondered at the prospect of someone gathering folklore, "to digest and assimilate these original lispings of an unsophisticated people while they were yet close—so close—to nature and to nature's God."[36]

If she dwelled excessively, and to contradictory effect, on images of humble, Christian blacks more worthy of pity than fear, Cooper also trenchantly analyzed the motives behind "A Voodoo Prophecy," a poem by Maurice Thompson that appeared in the *New York Independent* in 1892. Cooper denounced the poem as a hypocritical white man's fantasy of black male revenge through rape:

> As you have done by me, so will I do . . .
> Your snowy limbs, your blood's patrician blue
> Shall be
> Tainted by me
> And I will set my seal upon your face.

Cooper dismissed such inflammatory fears, assessing Thompson's poem as a perverse fantasy, arising from the northern white's lurid fascination with the white South's practice of rape, and Thompson's apparent desire, camouflaged by his use of a black male persona in the poem, to entertain vicarious fantasies of sexual domination and possession. To Cooper, the sexual terrorism practiced against black women in the South made this slander against black men all the more pernicious and hypocritical.[37]

Given the existence of such dubious texts as Thompson's poem in mainstream discourse, issues of sexuality, as we have seen, were a volatile topic among black writers. Insofar as patriarchal authority and home life signified to many middle-class blacks freedom from the unbearable realities of sexual domination of black women by whites, these were ardently sought goals of racial uplift. There were aspects of the enslaved past and the not fully emancipated present too painful to be remembered, and openly discussed. Such emphasis on family life as a racial panacea often treated the problem as a failure of blacks to conform to Victorian sexual mores, instead of as an outgrowth of ongoing, systematic repression. Thus, as lynching, a barbarous practice, was defended by whites as necessary to maintain racial purity by curbing so-called criminal black lust, and as black women were stigmatized as sexualized beings rather than the victims of criminal whites' lust, so it seemed that uplift ideology required relegating black women to the protective custody of the home. The proverbial sanctity of white womanhood was intertwined with the moral devaluation of black women, all of which abetted the terroristic component of white supremacy, and the dispossession of blacks, practiced in the name of "civilization." Statutes forbidding intermarriage in the South enabled white obsession with the so-called criminal lust and immorality of blacks when it was whites who remained free to be the aggressors. Until Ida B. Wells's antilynching campaign began in 1892, and outside of the occasional militant black editor, advocates of uplift rarely alluded to, let alone analyzed, the hypocrisy behind the white South's preoccupation with rape. Cooper's demystification of Thompson's poem departed from the Victorian reticence of many black commentators intent on maintaining an appearance of respectability by condemning black sexual improprieties, and by implication, exonerating white men—and some white women, according to Wells—of sexual aggression.[38]

Yet Cooper's identity as a southern writer also led her to contrast the hypocrisy of northern whites such as Thompson with what she at times wishfully perceived as the generosity and goodwill of southern authorities. Though admitting that "the South presents a solid phalanx of iron resistance to the Negro's advancement, still as individuals to individuals they are warm-hearted and often tender." Such interracial cooperation sought friends wherever they might be found, reducing race conflicts to the realm of harmonious interpersonal relations and the hope that black and white elites might find some common ground. In this instance, Cooper's overture was a variation on paternalistic whites' theme that considered blacks "like one of the family." Citing the folly of southern whites' fears of "Negro political domination" and the "horror of being lost as a race in this virile and vigorous black race," Cooper dismissed the prospect of black supremacy given that "the usual safeguards of democracy are in the hands of intelligence and wealth in the South as elsewhere." Cooper believed southern benevolence would ensure that "she [the South] will find herself in possession of the most tractable laborer, the most faithful and reliable henchman, the most invaluable co-operator and friendly vassal of which this or any country can boast."[39]

Cooper's final chapter, entitled "The Gain from a Belief," was an impassioned defense of religious faith against "lofty, unimpassioned agnosticism." Against agnosticism, Cooper argued for an evangelical crusade of social reform and uplift. She refused to accept the "eternal silence" of a Godless universe. Through the agnosticism of such men as the charismatic reformer Robert Ingersoll, "God and Love are shut out," eliminating all moral basis for social reform and activism. Against skepticism Cooper asserted "just this one truth:—The great, the fundamental need of any nation, any race, is for heroism, devotion, sacrifice" founded on religious faith, "particularly urgent in a race at almost the embryonic stage of character-building." Noting that at such times, "most of all, do men need to be anchored to what they *feel* to be eternal verities," Cooper asserted the pragmatism of religious faith for racial uplift. "Do you not *believe* that the God of history often chooses the weak things of earth to confound the mighty, and that the Negro race in America has a veritable destiny in his eternal purposes," Cooper asked as she exhorted both elite blacks and whites to "let go your purse-strings and begin to *live* your creed." Cooper's declaration of boundless, messianic faith undoubtedly had its roots in bodily oppression and worldly despair. Her vision resembled, for all her criticism of imperialism, the rhetoric of the civilizing mission: "There are nations still in darkness to which we owe a light. The world is to be moved one generation forward—whether by us, by blind force, by fate, or by God! If thou believest, all things are possible; and as thou believest, so be it unto thee."[40]

The possibility of the "eternal silence" of a godless universe meant to Cooper that the nameless, numberless crimes against black women and men, consigned to silence and invisibility before the bar of an unjust and complicit legal system, would forever remain silent, and unredressed. Those often unmentionable horrors—sins, really, to Cooper—that black women and men had endured in the South that had to be forgotten in the name of uplift, swallowed along with the unrighteous rage they provoked, cruelties that only God could know and reconcile—these horrors would have for Cooper no hope for redress and redemption if religious faith were meaningless. Cooper's piety lent meaning and moral strength, despite the decline in religious and ministerial authority she was witnessing. It was perhaps only through such a vehement declaration of spirituality that Cooper could hope to resolve all the contradictions of her experience, and reclaim the virtue and moral authority that American institutions withheld from black men and women. To Cooper, racial purity, uplift, and religious faith joined in a desperate prayer to divine will for deliverance, somewhat analogous to her appeal for the goodwill and material assistance of paternalistic New South industrialists.

During a period of violent labor confrontations, economic depression, and escalating racial segregation and harassment, Cooper's vision of social reform was personified by Christ's chaste love that must have represented to her the triumph over the patriarchal aggression to which she owed her very existence. The difficulties she faced as a southern black woman and intellectual to secure for herself the status of middle-class womanhood led her at times to adopt the unsympathetic stance of class privilege she had criticized elsewhere in *A Voice from the South*. Animated by service ideals, Cooper based her appeal for authority on the derogation of others. Uplift's strategy of class differentiation may have provided blacks like Cooper with some defense against racism, but in pursuing its strategy to its utmost, speaking for the black masses as compliant labor, Cooper risked muting the critical voice she herself raised to break the silence.[41]

6

URBAN PATHOLOGY AND THE LIMITS OF SOCIAL RESEARCH

W. E. B. Du Bois's The Philadelphia Negro

Every one knows that in a city like Philadelphia a Negro does not have the same chance to exercise his ability or secure work according to his talents as a white man.

W. E. B. DU BOIS, *THE PHILADELPHIA NEGRO*

(((

"Of greatest importance," wrote W. E. B. Du Bois of his two years of graduate study at the University of Berlin, "was the opportunity which my *Wanderjahre* in Europe gave of looking at the world as a man and not simply from a narrow racial and provincial outlook." His participation in middle-class German youth's postcollegiate interlude of travel had followed undergraduate work at Fisk University in Tennessee, where he spent summers teaching the children of black farm workers in rural schools, and graduate study at Harvard. Du Bois's wide-ranging experience surely fed his romantic, mystical temperament, which may have compensated for his humble beginnings in Great Barrington, Massachusetts, as the only child of a single mother (his father deserted the family during Du Bois's infancy). But an international outlook ultimately led Du Bois back to race ideals. As part of a ritualistic, solitary celebration of his twenty-fifth birthday in Germany, complete with candles and incense, he pledged to devote himself to racial uplift: "I [will] therefore . . . work for the rise of the Negro people, taking for granted that their best development means the best development of the world." Du Bois's retrospective description of his developing race consciousness, certainly the product of a uniquely privileged education, disclosed his firm belief, shared by many educated blacks, that the black intelligentsia held the key to race advancement.[1]

While in Germany he had awakened to the possibilities of applying to the study of America's "Negro problem" the social science methods he had learned from the sociologist Max Weber, the economist Rudolf Virchow, and the nationalist historian Heinrich von Trietschke. Du Bois returned to America in 1894 and joined the faculty of Wilberforce University, the African Methodist Episcopal church school in Xenia, Ohio. He found the religious school unsympathetic to social research. Thus in 1896, he eagerly accepted a one year appointment at the University of Pennsylvania to conduct a study of Philadelphia's black community. Influenced, like the many educated blacks of his era, by the boundless idealism of uplift ideology, Du Bois had hoped to provide as much of a solution to the Negro problem as could be accomplished by a single book.

Du Bois's landmark social study *The Philadelphia Negro* (1899) was the product of his stay in "the worst part of the Seventh Ward . . . where kids played intriguing games like 'cops and lady bums'; and where in the night when pistols popped, you didn't get up lest you find you couldn't." Having moved there just after his marriage to Nina Gomer, Du Bois had undertaken, with the help of an assistant, Isabel Eaton, a thorough canvass of the homes of the Seventh Ward, where he claimed to have personally "visited and talked with 5,000 persons." Much later, in his autobiography, Du Bois recalled that the study's sponsors at the university had sought scientific validation of the view that "the corrupt, semi-criminal vote of the Negro Seventh Ward" should be the target of the latest of the city's "periodic spasms of reform." Instead, his study hoped to reveal "the Negro group as a symptom, not a cause; as a striving, palpitating group, and not an inert, sick body of crime." Du Bois was only partially successful in this endeavor.[2]

In 1896, however, Du Bois probably had little idea of the intentions of the study's sponsors. He regarded social research as the basis for "A Program of Social Reform," which was the subject of a lecture he gave in 1897 while conducting his research. Sharing the progressives' confidence in the reformist potential of applied intelligence and expertise, Du Bois sought to promote a more enlightened approach to issues like crime, linking it to poverty and a low standard of social justice, within which "selfishness and greed prevail[ed]." Writing in the *Independent*, Du Bois took pains to dissociate his approach from stereotypes and argued that "the first and greatest cause" of Negro crime in the South "is the convict lease system," suggesting that strict criminal codes and overzealous enforcement inflated statistics of black crime.[3] As for the causes of urban crime ("misfortune, disease, carelessness, selfishness or vice"), Du Bois maintained that "ignorance of the cause is the greatest cause." A reform program that sought "individual regeneration aided by ability and knowledge" was "social opportunism which strives toward social science as its goal." Fusing missionary ideals of social service and education with a boundless faith in reason and positivism, the work was not only important for the development of empirical sociology in America, but it also brought a rare sophistication of social and historical analysis to racial uplift ideology.

More typical was its earnest attempt to demonstrate the social stratification and complexity of the black community, and the indispensable leadership role of its "better class." The tenor of Du Bois's thinking at the time, pursuing an ethical vision of social organization in vaguely religious terms reminiscent of the abolitionist reform spirit, led him to propose "the raising of the present popular ideal from mere money-getting to that of common property—common weal." Such romantic antimaterialism would soon find its way into *The Souls of Black Folk*. Indeed, as Arnold Rampersad has observed, it was while researching *The Philadelphia Negro* that Du Bois had first published that work's central idea of "double consciousness," with its warring Negro and American ideals and the spiritual strivings of elite blacks to forge a de-essentialized identity that transcended white prejudice.[4]

William Ferris, Anna Cooper, and Du Bois illustrate the complex struggles over black consciousness, both individual and collective, within racial uplift ideology. This struggle against and within a manichean binary logic of race, reflecting an ever-changing sociohistorical context, underscored the untenable nature of its avowed pursuit of a unified black middle-class subject predicated on historically static, and implicitly racialized, ideals of bourgeois morality. Black identity, and the politics that issued from it, remained highly situational, despite black elites' attempts to ground uplift ideology in what they considered to be the eternal verities. From this perspective, Du Bois becomes much more than the militant antagonist of conservative black leadership led by Booker T. Washington. Over the course of his long life, Du Bois embraced a wide range of positions that departed from his image as an egalitarian champion of civil rights. Readers of David Lewis's magisterial biography realize that Du Bois congratulated Washington after his Atlanta Exposition speech in 1895 and was in turn offered a teaching job at Tuskegee by the Wizard shortly after he had accepted the position at Wilberforce. As a delegate at a meeting of the Afro-American Council, Du Bois sided with Washington against a militant faction, telling reporters that the organization would be "very sorry if it went out into the world that this convention had said anything detrimental to one of the greatest men of our race."[5] Du Bois's Bookerite period ended with *The Souls of Black Folk*, which the *Southern Workman* dismissed as "unhealthful," claiming that "conditions in the South are not so bad as they are pictured here" by one whose northern background and elite education disqualified him as an authentic spokesman on race relations in the South.[6] Indeed, Du Bois's Philadelphia study may have been crucial in the intellectual transformation culminating in his public criticism of Washington's leadership. Later, during World War I, and a period of racial polarization which saw the segregation of federal employment facilities instituted under Woodrow Wilson's administration, Du Bois raised eyebrows and ire among black militants with an editorial in the *Crisis* asking African Americans to "forget our special grievances and close our ranks shoulder to shoulder" with white citizens and the allied nations "fighting for democracy." Mark Ellis has documented the link between the prowar editorial and Du Bois's behind-the-scenes campaign for an officer's commission from the War Department. Hubert Harrison, the West Indian socialist and black nationalist, had suspected as much. Although remembered as an integrationist for his work with the NAACP, Du Bois was ousted from the organization in 1934 by Walter White for his view that segregation held potential economic and political benefits for African Americans. In his last years, when he joined the Communist Party, Du Bois was an unrepentant Stalinist, goaded by the virulent racism of the Cold War era's unholy alliance between liberal and segregationist democrats and the harassment he suffered at the hands of the State Department, which arrested him in 1951 for his anticolonial and pacifist activities. Although acquitted, he was abandoned by the civil rights establishment and its leadership. Past ninety, Du Bois exiled himself to Ghana, where he died in 1963, on the day before the March on Washington.

Du Bois wrote a final autobiography in Ghana, subtitled "A Soliloquy on Viewing My Life from the Last Decade of Its First Century." In this work, the Marxist Du Bois subjects the political ideals of his youth to a withering auto-critique. He had truly been a benighted product of the nineteenth century. Recalling the establishment of the Congo Free State by Belgium, and the contemporary view that the Berlin conference of 1885 would benefit an African continent racked by the slave trade and liquor, Du Bois recalled, "I did not question the interpretation which pictured this as the advance of civilization and the benevolent tutelage of barbarians." Like many others, he considered strikes "ignorant lawlessness," and only with hindsight was "rich and reactionary" Harvard revealed to him as "the defender of wealth and capital, already half ashamed" of the radical abolitionists Charles Sumner and Wendell Phillips.[7]

Du Bois's utterances from the 1890s show that he espoused uplift ideology in its more conservative aspects, much of which echoed the values of the ruling Anglo-American bourgeoisie. As a youthful scholar seeking admittance into the black intelligentsia, his outlook shared a great deal with that of his more established elders. Addressing the American Negro Academy, which was founded in 1897 to foster academic research into race questions, Du Bois warned that the organization "ought to sound a note of warning that would echo in every Black cabin in the land: *Unless we conquer our present vices they will conquer us*; we are diseased, we are developing criminal tendencies, and an alarmingly large percentage of our men and women are sexually impure."[8] This is not the militant Du Bois we are accustomed to. Years later, Du Bois summed up the limitations of his utilitarian, scientific approach to reform and uplift: "I did not have any clear conception or grasp of that colonial imperialism which was beginning to grip the world."[9] His confidence in social science research as an antiracist panacea would help him negotiate his anxieties

William Edward Burghart Du Bois, ca. 1910.

surrounding urbanization among African Americans. The background to *The Philadelphia Negro* is Du Bois's incipient consciousness of a global imperialism that, combined with the progressive disfranchisement and segregation of African Americans, would reveal the fault lines and parochialisms of moralistic, self-help uplift ideology, and its intimations of urban pathology.

The very moment of the production of *The Philadelphia Negro* is thus fraught with ideological tension. Often asserting uplift's doctrine of class stratification and, therefore, the duty of privileged blacks to set a high moral tone for the black masses, Du Bois's analysis of discriminatory wages, rents, and living conditions for blacks in Philadelphia nevertheless rendered the usual exhortations of self-help, individualism, and the moral pieties of uplift quixotic at best. Just as uplift's function for black elites was in part to impose a sense of control and order on the overwhelming problems facing blacks in cities and elsewhere, Du Bois's study aspired to similar ideals of organized intelligence. He set out "to lay before the public such a body of information as may be a safe guide for all the efforts toward the solution of the many Negro problems of a great American city." Yet the overwhelming pattern unearthed by his reformist empiricism was a degree of white prejudice and systemic exclusion impervious to his ideals of enlightened reason.[10]

While brilliantly advancing sociological research methods, Du Bois's study also exhibited the moral and religious animus underlying much early social science writing. *The Philadelphia Negro* broke tentatively with the usual perception of the cultural and moral shortcomings of urban blacks and rejected prevailing hereditary explanations of poverty and crime. But at the same time, Du Bois's construction of class differences among blacks was predicated on cultural and moral distinctions measured by the degree of conformity to patriarchal family norms. This dominant perspective behind Du Bois's reading of urban poverty anticipated the work of subsequent studies, most notably those of E. Franklin Frazier, which characterized black poverty as an irregular preponderance of matriarchal authority. Frazier's work, like Du Bois's, had intended to demonstrate the harmful effects caused by discrimination. Frazier's theme of family disorganization had its greatest impact with the Moynihan report, published in 1965, which gave new impetus to the myth of black matriarchy, and reentered mainstream media discourse on race as the "culture of poverty" thesis advanced by a legion of informal social commentators, journalists, and policy makers. The contentious discussions of race, social class, gender, and urban poverty since the Moynihan report have their origins in the contradictions of Du Bois's study, which represented blacks as both discriminated against and morally suspect, subject to inegalitarian constructions of deviance.

In its day, Du Bois's study was seen as fair-minded and objective, insofar as it seemed to confirm its reviewers' preconceptions about race. Hampton Institute's *Southern Workman* welcomed the author's unwillingness "to withhold ugly facts, such as those relating to crime and pauperism and low standards in family life." While the *Nation* acknowledged that color prejudice "is a far more powerful force than is commonly believed," it strangely concluded that "the lesson taught by this investigation is one of patience and sympathy towards the South, whose difficulties have been far greater than those of the North."[11]

Elite blacks may have found poor blacks in urban slums embarrassing in-carnations of minstrel stereotypes. Or, they might have been sincerely moved by their plight and committed to settlement work. But often, formulaic rep-resentations of urban pathology were crucial to their self-image of racial re-spectability. As African Americans left the South for cities and towns in the region, and later, for the urban North, to compete for industrial and domes-tic jobs in a labor market as restricted as the one they left behind, social and demographic change challenged black elites to reconsider their relationship to "the race." Several ideological currents merged to produce the image of urban pathology: the view of race progress as epitomized by home life and pa-triarchal authority, combined with the cultural inertia of the plantation leg-end, which claimed that African Americans were morally better off in the rural South close to the soil; the negrophobic commentaries of social science writers who perceived the race as diseased, criminal, and immoral; longstand-ing popular traditions of minstrelsy that mocked the urban black male as a buffoon or branded him as a sexual menace; white prejudices against urban blacks as economic competitors with white workers for industrial jobs; the corollary expectation that African American labor remain tied to agricultural cotton production; and the preponderance of single, independent women in cities. African American elites who invoked images of urban pathology did not necessarily endorse this entire battery of assumptions. Accusations of urban pathology implied a normative view of social order and labor organiza-tion that perhaps carried moral authority in the minds of black elites. Never-theless, to speak of urban blacks as immoral or beset by family disorganiza-tion was in Du Bois's day to risk unleashing an avalanche of racist metaphors. Ultimately, however, uplift's moral assumptions of urban pathology reflected a developmental construction of race and class that bestowed on "better class" blacks an illusory sense of self-importance as it divested poor urban blacks of agency and humanity.

Prejudices against blacks on urban terrain were longstanding in the U.S. political culture. Carried over from minstrelsy's image of the dangerous ur-ban black dandy, these prejudices found respectable expression in social stud-ies which purported to document black disease and mortality, as well as the race's alleged predisposition to crime, vice, and immorality. Late-Victorian progressive reformers associated city life with dubious leisure activities such as visiting saloons (which, in Philadelphia, were also headquarters for black political organizations and patronage) and dance halls, along with prostitu-tion and gambling. As these illicit pleasures and pastimes were increasingly confined to black neighborhoods, urban immorality was frequently imbued with a racial stigma. Moral reformers focused their efforts on black sections as those most contagious portions of the social organism.[12]

Black writers opposed the most unscrupulous attempts at empirical demonstration of racially defined pathology in cities. An example was *Race Traits and Tendencies of the American Negro* (1896), by Frederick L. Hoffman, an insurance company statistician. Hoffman predicted that diseases resulting from the immoral nature "of the vast majority of the colored population" would eventually lead to the race's extinction.[13] Such prejudices found support in theological circles as well, such as in Rev. C. G. H. Hasskarl's book *The Missing Link: Has the Negro a Soul?* (1898). To Hasskarl, blacks were beasts bereft of a soul and the finer human attributes. Interestingly, as if to divert attention from assertions of urban pathology, Du Bois devoted part of *The Souls of Black Folk* to the virtuous black peasants he taught in rural Tennessee. In Philadelphia, however, Du Bois pursued a vision of scientific truth that might undermine racist representations, and that by focusing on changing social conditions, might disarm the race's enemies, intellectual and otherwise.[14]

Du Bois's historical analysis of blacks in Philadelphia reflected what many blacks, and for that matter, many others, were experiencing at the turn of the century—the class and cultural conflicts that the era's general bromides of progress attempted to contain. Du Bois chronicled the black community's struggles to first secure, and then maintain, whatever material and political gains it had achieved. He regarded the waves of European immigration, and the competition that ensued, disastrous for continued black advancement. Since their introduction to Philadelphia as slaves by the Dutch colonists during the seventeenth century (along with white indentured servants), "the Philadelphia Negro has, with a fair measure of success, begun an interesting social development," only to be checked, as "twice through the migration of barbarians a dark age has settled on his age of revival." Du Bois's reference to immigrants as "barbarians" sounded a well-worn theme of black writers who associated racism at its most brutal, usually in the South, with a backward, barbaric feudalism identified solely with poor whites or immigrants. He recounted the violent mob disturbances and the economic competition that characterized blacks' relations with immigrant groups in that city in the mid-nineteenth century. Identifying immigrants with social disorder, Du Bois, like many blacks, resented the presumption of white superiority so quickly learned by so many foreigners. Du Bois's thinly veiled nativism, fueled by white racism, sought interracial cooperation with white Protestant elites. This did not change the fact, however, that immigrants were not the sole purveyors of race hatred. Still, Du Bois's unvarnished portrayal of the retrograde trajectory of blacks' changing status challenged uplift's teleological assumptions of evolutionary progress.

Du Bois rooted the "Negro problem" in Philadelphia in a history of oppressive state actions. By 1750, the black population there had reached eleven thousand, and ordinances seeking to control and police the slave population were enacted throughout the eighteenth century. An act of 1726 sought to appease angry mobs of free white laborers by banning the hiring out of black slave laborers and mechanics. The act (suggesting an earlier version of urban pathology) declared that "it too often happens that Negroes commit felonies and other heinous crimes," and it sought to restrict the emancipation of blacks, fearing an increase of pauperism. The basis for such legislation was the claim that equal rights for blacks would be injurious to social order. City ordinances of 1738 and 1741 considered the black population innately "disorderly." Despite these restrictions, the antislavery agitation of the Quakers and the "broader and kindlier feeling toward the Negroes" brought by the war for independence aided the passage of the Act for the Gradual Abolition of Slavery in 1780. For Du Bois, a historical, environmental perspective, viewing changing race relations through the prism of the American Revolution, might refute the plantation legend.

Du Bois regarded the antebellum years following gradual emancipation as a time of advancement for blacks, followed by an initial period of "widespread poverty and idleness." Lack of opportunities propelled "a rush to the city," where "a secure economic foothold" was achieved through domestic service, and skilled and unskilled labor: "The group being thus secure in its daily bread needed only leadership to make some advance in general culture and social effectiveness." Du Bois praised Absalom Jones and Richard Allen, former slaves who had purchased their freedom, for their role in founding the Free African Society in 1787, after white Methodists excluded black congregants. Besides offering a space for worship, the Free African Society provided for the relief of the sick, widows, and orphans, and provided burial expenses for its members. Allen, a blacksmith, went on to found the African Methodist Episcopal church, serving as the first bishop of "the vastest and most remarkable product of American Negro civilization."[15]

Besides Allen and Jones, Du Bois mentioned James Forten, the Quaker-educated black businessman, as exemplary of the antebellum era's brief heyday of self-help and institution building. Forten, Jones, and Allen helped muster black troops during the War of 1812. By 1820, Du Bois noted, the industrial revolution, economic stress after the war with Britain, the rapid influx of foreign immigration, the increase of free blacks and fugitive slaves, and the rise of the abolitionists all strained social tensions, "prov[ing] disastrous to the Philadelphia Negro." Economic dislocations, combined with antislavery agitation, led to a renewed effort to displace black workers—"an effort which had the aroused prejudice of many of the better classes." In sketching a vision of the past that was to serve as a metaphor for the present, Du Bois stressed the complicity of white elites in their failure to exercise leadership and restore order: "So intense was the race antipathy among the lower classes, and so much countenance did it receive from the middle and upper class, that there began a series of riots . . . against Negroes, which recurred frequently until about 1840, and did not wholly cease until after the war." Du Bois devoted the next few pages to accounts of mob terror and rioting by the surplus population of rootless urban white males during the era of Jacksonian democracy. By 1837, the city constitution had deprived black men of their voting rights, which they had previously enjoyed for fifty years. Du Bois's description of antebellum riots, the racism of immigrant groups, including many Americans recently arrived from the South, and of disfranchisement in the North mirrored contemporary threats to blacks.[16]

Du Bois confronted the perception among erstwhile white allies that urban black communities represented the antithesis of progress. Noting that "the development of the Philadelphia Negro since the [Civil] war [has] on the whole disappointed his well wishers," he argued that immigration and "the development of large industry and increase of wealth" intensified competition for jobs, as "the little shop, the small trader [and] the home industry have given way to the department store, the organized company and the factory."[17] Du Bois lamented that racial exclusion accompanied industrialization. He observed ambitious blacks trying to better their condition, but found their opportunities for work "not only restricted by their own lack of training but also by discrimination against them on account of their race. . . . [T]heir economic rise is not only hindered by their present poverty, but also by a widespread inclination to shut against them many doors of advancement open to the talented and efficient of other races." Thus, assumptions of free will and an equally free market characterized by "untrammeled competition" were inaccurate: "One never knows when one sees a social outcast how far this failure to survive is due to the deficiencies of the individual, and how far to the accidents of his environment. This is especially the case with the Negro."[18]

In addition to demonstrating economic racism, Du Bois insisted on an environmental perspective, seeking "the tangible evidence of a social atmosphere surrounding Negroes, which differs from that surrounding most whites; of a different mental attitude, moral standard and economic judgment shown toward most other folk." He believed such social bias could "plainly be seen" but sought to determine through "careful study and measurement . . . just how far it goes and how large a factor it is in the Negro problems." He seemed to assume that instrumental rationality might cut race prejudice down to size.[19]

Du Bois was well aware of the pervasiveness of race prejudice. In a footnote, he rejected the usual practice of lowercase textual references to "the negro," insisting that a group of nine million deserved a capital letter. His emphasis on the role of black leadership as teachers and moral guides to the black masses, and agents of uplift, anticipated his Talented Tenth theory of black leadership, a secularized missionary ethos in which he argued that only educated "exceptional men" could "save" blacks. But within the pages of *The Philadelphia Negro*, Du Bois struggled to reconcile self-help strategies of social control with racial polarization. In the antebellum period, self-help meant emancipation, but with the dawn of monopoly capitalism, business elites and philanthropists exercised a considerable voice in dictating the political and economic conditions of "self-help." The tradition of self-help, Du Bois realized, was hard-pressed to withstand the struggle black entrepreneurs and service workers waged to survive competition with big business and hostile white workers.

Behind Du Bois's exhortations to self-reliance loomed the problem of powerlessness and the obstacles to the accumulation of wealth among blacks. Indeed, blacks' economic gains and resources, never large to begin with, were eroding. Black dominance of the catering business was on the wane, yielding to the preference of its upper-class clientele for white competitors. And even if color barriers were not insurmountable, the concentration of corporate power diminished opportunities. Small businesses run by blacks were being squeezed by the "development from the small to the large industry, from the house-industry to the concentrated industry, from the private room to the palatial hotel." Du Bois grimly noted the exclusion of black men from trades and organized labor, and the competition from German and Italian immigrants that reduced the number of barbering and personal service jobs for black men. In many cases, white competitors displaced longstanding relationships with white employers "and a larger place for color prejudice was made." Prejudice had become more than a fact of life for black Philadelphians, as black-owned cemetery companies had evolved out of "the curious prejudice of the whites against allowing Negroes to be buried near their dead."[20]

Du Bois's claims of class differentiation among blacks, delineating a complex taxonomy of groups within the group, were none-too-subtle prods aimed at the slumbering moral sense of many white elites. Noting that "every group has its upper class," he observed that "as it is true that a nation must to some extent be measured by its slums, it is also true that it can only be understood and finally judged by its upper class." Du Bois argued that "nothing more exasperates the better class of Negroes . . . than this tendency to utterly ignore their existence." Attributing the chronic invisibility of the black intelligentsia to "so much misunderstanding or rather forgetfulness and carelessness," Du Bois insisted that the "aristocracy of the Negroes" formed the "realized ideal of the group." He demanded that black Americans be judged by exemplary, accomplished individuals. "In many respects it is right and proper to judge a people by its best classes rather than by its worst classes or middle ranks. The highest class in any group represents its possibilities rather than its exceptions, as is so often assumed in regard to the Negro."[21]

Du Bois further challenged the homogenizing slanders of racism by documenting the uneven social development within the black community in the incidence of illiteracy and mortality, which he attributed to socioeconomic and geographical factors, not racial traits. He found a general decline in illiteracy among blacks, led by the achievements of the postbellum generation of black Philadelphians. Comparing the illiteracy rates of blacks to those of foreign immigrant populations in Philadelphia, Du Bois and Eaton found that blacks had a lower rate of illiteracy, at 18.56 percent, than the Irish (25.79 percent), Hungarians (30.84 percent), Poles (40.27 percent), Russians (41.92 percent), and Italians (63.63 percent). Only German immigrants (14.74 percent) scored better than blacks. This sort of comparative argument, marshalled for antiracist purposes, would be taken up by other students of race and urban poverty, including Du Bois's future ally in the NAACP, Mary White Ovington. The socialist reformer conducted social research on blacks in New York City. Much later, such comparative arguments, marshaled within liberal sociological discourse on race and ethnicity at the height of the civil rights movement, might serve the dubious end of contrasting a maladaptive black "culture of poverty" unfavorably with the perceived cultural adaptation and social mobility enjoyed by previously marginalized ethnic groups.[22]

On the subject of mortality, Du Bois sought to discredit the "disposition among many to conclude that [black mortality] is abnormal and unprecedented, and that, since the race is doomed to early extinction, there is little left to do but to moralize on inferior species." He rejected claims of black mortality, citing, for one thing, the unreliability of previous statistical records. He speculated that black mortality was insignificant compared to what "must have been an immense death rate among slaves, notwithstanding all reports as to endurance, physical strength and phenomenal longevity." Du Bois suggested the extent to which claims of black mortality fed nostalgic plantation myths of coddled, contented slaves. He detected a decline in black mortality, from an annual average of 47.6 deaths per 1,000 from 1820 to 1830 to 28.02 from 1891 to 1896, a figure that included stillbirths. Again, he found comparison with European nations instructive: "Compared with modern nations the death rate of Philadelphia Negroes is high, but not extraordinarily so." Hungary, Austria, and Italy were found to have comparable figures. Although black mortality surpassed that of whites, mainly in cases of such pulmonary diseases as tuberculosis and pneumonia, Du Bois saw this as a function of substandard, unsanitary living conditions, "partly by their own fault, partly on account of the difficulty of securing decent homes by reason of race prejudice." He also cited poverty and its attendant evils—insufficient clothing, poor diet, and inadequate access to medical care as factors. "There are still many of the old class of root doctors and patent medicine quacks with a lucrative trade among Negroes," Du Bois lamented (the Frederick Douglass Memorial Hospital and Nurse Training School, which served blacks, was founded by Dr. Nathan Mossell in 1895).[23] In addition, Du Bois brought a historical perspective to his analysis of mortality. Regarding "consumption [tuberculosis] it must be remembered that Negroes are not the first people who have been claimed as its peculiar victims; the Irish were once thought to be doomed by that disease—but that was when Irishmen were unpopular." He concluded that mortality "should . . . act as a spur for increased effort and sound upbuilding, and not as an excuse for passive indifference, or increased discrimination."[24]

By calling attention to social change and statistical variations within a socially stratified black community, Du Bois effectively countered homogenizing racist assumptions. Still, this strategy was fraught with difficulties. When his scheme of social classification strayed from quantitative methods, venturing into the more nebulous realm of observation of the sexual morality and behavior of blacks, Du Bois risked echoing caricatures of immoral and disorderly black masses. "Among the lowest class of recent immigrants and other unfortunates," Du Bois observed, "there is much sexual promiscuity and the absence of a real home life." While he cautioned that "of the great mass of Negroes this class forms a very small percentage and is absolutely without social standing," his view that "they are the dregs which indicate the former history and the dangerous tendencies of the masses" suggested that respectable blacks claimed their status and humanity somewhat parasitically. This may have earned Du Bois a measure of moral authority to some readers, but to less friendly others, such statements might confirm what they already "knew" about blacks, in Philadelphia and elsewhere.[25]

Du Bois's description of the Seventh Ward, represented in the form of a walking tour, read like a descent into an urban heart of darkness, striking a tone that shed doubt on his scholarly detachment: "The corners, night and day, are filled with Negro loafers—able-bodied young women and men, all cheerful, some with good-natured, open faces, some with traces of crime and excess, a few pinched with poverty. They are mostly gamblers, thieves and prostitutes, and few have fixed and steady occupation of any kind." To observe and "know" was inescapably to judge and condemn. Even worse, Du Bois's attempt to measure blacks' respectability was complicated by "a curious mingling of respectable working people and some of a better class, with recent immigrations of the semi-criminal class from the slums."[26]

Du Bois's highly distanced and subjective figurations of the poor reflected his personal social anxieties and rhetorically advanced his claims for class differentiation.[27] But such bourgeois-tinged rhetoric risked undermining his findings attributing blacks' condition to a discriminatory social environment. Du Bois's analysis of the percentage of blacks who worked for a living, for example, was clearly intended to disprove stereotypes of black idleness and criminality. But such an analysis invariably leaves the reader where he started; the impressionistic character of many of Du Bois's observations—of "able-bodied loafers," faces with "traces of crime and excess" and the notion of "respectability"—reveal the extent to which the sociologist's questions, let alone the conclusions, are dictated by images of urban pathology.[28] Du Bois's descriptions of the impoverished residents of the Seventh Ward show little of the moral resiliency and heroism with which he endowed the peasant families of rural Tennessee in *The Souls of Black Folk*.[29] Lacking redemptive ties to the soil and farming, the abject urban dwellers Du Bois depicted seemed even more dependent on the saving presence of a black elite.[30]

Du Bois's (and racial uplift ideology's) argument of class stratification as a sign of progress was riddled with contradictions. Social distance between elites and masses was reconciled by uplift's contested ethic of responsibility. Indeed, Du Bois rather dubiously believed that this "better class" of blacks was ignored by whites because black elites failed to cultivate "strong ties of mutual interest" with the black masses. He noted the lack of a proper spirit of noblesse oblige: "[Elite blacks] are not the leaders or ideal makers of their own group in thought, work, or morals. They teach the masses to a very small extent," and generally lack contact with them. This "anomalous position" of elite blacks in the North must have clashed with a view of uplift partly modeled after the progressive moral reform crusades of the day, but also informed by a not so distant antebellum tradition of service and self-help within the black community of teaching, cooperation, and resource sharing, intellectual and material. Although he argued that whites recognize class differences among blacks, he sensed that this recognition itself was inimical to the goals of uplift and racial solidarity: because "the first impulse of the best, the wisest and the richest is to segregate themselves from the mass," there was "more . . . dislike and jealousy on the part of the masses than usual." He argued that the "better classes" among blacks "have their chief excuse for being in the work they may do toward lifting the rabble." In his study of Du Bois's social thought, Joseph DeMarco called the work's rhetoric of social classification "a condescending provision of social responsibility" and noted that the necessary schism had become even more rigid in a 1901 essay, "The Black North": "A rising race must be aristocratic; the good cannot consort with the bad—not even the best with the less good." Such statements revealed more about the anxieties of Du Bois's elite perspective than about the social condition of the masses.[31]

The problem was that this sort of separate-but-equal claim for cultural authority simply didn't deliver the status and influence it promised black elites, to say nothing of what little it had to offer less privileged blacks. How could a bourgeois ideology that was itself steeped in racial categories slay the hydra of racism? The biggest obstacle to this ideology of mutual solidarity and altruistic service was the vicious circle of institutionalized racism and white prejudice: "This feeling [of repulsion] is intensified by the blindness of those outsiders who persist even now in confounding the good and bad, the risen and fallen, in one mass." Although Du Bois realized that "the uncertain economic status" of relatively privileged blacks made it difficult for them "to spare much time and energy in social reform," the fact remained that these blacks were as vulnerable to being regarded as social outcasts as those unassimilated, immoral blacks upon whom they sought to prop up their own status within the social hierarchy. Uplift was an ideological response by blacks to a segregated, deeply racist society that prescribed their subordinate place and thus circumscribed their opportunities. In effect, when Du Bois employed uplift ideology to mobilize the missionary zeal of "better class" blacks, hoping to gain the respect and recognition of influential, progressive whites, he was exhibiting a variant of double-consciousness.[32] It is important to recognize both the difficulties Du Bois contended with and his uneasy relationship to the community he studied.[33]

Bourgeois sexual morality provided Du Bois with a crucial means of articulating class differences among blacks, facilitating in his study a problematic linkage of poverty and immorality, and equating the disturbing presence of unmarried black women with promiscuity. He associated unemployment with idleness and sin, but his vision of lower-class status especially faulted all signs of the absence of the patriarchal black family. The problem was that many blacks suffered from "the lack of respect for the marriage bond," from which "sexual looseness . . . adultery and prostitution" soon followed. Consequently, Du Bois often described the struggles and low status of urban blacks in terms of improper sexual behavior and viewed everything short of "the monogamic ideal" as a lapse in female chastity, sometimes viewed in isolation from any male complicity. Although he called for compassion in undertaking social research as a guide to reform,[34] his approach was not always conducive to empathy with the subjects of his study.[35]

Du Bois's discussion of the weakness of the family stemmed from the uplift assumption of the home and family as signs of progress and security, and sources of strength. Indeed, much commentary on urban poverty targeted the status of the family as the barometer of social health or pathology. To many blacks, home life represented a realm of security, stability, and success, however modest, and it affirmed respectable manhood and womanhood. For many, the patriarchal family meant freedom from the domination that had kept black men and women divided, demoralized, and homeless.

It is likely that the difficulties he faced as a black man struggling to make a decent home for his new bride in the midst of the Seventh Ward's slums contributed to his judgmental stance. An uneasy realization of his own tenuous place within a social equation arrayed against him and untold others doubtless required a strenuous effort to maintain at the very least, a psychic distance from his objects of inquiry and their plight. Racial and social oppression stunted the lives and aspirations of many educated and elite blacks, but the masses' poverty was nobody's fault but theirs, by virtue of their moral shortcomings. This same logic applied to gendered representations of black oppression. As black progress had traditionally been defined in male-centered ways, Du Bois defined racial oppression as a process of emasculation. He noted the devastating blow to male self-respect dealt by the social impediments to the protection and support of black women in bourgeois families and homes. But if black men could be so victimized, unprotected black women were cast as culpable outside the sanctions of marriage and the patriarchal family. Du Bois occasionally singled out poor black women as blameworthy for family instability. This ran counter to his environmental approach. Blacks faced a severely restricted labor market in low paying menial and domestic jobs, and their confinement and crowding within slum areas made them vulnerable to exorbitant rents. Such discrimination, in rendering the support of families difficult at best, faded from an analysis that often stressed debased morals.

The Philadelphia Negro illustrated the tension within uplift ideology that combined altruistic ideals of compassionate service with unforgiving condemnations of those who appeared not to heed uplift's moral prescriptions. Du Bois was casting out society's most visible outcasts even further from "respectable" society: "Let us glance at the general character of the ward. . . . we can at a glance view the worst Negro slums of the city. . . . here once was a depth of poverty and degradation almost unbelievable. Even today there are many evidences of degradation, although the signs of idleness, shiftlessness, dissolutenenss and crime are more conspicuous than those of poverty."[36]

To his credit, such value judgments did not prevent Du Bois from an exhaustive investigation of urban conditions. He compiled detailed evidence of the economic discrimination that prevented blacks from meeting the cultural dictates of upright moral behavior—chastity and matrimony. He found employment opportunities for black Philadelphians in 1896 largely restricted to low-paying domestic and personal service jobs. Of employed blacks, 73 percent worked as servants; of this percentage, 61 percent were men and 88.5 percent women. Higher up the occupational ladder he found barely 2 percent of employed blacks were learned professionals, "represented among Negroes by clergymen, teachers, physicians, lawyers and dentists, in the order named."

Du Bois's findings, particularly in comparison to the rest of the city, may have run counter to some expectations. Whatever signs of idleness and shiftlessness he reported, he found that 78 percent of blacks worked for a living, as against "55.1 per cent for the whole city, white and colored." He took these figures as evidence of a lack of accumulated wealth among blacks "arising from poverty and low wages; the general causes of poverty are largely historical and well known." Du Bois attributed low wages to the lack of job opportunities for blacks and "the competition that must ensue." These impoverished conditions were disastrous to conventional moral standards. Black women's "chances of marriage are decreased by the low wages of the men" and the "large excess" of black women in the city. For men, low wages meant the unpleasant choices of either "enforced celibacy" or "dissipated lives," or "homes where the wife and mother must also be a bread winner."[37]

To Du Bois, joblessness meant immorality, and the consequences of all this were clear on the "conjugal condition" of the residents of the Seventh Ward, as he focused on the "widespread and early breakup of family life." Even those who tried to fulfill the dictates of the work ethic found it hard to stay afloat. Du Bois went on to describe the struggles of black servants to live respectable lives: "The economic difficulties arise continually among young waiters and servant girls," who, lonely and isolated, "thoughtlessly marry and soon find that a husband's income cannot alone support a family." This led to "a struggle which generally results in the wife's turning laundress, but often results in desertion or voluntary separation." Noting that one-third of black Philadelphians were servants, Du Bois considered it a "maladjustment in social relations" that so many were forced to earn a living in domestic service, "adding a despised race to a despised calling." Still, even as he argued that matters might be improved if whites regarded domestic service and their black employees more highly, he wrote poignantly of how the humiliations of domestic service clashed with the aspirations of even the ablest and most ambitious blacks, breeding in them sufficient resentment to affect the quality of their service: "All those young people who, by natural evolution in the case of the whites, would have stepped a grade higher" than their parents "in the social scale, have . . . been largely forced back into the great mass of the listless and incompetent to earn bread and butter by menial service." Noting at the same time a trend toward the displacement of black servants by white immigrants, which exacerbated "crime, pauperism and idleness among Negroes," Du Bois finally called for better training and urged employers to "recognize more keenly . . . the responsibility of the family toward its servants" in allowing them to live on the premises as members of the family. Even as he wrote with some empathy for the plight of servants, he tended to speak of them paternalistically, as if they lacked virtuous self-reliance. Again, the problem became a matter of moral blight and disease centering on blacks: "Thousands of servants no longer lodge where they work but are free at night to wander at will, to consort with paramours, and thus to bring moral and physical disease to their place of work." Such statements were unlikely to gain sympathy or job security for black domestic workers.[38]

Urban Pathology as Family Disorganization

The destruction or absence of the patriarchal family among blacks was symptomatic of exclusion from unions and industrial wage labor. Racist minstrel and journalistic discourses trumpeted images of absent patriarchy as evidence of black inferiority. As part of a patriarchal U.S. culture, African Americans understandably regarded conformity with patriarchal gender norms as the crucial standard of race progress. But black nationalist intellectuals, haunted by the memory of slavery and its destruction of the family, restricted their idea of the race's oppression to the terms dictated by minstrelsy. To be the patriarch, the master of one's family, was ardently desired by African American men, who considered this an essential prerequisite of respectability, civilization, and progress. This defensive preoccupation with the family, bourgeois morality, and individual behavior as preconditions for humanity was a distraction from the excesses of monopoly capitalism and its gross disparities in wealth and power.

Du Bois tried to place his discussion of the black family within a broader, environmental context. In explaining the weakness of the family, he sought a precarious balance of both discrimination and moral weakness: "The causes of desertion are partly laxity in morals and partly the difficulty of supporting a family." The iron fist of his Darwinian Calvinism was cushioned somewhat by a velvet glove of compassion. Aware that opportunities for talent and ambition were "confined to the dining room, kitchen and street," Du Bois nonetheless sometimes pointed an accusing finger at black women whose condition as "unmarried mothers . . . represent[s] the unchastity of a large number of women." Social phenomena such as the excess numbers of "single females" in the city, but also their prevalence in exploitative domestic jobs, only served to provide Du Bois with further evidence of faulty morals. In Du Bois's scheme, working black women embodied the weakness of the patriarchal family, a condition from which prostitution seemed only a short plunge. Patriarchal authority remained the crucial criterion of black bourgeois stability.[39]

Within racial uplift ideology, however, status classifications based on the wife's presence in the home presented an unattainable standard for many black women and men. While Du Bois certainly dwelled on the moral failings of black men, referring often to gamblers, criminals, rogues, and rascals, women who failed to meet the lofty standard of motherhood appeared to bear the brunt of his findings on family instability. Ranked slightly above the unmarried in moral status were married women who worked outside the home—respectable, but less so. Black wives who were homemakers represented the highest status, signaling decent homes sustained by male support.[40]

Du Bois's placement of poor urban blacks within a lower state of moral development by virtue of the relative absence of family stability was linked to the moral double-standard to which black women were particularly vulnerable. Black women often worked to support themselves, under circumstances, as during slavery, and later, in domestic jobs, that obliterated the boundary between public and private life that bourgeois selfhood required. In a footnote Du Bois gave a fairly concise view of racial oppression, construing female immorality as the outcome of black emasculation. The general lack of social protection for black women and girls not only left them vulnerable to "peculiar temptations," but also, because "the whole tendency of the situation of the Negro is to kill his self-respect," black women thus lost the protective, saving benefit of "the greatest safeguard of female chastity." The plight of black men thus led to the fall of black women to unchastity and promiscuity.[41]

Du Bois's discussion of gender relations revealed the problematic presence of black women within black middle-class ideology. Glowing uplift ideals of motherhood were at bottom injunctions to monogamous marriage and domesticity. Black women's respectability and moral authority were contingent on their relationship to black men. Thus, the requirement of black wives to tend families in the home signified progress for all concerned. Of course, the symbolism of the family and motherhood also had a compelling material and historical basis, as black men and women believed that it was preferable for a black woman to be supported and protected at home than to work for white employers outside it. Economic necessity, however, required many married black women to work to help support their families while also performing household duties.

Yet these ideals of home, family, and motherhood could just as easily be turned against black women, and all blacks. By condemning all black women outside of marriage, Du Bois echoed dominant assumptions of black immorality. He was hardly alone in assessing black women who did not live up to the status of respectable motherhood as morally suspect. If black men were slow to marry, a grave tendency that threatened "race suicide," it was because black "women, by entering business and trades, have so reduced man's means of a livelihood that, he finds the task of supporting a family a most difficult one. . . . The rule applies more to the cities than to rural districts where living is simpler." From this perspective family stability required that black women withdraw from competition for scarce economic resources.[42]

A 1908 editorial from the *Colored American Magazine* entitled "How to Keep Women at Home" is relevant, although somewhat parodic in tone. It contains no explicit reference to black women, or race in general, but its very presence in a black publication indicates that it held significance for middle-class blacks. The author noted with growing dissatisfaction that "women will not stay at home," choosing instead to frequent clubs, stores, theaters, societies, and lectures. The problem threatened "the final destruction of our American homes, because of its abandonment by its queen, the American woman." Women's independent behavior was clearly an affront to this author's image of the civilized male: "Women are getting very bold, and instead of using the freedom that civilized men are allowing them, for adding to the comforts of man, they are abusing them. This is the thanks that civilized man is getting for giving his women more liberty than women get in half civilized countries. . . . And what is coming next nobody knows. Women always know how to take the ell if they are given the inch. They are selfish creatures and think everything a man has belongs to them because they tell him they love him."[43] For this writer, "freedom" for black wives means the leisure to stay at home and be supported, which, as we have seen, is no small task for the "civilized" black man. Interestingly, he resorts to an allusion to Frederick Douglass's autobiography, describing women's so-called freedom with words from Douglass's bondage ("if you give a nigger an inch, he will take an ell").[44] Fulfillment of the white bourgeois ideal of separate spheres as a sign of advanced civilization requires that he keep his wife at home. His status and identity as a civilized, bourgeois male depends on it. The interesting thing here is how the emphasis on the male prerogative of woman's place in the home serves to transcend race. To black men desirous of maintaining a middle-class, patriarchal identity, the attainment of economic independence usually meant protecting their wives from domestic service, and the threat of sexual abuse by white men. The author represses this anxiety, imagining instead a universalized male complaint against all women through which racial conflicts are suspended by invoking gender-related anxieties. This ideal arrangement, so "abused" by "selfish" women, represented the level of civilization, or upright moral behavior, that middle-class blacks had struggled to achieve, and which presumably distinguished them from "half-civilized" peoples.[45]

The Limits of Black Leadership

In addition to anxieties over patriarchal authority, Du Bois seemed at a loss to account for the agency and self-determination implicit in racial uplift ideals and what he regarded as the shortcomings of the leadership of "the better class." He had a difficult time reconciling his ideals of a truly legitimate black leadership with existing institutions and leaders. Like many white progressives, he disapproved of machine politics, which were associated with corruption, patronage, drunkenness, and prostitution. At the same time, however, he admitted that politics afforded black men rare opportunities for status, power, and race pride. "What if some of these positions of honor and respectability have been gained by shady 'politics' . . . ?" he asked. Consequently, he thought it too much to ask that blacks "surrender these tangible evidences of the rise of their race to forward the good-hearted but hardly imperative demands of a crowd of women." Given that uplift ideology in some respects represented a style of reform that coincided with nineteenth-century evangelical notions of women's moral influence, Du Bois's mocking reference to white women reformers is ironic, but also indicative of his desire to protect nascent black political culture and institutions from such root-and-branch reform efforts.[46]

Generally, however, Du Bois was so adamant on the need for irreproachable, socially responsible black leadership that he went well beyond condemnations of machine politics, poor, desperate blacks, and "fallen" black women. The class stratification he observed among those black Philadelphians who had apparently succeeded in the struggle of getting a living appeared in some instances to him to be the antithesis of progress. Far from being guardians of purity, the black elite seemed to him to have been infiltrated by people whose ability to give an appearance of outward success nevertheless masked a basic moral delinquency. He noted that within the Seventh Ward, "intermingled with some estimable families, is a dangerous criminal class." These were not the unemployed "low open idlers" of the slums, "but rather the graduates of that school: shrewd and sleek politicians, gamblers and confidence men, with a class of well-dressed and partially undetected prostitutes." Ever vigilant, and preoccupied with rooting out all vestiges of impurity, Du Bois witnessed such "undesirable elements" in conducting his "house-to-house visitation" of the ward in 1896, noting every apparent transgression of uplift ideals and Victorian morals. Du Bois seemed concerned, to the point of distraction, with the anonymity of urban life, where the deceptive nature of outward appearances rendered his project of moral and social classification all the more dubious.[47]

Despite all his criticism of the morals of lower-class blacks, for the sake of delineating a black "better class," Du Bois reserved his harshest judgments for the black community's nominal leaders. He was disillusioned by the quality of black ministers because the church had historically been such a crucial institution serving "to promote the intelligence of the masses." Although careful to insist that blacks were not "hypocritical or irreligious," their church was "to be sure, a social institution first, and religious afterwards." Having escaped the pietism of Wilberforce University, Du Bois believed black ministers fell short of the enlightened, reform ideals of uplift, forsaking "the chance to be a wise leader or a demagogue, or, as in many cases, a little of both." He sarcastically viewed many ministers as "good representatives of the masses of Negroes," followers instead of leaders. He likened black Methodist ministers to businessmen and politicians, "sometimes . . . inspiring and valuable leader[s] of men," but at other times parasitic charlatans who induce "the mass of Negroes to put into fine church edifices money which ought to go to charity or business enterprise." The reversal of moral values that brought "undesirable elements" into contact with respectable blacks had also contaminated black church life, which Du Bois perceived as antagonistic to home life. "The congregation does not follow the moral precepts of the preacher, but rather the preacher follows the standard of his flock, and only exceptional men dare seek to change this." Seldom preaching an uplifting social gospel, the preacher often pandered to his congregation, and was on the average, "neither learned nor spiritual, nor a reformer."[48]

The black minister had become the equivalent of the demagogic machine boss to Du Bois, who perceived a disturbing lack of vision among the race's putative leaders. To him, the church life of black Methodists offered no more substance than the "host of noisy missions which represent the older and more demonstrative worship." The negative impact of religion even extended beyond the church, extending into charity organizations: "A Young Men's Christian Association which would not degenerate into an endless prayer meeting might meet the wants of the young men." Even the *A.M.E. Church Review*, published in Philadelphia, the birthplace of the independent black church, while "probably the best Negro periodical" of its kind, was not above criticism. To Du Bois, the *Review* was "often weighted down by the requirements of church politics" and was obligated on occasion to publish "trash" penned by ambitious churchmen. Du Bois's criticisms were indicative of the tensions within black leadership circles between the church and more secular ideals and institutions, embodied, for example, in the black press, in schools, and in the mass culture and entertainment industry.[49]

While lamenting the lack of truly exceptional men, Du Bois saw the deteriorating occupational situation for black entrepreneurs, tradesmen, and workers as further evidence of the abandonment and betrayal of white elites. As he found only inconsistency in his search for able black leadership, Du Bois also doubted that disinterested moral authority rested with so-called progressive whites. "There was," he noted, "no benevolent despot, no philanthropist, no far-seeing captain of industry to prevent the Negro from losing even the skill he had learned or to inspire him by opportunities to learn more." The benevolence to which Cooper and other black spokespersons had appealed had not materialized, as the "simple race prejudice" of both workers and capitalists provided the motive for the systematic exclusion of blacks from jobs. Du Bois denounced justifications of black exclusion that claimed that hiring blacks was bad for business.[50]

For Du Bois, Cooper, and progressive reformers in general, uplift was a matter of social equilibrium, of constructive, mutually rewarding relations between the classes of society, leaders and masses, and between the "better classes" of blacks and whites. Holding out little hope for improved race relations with white workers, black intellectuals such as Du Bois and Cooper were even more resentful of the contempt of those supposedly enlightened middle-class whites whose values they shared. Du Bois's case studies in the section titled "Color Prejudice" showed enterprising, persistent blacks confronting the white monopoly on trades, clerical, and business opportunities in Philadelphia with few victories. "No matter how well trained a Negro may be," he wrote bitterly, "or how fitted for work of any kind, he cannot in the ordinary course of competition hope to be much more than a menial servant."[51]

A crucial problem of black leadership was its difficulty in reproducing black business and entrepreneurship across generations, a situation tied to the economic dependence of that class on white consumers and patronage. Prejudice and exclusion, while providing a market for such enterprises within the black community as funeral parlors, newspapers, grocery stores, hair salons, and restaurants, had thinned the ranks of those black barbers, caterers, and entrepreneurs who had thrived serving an upper-class white clientele. Although Du Bois bemoaned such economic isolation, he also realized the extent to which blacks' "economic activities have been directed almost entirely to the satisfaction of the wants of the upper classes of white people." The combination of a lack of business training, prejudice, and Du Bois's observation that "Negroes are unused to co-operation with their own people" spelled dim prospects for black merchants. The disturbing void he found in his search for capable black leaders was evident here, too, as he saw a heroic antebellum generation of successful black entrepreneurs dying off. Indeed, as he lamented the tendency of the businesses of ambitious blacks to die with the charismatic personalities who built them, Du Bois also noted the additional impact of the ruthless competition of large enterprises on the small businesses of black entrepreneurs. Department stores and factories (whose jobs were generally closed to blacks) "almost preclude[d] the effective competition of the small store." Du Bois found many obstacles to the reproduction of blacks' wealth and enterprise across generations.[52]

In spite of everything, the burden fell upon blacks to improve their morals. Black homes "must cease to be, as they often are, breeders of idleness and extravagance and complaint." The black middle-class concern for the preservation of family life, though related to middle-class white anxieties on the matter, arose from blacks' sense of deprivation of secure homes and family relations that were immune from white invasion. The home was thus a sign of racial integrity and conservation, with unmistakable implications for the reproductive control of black women. Beyond it, blacks also faced, according to Du Bois, "a vast amount of preventive work," mainly in chaperoning young women and girls and protecting them from the evils of the streets. Despite past and present hardships, blacks were required to make "every effort and sacrifice possible on their part" toward something achieving "complete civilization." Du Bois's skepticism regarding black ministers notwithstanding, he set for black leaders a messianic challenge of moral spotlessness and forgiveness.

Perhaps because he sensed few people were capable of bearing such a burden (and he would eventually tire of it himself), Du Bois saved for last a discussion of the duty of white Philadelphians, arguing that whites "must hold themselves largely responsible for the deplorable results" of discrimination. He baldly stated what his previous moralism against blacks had perhaps laid a foundation for: "Such discrimination is morally wrong, politically dangerous, industrially wasteful, and socially silly. It is the duty of the whites to stop it, and to do so primarily for their own sakes." Whites also needed to realize that much of the "sorrow and bitterness" among blacks "comes from the unconscious prejudice and half-conscious actions of men and women who do not intend to wound or annoy." Deeply attentive to the sentiments of whites, Du Bois appeared almost to be excusing his white middle-class audience, forgiving them in somewhat Christlike fashion for "unconscious" actions that caused unintended harm.[53]

The rhetorical strategy of Du Bois's study, directed toward alerting reasonable, right-thinking whites to intraracial class stratification, and to the existence of a racially oppressive social environment, suggests the extent that blacks were judged guilty by the dominant culture, either as outright criminals or, perhaps more benignly, as an "undeveloped" people. Although he provided a subtle and innovative analysis of the psychological impact of race hatred on blacks, Du Bois made the dubious suggestion that it affected elite blacks more than others: "All this of course does not make much difference to the mass of the race, but it deeply wounds the better classes, the very classes who are attaining to that to which we wish the mass to attain."[54] Du Bois's claim that black elites felt the sting of prejudice and exclusion more acutely than did less privileged blacks recognized white society's backlash against black social advancement. But although he undoubtedly spoke from experience concerning "the better classes," Du Bois's distinction nonetheless illustrated the self-serving, class-bound assumptions of racial uplift ideology.

Yet even as Du Bois cited socioeconomic and historical causes in explaining black poverty, *The Philadelphia Negro* set the standard for a sociological version of racial uplift ideology. His study employs a view of class predicated on

racial essentialism, displacing one rooted in social structures and power relations. Despite his thorough survey of discrimination, Du Bois echoed the
general tendency to emphasize moral, behavioral issues of individual adjustment and assimilation to "modern civilization," a euphemism that effaced the
power relations reproducing class. In the aftermath of black migration to the
North, this reformist discourse of uplift prized instrumental rationality in
seeking "the adjustment of the Negro to the problems of urban life." These
urban "problems," measured by family "disorganization," were understood as
deviations from blacks' presumably natural state of rural life, which was assumed to be qualitatively better on the farm.

Such rural nostalgia, a mood reflected in *The Souls of Black Folk*, was rooted
in a notion of an organic society, jolted out of its functional order by urbanization. But even within such conventions and sensibilities there was room
for innovative social analysis. That work, interestingly enough, might be read
as a critique of the sociological animus of its predecessor, and as an elabora-
tion on some of its more effective analytical strategies. Denouncing the "car-
window sociologists" whose superficial knowledge of the southern Negro
owed more to minstrel stereotypes than careful study, Du Bois urged his
readers not to forget that "each unit in the mass is a throbbing human soul,"
and that the "great mass of them work continuously and faithfully for a return" under exploitative conditions. Du Bois's discussion in *Souls* of the re-
placement of the landlord with the merchant—"part banker, part landlord,
part contractor, and part despot,"—struck at the heart of the conditions of
debt slavery in the "cotton kingdom" of the black belt. Noting the conditions
of peonage, convict labor, laws prohibiting agents seeking to entice black migration, the paternalism that rendered black men powerless before the courts
unless a white man, usually his employer, vouched for him, the prevalence of
child labor, and the denial of public education, Du Bois insisted that these
conditions of "modern serfdom," not the proverbial charge of indolence, had
sparked urban migration. "Such an economic organization is radically
wrong," he declared. "Whose is the blame?"[55]

In posing the question in this manner, Du Bois demonstrated a grasp of his
white readers' sensibilities that owed a great deal to Washington's pseudo-
empirical rhetorical style. Here Du Bois's mode of analysis surpassed a racial
essentialism designed to tighten the shackles on black labor. Du Bois challenged the widespread view, endorsed by Washington and so many others, of
black indolence, countering that "a system of unrequited toil" was fatal to the
industry and efficiency of black field hands: "Nor is this peculiar to Sambo; it
has in history been just as true of John and Hans, of Jacques and Pat, of all
ground-down peasantries." However regressive his use of ethnic stereotypes,
Du Bois's comparison of the exploitation of black labor with that of European peasants attacked assertions that subservience to white employers was a

racial trait of southern black laborers. Instead, Du Bois warned that crime and socialism (a telling juxtaposition) were inevitable within such an arrangement, and, by way of confirmation, offered an anecdote that seemed more indebted to underground black folklore than minstrelsy: "I see now that ragged black man sitting on a log, aimlessly whittling a stick. He muttered to me with the murmur of many ages, when he said: 'White man sit down whole year; Nigger work day and night and make crop; Nigger hardly gits bread and meat; white man sittin' down gits all. *It's wrong.*'" Here, Du Bois was revising Washington's text, and his own. His discussion of class stratification among African Americans in the black belt was strictly economic, representing an advancement from the racialism implicit in his stress on gender relations, patriarchal authority, and sexual morality as the measure of class stratification in the Philadelphia ghetto.

In noting both the similarities and subtle, yet crucial differences in Du Bois's perspective that are evident in the shift from northern urban to southern rural fields of inquiry, it is imperative that we distinguish between the impact of situational identity along with the additional movement of history on Du Bois's intellectual production, and the less reflective processes inherent in the institutionalization of a sociological discourse of uplift, which, despite its environmental impulse, nonetheless carried racialized overtones. That said, the main contribution of Du Bois's study—its environmentalism—was generally undermined by its anxiety over the morals of black migrants to the city, particularly single black women, whose existence outside the family threatened reproductive norms that privileged paternity. This approach represented the intertwining of older pietistic and secular outlooks in the evolving professional uplift discourse, whose moral prescriptions, inherited from dominant cultural codes, cannot be understood apart from the social conflicts of industrialization, racist social science, and even minstrel vulgarisms.[56] At any rate, the academic sociological discourse of uplift, the urban counterpart to industrial education, called for the supervision and adjustment of black workers to industrial capitalism by social work professionals, who also sought to inculcate a complementary domesticity for black women. In short, this "black" sociological approach echoed mainstream notions of social pathology, measured not solely by family disorganization but also in accordance with the view that urban pathology entailed a failure to reproduce an industrial labor force.[57] Descended partly from the approaches of both Du Bois and those of reformers and academics, the sociological component of uplift ideology was promoted within the sociology departments of the University of Chicago, as well as Fisk, Atlanta, and Howard Universities. Subsidized by foundations and other forms of white philanthropic largesse, variants of it would remain influential within professional and journalistic discussions of race, migration, reform, and urban poverty well into the twentieth century.

Upon completion of his research in Philadelphia, Du Bois established a sociology program for both graduates and undergraduates at Atlanta University. His series of social studies, produced from 1896 to 1914, rarely met the
standard set by *The Philadelphia Negro*, due to a lack of funds and the necessity
of using untrained assistants. Still, it represented the only work of its kind and
attracted wide and sometimes favorable comment. In 1900, Du Bois used his
studies to prepare for the Paris Exposition an exhibit of the social progress of
black Americans that won universal praise from the American press and the
exhibition's grand prize for its author.[58]

A year before, however, Du Bois's faith in dispassionate social research had
been irreparably shaken by the lynching of Sam Hose, a black sharecropper,
in the outskirts of Atlanta. While carrying a letter to the *Atlanta Constitution*
defending Hose against charges of rape, Du Bois learned that Hose, who had
killed his landlord in a dispute over payment for his crop, was taken from jail,
tortured, and lynched. "I began to turn aside from my work," Du Bois recalled. In another memoir, he recalled the impact that his return to the South
and its brutal customs had on him: "One could not be a calm, cool, and detached scientist while Negroes were lynched, murdered and starved." In addition to what he called "the crucifixion of Hose," the racial violence of 1898,
with the Wilmington riot, the killing of postmaster Fraser Baker, and the
mistreatment of Negro soldiers in the recent war surely played a part in his
shift to a more militant posture.[59]

Another outbreak of racial violence—the riot in Springfield, Illinois, in
1908, would provide the catalyst for Du Bois's transition from academic to
agitator, and his subsequent career with the NAACP. Its contradictions notwithstanding, *The Philadelphia Negro* demands our recognition of its continued relevance, as urban blacks still contend with disproportionate poverty, ill
health, unemployment, and inadequate city services, with their life chances
additionally restricted by de facto residential segregation and ineffective public schools. "How long can a city teach its black children that the road to success is to have a white face? How long can a city do this and escape the inevitable penalty?" wondered Du Bois in 1899.[60] Perhaps because we cannot
read it today without perceiving the limitations of bland assertions of racial
progress and uplift, *The Philadelphia Negro* retains a sobering, prophetic impact that Du Bois could not have foreseen.

7

BETWEEN UPLIFT AND MINSTRELSY

Paul Laurence Dunbar, James D. Corrothers, and the

Ambivalent Response to Urbanization, 1900–1916

She's the leader of the color'd aristocracy
And then I'll drill these darkies till,
They're up in high society's hypocrisy
They'll come my way to gain entree . . .
To the circle of the color'd aristocracy.

JAMES WELDON JOHNSON, "IN DAHOMEY"

When dey hear dem ragtime tunes, White folks try to pass fo'
coons on Emancipation day.

PAUL LAURENCE DUNBAR, "IN DAHOMEY"

❨ ❨ ❨

As we have seen, the dread of racial stigma colored much of what the black intelligentsia did or said about the so-called Negro problem. Still, black intellectuals found ways to challenge white constructions of blackness: Ida B. Wells, Anna Cooper, W. E. B. Du Bois, J. Max Barber, T. Thomas Fortune, and many others were able to do this, on occasion. Omnipresent as it was, however, racism might be challenged, but not easily refuted. As we have seen with the confluence of minstrelsy and social science conceptions of pathology, the urban setting was the location upon which black writing on race waxed apologetic or, at best, ambiguously oppositional. At the turn of the century many black intellectuals and leaders expressed alarm at the impact of urbanization, migration, and the homogenizing forces of mass, consumer culture on the black community. Like many bourgeois whites, they associated tenements and slums with social and cultural decay. For blacks, social change also meant challenges to religious traditions of black leadership and authority by new secular pastimes and attractions. As early as 1885 Alexander Crummell noted with dismay what he saw as "an addiction to aesthetical culture as a special vocation of the race." To Crummell, such secular cultural and artistic activities had come at the expense of strengthening the family and improving the conditions of labor and morals for blacks. Curiously, however, Crummell held the black poet Paul Laurence Dunbar in high regard, despite the fact that Dunbar was implicated by the commodification of blackness in mass culture industries of literature and musical comedy.[1]

Well before the major urban migration of Southern blacks to the North during and after World War I, the black population in northern centers like Philadelphia and Chicago increased substantially. In New York, the black population grew by twenty-five thousand between 1890 and 1900. Real estate agents were often unconcerned with preserving the middle-class character of black neighborhoods and profited from the residential segregation that produced crowded slums. This, combined with municipal policies confining prostitution, saloons, and gambling to black sections, away from white residential and commercial areas, led elite blacks to see a correlation between urbanization and moral chaos. The Chicago clubwoman Fannie Barrier Williams thus described the struggles of the black elite: "The huddling together of the good and the bad, compelling the decent element of the colored people to witness the brazen display of vice of all kinds in front of their homes and in the faces of their children, are trying conditions under which to remain socially clean and respectable." Williams was hardly alone in her concern to demarcate with utter clarity their moral and class superiority over the faceless, penniless "greenhorns" and the various pretenders to elite status among black newcomers to the urban scene. And class anxieties were exacerbated by the racial violence that erupted in New York in the summer of 1900 as blacks were mobbed and beaten in the West Sixties' San Juan Hill district by Irish gangs and police.[2]

This influx of southern blacks, combined with European immigration, into cities already fraught with explosive labor strife throughout the 1890s had heightened general fears for the maintenance of social order. Northern migration—"voting with one's feet"—provided one of the few opportunities for powerless, impoverished blacks in the Deep South to escape subordination. To many elite blacks, however, the movement to the North had worsened the black elite's already considerable sense of dislocation. Themselves ill-equipped to assist the migrants, they were largely incapable of viewing the migration positively. Their outlook, rooted in the philosophy of industrial education, often characterized blacks as disorderly, unfit for citizenship, superstitious, criminal, lazy, immoral, and needing to be compelled to work. White supremacists and even some of their moderate allies had argued along similar lines that blacks needed to be discouraged from migrating, and controlled through racial segregation, or more drastic measures.[3]

Unaware that more privileged elements were well represented among black migrants, elite blacks feared that urban leisure and consumerism were undermining the eternal verities. In this, they were strongly influenced by culturally dominant fears of black immigrants. The migration had a corrosive effect on black institutions; Orishatukeh Faduma, a West Indian–born pan-Africanist educated at Yale, criticized the black church for its "outwardness" and what he saw as its lack of enlightened spirituality. The urban black church promoted materialistic values and a tendency among worshippers of "valuing oneself from appearance" and making religion "a puppet show." Several black commentators even relied on minstrelsy's debased images of blackness to disparage the trend of migration and the urban proletariat it produced. Such jeremiads by members of the black intelligentsia reflected their own marginality and their bid for cultural authority. At the same time, however, their criticisms arose from the deep conviction that in a racist society, it was incumbent on African Americans to adhere to standards of moral perfection. Still, the question remained, precisely who set the standards for the proper moral conduct of African Americans in cities?[4]

Dunbar, whose lyrics and stories often portrayed the simple joys of pastoral life, offered a bleak assessment of the condition of urban black migrants. In an account of "The Negroes of the Tenderloin," Dunbar summoned all his literary powers to sketch a lurid Darwinian vision of moral peril. The crowds of "idle, shiftless Negroes" he observed there led him to despair that nothing could be done to prevent them from "inoculating our civilization with the poison of their lives." They cared nothing for socialism or anarchism, and yet, these seemingly "careless, guffawing crowds" posed a "terrible menace to our institutions." Their environment promoted crime and obliterated the moral sense, and the occasional "mission," or social settlement, was as inadequate as a gauze fan against the furnace blasts of hell. Black migrants to New York were "giving up the fields for the gutters," the "intelligent, moral and industrious" class of blacks was powerless to rescue these fallen masses, and although Dunbar feared for civilization, he expressed pity for the defenseless migrants. Until they demonstrated a better capacity for urban civilization, he concluded, "I would have them stay upon the farm and learn to live in God's great kindergarten for his simple children!" As with other black commentators on the subject, Dunbar's perspective was informed by the plantation legend, which held rural surroundings as the natural environment for undeveloped African Americans.[5]

Dunbar's observations on the black residents in the Tenderloin are even more intriguing when superimposed against what is known of his personal life. He divided his time between New York, where his fiancée, Alice Moore, lived and taught in Brooklyn, and Washington, D.C., where he worked as an assistant in the Library of Congress reading room. Paul and Alice were married in 1898 after a long and difficult courtship, prolonged by their separation, the opposition of her parents to the engagement on grounds of class and perhaps color, and tensions related to Dunbar's alcoholism. After a brief honeymoon, they returned to their respective homes. As a popular "literary lion," Dunbar toured the country giving readings and was worshipfully feted by black socialites. Knowing him better than others, Alice was concerned about his reputation, and clearly, hers as well. Just before their wedding, Alice had implored him to avoid the Tenderloin when he visited the city. "I want you to be dignified, reserved, difficult of access," she wrote, and she bluntly urged him to keep away from the section's undesirables, the category in question rendered with a choice epithet so as to avoid misunderstanding. It appears that Dunbar's personal frailties and his constant touring prevented the realization of Alice's hopes for their marriage. But she had her own ambitions. Besides her employment, Alice held literary aspirations as a poet, essayist, and author of short fiction.

As his writings, and records of his relationship with Alice suggest, Dunbar was deeply ambivalent, if not tortured, on matters of race and class. Although a national celebrity and a culture hero for African Americans since his recognition by the literary critic William Dean Howells, he chafed at the popularity of his dialect poems. There is enough evidence to suggest that despite his fame, Dunbar bore considerable despair for which his intimate relationships provided little relief. In 1899, he contracted a disease reported as pneumonia, and Alice nursed him back to a semblance of health and took charge of his business affairs as a collection of her own stories, *The Goodness of St. Rocque*, was published by Dodd, Mead and Company. In 1902, the Dunbars separated, and they remained unreconciled at the time of Dunbar's death in 1906 of tuberculosis. James Weldon Johnson, who greatly admired Dunbar, recalled that beneath the latter's politeness dwelled a "bitter sarcasm," adding that Dunbar felt aesthetically limited by incessant demand for his dialect poetry. Dunbar's reputation was the captive of whites' fixed image of blackness as minstrelsy, a view that pursued him to the grave. The *Southern Workman*'s obituary carped that "his work in dialect seems to us far superior to his other writing and his special talent was for poetry rather than prose."[6]

Given what is known of his personal history, Dunbar's views on black migration provide a striking context for a reading of his 1902 novel, *The Sport of the Gods*, which assayed urban life among African Americans in New York City. Although the novel conveyed a gloomy apprehension toward the debased ideals of urban black youth, and voiced the usual contempt for the black and white pleasure seekers who inhabited the city's cabarets, his naturalistic treatment of these issues was much more complicated than the stance of outright condemnation he and others took elsewhere. Whatever his motives in penning the newspaper sketch, it is clear that Dunbar, the son of

Paul Laurence Dunbar, ca. 1900.

former slaves, lived at the margins of the black leisure class and of racial uplift ideology. Although he, as the rising poet of the race, had spent many social hours with the intellectuals of the American Negro Academy and Washington, D.C., black society, he could simultaneously bask in their attention while maintaining a fascination for "low life" that others, particularly Alice, would find abhorrent. Dunbar conformed to, but was skeptical of the uplift pieties voiced by many black spokespersons. It wasn't only that black elites were powerless to dissuade southern blacks from coming north. Even more decisive for Dunbar was the sense that uplift's self-help, leadership ideals paled before the magnitude of social conditions in cities.

As some of the Harlem Renaissance writers were to discover years later, creative intellectuals like Dunbar found that their productivity and livelihood were seldom free from the constraints of white audiences and patronage. Dunbar applied these lessons in *The Sport of the Gods*, manipulating and challenging the conventions of plantation fiction that had characterized much of his work. His struggles for creative integrity led him to pursue a comprehension of the historical and social relations that underlay class relations among blacks that bordered on parodic treatments of the verities of racial uplift and migration.

Northern writers such as Dunbar and his contemporary, James D. Corrothers (1869–1917), a minister, journalist, and poet based in Chicago, charted alternative paths in African American literature away from the didactic historical fictions of writers such as Pauline Hopkins and Sutton E. Griggs. They, along with James Weldon Johnson, tackled difficult subjects and grounded their work in the mass culture of Progressive Era journalism and popular music and stage shows, whose racial content, minstrel trappings, and working-class settings writers of uplifting race literature would have scoffed at. Ironically, such writings caught on with white audiences predisposed to seeing their authors as "authentic" black writers of dialect verse derived from the plantation and minstrel stereotypes of urban blacks. There were obvious pitfalls to such an approach. Any divergence from sentimentalized white perceptions of blackness might inspire a dismissive review such as the one Dunbar received in the *Independent* in 1899: "The negro, pure and simple, is not here."[7] Both Dunbar and Corrothers expressed frustration with the mass publishing market's hostility to their more assimilationist literary aspirations. They shared a tragic awareness of the failures inherent in the success bestowed only on those black writers who worked within demeaning literary and popular conventions.[8]

Given their willingness to both exploit and flout both dominant and oppositional racial conventions, Dunbar and Corrothers condemned themselves to marginality within the discourse of uplift, which tended to stress positive portrayals of blacks as paragons of success and refinement. Yet they also shared a deep interest in representing the impact of urbanization on cultural and class divisions, and aspired to a level of social realism that William Ferris, for one, would have termed pathological. More than many of their contemporaries in literature, they were exploring social and cultural change and scrutinizing its effects. Their urban writings seem all the more adventurous when compared with W. E. B. Du Bois's figuration of a vanishing black rural folk culture, which emphasized, along the lines of the Volksgeist of German nationalism, the folkloric and musical expression of African Americans' racial soul.

Du Bois's conception in *The Souls of Black Folk* of African American folk culture embodied in the slave spirituals—the "sorrow songs" sung by those "who walked in darkness,"—makes an interesting comparison with Dunbar's invocation of the plantation legend in his discussion of urban blacks in the Tenderloin. By equating spirituals with the Volkslied of German romanticism, Du Bois departed from minstrelsy, creating an international context for his definition of black high culture. He was determined to distinguish from minstrel songs what he called "not simply . . . the sole American music, but . . . the most beautiful expression of human experience born this side the seas." To his aesthetic argument that held the spirituals as proof of black beauty and humanity "as the singular spiritual heritage of the nation and the greatest gift of the Negro people," Du Bois added a folkloric argument for race progress. Drawing on what he felt to be the omissions and silences of the spirituals, he noted that "mother and child are sung, but seldom father; fugitive and weary wanderer call for pity and affection, but there is little of wooing and wedding; the rocks and the mountains are well known, but home is unknown." Even as Du Bois believed the spirituals would affirm blacks' claim to equal rights ("Actively we have woven ourselves with the very warp and woof of this nation. . . . Would America have been America without her Negro people?"), hoping that "America shall rend the Veil and the prisoned shall go free," his sense of loss at the songs' absence of patriarchy allowed him to contrast folk traditions with uplift's prescription for the race's arrival into the fatherland of modernity through patriarchal home and family life. The force of Du Bois's argument for African Americans' humanity is not diminished by the realization that in a society uncontaminated by racism such arguments would have been unnecessary. Still, Du Bois's vision of the spirituals operated at several levels: as an appeal for recognition, an affirming claim of cultural autonomy, and a construction of African-Americans' collective messianic purpose in redeeming American democracy.[9]

Du Bois's renaming of black folk culture using the spirituals as the Negro equivalent to Germanic folk culture came at a time when European composers were adapting folk melodies for orchestral music, and it represented a flight from the pejorative racial connotations of American minstrelsy and the urban setting. Although Du Bois praised the Fisk Jubilee Singers as the true bearers of the spirituals, he noted the all-too-frequent "debasements and imitations—the Negro 'minstrel' songs, many of the 'gospel' hymns, and some of the contemporary 'coon' songs." The potential for misunderstanding was magnified by the fact that virtually every southern black educational institution sent out a vocal group of this sort for fundraising purposes. Along with the spirituals, some of these groups performed minstrel and vaudeville songs and routines. One such group was the Dinwiddie Quartet, organized to sing on behalf of the John A. Dix Industrial School of Dinwiddie, Virginia. Founded in 1902, they toured in support of the institution, went into vaudeville, and disbanded in 1904. James Weldon Johnson had such deviations from the assimilationist cultural aesthetic of uplift in mind when he wrote, in 1928, "Many persons . . . have heard these songs sung only on the vaudeville or theatrical stage and have laughed at them because they were presented in humorous vein. They have no conception of the Spirituals. They probably thought of them as a new sort of ragtime or minstrel song." [10]

While well acquainted with black bourgeois values, Dunbar, Corrothers, and even Johnson, along with those quartets that straddled the line between spirituals and minstrelsy, were less than wholly faithful to elite Western cultural values. Dunbar, writing in the *Saturday Evening Post*, had urged whites to recognize the existence of an exclusive black leisure class in Washington, D.C., but his days there and in black Manhattan brought home for him an understanding of the rhetorical nature of the dichotomy between "the classes" and "the masses," and its irrelevance in the face of white violence. Dunbar had himself visited San Juan Hill in an attempt to quell the bloody violence of 1900. For Corrothers, such class distinctions, based largely on character, were fodder for satire, except where he employed them to his personal advantage in his autobiography. In Dunbar's novel, and in Corrothers's autobiography *In Spite of the Handicap* (1916), these writers examined the extent to which white betrayal and exclusion had not produced an ameliorative class differentiation, as other writers had insisted, but instead, bitter internecine conflict and resentment within the black community. Their works illuminated the dirty laundry of internal conflicts that uplift ideology had sought to explain away. [11]

Incorporating not simply dialect but also aspects of black vernacular and popular culture into their writing, Dunbar and Corrothers sought to hold a mirror up to social and cultural change in their work, rather than merely rail against it. In this they departed from the prevailing moralistic approach to urban black society. As precursors to the literary activity that emerged out of New York and Chicago after World War I, they and others were more receptive than older black intellectuals to literary experimentation that incorporated popular forms and addressed changing social conditions in novel ways.

Corrothers was a keen observer of the cultural diversity of ethnic politics in Chicago in the 1890s. His writings represented the competitive struggles of working-class, immigrant whites and blacks who occupied the same morally charged urban public spaces in the Progressive Era, with saloons and other disreputable enterprises becoming bases for political influence and entry into machine politics. Dunbar and Corrothers refigured and broadened racial representations with secular, critical positions that addressed the inconsistencies of uplift ideology as a blueprint for black progress.[12]

Dunbar's *Sport of the Gods* is yet another meditation on the theodicy of American racism, its title serving as an ironic displacement of the narrative's sustained critique of whiteness, and the institutional apparatuses that upheld white privilege, particularly the courts. Dunbar addresses the social and cultural pressures facing the black community, North and South, both internally and from without. Like the work of William Ferris, the novel reads almost as an atonement for previous failures and transgressions, and an act of self-justification. It spans blacks' historical movement from the rural South to cities, the destination being New York, the mecca of all aspiring young men and women from the provinces, much as it had been for the Ohioan Dunbar, and for many others, including such southerners as T. Thomas Fortune and James Weldon Johnson. Dunbar endorsed the prevailing view among prominent blacks that this move to the cities was hardly progressive, although he made the move himself.

The ineluctability of Dunbar's account of the disintegration of a black family, combined with his title, has led several critics to dwell on his unrelieved pessimism and the complete subordination of his characters to fate. The novel's sense of the futility of human agency against inexorable social and economic forces shared the bleakness of the novels by Theodore Dreiser and Frank Norris. The novel has more in common with these works of social realism than with the optimism of the uplift romances of Pauline Hopkins and the autobiographical success stories of Booker T. Washington and Amanda Smith. But as D. D. Bruce has argued, such an emphasis on a relentlessly deterministic fate blatantly ignores Dunbar's confrontation with that other form of human agency—oppressive white power and societal racism. Dunbar systematically attacks legal injustice, myths of southern paternalism, evolutionary theory, and the cynicism of yellow journalism. Having constructed an all-too-real fictional universe of societal prejudice, Dunbar ironically (for reasons to be more fully discussed later) describes hapless black migrants as "the Sport of the Gods."[13]

Dunbar's depiction of the novel's central characters, the Hamilton family, captured the struggles of right-living, pious southern blacks to maintain a modicum of security. In an unspecified location, probably in the upper South, Berry and Fannie Hamilton met and married in their earlier lives as slaves, and after emancipation, remained as servants for the southern white planter and businessman Maurice Oakley. With their children, Joe and Kitty, the Hamiltons made their home in the little servant's cottage in Oakley's yard. Eighteen-year-old Joe worked as a barber for the town's white gentlemen, and Kitty, an attractive and well-attired sixteen year old, sang recitals for the AME church and her father's lodge. The family's security was shattered when Berry was accused of theft by Oakley at a farewell dinner for Oakley's weak-willed younger brother Francis, who was leaving for Paris to become an artist.

In Dunbar's scheme of social relations, white mistrust, betrayal, and moral cowardice were clearly implicated in the Hamiltons' exile from the South. Francis, a womanizing dilettante, in Dunbar's words, "an unruly member," had gambled his money away, and unable to confess the truth, claimed he had been robbed. Berry conveniently becomes the prime suspect, and the pallid Francis watches his swift arrest in silent horror. When it is learned that Berry has eight hundred dollars in the bank, this is used against him, although his life's savings was in small bills and coins. In Dunbar's New South, the virtues of thrift could just as easily incriminate blacks, as Oakley's paternalism turned into hateful prejudice in an instant. When a piece of circumstantial evidence proves decisive, Dunbar's omniscient narrator wryly observes, "Frank's face was really very white now." As if Dunbar's sly rendering of whiteness as duplicity had dawned on him, a disbelieving Berry, his final appeal to the trust and goodwill of his employer rejected, exploded, "Den, damn you! damn you! ef dat's all dese yeahs counted fu', I wish I had a-stoled it." Berry's tirade, voiced by Dunbar in dialect, undermined the sentimental plantation tradition, with its paternalistic assumptions of happy, docile blacks. By inscribing a dissonance between dialect form and angry content, Dunbar may have also wished to justify his previous dialect writings to himself and those blacks, including his wife, Alice, who had equated them with demeaning minstrel stereotypes.[14]

Dunbar's narrative flatly rejected the paternalistic claims of New South spokespersons that the white people of the South were the Negro's best friends. Even more relevant to this critique was his view that the Hamiltons, while privileged within the black community, were so dependent on white power that they could hardly be accurately described as middle-class. In addition, sisterhood proved no match for patriarchy tarnished with the self-righteous arrogance of whiteness, as Fannie's desperate appeal to Mrs. Oakley for clemency fell on unsympathetic ears. Maurice Oakley had his servant jailed, and evicted his family from their cottage, hours after they had enjoyed the leftovers from the previous night's dinner.

Oakley's willingness to divide and disperse the Hamiltons suggested that enslavement had never ended for southern blacks. Dunbar described the tenuous status of those who may have existed in lordly relation to poorer blacks, but always at the sufferance of more powerful whites.[15] As house servants to the Oakleys, the Hamiltons had been upstanding, if secretly envied, members of the black community. Having incurred the whites' displeasure, however, their downfall unleashed the hostility of those blacks in whom "the strong influence of slavery was still operative . . . with one accord they turned away from their own kind upon whom had been set the ban of white people's displeasure." The AME church "hastened to disavow sympathy with him, and to purge itself of contamination by turning him out." Here, class differences, or rather, the resentments among those for whom privileged status was merely a heritage of slavery, were seen as anything but progressive. If their neighbors had any sympathy at all for the high-toned Hamiltons, they dared not show it. "Their own interests," Dunbar wrote of the Hamiltons' neighbors, "the safety of their own positions and firesides, demanded that they stand aloof from the criminal." In his eyes, respectability, class differentiation, and the protection of secure homes and firesides were hardly unmixed assets for the race. The security of such homes, hard-won prizes from a punitive white society, seemed inescapably tied to the dispossession and homelessness of others. Among vulnerable blacks, such misfortune was commonly explained not so much by legal racism as by the absence of a virtuous reputation that had distinguished the privileged few.[16]

Dunbar extended his criticism beyond the dependency of a black community, divided by moralism and resentment. These effects of oppression were part of a parodic treatment of those racist evolutionary theories that had informed the views of not only whites, but also, many a black spokesman. In a chapter mockingly entitled "The Justice of Men," Dunbar staged a discourse on race relations among whites "at the bar of the Continental Hotel." Here, with faculties of reason unhinged by whiskey, the Old South's self-righteous racism and moral decadence are seen to be well preserved. Talbot, an old southern gentleman "who was noted for his kindliness towards people of color," advanced a deterministic view of powerless blacks overwhelmed by fate. The Hamiltons, indeed, the slaves, should never have been freed in the first place, so unfamiliar were they with freedom and responsibility: "They are unacquainted with the ways of our higher civilisation, and it'll take them a long time to learn. You know, Rome wasn't built in a day." Reflecting the prejudice masked by the seigneurial benevolence of Maurice Oakley, Talbot's paternalism was actually not so distant from that of his drinking partner, "Mr. Beachfield Davis, who was a mighty hunter." Davis insists, offering a clue as to what his hunting preference was, that "it's simply total depravity, that's all. All niggers are alike, and there's no use in trying to do anything with them." Where some black writers had accepted and internalized racist evolutionary discourse in their discussions of class distinctions, migration, and vice and immorality among blacks, Dunbar attacked the stereotypes at their source, spelled out the implications of their dehumanizing logic, and repudiated their authority.[17]

After the Hamiltons are driven from the Oakley house, all their efforts to find work and a new home come to naught, despite their innocence, within a black community obsessed with respectability. Already throwing off the religious piety of his parents' generation, Joe proposes that the family move to New York, "a city that, like Heaven, to them had existed by faith alone." What awaited the Hamiltons there made a mockery of the Christian idealism of the spirituals to which Dunbar sarcastically alluded. Despite Fannie's misgivings, the family moved and settled into a rooming house, where William Thomas, an urbane railroad porter, promptly took an interest in them, especially Kitty. Dunbar described Thomas as "a loquacious little man with a confident air born of an intense admiration of himself." Dunbar described Thomas, not coincidentally the namesake of the black man who had published that scandalously antiblack book of essays in 1901, as "the idol of a number of servant-girls' hearts, and altogether a decidedly dashing back-area-way Don Juan." Dunbar's disdain for Thomas, who "looked hard at Kitty," and eagerly offered to introduce the new arrivals to the dubious pleasures of ragtime, buckets of beer and coon shows, was evident.[18]

Historical references aside, Dunbar's novel seemed propelled by autobiographical concerns. New York cabaret life was a world that Dunbar knew intimately, and a site charged with Dunbar's ambivalence around black culture. Dunbar's assessment of black musical comedy reflected the frustrations he experienced as an aspiring poet working both within and against the stereotyped expectations of white audiences. His account of the musical "coon shows" was deeply ambivalent. He saw value in blacks performing their own syncopated songs and dances for black audiences even while it galled him that they so avidly consumed the stereotyped entertainments that he believed were foisted on them. The avid interest of the audience indicated a popular desire for an autonomous cultural sensibility not unlike that which Du Bois located in the spirituals. Quite possibly the audience revelled in the display of black performance styles; moreover, in such a setting, their minstrel trappings may have been appealing partly by virtue of their parodic tweaking of black bourgeois pretensions. Dunbar was disinclined to ruminate at length on such matters, noting that the blacks in the audience, "because members of their own race were giving the performance . . . seemed to take a proprietary interest in it all." The theater, while garish and cheap, looked "fine and glorious" to the Hamiltons, whose less than exalted standard had been set by the filthy "peanut gallery" of their segregated southern theater. Dunbar's description conveyed his deep ambivalence over his own involvement in such productions, and over his poetic struggles, waged within the formal restraints of dialect: "They could sing, and they did sing, with their voices, their bodies, their souls. They threw themselves into it because they enjoyed and felt what they were doing, and they gave a semblance of dignity to the tawdry music and inane words." Like caged birds, the black performers on stage were struggling heroically to break out of the insipid material. Still, despite his sympathy for the performers, Dunbar regarded popular entertainment as an opiate for the masses. Kitty found the spectacle enchanting, and "if ever a man was intoxicated, Joe was." In Dunbar's mind, at least for the moment, assimilationist critical standards, and the desire to distance himself from the crude coon songs, held sway. Ragtime, dancing, and dialect were of the same inferior order to him. Later, with the setting transported to a black nightclub, a slumming white journalist, watching couples dance to ragtime music, remarks that "dancing is the poetry of motion." His black companion, a dour man nicknamed Sadness, sardonically replies, "And dancing in rag-time is the dialect poetry." Dunbar had a difficult time distinguishing the creative possibilities of black culture from his hostility toward its consumption by uncultivated blacks and deluded white tourists and its expropriation by white popularizers—journalists, composers of coon songs, and publishers—the latter lured by their stereotyped, popular images of "authentic" negroness. Such feelings were no doubt complicated by Dunbar's own role in promoting the genre: he himself had written the book and lyrics to "Senegambian Carnival," an all-black show starring the popular comedy team of Bert Williams and George Walker.[19]

A Victorian sense of sexual propriety, and a vaguely expressed disapproval of the sexual objectification of light-complexioned, "high yellow" black women, informed Dunbar's portrayal of events both onstage and in the audience. The narrative turned swiftly from the performance on stage, and Joe and Kitty's rapturous enjoyment of the show's "delusions," to Mr. Thomas, who "was quietly taking stock" of Kitty, "of her innocence and charm." In this garish setting of tawdry ideals and illicit pleasures, anonymous members of the audience were as much of a spectacle as the chorus of fair-skinned black women. Dunbar described the predatory gaze of Thomas, condemning the latter's designs on Kitty, as well as the status light-complexioned black women companions conferred on black men. Still, Kitty stood a greater chance of resisting Thomas's seductive attentions than did Joe, who was "so evidently the jest of Fate." Mitigating this deterministic view, however, Dunbar added that in Joe's job as a barber for whites in the South, he had "drunk in eagerly their unguarded narrations of their gay exploits," and thus had begun "with false ideals as to what was fine and manly." The "moral and mental astigmatism" Joe inherited from the white "wild young bucks" of his hometown found its counterpart in the admiration Thomas elicited from passing acquaintances whose tastes were equally suspect: "I wonder who that little light girl is that Thomas with tonight? He's a hot one for you."[20]

The musical stage and cabarets constituted an underworld where jaded hustlers preyed upon naive, impressionable young men like Joe. Hoping to insinuate his way into Kitty's affections, Thomas introduced Joe to his gambling associates at the Banner Club. Capitalizing on Joe's eagerness to prove himself as a man of the world, the gamblers "treated him with a pale, dignified, high-minded respect that menaced his pocket-book and his possessions." Over several rounds of drinks, the men welcomed Joe as an old friend. In a didactic aside, Dunbar noted that the Banner Club "was an institution for the lower education of negro youth," attracting people of all races and classes. "It was the place of assembly for a number of really bright men, who after days of hard and often unrewarded work came there and drunk themselves drunk in each other's company, . . . and talked of the eternal verities." Dunbar exhibited a bohemian's mordant compassion for those with defeated aspirations, whose troubles could not be fully explained by personal weakness. Throughout the novel, such ironic moralism often functioned for Dunbar as a stoic shield against his own disappointments and alienation.[21]

Joe's downfall is almost complete. He is fleeced by the gamblers, drinks heavily, and takes up with a showgirl, Hattie Sterling, who is the only trustworthy, decent character at the Banner Club. Hattie tries to help Joe recover his senses, and perhaps her character provided Dunbar an outlet for autobiographical reflections on his relationship with Alice.[22] Be that as it may, Joe cannot be rescued from his disastrous course, and when Hattie finally leaves him, he murders her in a drunken fit of rage and goes to prison. Watching Joe's descent helplessly, Mrs. Hamilton tries to save Kitty, and is devastated when, encouraged by Hattie's coaching, she begins to perform on the musical stage. Lacking the financial support of her children, Mrs. Hamilton marries a boarder, in an unhappy, abusive union that Dunbar describes as purely utilitarian. Meanwhile, years after Berry's imprisonment, Francis confesses his guilt and Berry's innocence in a letter to his brother Maurice, who, although stricken feeble with the news, stubbornly refuses to let the truth be known. Through an unlikely sequence of events, Skaggs, a white journalist who frequented the Banner Club and had witnessed Joe's dissipation, investigates Berry's case, and sensing adventure and a scoop, heads south. He storms upon the Oakleys, and seizes the letter of evidence from Oakley (in the process fending off Mrs. Oakley, who attacked him with teeth and nails, "pallid with fury"). The sensational exposé he writes for his newspaper secures Berry's release from prison. Dunbar notes that the "yellow" paper's apparent liberal progressivism in gaining Berry's release was motivated by little more than commercial opportunism. The novel's bleak conclusion found Berry and Fannie reunited, after the opportune passing of Fannie's second husband, and back at their cottage near the Oakley house, where they spent many nights thereafter "listening to the shrieks of the madman across the yard and thinking of what he had brought to them and to himself."[23]

The utter pessimism over the state of race relations of Dunbar's novel is only slightly relieved by his narrator's ironic tone. Indeed, Dunbar seemed so thoroughly disenchanted with the urban scene that irony presented to him the only viable response to the resignation and helplessness of his characters. This ironic voice surely blunted the force of his social criticism, giving his jaded omniscient narrator some distance from his unpleasant tale. That same stance of withdrawal was served by his ironic title. For the entire plot of his novel contradicted the premise of resignation to an omnipotent divine will. If anything, human depravity and white exploitation wrecked the Hamiltons' lives and were the root of the problem of evil, according to Dunbar. In a pivotal passage revealing Dunbar's skepticism toward uplift pieties, the disreputable gamblers of the Banner Club, the architects of Joe's destruction, become mouthpieces for the moralistic arguments of uplift advocates. "Here is another example," they preached, "of the pernicious influence of the city on untrained [N]egroes. Is there no way to keep these people from rushing away from the small villages and country districts of the South up to the cities, where they cannot battle with the terrible force of a strange and unusual environment?" The gamblers continued to sermonize in their unlikely role as purveyors of the moral discourse of Darwinian determinism and social control, cynically abdicating responsibility for their exploitation of Joe. Through the parasitic gamblers, Dunbar unmasks conservative black opinion in its usual function articulating class-specific interests, and parodies denunciations of urban migration (one recalls that the Hamiltons were forced North by the Oakleys, and like many black migrants, had fled intolerable living conditions). Fearing that the migration northward would continue, the Banner Club regulars disingenuously concluded that "until the gods grew tired of their cruel sport, there must still be sacrifices to false ideals and unreal ambitions." Spoken by disreputable men with few illusions, divine or otherwise, about their world, Dunbar's title was a profoundly ironic euphemism for a network of exploitative social relations that was anything but God-given.

James Corrothers's Literary Quest for Black Leadership

The black autobiographical tradition, dating back to the slave narratives, has often been synonymous with the freedom struggles of black Americans. By the Progressive Era, some black autobiographies not only embodied the collective goals of freedom, literacy, and Christian piety but also showed a relentlessly secular preoccupation with the success myth of the self-made man. In Booker T. Washington's *Up From Slavery*, the Protestant work ethic and public achievement were central themes. Far less convincing in applying this type of formula was James D. Corrothers, who published his own auto-biography, *In Spite of the Handicap*, in 1916.[24]

Corrothers's autobiography was his solution to the racial constraints of the literary market that faced black writers of his time. In pursuit of white audi-ences and publication in the better paying magazines, Corrothers, like many others, tried to carve out, through Negro dialect, a narrow space for expres-sion between the minstrel-derived representations of blacks in popular litera-ture and journalism and the defensive response of those black writers and spokespersons who espoused the assimilationist, developmental ideology of racial uplift. Unlike Du Bois and most other advocates of uplift, however, Corrothers carried class stratification to divisive extremes. He used Negro dialect and minstrel images of other black men in his autobiography to vali-date his class authority and fitness for leadership. Instead of choosing the re-sponsible path of racial uplift over minstrelsy, Corrothers's autobiography often merged the two, as he employed minstrelsy to affirm himself as the em-bodiment of assimilation and race progress. As if to atone for his self-serving use of minstrelsy, and in the process suggesting the protean character of black identity at its most playful and uncategorizable, at rare moments in his auto-biography—as he had done earlier in the irreverent *The Black Cat Club*—Cor-rothers refigured minstrelsy with sympathetic representations of urban black vernacular cultures. Both unique and representative, Corrothers's works tell us a great deal about the intertwining of various versions of racist discourses in his day, specifically the largely unexamined minstrel nonsense residing within "respectable" race theories described by the ostensibly benign concept of assimilation.

Corrothers was a man of considerable energy and talent, a self-portrayal borne out by writings on race displaying the audacity of an escape artist. He was born in southern Michigan in 1869 in a community founded in the ante-bellum period by fugitive slaves, free blacks, and abolitionists. His mother died in childbirth, and he was raised by aunts and his paternal grandfather, a man of Scottish-Cherokee background who fought Indians. He attended the public schools there and recalled that "as the only colored boy in the village I had actually to thrash nearly every white boy in town before I was allowed to go to school in peace." When his grandfather died, James supported himself by taking on a number of jobs, including work as a lumberjack, mill hand, waiter, amateur boxer, and coachman. An athletic and precocious youth, he worked in the sawmills of a Michigan town "full of rough men who loved . . . a fight."[25] Estranged from his father, Corrothers devoted himself to self-improvement, traveled throughout the region in search of work, and eventually reached Chicago in his late teens. There, he met the reformers Henry Demarest Lloyd and Frances Willard. With their assistance, Corrothers attended Northwestern University from 1890 to 1893. After a brief stint at Bennett College in North Carolina, Corrothers returned to Chicago, and, from a janitor's job, he rose to become an occasional contributor to the *Tribune*. As a contributor to other newspapers, his work was often revised and published under the names of white authors. He was ordained a Methodist minister in 1894 and pastored churches in New York, New Jersey, Michigan, and Virginia. He lectured as an elocutionist and temperance advocate. Inspired by Dunbar's success, he began to publish his own Negro dialect poems. For more than twenty-five years his poems, stories, and sketches appeared in leading newspapers and journals and in the black press. Fannie Clemons, his first wife, who bore him two sons, died in 1894. He married Rosina B. Harvey in 1906, and, at his death in 1917, he left her, their son Henry, and a surviving son from his first marriage.[26]

Although black writers generally used Negro dialect to figure the class and cultural differences that elite blacks insisted whites recognize, their use of dialect was not always a capitulation to racial stereotypes. Still, Corrothers's assimilationist persona relied on dialect that went further into the forbidden terrain of minstrelsy than most other black writers dared. His autobiography thus pandered tacitly to distorted images of blacks and to the very prejudice the work bitterly denounced. Yet, reflecting the contradictory and ambiguous content of his writings, Corrothers at moments in the autobiography seemed to admit the limits of such a vision of assimilation, and located resistance in a black folk consciousness that masked its true intentions from more powerful whites. This work is unique in its blend of anger and accommodation, of aggression modulated by irreverent humor.

An examination of Corrothers's writings, particularly the contrast between the assimilationist autobiography and the earlier *Black Cat Club*, with its urban setting and its use of black vernacular culture, marks Corrothers as bold, distinctive, and ambitious, if not foolhardy in his willingness to violate literary and aesthetic canons and exploit and subvert minstrelsy. Occurring when the urbanization of black communities created new audiences for black popular entertainments, Corrothers's career also illustrates the complexities and contradictions within assimilation and racial uplift ideology. In the final analysis, Corrothers's assimilationist writings were torn between an oppositional folk consciousness and a quest for individual success and authority articulated through strenuous masculinity. Corrothers's self-construction remained subordinated to the paternalistic dictates of an exemplary, instrumental black leadership, loyal to the social order and the American nation.

Through uplift ideology, black spokespersons essentially accepted the prevailing view that "the race" was on trial against widespread negrophobic accusations of urban deviance and criminality. Yet at the same time, other blacks less burdened with the demand to be respectable were also manipulating and reclaiming minstrelsy and were exploring different modes of cultural expression in ragtime, blues, and Negro dialect literature and in the performances of barnstorming Negro vaudeville troupes.[27] For his part, Corrothers seized upon assimilation as his greatest asset in an apparent bid for legitimacy as a black spokesman. He stressed his northern background, claiming that he had "never talked Negro dialect, nor done plantation antics." And during his youth, he said, "My speech and ways were those of the white community about me." To Corrothers, assimilation meant behaving like whites and avoiding those grotesque signs of blackness that one might see at a minstrel show.[28]

Washington's success story, *Up From Slavery*, was Corrothers's model. Like the Wizard of Tuskegee, he was not above telling a minstrel joke and passing off stereotypes as social truth. But Corrothers's autobiography sought to turn his lack of success and his suffering into a sign of character and virtue. His career poignantly reveals (in a manner reminiscent of the more famous Dunbar) the burden of being an "authentic" black writer of Negro dialect, as genteel magazines such as *Harper's*, *Scribner's*, and *Century* often carried racial and ethnic stereotypes represented through dialect and illustrations. Since there was only enough room for one "poet of the race" in the eyes of the white public, Corrothers never achieved much more than scattered notice through his fiction writing. His solution was producing an autobiography that might reverse and redeem a lifetime of material hardship. In this work, and in two autobiographical short stories published just before it, Corrothers was anxious to identify himself with a strenuous but refined masculine authority and responsible black leadership. He believed that this strategy, aided by his fluency in Negro dialect, would gain him a sympathetic hearing from white readers.[29]

If Washington influenced Corrothers's autobiography, it is just as likely that the success of minstrel comedians such as Bert Williams and Bob Cole provided a model for Corrothers's earlier use of Negro humor in *The Black Cat Club*. Here, Negro humor represented an attempt to infuse minstrel forms with black content and resonances, purging minstrel narratives of white racism. The book was a collection of humorous, fictional sketches about a black Chicago literary society whose unlikely members were shady urban denizens still close to southern folk ways and ready to draw their razors at the slightest provocation. The club took its name from its mascot, a black cat that the members sometimes employed, in keeping with southern black folk belief, to intimidate superstitious persons deemed unfriendly to the society. His remorse over its appearance notwithstanding, Corrothers twice mentioned the volume in listing the achievements of his literary career, and was apparently proud that it "was published by a New York firm."[30]

Black writers and audiences were divided on the merits of Negro dialect writing. Although many agreed with the view that "it can scarcely be believed . . . that great poetry can ever be clothed in the garb known as Negro dialect,"[31] for others, Negro dialect symbolized an enduring black folk wisdom and provided a vehicle for articulating rage against past and present cruelties of enslavement and lynching. D. D. Bruce, in noting the widespread use of Negro dialect by black writers from about 1895 to 1906, asserts that instead of finding the form limiting, authors found it amenable to a variety of sentiments, including protest. Black writers employed dialect in work that appeared in such genteel periodicals consumed by blacks as the *Colored American Magazine* and *Voice of the Negro*.[32] Clearly, Negro dialect was in some forms permissible to black editors and audiences and did not inherently entail minstrel stereotypes. But while *The Black Cat Club* trafficked in the usual stereotypes, its dialogue often a barrage of malaprop humor, the work also revealed minstrelsy to be a pliable sign whose meaning might diverge from the work of white imitators.

Its urban setting distinguished Corrothers's dialect writing in *The Black Cat Club* from the plantation nostalgia that had brought success for white journalists Thomas Nelson Page, Joel Chandler Harris, Harry Stillwell Edwards, and a spate of other scribes of so-called Negro authenticity. Corrothers reveled in the image of the razor-wielding urban dandy, just comical enough to reassure whites' subliminal fears at the implication of violence. He played upon such anxieties and put whiteness on the table for equal opportunity representation, as he sent the members of the club, razors at the ready, on a cultural exchange visit to a German saloon on the north side. Upon arrival, the threat of conflict was washed away in a torrent of beer, and Corrothers demonstrated his cultural ambidexterity with verses written in German dialect. At the same time, however, he seemed to criticize the popularity of dialect writing among a black middle class all too willing to celebrate public success and status in any guise. Corrothers's hero, the president and poet laureate of the Black Cat literary society, Sandy Jenkins (a name familiar to readers of Frederick Douglass's autobiography who remember the plantation conjurer whose powers the skeptical, assimilationist Douglass grudgingly acknowledged)[33] is lionized among blacks in the novel for his diamond-accented fine dress as much as for his verse. Jenkins, who is also a gambler, regales a saloon crowd with his acknowledged masterpiece, "The Carving," a mock-epic dialect poem about a razor duel over a light-complexioned black woman. Perhaps the transgressive implications of Corrothers's view that black men like those in the Black Cat Club could exist freely outside the boundaries of law and respectability led him to end the book on a note of moral uplift with Jenkins's marriage to a daughter of the black middle class, and his establishment of a catering business.[34]

The Black Cat Club's carnivalistic conflation of black middle-class and vernacular cultures and its sympathy toward black migrants as heirs to a tradition of slave resistance satirized uplift's, and the social order's, repressive images of work and respectability. Men of the Black Cat Club boasted of their skill at avoiding exploitative work ("Ain't nothin' in it, no way!"). Sharing a laugh at their exploits as heroes of their own urban trickster tales, they duped political machines at election time and took bribes and patronage from corrupt white Democratic aldermen, while amongst themselves vehemently denouncing the Democratic Party as racist. Such tactics were, to Corrothers, merited by the racism of both political parties. Club members regarded such actions as guided by the "Chicago Golden Rule—'*Do de other feller, befo' he do you.*'" Humor also masked a critique of Washington's conservative philosophy; Sandy Jenkins, in the midst of a Bookerite tirade against "De Eddicated Cullud Man," described an unlikely scenario that parodied economic self-help: "Now s'posin dey wuz a lynchin' 'bout to take place, an' de curly-headed brunette whut was to be de pahty acted upon hel' a fust mo'gage on de home uv evah man in de lynching pahty. An' s'posen mose o' dem mo'-gages wuz 'bout due er ovah due; an' s'posen jes' 'fo' dey lit de fiah er strung 'im up, de cullud man wuz to say: 'Genamuns, ef you lynches *me*, ma *son* 'll fo'close all ma mo'gages t'morrer! *Dis am ma ultimatum!*' Do you thaink dey would have any lynchin' 'at day? No sah! Now, whut could de college dahkey do?—Nothin' but say his prayers." Through Jenkins, Corrothers went on to damn Washington's leadership with ostensible praise: "I tell you dat man's doin' a heap mo' good in de Souf den all de graddiates whut's a-slanderin' uv 'im an' writin' resolutions." As proof, Jenkins dubiously urged his audience to "look at de genamus uv dis club! We ain't got much book l'arnin', but we has lit'a'ly cahved ouh way to fame an' fortune."[35] Although the combination of dissent and the work's minstrel trappings made this sort of thing sacrilegious to many, such humor created possibilities as a vehicle for protest from the margins, the lower frequencies, so to speak.

Corrothers's portrayal of violent competition among blacks for status and prestige, mediated by farce in *The Black Cat Club*, was a theme that received far more serious and embittered treatment in his autobiography. In the later work, Corrothers also addressed the apparent contradiction between his professed commitment to assimilation and his past success as a dialect writer. Dialect in the autobiography served as racial raw material, fueling his quest for a higher style of writing, a quest that, among other factors, would confirm Corrothers's fitness as a race leader. Even as he tried to dissociate himself from dialect and its stereotypes, he repeatedly used the form to strategic advantage by trying, as Washington had done, to construct a civilized leadership persona over the primitive, dialect-speaking "Old Negro." But where Washington's use of dialect exploited plantation stereotypes, for Corrothers, dialect was also a sign of a covert political consciousness that could resist whites. Just as the melodious sound of Negro spirituals enthralled abolitionists as their meaning masked internal codes of resistance, Corrothers, like Dunbar and the Du Bois of *The Souls of Black Folk*, were well aware that white audiences' fascination with minstrelsy might be turned to blacks' advantage. For his part, Corrothers used assimilationist minstrelsy to figuratively mask his actual blackness, and, in his autobiography, dialect enabled him, like whites who were quite free to do so on the stage, to figuratively don the mask. He could invoke the spectre and threat of unregenerate blackness and reassert his controlling presence at will in his narrative.[36]

Corrothers's autobiography, a peculiar kind of success story, dwelled on the contradiction between uplift's lofty civilizationist aspirations and the material struggles of black Americans. Corrothers laid bare what many elite and aspiring blacks were reluctant to speak of and preferred to submerge beneath respectable appearances: the painfully enormous gulf between literary and leadership aspirations and a lifetime of ill-paid, itinerant toil at an endless series of menial jobs and ministerial positions. Despite his poverty, he portrayed his ultimate "triumph" as his ability to profess faith in American society. This stance was convincing to Corrothers's literary patron, journalist and editor Ray Stannard Baker, who noted in the introduction to the work that Corrothers's book was "singularly without rancor" and that its author "in spite of difficulties has maintained a cheerful and helpful outlook toward life." Baker seemed willing to ignore much of Corrothers's anger in presenting him as an authentic black spokesman.[37]

Despite Baker's disclaimer, Corrothers was not blind to the injustices of white society. Indeed, the lightness of his prose style allowed a considerable amount of anger, marking the autobiography as a bold venture. He noted that "the first mobbing of Negroes of which I ever heard did not occur in the South, but in Michigan," in the town where he was raised. Suggesting the extent to which national ideals were contaminated by race hatred, Corrothers observed that the riot spoiled what was to have been a Fourth of July celebration. No one was killed, but "a number of coloured people were severely beaten and scarred for life." Later, in Chicago, he vividly recalled how his ambitions as a journalist and poet clashed with the minstrel stereotypes promoted by the majority press. As a young reporter for the *Chicago Tribune* in the 1890s, Corrothers had the horrifying experience of seeing his piece on prominent Chicago blacks rewritten by a white editor in a demeaning dialect style. His promise to those he interviewed, including the eminent black surgeon Daniel Hale Williams, that they would be depicted favorably, compounded his humiliation when the insulting buffoonery reached print. Angrily protesting this incident, Corrothers was fired, and he latched onto work as a waiter at a lunch counter.[38]

Corrothers situated himself in the middle-class culture of progressive reform. In doing so he was hardly leaving the racial assumptions of minstrelsy behind. In an account of his first meeting with Frances Willard, Corrothers recalled swapping dialect jokes with the temperance and women's rights advocate. As Willard joked at the expense of Irish Americans, Corrothers answered with the old, inside joke about the chronic lateness of blacks. Duly impressed, she offered him financial support toward his (incomplete) studies at Northwestern University. Corrothers recalled meeting Willard at an address he gave before the Women's Christian Temperence Union while at Northwestern. Corrothers's silence concerning how he came to become a temperance worker belies his coy assertion that he did not know "what on earth she came to hear me for." Perhaps he was asserting his moral superiority by alluding to Dunbar's alcoholism; in any case, such reticence downplayed his role as Willard's protégé and defender in the wake of her controversial stand condoning lynching, and its crucial myth of the black rapist, a position that had elicited the wrath of another prominent Chicago reformer, Ida B. Wells.[39]

If Corrothers sought to popularize his fictive racial persona by manipulating the tension between assimilation and minstrelsy, far more overt, indeed exaggerated, was his emphasis on masculinity. This strategy was rooted in minstrelsy's relentless attack on black manhood. Given the historical denial of the normative status of patriarchal protector to black men, advocates of racial uplift sought to escape this "feminized" image by asserting manliness as the epitome of rights and bourgeois respectability and as an antiracist panacea. In doing so, however, many black men internalized the myth that their perceived lack of manliness was a personal, moral failing, rather than a result of their historical and social condition. While the rhetoric of manhood rights was a staple of militant black protest, to many, manhood itself became synonymous with the progress of the race and thus extended its mission of social control to the lives and sexuality of black women in the name of protection. For Corrothers, however, black women were virtually invisible in his appropriation of the popular literary conventions of white working-class manliness, as seen in his frequent references to fistic duels, boxing, and to his own athletic prowess and capacity for heavy physical labor. Indeed, Corrothers sought at some level to incorporate blackness and white manliness in the same strenuous male body. If working-class white men built their identity on distorted minstrel images of black males, Corrothers felt entitled to construct his autobiographical persona through an appropriation of the blackness of white masculinity.

Corrothers's self-proclaimed superiority and "goodness" depended heavily on his accounts of physical combat with dangerous, razor-toting black men textually signaled by the Negro dialect he had them speak. Such roguish stereotypes served as foils for his bourgeois aspirations to self-improvement as a poet and minister, as Corrothers stressed the dignity of labor and the work ethic and portrayed himself as a paragon of tough, if refined and chaste, manliness. Revelling in his physique, Corrothers noted that he personally brought an athletic program and "physical culture" to Bennett College, where "the teacher of physiology invited me to pose in sleeveless boxing costume before her class, that they might, as she expressed it, 'observe the development and play of the muscles.'"[40] Careful to avoid the implication of overt sexuality in such displays, Corrothers professed to be "a novice at Cupid's game." However idiosyncratic, Corrothers's depictions of his chaste, aestheticized body clearly fit the pattern of uplift's attempts to establish fraternal, as well as middle-class, solidarity across racial lines with white males and reflected his literary quest to portray respectable black manhood. His emphasis on masculinity was solidly in the tradition, within racial uplift ideology, of defining "the race" as a masculine collectivity, a construction partly explained by black male writers' anxiety over the harsh realities of the sexual exploitation of black women by white men.[41]

Repeatedly, Corrothers took an antagonistic stance in his autobiography toward the image of those blacks he viewed as the antithesis of the assimilationist ideals of uplift. Even as he denounced Jim Crow railroad cars for their failure to respect the claims of middle-class black women to protected femininity, he insisted that "white people . . . are not entirely to blame for the bringing about of these conditions in the South." Instead, he saw "rowdy Negroes . . . [and] disgusting and dangerous displays of black savagery" as spoiling things for "decent and intelligent coloured people."[42] Surpassing the uplift strategy of insisting on a distinction between "better" and "undeveloped" classes of blacks and following the pattern of Washington's autobiographical attempts to discredit rival black leaders, Corrothers represented most other black men, leaders and masses, as his enemy. In this, he epitomized the individualistic psychology of oppressed minorities for whom nothing could be more foreign, or undesirable, than a collective consciousness. Of course, the American context for messianic notions of black leadership ("the Moses of his race") and uplift ideology's vanguardist assumptions did little to discourage this way of thinking. Be that as it may, Corrothers portrayed himself as the victim of scandals and disputes, engineered by his cultural inferiors, which cost him ministerial positions. Indeed, he served in three denominations, African Methodist Episcopal, Baptist, and finally, Presbyterian.

Just as humor, as a self-conscious narrative strategy, might channel anger, so did his eruptions of anger, when directed against black rivals, real and imagined, contain a measure of insight. Uplift declarations of race solidarity masked a brutal individualism. Corrothers made the painful realization that black institutions were so marginal that control over their limited resources was necessarily a competitive endeavor. With so few professional and leadership opportunities to go around, leadership was primarily a matter of dominance. He knew that black men like himself wielded such power and influence as they were able to obtain in fierce, often covert competition with their would-be allies. Repeatedly, he complained of black congregations unable to pay his salary, and he claimed to have staffed, practically singlehandedly, a black newspaper in Chicago, which could not pay him much before it failed. Painfully aware that "my race could not employ me," Corrothers wrote gratefully of the assistance he had received over the years from whites.[43]

Yet there was something more complicated about Corrothers's quest for vindication as a truly representative black leader. As if to reflect his many reversals of fortune and to recall the mischief of *The Black Cat Club*, his narrative contains moments that dislodge assimilation as a privileged strategy. On the one hand, recalling his days at Bennett College, he disdainfully described southern black college presidents as "so many . . . ignorant frauds" and carped on the "Negro mannerisms" of a Greek and Sanskrit professor who "invariably said 'dis' and 'dat' and mispronounced a number of common words." Yet later, he was surprised to discover that this same professor of the "infelicitous speech" was capable of a rousing and eloquent address protesting Jim Crow.[44]

Here and elsewhere, in a manner that recalled *The Black Cat Club*, Corrothers suggested that to be unassimilated meant an inclination to resist and challenge, however indirectly, white supremacy. He described being rescued from a confrontation on a Jim Crow car by a dialect-speaking Pullman porter and recalled with approval the cunning of a "half-savage" African prince who successfully defrauded white colonial investors. "From the viewpoint of the prince," Corrothers remarked, "it had been a game of wits." Here Corrothers suggested that the moral bankruptcy of colonialism justified turning the shears against those wolves willing to take up the white man's burden. Given the vulnerability of blacks to this sort of exploitation, success for a black man, following the Chicago golden rule, could be as much an amoral, duplicitous con game as it was a matter of meritorious assimilation.[45]

In one crucial instance, he saw his own assimilation as a liability. As a minister, he often regretted his "lack of early contact with the masses of my race." Finding himself at a disadvantage in discerning "their moods and methods of thought," he noted that "the unschooled Negro, when he premeditates church meannesses, either talks in riddles or assumes a sullen, enigmatic manner quite difficult for me to fathom." Immediately, in the next breath, Corrothers rendered the folksy dialect voice of the black preacher: "Often, I have envied," he wrote, "the reassuring confidence of the old plantation preacher" who warned his new congregation, "Chilluns, you cain't fool me; 'ca'se I has good, bo'n undahstan'in o' mah people: When a niggah sneeze, *I knows whah he cotch his col'*." His sense of alienation made it difficult for him to compete with the folk preacher's ability to enthrall his congregation. Wishing he could "get over" on his congregations before they could send him packing, Corrothers's resentment communicated his own thwarted desire for mastery and control over other blacks.[46]

Corrothers sought power and legitimation outside the black community, compromising the antiracist aspects of his narrative. The construction of an authoritative black public persona paradoxically necessitated cleansing himself of the stigma of racial difference. Here is his recollection of a stint working with a group of black workingmen on a freight boat over the Great Lakes: "They were of the 'razor-toting' class. . . . Their ways were not my ways. . . . Their conversations fairly reeked with lasciviousness and vulgarity. They were not Northern Negroes, but Southern Negroes, come North and gone to the devil. The first night of my association with these men I was speechless with the horror of it. I thought I had almost reached the confines of hell. . . . Before the end of my second trip, I had thrashed the bully of the boat in a combat which came near ending fatally for me."[47] More than once in his autobiography, he represented his quest for supremacy among blacks as a violent struggle among black male rivals, enacted before a judging white readership. Zealously guarding his own image, lest he be mistaken for one of those boat hands, Corrothers noted that he abhorred liquor, found dancing "a silly waste of time," and followed inner promptings to keep his life clean and decent. His account of the dangerous black boathands was in marked contrast to the nostalgic remembrance of those white lumberjacks with whom he had grown up "rough and unafraid . . . thoroughly at home in [the] rough company" of men who loved strong drink and fighting.[48]

By his own account, ability, spotless character, and refined speech were apparently insufficient in themselves. For Corrothers, self-improvement and leadership meant a willingness to fight and subdue other blacks, though he suggested in one instance that white manipulation lay behind violence among blacks. Corrothers recalled that during his young manhood, he fought into submission what he called "a big Negro of the lumbering fieldhand type" whom an angry white former boss had set upon him. Lest (white) readers feel threatened by all the fighting, Corrothers assured them that he lacked a "blood lust" for fighting: "My youthful fistic encounters were experiences which have seemed to me like reassuring milestones on my road to higher achievements and development. Because of them I have said to myself: 'I can do this other, better, nobler thing!' They have given me courage, often, to fight on against odds."[49] Violence was central to his narrative of self-improvement, despite Corrothers's attempt to portray his development as something more benign.

Professing shame for *The Black Cat Club* and much of his earlier dialect verse, he aspired to what he viewed as a higher style of writing, modeled after Swinburne, which became the object of his prodigious work ethic and his quest for self-improvement. At last, he recalled: "I was working for my *race*, as well as for myself and my family. . . . I was doing a higher class of work than I had ever done before. . . . I felt that I had mastered Negro dialect; but I was far from having mastered the art of expressing worthy thoughts in literary English. Besides, I moved in an element of society which, for the most part, did not use good English."[50] Such statements, presumably reconciling personal ambition with rhetorical concerns for the race's welfare, failed to do justice to Corrothers's literary achievements. Middle-class aspirations led him in his autobiography to defer to assimilationist cultural standards for his writing. Corrothers's literary ambitions suggested the anxiety of the American artist in relation to Europe, as well as the torn, contradictory identities produced by writing for both black and white audiences. The fact remained, however, that his poems, like the work of most black writers, advanced political priorities and black formal alternatives that often rendered such imitative aesthetic considerations less significant. The Victorian stoicism and forebearance of the protest poems (which would soon find their apotheosis in Claude McKay's "If We Must Die," penned to protest racial violence in 1919) Corrothers published in W. E. B. Du Bois's *Crisis* found their formal opposite in the dialect poems he published in the *Century Magazine* at the same time. As with *The Black Cat Club*, humorous dialect verse voiced protests belied by his ambition to express "worthy thoughts in literary English."

In "An Indignation Dinner," Corrothers couches a demand for redistributive justice for blacks in dialect verse. The poem's speaker tells of "a secret meetin', whah de / white folks could n't hear" over how to ensure a good Christmas dinner in the face of hard times. However softened by humor, the poem depicts an angry group consciousness. At the meeting, one man points out that "de white folks is a-tryin' to keep us down," and that "dey's bought us, sold us, beat us; / now dey 'buse us ca'se we's free." Facing the holiday indignant, poor, and desperate from low wages, the bounteous livestock and crops "on a certain genmun's fahm" spurs the group to form "a *committee* foh to vote de goodies here." Speaking significantly in the first-person plural voice, the poem's narrator describes the festive, capacious Christmas dinner enjoyed by the group, "Not beca'se we was dishonest, but indignant, sah. Dat's all." As in *The Black Cat Club*, a sense of injustice animates blacks' seizure of whites' property, and challenges stereotypes of chicken stealing and criminality.[51]

The political content of such dialect works found a counterpart in even a standard English work like "In the Matter of Two Men," published in the *Crisis* in 1915. The poem's protest rehearses the exaltation of manly physical prowess in his autobiography. In the poem, Corrothers posits a Darwinian teleology created by slavery and Jim Crow in which whites would lose vitality and blacks would become a masterly race:

Though the white storm howls, or the sun is hot,
The black must serve the white.
And it's, oh, for the white man's softening flesh,
While the black man's muscles grow!
Well, I know which grows the mightier,
I know; full well I know.

Here evolutionary theory is thus pressed to the service of upsetting the social order, revising dogmas of developmental tutelage and uplift:

Ingenious grows the humbler race
In oppression's prodding school.
And it's oh, for a white man gone to seed,
While the Negro struggles so!
And I know which race develops most, I know; yes, well I know.

The accommodations of his autobiography are absent here, as Corrothers exposes the racist double standard used to discredit black political aspirations.

The white man votes for his color's sake,
While the black, for his is barred;
(Though "ignorance" is the charge they make),
But the black man studies hard.

Reviving the old antislavery argument that southern society had regressed to a backward condition as whites had grown feeble, lazy, and immoral by enslaving blacks, Corrothers concluded: "So, I know which man must win at last, / I know! Ah, Friend, I know!" Corrothers seemed to fuse evolutionary theory with Christian teleology, as in his autobiography, where his elaborate descriptions of hard menial labor evoked the suffering of the stations of the cross. Unloading cargoes of salt and flour from freight barges, Corrothers described working without food or rest "for forty-eight and fifty-two hours at a stretch." Handling heavy, dripping barrels of wet salt, Corrothers wrote "my hands would crack open and drip blood. But I stuck it out."[52]

Corrothers's autobiographical theme of the betrayal of his leadership by irresponsible, unassimilated blacks was central to his 1914 short story "At the End of the Controversy." Its protagonist, Grant Noble, a black minister in New England, had successfully defended the black community from a prominent white minister's public accusations of vote-selling and criminality. Having prevailed against one adversary, Noble, "broad-shouldered, erect, . . . a personality to be reckoned with, a man among men," met his match in a conspiracy among members of his congregation seeking to defraud white philanthropists on the pretext of rebuilding the church. "The plan now was to use the popularity of the pastor to make a 'killing' from the whites," Corrothers wrote, representing the conspirators—"a certain brand of negroes"— with dialect: "'We will ast de pastah to do mose o' de solicitin',' said Conspirator No. 1." When Noble, a man of integrity (who had excelled at varsity football in college), refused to take part, the angry conspirators ousted him from the church despite the fatal illness of his wife and one of his two sons. "For doing *right*, he was exploded forth into the great army of the unemployed." The story was accompanied by illustrations, including one depicting the pastor's departure amidst a throng of grotesque Negro stereotypes: "And straight through the crowd he went; overblowing this spawn of savagery with an awing look he passed out and was gone." Corrothers's story ultimately affirmed the accusations that the exemplary Noble had refuted, as his omniscient narrator confessed that Noble's flock had actually been engaged in political corruption all along.[53]

While "At the End of the Controversy" laid the groundwork for the later autobiography's attempt to portray Corrothers as a natural aristocrat exiled by resentful black ministers, a story that appeared in the NAACP organ *Crisis* in 1913, "A Man They Didn't Know" situated the problems of black leadership within global affairs by imagining a military alliance of Japan and Mexico against the United States, further supported by black deserters from the U.S. Army and the secession of Hawaii, led by angry Japanese Americans.

Drawing on such contemporary events as the rise in domestic racism under the Wilson administration, black antilynching agitation, the Mexican Revolution, and the advent of Japan as an imperial and military power, Corrothers's imaginary threat to domestic security was ambiguous. While transgressive in raising the militant specter of black Americans' angry willingness to side with foreign powers against the United States on grounds of racial solidarity, the duty for the pacification of this uprising fell to black leadership, personified again by Corrothers's alter ego, Grant Noble. Summoned by a panicked President Nefferman for advice on how "to win the Negroes over," Noble urged the president not to rely on the Bookerite Dr. Packer T. Jefferson to marshal blacks' support. The only "mighty black man," according to Noble, "whom my people would follow into death . . . is Jed Blackburn, the discredited Negro boxer." Noble was certain that Blackburn, whom Corrothers modeled after the black heavyweight champion Jack Johnson, would lend his support in search of "*redemption*, through the battlefield." Approached by Noble, the down-and-out fighter initially balked, echoing Corrothers's Darwinian view of black male strength: "Fightin' fer white folks is whut ruined *me*! They say I'm a bad man. Well, I'm just whut white men developed me into. . . . After I licked the champeen, th' white folks got it in for me." Reminded by Noble of his disgrace (the precise nature of which is never fully explained), Blackburn tearfully relents—"if I've hurt my race, I'll atone"—and with his commission as colonel adapts his ring technique to military strategy: "Always let your man come *to* you. . . . Jes' like boxin'!" Blackburn led a force of ten thousand black soldiers on a suicidal counterattack of Japan's invasion of southern California. "If we die in this fight," Blackburn told his troops, "we'll be dyin' fer our race. Maybe we'll make it better fer them that's lef' to tell." Integrationist ideals of race loyalty, pluralism, and national unity yielded victory as Blackburn's advance guard, followed by Noble and reinforcements of ninety thousand black soldiers, was joined by Germans, Jews, Frenchmen, Italians, Irish, and Swedes. When Noble was praised for his role in averting the crisis, he "pointed to a gigantic black man lying among the slain. "'There, gentlemen,' he declared, 'is a man they didn't know.'" Here, Blackburn represented the primal black male, his dangerous presence domesticated by his, and other black soldiers', willing martyrdom to the American nation.[54]

Like Corrothers's autobiography, the story contained the extremes of black anger and accommodation. The story's sentiment was echoed in Corrothers's poem "At the Closed Gate of Justice": "To be a Negro in a day like this / Demands forgiveness" as well as a "strange loyalty." Like much of uplift ideology, the poem functioned as an appeal to the conscience of white elites for recognition of blacks' Christlike humanity and as an expression of controlled fury at white betrayal, as blacks knocked, "unheeded, at an iron gate." In both the poem and the story, Corrothers anticipated the mood of anger and betrayal that informed hotly contested debates among blacks over their participation in World War I.[55]

The writings of Corrothers and Dunbar, as well as those of Du Bois, James Weldon Johnson, and others, situated within the historical and cultural transformations of migration, imperialism, industrialism, immigration, the woman's movement, and minstrelsy and the mass commodification of blackness, mark the internal contradictions of racial uplift ideology, and the extent to which it contained the seeds of black modernism conventionally associated with the Harlem Renaissance. Far from the least significant aspect of this black modernism was the flourishing of contestation around racial representation, even within racial uplift ideology's ostensible project of assimilationist conformity. Such confrontation with the centrality of minstrelsy as a foundation for both black *and white* middle-class subjectivities anticipated perhaps the most crucial contribution of the black diaspora intellectual tradition: the critique of race stressing the interrelatedness of construction of blackness and whiteness that has been advanced by, among others, Ida B. Wells, Du Bois, Ralph Ellison, James Baldwin, and Toni Morrison.

Corrothers, had he lived, might have surpassed his far humbler role as protean pretender to the throne of black leadership, thus escaping the invisibility that quickly shrouded his career. His stoic rendering of assimilation as the recipe for black success and leadership in his autobiography was ultimately half-hearted and unconvincing. Ironically, his espousal of assimilation served as its own critique insofar as it repeatedly summoned forth the violent conflict and racial difference that it sought to repress, and exposed the competition, dominance, and minstrelsy behind the benign image of racial uplift ideology as a civilizing mission of racial self-improvement. In this sense, Corrothers's literary persona was jerry-built from fragmented images of blackness handed down by whites. To him, assimilation and uplift, ostensibly beneficial for the race and humanity, were virtually synonymous with self-interest, pursued as a battle for hegemony over other blacks. His personal struggles (as well as his transgressive Negro humor sketches) made a mockery of the conventions of success literature, even as he sought to capitalize on them. He bitterly complained of the exclusionary tactics of whites and their refusal to admit blacks on terms of equality, yet he often tailored his narratives to white prejudices.

Corrothers's writings render visible the stigma of blackness and undermine an ostensibly neutral assimilationist ideology that has nevertheless been hostile to black advancement and has made the melting pot and dreams of a color-blind society illusory ideals for African Americans. Corrothers's politically ambiguous formal experimentations with minstrelsy, his Darwinian pretensions to cultural superiority as a northern writer, and his preoccupation with solidifying his assimilationist persona with masculine toughness indicate the need to further interrogate seemingly neutral racial categories such as assimilation. Indeed, Corrothers's life and work suggest the extent to which some blacks, as Du Bois argued, struggled to achieve true self-consciousness and to forge a black cultural sensibility against racist representations of blackness. Perhaps the sum of Corrothers's and Dunbar's writings enables an understanding of how ostensibly rational, color-blind assumptions on race and class in the United States were, and continue to be, unsuspectingly haunted by the indelible, pathological distortions of minstrel stereotypes.

8

THE EVERYDAY STRUGGLES AND CONTRADICTIONS

OF UPLIFT IDEOLOGY IN THE LIFE AND

WRITINGS OF ALICE DUNBAR-NELSON

> You long to explode and hurt everything white: friendly; un-
> friendly. But you know that you cannot live with a chip on your
> shoulder even if you can manage a smile around your eyes—
> without getting steely and brittle and losing the softness that
> makes you a woman.
>
> MARITA O. BONNER, "ON BEING YOUNG—
> A WOMAN—AND COLORED"

(((

Gloria T. Hull's discovery of the diary and writings of Alice Dunbar-Nelson is a major contribution to African American historiography: for the diary, which covers Dunbar-Nelson's life from 1921 to 1931, from age forty-six to fifty-five, records her comments on America's (and the world's) major historical transformations and events, and perhaps just as importantly, her reflections on her daily life and her multifaceted identity as a black woman. In many ways a wallflower of history, Dunbar-Nelson's private writings, uncontaminated by the self-protective distortions of memory, and ranging from a serious quest for historical and personal truth to a penchant for gossip, rescue from obscurity her spontaneous perceptions of a wide array of contemporary issues: the ideology of racial uplift, the rise of consumer culture, Progressive Era reform, spiritualist and occult groups, the women's suffrage and peace movements, World War I, black urban migration, the Jazz Age, motion pictures and cabarets, the New Negro (Harlem) Renaissance, Marcus Garvey, Jack Johnson, the phenomenon of blacks "passing" for white, the complexities of lesbian sexuality, playing the numbers, the debate on the Dyer anti-lynching law, and communism, to name but a few.[1]

Alice Dunbar-Nelson was born Alice Ruth Moore in New Orleans on July 19, 1875. Her mother, born a slave in Opelousas, Louisiana, was a seamstress who raised her and an older sister after their father, Joseph Moore, a merchant marine, deserted the family. Alice Moore attended public schools and graduated from Straight University in New Orleans in 1892. Intellectually gifted, ambitious, and marked for future greatness, she wrote for local newspapers and published in the *Woman's Era*, the Boston periodical edited by Josephine St. Pierre Ruffin. In 1896, she moved North to attend a number of elite colleges over the next twenty years, studying English Literature at Cornell, Columbia, and the University of Pennsylvania. In 1897, while living in New York City and working at the White Rose Mission (a settlement house for young black girls founded by Victoria Earle Matthews with the assistance of Booker T. Washington), she began her courtship with Paul Laurence Dunbar. Dunbar had written to her after seeing her picture and a poem of hers in the *Woman's Era*. They married in 1898, eventually settled in Washington, D.C., and had what might be fairly described as a difficult relationship over the next four years. After her separation from Dunbar in 1902, Alice Dunbar moved her family (her mother and sister) to Wilmington, Delaware, where she taught at all-black Howard High School for the next eighteen years. In 1920, she lost her position as head of the English department there when the school's new principal locked her out of her classroom. The grounds for her dismissal, according to Hull, were Dunbar-Nelson's "political activity" and "incompatibility."[2]

In 1910, approximately four years after Paul Dunbar's death from tuberculosis, Alice Dunbar secretly married a colleague at Howard High School named Henry Arthur Callis, a man twelve years her junior. (He was twenty-two to her thirty-four, and the age difference, combined with her celebrity, would have been enough to brand the union improper in the eyes of many if it were known. The brief marriage may also have been kept secret for fear that Dunbar-Nelson might lose her job. After they both remarried, Dunbar-Nelson and Callis, a physician and a founder of the Alpha Phi Alpha fraternity, remained close friends.)[3] In 1916, Alice Dunbar married once again, this time publicly. Her husband, Robert Nelson, a widower who had also lost a spouse to tuberculosis, was a journalist from Pennsylvania, and the union lasted until Alice's death in 1935. With Nelson, she coedited and published the *Advocate*, Wilmington's black newspaper, from 1920 to 1922, an enterprise maintained, like many black newspapers, by Republican Party patronage. After the *Advocate* collapsed, the victim of a political reprisal that saw the withdrawal of GOP support, Robert Nelson lived and worked in D.C. as the editor of the *Washington Eagle*, the national newspaper of the Improved Benevolent and Protective Order of Elks of the World, a black fraternal organization. Dunbar-Nelson remained in Wilmington, where she managed the household that she shared with her mother, sister, and nieces. There, she maintained a crowded schedule of public activities, including her post, after 1920, as the first black woman on the State Republican Committee of Delaware. In 1927, she joined the Society of Friends' American Interracial Peace Committee, a pacifist organization based in Philadelphia. As executive secretary, her duties included publicity and fundraising through speaking appearances.[4]

With her education, celebrity credentials, and looks (she was of near-white complexion with auburn hair) Dunbar-Nelson represented to many, herself most of all, the grandest hopes and ambitions of racial uplift ideology. She was active in black uplift institutions. In the 1890s she wrote a column for the *Women's Era*, and during 1913 she helped edit and wrote for the *A.M.E. Church Review* in Philadelphia. She earned her living primarily as a teacher, and in addition to this, and her membership in the National Association of Colored Women, Dunbar-Nelson advocated bourgeois uplift ideals in her newspaper columns syndicated in the black press, as well as in the two entre-preneurial volumes which she edited: *Masterpieces of Negro Eloquence* (1914) and the *Dunbar Speaker and Entertainer* (1920). These collections were more than commercial ventures meant to capitalize on her celebrity as the widow of the famous black poet. Like many other books of their kind, they were also teaching and inspirational guides for black youth. Yet, her attempts to build a canon of black writing and oratory for the instruction of the race's youth met with disappointment.[5] Such frustrations aside, Dunbar-Nelson worked to bring the gospel of uplift to numerous school assemblies and church groups as a platform lecturer, a career she avidly pursued after she was forced to leave Howard High. In addition to these activities, Dunbar-Nelson also founded and helped administer, from her own limited funds, the Industrial School for Colored Girls in Marshaltown, Delaware. This whirlwind of public activities certainly yielded Dunbar-Nelson more in status than actual remuneration.

The tragedy and pathos inherent in the situation of elite blacks taught to equate their personal aspirations with those of the group is forcefully appar-ent in Dunbar-Nelson's case. Dunbar-Nelson began her diary in 1921 during a period of financial and emotional stress. We see her with her defenses down, a vulnerable condition that would remain fairly constant throughout the document: "Times are hard. Money tight. Debts staggering." Assessing the insolvency of her newspaper, she figured that "we are running behind about $360 a month." The diary was one of several strategies she employed to pull together what seems to have been a great deal of inner strength, though Dunbar-Nelson seemed unable to give herself credit. Instead, most of her at-tention is claimed by attempts to manage crises, impose self-discipline, and unburden herself of the discouragement that she could not share with a household full of dependents. "I lay in bed this morning thinking, 'forty-six years old and nowhere yet. It is a pretty sure guess if you haven't gotten any-where by the time you're forty-six you're not going to get very far.'" Around

Alice Moore Dunbar-Nelson, ca. 1900. (Courtesy of Carlson Publications)

this time, Dunbar-Nelson became involved with Unity, a quasi-religious self-help organization, to achieve self-control, peace of mind, and to focus her energies. "How am I going to control the Infinite Universal when I am wedded to the same slip-shod habits?" she wrote. "I dawdle and waste time day after day. . . . I shall begin to discipline myself severely. . . . I shall castigate myself until I can work without dawdling and can do this little bit of room-cleaning, washing, ironing etc. in double-quick time and leave time for writing and real work." Through Unity, Dunbar-Nelson hoped to strengthen her faith in individual achievement through hard work. But worried by debt and shouldering the added burden of domestic labor, Dunbar-Nelson's interest in spirituality was also rooted in her desire to "think constructive thoughts and attract wealth, and meanwhile indulge in some self-discipline." Throughout the year she attempted (without success) to get her original film scripts produced by the black independent filmmaker Oscar Micheaux, and briefly considered studying law. Through Unity, an already oversubscribed Dunbar-Nelson appeared to be castigating herself for her quite natural desire for more leisure to pursue her literary and intellectual interests.[6]

Besides money worries, Dunbar-Nelson's diary entries reveal her constant struggles to stay abreast of the times. The diary also provides a document of the painful truths masked by dissemblance, as the record of her daily life captures the complex relationship between public and private life for many privileged blacks. The pressures of genteel poverty fed the gnawing doubts she harbored about her self-worth, public life, and leadership status, doubts she was disinclined to raise in public. Much in demand, an overextended Dunbar-Nelson cynically noted the hollowness of racial uplift rhetoric. When another clubwoman wrote to ask her to "save the womanhood of Delaware," a weary Dunbar-Nelson confided to her diary, "Nothing doing. . . . I'm not bothered about the womanhood of Delaware. It will have to go unsaved." Aired publicly, such a statement was heresy; such ideals of uplift were held sacred because other reliable sources of status for elites were unimaginable. There were other reasons for putting the best foot forward. Although blacks' achievements were heralded in the black press as triumphs for the race, failures of any sort cast suspicion, not just on themselves as individuals, but on the moral worth of all black people. Therefore, the judgmental gaze of the dominant culture, absorbed by many elite blacks, necessitated the concealment of personal doubts and inadequacies. Only in private writings do we find frank expressions of anxiety, despair, and resentment among elite African Americans. One gets a sense not only of the seemingly endless slights and petty humiliations resulting from the inevitable encounters with race prejudice, but also the bitter tensions of intraracial class and color conflicts. Dunbar-Nelson recalled that as her train changed into a Jim Crow car while she was traveling to Maryland, a "fresh white youth wanted me to move out, to the hysterical delight of the colored passengers, who knew me."[7]

Dunbar-Nelson's life, while unique in many respects, was nonetheless typical within a black middle-class milieu. Indeed her diary and writings record the limited satisfactions, material and otherwise, of racial uplift ideology, and the extent to which African Americans' class aspirations routinely clashed with Jim Crow. Dunbar-Nelson's struggles epitomize the very tenuous nature of bourgeois identity, particularly among blacks, and for whites as well. Since the turn of the century, claiming a bourgeois identity had been a struggle for blacks, fought on several fronts. Elite blacks found themselves trapped between the racism of whites and the resentment of less-privileged blacks, who, on the one hand, may have objected to elite blacks' false sense of superiority, but on the other, may also have internalized dominant white resentments against blacks in positions of authority. And within uplift ideology, black elites mediated their racialized vision of class differentiation vis-à-vis the black masses by constructing their privilege in relation to what they considered an uncouth, racist white working class, as well. Still, as members of an oppressed group struggling to cling to what little they had, bourgeois African Americans' political powerlessness and the constant reality of economic hardship and violence frustrated their claims to elite status. Their plight was worsened by the extent to which middle-class identity for all Americans was rooted not only in economic inequality but also in the phenomenon of race—symbolized by whiteness. Be that as it may, the activities of Dunbar-Nelson and other black leaders, representing a shift from racial uplift ideology to a New Negro militant consciousness, were inescapably a response to the elevation of segregation to the level of national policy in the years preceding the war, and later, racial polarization, with an attendant rise in black consciousness in the northern urban black communities created by the mass migration of southern blacks.

As blacks crowded into northern cities, propelled by lynching and peonage and drawn by the labor shortages during World War I, racial violence and the Ku Klux Klan spread to the North and Midwest. Immigrants and native-born white migrants from the South had either learned or brought with them older racial antipathies. Indeed, racial violence had erupted in the North earlier over conflicts between black and white industrial workers. Mob violence in the birthplace of Lincoln, Springfield, Illinois, in August 1908 provided the catalyst for the founding of the National Association for the Advancement of Colored People, enacting the interracial cooperation against racism advocates of uplift had long sought. But the NAACP, which devoted its early efforts against peonage, lynching, and segregation, faced overwhelming odds in securing justice in southern courts. In 1911, a southern correspondent described the system of peonage for the readers of the NAACP organ, the *Crisis*, in a manner that underscored the symbiosis of racial and economic oppression: "The court and the man you work for are always partners. One makes the fine and the other one works and holds you [in debt], and if you leave you are tracked up with bloodhounds and brought back." The Supreme Court had upheld federal antipeonage legislation in 1911, but the practice persisted in the South for years afterward. Northern courts were no better, even when the rights of more privileged blacks were at stake, as Booker T. Washington discovered when his assailant was acquitted after dealing the Tuskegee educator a bloody beating with a cane in New York City in 1911.[8]

Federal segregation under the Wilson administration gave further comfort to the spread of racial hostility, eliciting angry protests among black leadership. Having earlier abandoned all faith in President Taft and the Republican Party, black leadership and opinion shifted to the Democrats, as W. E. B. Du Bois and William Monroe Trotter supported the southern-born Woodrow Wilson in 1912, hoping to influence policy as spokesmen for the race. But almost immediately, Wilson's administration put to rest whatever optimism existed among blacks. As a portent of things to come, just before his inauguration, the House passed a law making racial intermarriage a felony in the District of Columbia. In 1913, Wilson established segregation in federal office buildings. Throughout his administration, he effectively condoned outbreaks of racial violence with federal nonintervention. He ordered racist military interventions in the Dominican Republic and Haiti that effectively turned those Caribbean nations into plantations controlled by U.S. bankers and corporations. Then in 1915 he warmly endorsed the film epic *Birth of a Nation*, based on Thomas Dixon's anti-Reconstruction novel *The Clansman*.

Amidst carping between his organization, the National Independent Political League, and the NAACP, Trotter sought vainly to register his protest against the segregation of federal employees to Wilson. In November 1914, Wilson finally granted Trotter an audience, at which the two men argued for forty-five minutes. When Trotter called for the abolition of federal segregation, Wilson replied that "segregation is not humiliating but a benefit," and that African Americans were misled by their leaders to believe it a humiliation. Trotter countered that black and white federal employees had worked together for fifty years before Wilson took office and that black leaders were now being roundly denounced for having supported him. Interrupted several times by an increasingly nonplussed Wilson ("Your manner offends me. . . . Your tone, with its background of passion . . ."), Trotter pressed on: "Have you a 'new freedom' for white Americans and a new slavery for your African-American fellow citizens?" The confrontation made the front pages of both black and white newspapers, and it marked Wilson's first public admission of personal involvement in the policy.[9]

Trotter had a reputation even among black allies as a reckless instigator. Although many press accounts accused him of "bad manners," others, including the *Independent*, the *New Republic*, and, of course, the *Crisis*, criticized Wilson's policy. Wilson received staunch support from more conservative segments of black leadership. Presuming to speak for the race, as black spokesmen were wont to do, Robert Moton, who would succeed Washington as head of Tuskegee, assured the president that "the Negroes, generally, do not in any way approve of Mr. Trotter's conduct in the White House." Moton actually spoke for a dwindling few, however, as Trotter's coup marked the increasing militancy of black leadership, and the emergence of the NAACP as the preeminent race organization after Washington's death in 1915.[10]

Through public education and the exposure of lynchings, the NAACP campaigned for a federal antilynching bill introduced by Congressman Leonidus Dyer of Missouri after the race riot in East St. Louis, Illinois, in 1917. As racial violence spread, crucial to the militant New Negro consciousness was the fact, widely reported in the black press, that blacks fought back against their persecutors. A 1917 rebellion by black soldiers stationed in Houston, Texas, against harassment by police and local prohibitionists led to the court martial of the troops involved; thirteen were hanged, and forty-four were sentenced to life imprisonment. After white mobs rampaged in Washington, D.C., and Chicago in the summer of 1919, Dyer's bill passed in the House, but was filibustered to death in the Senate in 1920. Uniformed black soldiers discovered that their fight for democracy and freedom had only intensified in America upon returning from the war in Europe.[11]

Lynching had been a constant through the 1890s and the first decade of the new century. Georgia had the infamous distinction of leading the nation in lynchings from 1882 to 1923. By the 1920s, lynchings were less frequent, but more savage. James Weldon Johnson reproduced in his autobiography a grisly account of an Arkansas lynching in 1921, which might be seen as part of an antilynching discourse around the figure of the heroic Negro martyr. A man accused of murder was surrendered by authorities to a mob. More than five hundred persons, including a few women, watched as "inch by inch the Negro was fairly cooked to death." The victim retained consciousness, "even after the flesh had dropped away from his legs and the flames were leaping toward his face. . . . Words fail to describe the sufferings of the Negro. Even after his legs had been reduced to the bones he continued to talk with his captors, answering all questions put to him." Johnson noted that the incident was not unique, and the NAACP had sought to mobilize public sentiment against a number of equally atrocious cases. As had occurred in earlier periods of crisis, episodes of mob violence galvanized an oppositional united front among black leadership.[12]

Given the failures of the NAACP's pressure-group politics, and of black soldiers' participation in the war for world democracy to avert a resurgence in lynching and a national wave of urban mob violence, it is little wonder that Alice Dunbar-Nelson shared with many blacks a sense of political impotence, in addition to her personal disappointments and her frustration at talents largely unused and unappreciated. For many blacks, the sense of futility and of unredressed injustice held a heavy cost in rage for which there was no suitable public outlet. Things had not much improved since 1901, when Dunbar-Nelson herself had been beaten in Washington, D.C., by a policeman after an altercation during the funeral of President William McKinley. A persistent letter writing campaign by Paul Dunbar and the couple's friends in the government resulted in assault charges being brought against the policeman, who was later acquitted.[13]

Alice Dunbar-Nelson's writings document the contradictions within uplift ideology, specifically, the complex divisions within the group along class, color and gender lines. Black elites were well aware that they were on trial before the dominant society, and they labored to maintain a public image of respectability as representative leaders. Within racial uplift, however, based on the dominant society's racial and sexual double-standard, the strictures of respectability weighed heaviest on black women. In this light, Dunbar-Nelson's private discussions of her brief secret marriage and her clandestine desires for women have special significance. She existed between, never safely within, her society's repressive polarities of race, class, and heterosexual, versus lesbian, sexuality, a condition that disrupted the stable, privileged identity promised by black middle-class ideology.

Dunbar-Nelson also contended with the assumption that racial uplift was best served by bolstering patriarchal authority within the race. The sexual division of labor within black institutions that merely reflected patriarchal society is also a major concern in her diary, and in her public writings, too. Dunbar-Nelson attacked gender inequality in her newspaper columns, syndicated throughout the 1920s in the black press. She paid tribute to several of her female associates who, with little fanfare, had built lasting institutions for blacks, including Maggie Lena Walker, who founded and ran a black-owned bank in Richmond. A schoolteacher, Dunbar-Nelson, like Anna Cooper, was ousted from her job after clashing with male officials on the Board of Education in Wilmington, Delaware. In the diary, she described her encounters with male authority in her professional and reform activities, as well as within her daily life at home.[14] Her diary also discloses an attempt in 1930 to write a satirical novel based on her deeply contradictory experience, entitled "Uplift." Her attention to the novel faded as she joined a last ditch attempt to gain a new trial for Theodore Russ, a young black man sentenced to hang after being convicted of raping a white woman. In each case, her efforts were futile. Russ, who maintained his innocence, was hanged on August 22, 1930. Sometime that next year, Dunbar-Nelson destroyed the manuscript of what she had self-deprecatingly referred to as "The Great American Novel."[15]

As representative, then, for her disappointments as she was for her achievements, Dunbar-Nelson waged a constant struggle for intellectual mastery of a bewildering world. Nevertheless, Dunbar-Nelson's syndicated columns in the black press are important for assessing the public role she projected for herself as a "race woman," a role that meant both championing and criticizing black leadership. Within black leadership, to be a "race woman" was considered a contradictory proposition, given the concern for restricting women's sphere. Despite being warned off politics by her editors (reminiscent of injunctions leveled at southern black elites within the repressive context of disfranchisement), Dunbar-Nelson criticized reflexive black support for lily-white Republicanism. This analysis, when brought to the attention of a group of black male politicians, elicited a hostile response. As Dunbar-Nelson recalls, "They called [me] so many kinds of apostate, traitor, renegade, silly woman . . . and other vile names." Potential black solidarity on political questions shattered on the rocks of assumptions of male dominance.[16]

In other published editorials, Dunbar-Nelson upbraided black politicians for supporting antiblack forces. Her views coincided with the militant critiques of "hat in hand" black leadership on view in such black periodicals as the *Messenger*. In the *Advocate* she called Perry Howard, a black Mississippian and a Harding appointee to the Justice Department, a "Traitor to His Race" for attacking the NAACP and opposing the Dyer bill. Howard, it seems, retaliated by blaming Nelson and the NAACP for the defeat of the Republican Party in the Delaware senatorial contest in 1922. Howard may well have had a role in terminating GOP patronage for the *Advocate*, resulting in its demise. Despite tension between the Nelsons and the Howards, Dunbar-Nelson accompanied her perennially ambitious husband to Howard's summer house at Highland Beach, a vacation resort for blacks near Washington, D.C. Resigning herself to the visit, she wrote in her diary of her host as "mine old enemy" before leaving for the shore.[17]

Such entries reveal the extent to which a highly competitive scramble for the spoils of political patronage occurred within the inner circles of the black elite, even as its members maintained a public face of cordial relations. Black middle-class ideology, as a public doctrine of self-help and altruism, hardly transcended unseemly jockeying for patronage and philanthropy. The setbacks under Wilson's administration worsened an already dismal situation, as opposition to black office holding in the Senate caused a white man to receive the post of District Recorder of Deeds, an appointment which had gone to blacks since 1881. Under these circumstances, wolves like Booker T. Washington and functionaries like Howard might cloak themselves in the altruistic rhetoric of uplift, the better to quietly co-opt black rivals and punish dissenters through the control of few coveted patronage appointments.[18]

Dunbar-Nelson's exasperation at her husband's political disappointments (specifically, his hope for an appointment rewarding him for campaigning in state and national elections) touches on a different realm of politics, namely, marriage. For many African Americans, regardless of class, the health of relationships was fundamentally a matter of economics, as uplift's florid tributes to marriage could ring hollow when the rent could not be paid. It is important to note in this sense that the struggles of black women cannot be understood in isolation from the equally trying existence of black men.[19] Robert Nelson's decidedly modest earnings required his wife, like many black women, married or not, to become self-sufficient, and what is more, to tolerate his considerable frustration and "growling" with unfailing support. (Incidentally, Alice Dunbar had been generous in offering sympathetic understanding and support to Paul Dunbar, until their falling out.) Perhaps tensions between them eased when insolvency dictated that Robert Nelson live near his job in Washington, D.C. Since her first marriage, Alice Dunbar-Nelson had long been accustomed to such separations. Freed to pursue a range of activities, Dunbar-Nelson still could have found the extra time far more lucrative. In addition to her column, Dunbar-Nelson taught and performed administrative work at the Industrial School for Girls in Delaware, but at a low salary—work she considered drudgery and would have been glad to give up. Publicly she denounced the sort of office seeking that constantly preoccupied Robert Nelson, but she would have relished the security brought by such an appointment.

Dunbar-Nelson and her husband sought to supplement their income by playing the numbers, an illegal gambling game that the respectables (including Dunbar-Nelson) publicly denounced, even as many of them, in all probability, privately consulted their dream books. These were manuals, sold by druggists, and retailed in grocery stores, barber shops, and beauty parlors, which, in their perfect blend of spirituality and materialism, gave numerological betting advice based on dream symbolism. The numbers racket constituted a thriving underground economy in the black community, and its wealthy "bankers," however shady, generally commanded respect among blacks of all social levels as courtly civic and philanthropic leaders. Here, segregation, economic exclusion, and poverty, whether genteel or not, defeated attempts to draw the line between black middle-class and working-class cultures. But middle-class morality, by definition, masked behavior inconsistent with its dictates. Thus uplift ideology's espousals of the work ethic might tolerate, while outwardly condemning, the secret hopes of not a few respectable, but marginal persons that they would one day hit the number—an event which was about as likely as landing the plum political appointment.[20] In 1931, Robert Nelson finally got his long-sought appointment, to the Pennsylvania State Boxing Commission. With the cessation of the family's financial worries, Dunbar-Nelson's diary ends abruptly, and there are no subsequent extant entries in this period before her death in 1935 of heart disease.[21]

Because members of the black elite generally faced economic vulnerability, the community itself became a major arbiter in bestowing upon its members the crucial status of respectability. In many ways, its criteria for judging its members, for exclusion, as well as inclusion into its social circle, were generally similar to those of the white bourgeoisie. But among blacks, the most decisive factor besides access to power, was conformity to gender conventions of respectability—to bourgeois family structures of patriarchal authority and female domesticity. As with everyone else, power, money, and status were all important, but among blacks, the status and material opportunities that often accrued to symbolic whiteness, through assimilated and lighter-complexioned blacks, had long been a source of internal conflict. It is tempting to compare intraracial class tensions and prejudices with parallels among German Jewish and "lace-curtain" Irish elites against their less privileged counterparts. The distinguishing factor, of course, was that color differences informed class hierarchy among blacks, even within the black elite, ideals of racial solidarity notwithstanding. Gender complicated internal color biases, favoring light skin color, youth, and ornamental attractiveness in women as desirable characteristics.

Amid these dynamics of sex and color, often publicly unspoken but painfully familiar, Dunbar-Nelson, like many other middle-class blacks, craved the recognition that was withheld by whites. Hemmed in by segregation, many elite blacks demanded a compensatory deference from less privileged blacks. Dunbar-Nelson was forced to cope with the volatile, contradictory combination of light skin privilege on one hand, and on the other, her subordinate status as a woman. Thus, by merely showing up, Dunbar-Nelson could find herself alienated from those within the black community quick to snub and disown "dicties"—the term for elitist blacks, often those of lighter complexion. The main point here is that women were more vulnerable to such judgments than were lighter-complexioned men. Generally, and often, with good reason, light-complexioned blacks were suspected of practicing color prejudice against darker skinned blacks. Anxieties surrounding color difference might result in class tensions between black women paralleling those between black and white women. Dunbar-Nelson indicated as much when she complained in a column that "women in [beauty parlors] drag their social ambitions into their commercial life. A woman or girl from a class which they feel is superior socially to their own gets short shrift, poor service, and insulting discrimination." The beauty parlor (where the business of having one's hair straightened, while providing a crucial source of economic independence for black women, was nonetheless implicated in the equation of feminine beauty with whiteness) is revealed here as a site of class conflict among black women. Although it is impossible to determine who insulted whom in this encounter, it seems clear enough from her assumption of superiority, however cautiously phrased, that Dunbar-Nelson was writing about color, which was predominant among the other markers of class—including hair, dress, demeanor, and speech—in the beauty parlor. The experience was apparently so disconcerting for Dunbar-Nelson that she once risked visiting a white-owned beauty parlor in Wilmington, where she "didn't know whether I'd 'get by,' but evidently did. Nice place. Nice girls." Only by risking exclusion, it seems, could Dunbar-Nelson momentarily escape the painful color and class tensions among black women.[22]

As we have seen, color differences had been a sensitive topic in black leadership since the post-Reconstruction period. One of the results of the systemic rape (let us not prevent the likelihood of consensual relationships from facing this issue honestly) of black women during slavery and afterward was the birth of numbers of African Americans with access to wealth, education, and power, and many of the race's leaders during Reconstruction had emerged from the social advantages that accrued to whiteness. But although white ancestry diminished in importance when education became more widely accessible, and in the face of assertions of political conceptions of racial solidarity and uplift, color controversies could not be put to rest. Praising Frances Harper's *Iola Leroy*, the *A.M.E. Church Review* nevertheless questioned "the propriety of selecting a person so nearly white . . . to establish the virtues of a colored woman," but pardoned the "apparent error" because Iola's color, or lack of it, dramatized the discrimination visited upon even those with "one drop of black blood." So powerful was the obsession surrounding color that this commentator did not consider that Harper and other black writers such as Hopkins depicted "white" black characters for other purposes: to locate racial identity in one's political consciousness, rather than one's color, and to demonstrate to white readers their own moral agency and capacity to take an antiracist stand. After all, Iola, the daughter of a slave owner and his wife of invisible African ancestry, had spouted proslavery views when she believed that she was white. When suddenly remanded into slavery, and subjected to discrimination after emancipation, she embraced her African American identity through her commitment to racial uplift.[23]

But the narrative strategies of Harper and Hopkins could not conquer color tensions. Nannie Burroughs tackled the vexed issue of color and marriage when she observed in 1904 that "many Negroes have colorphobia as badly as the white folk have Negrophobia." She voiced a cultural nationalist sentiment when she insisted that this prejudice was baseless, given the "superior types of manhood and womanhood found in thoroughbred Negro men and women." Burroughs lamented that many black men married black women for their light skin color over their character, and noted the hypocrisy of those black men who accused black women of consorting with white men, while coveting the half-white daughters of such liaisons. Striking radically at assumptions about color and femininity, Burroughs frowned upon not only black men's vested interest in miscegenation but also the practice among black women of hair straightening and skin bleaching. Women so devoted to superficial matters of appearance, to Burroughs, could instead be developing a formidable and attractive character.[24]

Burroughs's outspoken analysis confirms that color conflicts among African Americans were inescapably gendered matters. "You're so beautiful, but you've got to die someday," went the popular blues lyric of unreciprocated male desire, and the role of color in joining sentiments of love and aggression is worthy of conjecture. The accusation of being "color struck" apparently plagued Dunbar-Nelson, based on a letter she received from her friend in Wilmington, Edwina Kruse. Kruse advised Alice to ignore murmurings accusing her of such selectiveness in her choice of suitors. Kruse reminded her friend that her marriage to the dark Paul Dunbar was "convincing proof" of her lack of bias. Kruse believed that class ought to be the determining factor in such matters, not color, a view with which Dunbar-Nelson concurred.[25] Although privileged by her light complexion, Alice was caught at the nexus of sex, color, and desire in a vulnerable position in which she could be the object of powerful desires that, if not returned, might instantly turn into resentful rage. The dilemma of color and sex preceded her, and all blacks, exerting on occasion an overdetermining impact on social interactions and intimate relationships, and dredging painful group memories of the legacy of slavery. Both worshipped and detested for her appearance, Dunbar-Nelson was constantly being judged by others, and in turn, judging others and not sparing herself.

Dunbar-Nelson's diary records a period in her life when color in itself was no guarantee of social success. In the diary, she confessed her worries that she was losing her popularity within the black elite. In 1929, she described an NAACP ball as a "very colorful affair, with plenty of ofays [whites]" but found "a curious selfishness on the part of the Jim Johnsons and Walter Whites and have my usual loneliness in the crowd. Oh, so pitiful." More than once, she struck a plaintive note about her "loss of social touch everywhere, save in Manhattan. People don't invite me to parties anywhere. Why?" After attending a meeting of the National Federation of Colored Women's Clubs in 1928, she wrote of a "stormy and bitter . . . session. . . . Terrible. Lots of dirty linen washed. Tears. Undercurrents that I knew not of. Realized sharply that I am an 'out.'" Despite all this, in Wilmington she socialized, though not always comfortably, with blacks of all social levels, and was hurt by her more snobbish friends' disdain toward her acquaintance with the former boxing champion Jack Johnson. "Guess I'll stick to high-browing," she wrote rather cynically in her diary at the end of 1928. Such entries reveal the extent to which her standing within the black bourgeoisie was a constant preoccupation.[26]

Her marginality within black society heightened her frustration at the barriers of segregation. In her columns, she railed against the invisibility of middle-class blacks who struggled vainly to impress whites with evidences of their progress. What was to be done? Like Anna Julia Cooper before her, Dunbar-Nelson questioned black spokespersons' incantations of statistical proofs of racial progress. Most whites, Dunbar-Nelson maintained, ignored statistics of property ownership and professional occupations, which only served the purpose of "bolster[ing] up our own crushed pride." A similar fate befell the letters of protest blacks sent to white newspapers, which usually ended up in waste baskets. Dunbar-Nelson believed that "there is no question that faces the Negro graver than just this one—the inability to get our message, propaganda, story over to our enemies." And even if one succeeded in this respect, as did Trotter with President Wilson, there was little to be gained from this increasingly outmoded style of leadership based on personal access and influence, instead of pressure politics backed by mass support. Throughout the post-Reconstruction era, blacks incessantly preached uplift ideology's reformist vision of black property ownership and interracial cooperation, believing that these achievements would usher in the millennium. Dunbar-Nelson, however, astutely recognized the limits of strategies that depended ultimately on whites' willingness to recognize blacks as equals.[27]

Dunbar-Nelson also soured on assimilationist beliefs that blacks must demonstrate their patriotism and loyalty to the nation through military service. Since the turn of the century, uplift ideology assigned the highest value to black participation in national wars as an opportunity for the race to prove its loyalty, its capacity for citizenship, and in a word, its "manhood." During World War I, W. E. B. Du Bois supported the Allies, shocking his militant comrades with the claim that black Americans could not remain idle in a war for world democracy. The belief that military service would diminish racism was dashed by the riots and mob violence that greeted black soldiers returning from Europe. The ardent pacifism that Dunbar-Nelson espoused in her columns and in her public duties for the American Interracial Peace Committee during the interwar years stemmed partly from the disillusionment that ensued when the sight of black men in uniform provoked not respect and gratitude, but murderous rage, from many whites.[28]

Thus, Dunbar-Nelson joined the radical internationalist trend among black leadership, linking the threat of global war to the ongoing imperialist global struggle along "the color line." Noting that the younger generation of black writers "has scrapped war with other useless and outworn traditions,"

Dunbar-Nelson argued in 1928 that the prospect of world destruction loomed "because so-called civilization wants oil, coal, rubber, iron. And so-called savagery does not see the necessity of being ruthlessly slaughtered to furnish" these commodities. Dunbar-Nelson's pacifism and anti-imperialism, contemporaneous with Garveyite and black radical anticolonialism, marked a departure from the militarism that for many had epitomized black progress since the Civil War. In the same editorial, she proclaimed that "now is about the time for the Negro to make his choice, whether he will join the ranks of the unthinking multitude who know not what they do, but will bring disaster upon the heads of their children—or of the true patriots, who will aim to keep the keel of the ship of state steady and true."[29]

Dunbar-Nelson and the New Negro Renaissance

Dunbar-Nelson's diary also coincides with the black literary and cultural movement that contemporaries dubbed the "New Negro renaissance." The massive exodus of southern blacks to northern cities like Harlem provided the basis for a resurgence of race-consciousness among black intellectuals. Bitter political rivals—Garvey, the silver-tongued socialist A. Philip Randolph, and even the apolitical godfather of black art and culture, Alain Locke—all waged a tug of war over the term "New Negro." While Garveyites and contributors to the black socialist magazine the *Messenger* spoke of the New Negro masses' militancy, Locke and others used the term to refer to an integrationist, middle-class cultural and artistic movement based in Harlem. The black journalist Lester A. Walton summed up Locke's vision when he asserted in 1925 that "art is slowly but surely knitting a closer kinship between white and colored Americans." Here was racial uplift ideology's old ideal of interracial cooperation, in a new setting, perhaps, but still solidly bourgeois in character.[30]

The historian David Lewis has noted that the emphasis placed on black artistic and cultural endeavors by men like James Weldon Johnson and Alain Locke reflected the extent that conventional politics was perceived as a dead end for black leadership. But for better or worse, culture has its political implications, and accordingly, Locke, Johnson, and others who promoted the contributions of black art and literature to American civilization were, in effect, reformulating uplift's sense of the mutuality of black elites and masses by stressing a symbiotic relationship between black folk culture and the Negro artist. It was a strategy which marginalized rival anticolonial diasporic articulations of New Negro militancy.[31] Black magazines, including the *Crisis* and *Opportunity*, sponsored literary prizes for black writers, some of them funded by the numbers racketeer Casper Holstein, in his own bid for respectability. Such prizes facilitated contacts between black writers and white literati and publishers in the 1920s. While her husband Robert waited for his political ship to come in, Dunbar-Nelson was generally receptive to the view of literary production as a forum for race-conscious protest activity and progress. Accordingly, she kept up her newspaper columns to maintain public visibility as a social commentator, literary critic, and potential contributor to the New Negro renaissance.[32]

What probably remained unknown to many of her readers was that she herself had pursued a literary career since the 1890s, prior to her marriage with Dunbar. She published *Violets and Other Tales*, a book of poems, short stories, and essays, in 1895, and *The Goodness of St. Rocque*, a volume of short stories, in 1898. Although she left behind many unpublished manuscripts, her diary suggests that financial pressures, combined with her housekeeping duties, prevented her from fulfilling her literary aspirations.

Dunbar-Nelson's literary and aesthetic values reveal the divided outlook of one who maintained an ambivalent attitude toward the profound cultural shifts in American life she had witnessed. Victorian sexual mores and ideals of the work ethic and self-control were being supplanted by a consumer culture and a sexual openness that were thriving by the 1920s. Dunbar-Nelson clearly sympathized with the growing independence of women in politics, education, employment, and fashion. She campaigned for women's suffrage. The diary reveals that she was an avid consumer of motion pictures, frequented department stores to treat herself to new hats and dresses, and remained, with her husband and friends, an unrepentant violator of prohibition. Still, she remained uneasy about the permissiveness of her society, and occasionally castigated herself—"I'm a shiftless colored woman," she wrote in her diary—for failing to live up to work ethic ideals.[33] Her literary and aesthetic tastes were modeled on Victorian standards of moral uplift and respectability. She commended Rudolph Fisher for showing in his novel *Walls of Jericho* (published in 1928) that "one does not have to wallow in filth to write about . . . Harlem," and she vehemently objected to modernist styles of abstract art like cubism. Like Du Bois, Dunbar-Nelson was guided by moral uplift values in her quest for a subtle and effective merger of what many perceived to be the polar opposites of art and politics, or racial propaganda. She believed that an ennobling literature devoted to black middle-class expression and concerns was more representative, and thus preferable, to portrayals of Harlem "low-life." Nonetheless, she praised the white writer Carl Van Vechten's highly controversial novel *Nigger Heaven*, published in 1926, and recommended that it be read in conjunction with its forgotten precursor, Dunbar's *Sport of the Gods*.[34]

Like those who believed in the elevating potential of bourgeois culture, Dunbar-Nelson also sought to enact her integrationist vision of racial progress through blacks' mastery of the fine arts. Of the black painter Laura

Wheeler, Dunbar-Nelson commented that "she gets at the heart of our people, delving down deep below the superficial gayety of the surface down to the sorrow-laden heart of a race." Joining those who believed in the redemptive, antiracist impact of beauty, she advocated the revival of the Negro spirituals, noting that "it is the music in our race that makes us great artists in other lines," and she praised such black concert soloists as Roland Hayes, Paul Robeson, Marian Anderson, and Jules Bledsoe. In 1929 she called attention to a performance by Bledsoe opposite a white *Aida*, which in failing to excite controversy, moved her to pronounce the event "a triumph of the Negro in art."[35] After the disappointments of the war and the failure of the Dyer bill, black achievements in the arts and literature were, it seemed, the last, best hope for shattering racial boundaries and removing obstacles to the success and status of the black intelligentsia. In this, there was certainly an aspect of the ambitious American artist's anxious relation to European culture and art. But among black Americans, this strategy was well within the class-bound uplift tradition by which blacks took up the burden of proving themselves, asserting both cultural distinctiveness and universality by mastering the elite culture of European civilization. This outlook was uppermost in Dunbar-Nelson's literary aspirations and efforts, expressed in the poetry she wrote steadily throughout the 1920s.

Her literary aspirations within the New Negro renaissance do not fully explain why she was moved to write poetry. Dunbar-Nelson sought in her poetry more than just the fame of a published poet. Indeed, as with much poetry, her verse provided a crucial outlet for the creativity and impassioned expression that her circumstances often denied her. Her poetry, like her diary, reflected the contradictions of her life. Many of her poems convey the popular romantic ideal of poetry as a form for the expression of intense, intimate feelings, with imagery and symbolism drawn from nature and affirmations of life and love. Edna St. Vincent Millay's love sonnets were perhaps a model for her poetry;[36] more certain is Dunbar-Nelson's enthusiasm for the verse of her friend, Georgia Douglas Johnson, whom Hull calls "the most popular Black woman poet of the 1920s."[37] A select few of Dunbar-Nelson's poems were meant only for her loved one's eyes. She wrote in her diary of sending sonnets, no longer extant, dedicated to her women lovers.[38]

Dunbar-Nelson's writing repeatedly tested the conventional distinction between public and private life so crucial to uplift ideology and its desire for representations of black respectability. Her class aspirations, combined with the period's literary standards of social realism, prompted Dunbar-Nelson to aestheticize the stark realities she faced. Her "social" poems, I would argue, were just as much a vehicle for the expression of suppressed personal longings and social anxieties as her love poems. Indeed, there was a direct, though complex, relationship between her material deprivation, her bourgeois aesthetics, her status anxieties and lack of public acclaim, and her desire for women. The latter was forbidden within a repressive society that for its women, enforced standards of compulsory heterosexuality. Thus, just as her diary provided an outlet for feelings of despair she could safely confide to no one, her relationships with women served a crucial function of providing the emotional support, romance, and pleasure that her circumstances often withheld from her. But because of the enormous risks of conducting affairs with women within this context of patriarchal support of women within marriage (her diary recounts the bitter divorce of one of her lovers), she endured painful separations from one of her lovers, with little hope of maintaining the relationship.[39]

Her ambivalent, assimilationist literary values found their counterpart in her political attitudes about racial uplift. While she was committed to public service and leadership within the black community, she also used her newspaper columns to promote interracial cooperation as a strategy toward racial equality and social reform. In a 1928 column, Dunbar-Nelson said that the idea of interracial cooperation had gained momentum since "the historic meeting of the white and colored women at Tuskegee in 1920, and the furor which it created." The column appeared during the National Interracial Conference at Howard University, which Dunbar-Nelson and her husband attended. Her support for reform organizations that bridged the racial divide did not prevent Dunbar-Nelson from acknowledging the difficulty of achieving mutual understanding at such gatherings. After a meeting of the Interracial Council of the Federal Council of Church Women in 1928, Dunbar-Nelson pointed out that "it was the colored women . . . who kept the discussions on a frank and open plane; who struggled hardest to prevent the conference from degenerating into a sentimental mutual admiration society, and who insisted that all is not right and perfect in this country of ours."[40]

Dunbar-Nelson struggled to remain committed to her work with the American Interracial Peace Committee. Initially a volunteer, she later drew a part-time salary as liaison to the black community, charged with recruiting, lecturing, fundraising, and on top of these, secretarial duties. Her diary enabled her to unburden her feelings of anger and frustration over internecine battles for status and authority, and over being unappreciated by her superiors. As a salaried worker, drawing a "pitiful $2000" in 1929, her status did not improve greatly. When a benefit concert she had organized failed to raise the expected amount, the committee's black chairman, Leslie Pinckney Hill, blamed Dunbar-Nelson in a "stormy" meeting. Hill "politely and subtly said I was inefficient, inept, etc. I almost burst with rage. . . . Wish I had another job." While it is not always clear how accurate Dunbar-Nelson's perceptions of herself and others were, more certain is that there were few settings, public or private, in which she had sufficient power and freedom to act independently of others, whether they were co-workers, social acquaintances, or family members.[41]

Sex and Color Revisited: Passing

Throughout her diary, Dunbar-Nelson provides evidence of the color line that existed within the black middle class itself, a topic that received considerable public debate and literary attention during the 1920s as "passing." By this time, with urbanization and the relative anonymity of cities, persons of black ancestry who passed for white had become a social phenomenon; Dunbar-Nelson estimated that twenty thousand blacks passed each year. The discourse surrounding passing in the 1920s was quite different from its earlier version of the 1890s when, in much of the racial uplift literature, black characters who were white in appearance routinely chose to identify with black people to affirm racial solidarity.[42]

For whites, passing, or what historian Joel Williamson referred to as "invisible blackness," raised the spectre of unwitting black genetic invasion.[43] For those nominal blacks who passed, it was the ultimate escape from a society structured on ideologies of racial difference, and an escape from the segregated black world, as well. It should be noted that there were degrees of passing. Many passed opportunistically, as Dunbar-Nelson occasionally did, to bypass public Jim Crow restrictions, indulging a fleeting, private transgression against racial barriers. In extremely rare cases, one might pass in the service of race partisanship, as Walter White did in his risky undercover sleuthing to gain intelligence on southern lynchings for the NAACP. And it was not unheard of, though equally rare, for darker blacks to "pass," as Mary Church Terrell recalled of one man who donned white robes, proclaimed himself a Hindu, and saw his social options enhanced. For many, however, passing violated the ideals of racial solidarity that the black middle class sought to promote through racial uplift ideology. Indeed, among blacks, passing turned a harsh light on the extent to which color served as a criterion for class differentiation, as degrees of whiteness in appearance held value as a sign of privilege. In the 1920s, especially within the nationalistic Garvey movement, passing was usually regarded as a betrayal, an abandonment of the race, particularly when it involved "black" women. Although her own race loyalty was never publicly questioned, Dunbar-Nelson herself admitted somewhat sheepishly in her diary to have passed as white out of convenience, as when she toured the South on a Jim Crow train during a speaking tour.[44]

Passing generated such intense debate among blacks in this period because it dramatized the unsettling juncture of race, sexuality, and class. For those willing to accept its risks, including the possibility, as Terrell noted, that one's children could become antiblack racists, passing created more economic and social opportunities, and a surer path to wealth and status, than did work in elite race organizations.[45] Passing not only defied the racial classifications that organized social relations but also thwarted blacks' efforts to assign or withhold bourgeois status within the group. To be sure, many blacks saw passing as an act of betrayal and complicity in a racist social order (and in this connection it is interesting to note that "to pass" is also a black expression for death). Still, those blacks who "passed" over to the other side not only transgressed "whiteness" as a viable legal racial classification, but also, concomitantly, racial uplift ideology's self-serving, inconsistent declarations of altruism and racial solidarity, and its internalization of racist and patriarchal values as, paradoxically, signs of status among blacks.

One of the primary motives for passing was marriage "outside the race." Thus, when fair black men and women passed, they were removing themselves from a partly status-driven marriage market among blacks. However imperceptible and individualistic passing was, it also defied widespread attempts to fix blacks in a socially subordinate "place." To manage its troubling implications, many blacks, like some white southerners, claimed the ability to detect others who were "passing," believing that they were not so easily deceived as many oblivious whites were on this matter. Although some might have regarded the ability as a natural talent, such powers of discernment were in fact encouraged by a social formation in which relative white appearance held potential rewards. It was also a matter of one's position within the color hierarchy, as mulattoes and lighter complexioned blacks unable to pass for white may well have been more preoccupied with the matter of passing than darker complexioned blacks.

For Dunbar-Nelson, passing triggered ambivalent feelings of guilt, betrayal, and alienation even as it conferred social advantages. It was yet another of many situations occasioning reflection on the complexity, and situational nature of black subjectivity, which refused to sit still for racial uplift ideology's attempts to stabilize black identity. Generally, she publicly condemned the practice: she compared the Republican Party's abandonment of blacks to "the fair colored person who 'passes for white,' and is most bitter in his denunciation and renunciation of his erstwhile friends." But in her review of white author Vera Caspery's novel *The White Girl*, she commended the portrayal of a black woman passing for white. Dunbar-Nelson remarked that the book was perceptive and realistic in its observation of the knowing, judgmental gaze by black men that took the specific form of a desire to reclaim black women sexually for "the race." This novel, she felt, was honest in explaining its protagonist's behavior not in terms of race loyalty, but simply for practical economic reasons. She referred to the novel's heroine as "a true modern, without so-called racial superstition." Dunbar-Nelson's equanimity on the subject may have served as a partial rebuttal to those who were quick to denounce black women who passed for white (and married outside the race) as traitors.[46]

The climate of literary realism doubtless enabled Dunbar-Nelson's even-handed discussion of passing, but national trends of racial polarization made hers a minority viewpoint. As passing defied dominant assumptions of racial difference, it invariably provoked white anxieties around questions of racial purity, marriage, reproductive sexuality, and inheritance. In 1926, these matters became the subject of scandal with the Rhinelander case. Leonard "Kip" Rhinelander, the scion of a wealthy New York family, sued his wife, Alice Jones, for divorce after learning that she was a black woman. The sensational trial, during which Mrs. Rhinelander was required to strip naked to the waist so the jury could determine whether Rhinelander could have known that she was black, was widely covered in the New York press, which cast Mrs. Rhinelander in the role of seductress. The *Crisis* editorialized that the racially naïve Rhinelander was forced to seek the divorce by his humiliated family. The Garveyite *Negro World* drew from the controversy the moral that inter-marriage was wrong. The court granted the divorce, and a settlement was paid to the former Mrs. Rhinelander.[47]

The Rhinelander case was also a lightning rod for concerns within the black middle class over racial identity and the imperative to ensure its own reproduction. Of course, this connection between racial identity and the reproductive sexuality of black women applied to all black women, not solely those light enough to pass. Kelly Miller, the Howard University professor, advocated traditional uplift values of motherhood as a racial duty to prevent race suicide. Miller's outlook, published in the *Negro World*, was rooted in evolutionary and eugenic theory, and indicated the convergence of black nationalism and racial uplift ideology on matters of race and reproduction. This was partly a response to declining black fertility rates in cities since the turn of the century, as black women and families increasingly exercised birth control for economic reasons.[48] The continued influence of evolutionary discourse among black commentators as a perceived source of cultural authority, however, finds no clearer illustration than in the fact that Alice Dunbar-Nelson reiterated Miller's argument. The survival of the "more cultured and . . . leisure classes" of blacks was imperiled by the falling birthrate among the race. Dunbar-Nelson earnestly felt that the problem was worth "the attention of the Negro woman." She saw the growing numbers of wage-earning black women diminishing the ranks of the race's mothers and children: "No race will amount to anything economically, no matter how high the wages it collects nor how many commercial enterprises it supports, whose ownership of homes has not kept proportionate pace with its business holdings."[49]

Dunbar-Nelson was drawing on the sociological discourse of urban pathology that measured black progress by conformity to the patriarchal family as the respectable race norm. This literature had its origins in the guarded response of black elites to urban migration. As we have seen, anxieties over urban migration often lingered on the image of the single black woman in the city.[50] Such an outlook reflected a partial internalization of racial and sexual stereotypes that branded black women outside marriage and the family as promiscuous, or potentially criminal. Such uneasiness certainly did not consider that, as Darlene Clark Hine has suggested, black women migrated to cities seeking not only economic opportunity, but also to escape the sexual exploitation of concubinage endemic within the sharecropping system.[51]

What is striking about the tension between black women's active public presence and their perceived reproductive and domestic roles is the concern for women's "place." Within uplift, black women cannot exist for themselves, but only insofar as they serve the utilitarian project of race building. That Dunbar-Nelson, who, incidentally, never had children, could endorse these views, indicates the status benefits of voicing them. Dunbar-Nelson's public and private writings, taken together, provide an example of the deference and dissemblance uplift ideology imposed upon black women. Her views on black women's reproduction also suggest the degree to which many advocates of racial uplift, even someone as critical of its ideals as Dunbar-Nelson, might nonetheless cling to outmoded, if not oppressive, ideas. Such antimodernism, expressed in the historical lag that was common to much of racial uplift ideology, was rooted in the class aspirations of its exponents, and in the equation of the patriarchal family with respectability and bourgeois stability.

The impulse to direct the matrimonial and reproductive choices of black women worked in two directions. In addition to enjoining black women to marry within the race, the ideology also served to determine whom, among blacks, a lighter complexioned black woman should *not* marry for fear of jeopardizing her own class status. This situation found poignant documentation in Dunbar-Nelson's diary in the experience of a longtime Wilmington friend, Arleon Bowser, whose family forbade her romance with a local minister because of his dark complexion. Though certainly not the stuff of the public discourse of racial uplift, such incidents were common enough among those blacks who associated color with status. When Bowser had a nervous breakdown in 1929, a distraught Dunbar-Nelson attributed it to this youthful trauma: "What caused it? Sex frustration? . . . Far better that she married Isaacs, or committed fornication with [others]."[52]

The matter of black women's status being dictated by men extended beyond the family into the public world of employment opportunities.[53] Dunbar-Nelson, like other assertive black women leaders, frequently pointed out the expectations of deferential self-sacrifice imposed on black women within the black community, despite their often considerable public accomplishments. Black women's prescribed role within uplift was no different from what was widely expected of white women. If black women managed to escape their idealized sphere within the home as mothers and homemakers, it was often to perform unpaid and anonymous organizational work within male-headed institutions like churches, homes, hospitals, schools, and charities. For women with leadership aspirations like Dunbar-Nelson, assumptions of male privilege were a constant source of frustration. Sometimes, the male leaders black women had to contend with were white, ensuring that little opportunity existed for them to move up in the administrative hierarchy. Generally, however autocratic the male leadership, gender and class conflicts within black institutions were neutralized by an ethos of service, which tended to place black women at the center of their communities, making them less aware of their subservient status in a male-dominated world. In the black church, for example, as Sharon Harley has pointed out, many black women undoubtedly regarded their volunteer organizational labor in broader terms as community service. Darlene Clark Hine has also brought to light the often unsung organizational and fundraising work performed by black community women, as in the building of the new Frederick Douglass Memorial Hospital and Nurse Training School in Philadelphia, in 1908. Such institution building, Hine argues, brought black women a sense of empowerment, and their gifts of time, effort, and funds, freely given, were hardly seen as exploitation. This premium on often unpaid domestic work, projected into the public sphere of black institutions, was to many blacks, men and women, far more preferable to the individualistic image of the independent, wage-earning black woman.[54]

It is clear from her diary that uplift ideals of altruistic service and sacrifice did not always provide Dunbar-Nelson with the fulfillment she sought. After speaking at a church in West Philadelphia, she recorded in her diary that it was the "usual 'cullud' affair. Freebies as usual. [The church paid] My expenses. That's all. The older I grow and the more I do, the cheaper I get." Although Dunbar-Nelson could publicly exalt the duty of motherhood over wage earning, she clearly sought more recognition and remuneration for her speaking engagements. When black women did manage to attract public notice, it often focused on the "abnormality" or undesirability of their behavior. In her diary, Dunbar-Nelson wrote of a posed newspaper photograph recording her presence in a black delegation visiting President Warren Harding at the White House in 1921, which sought to secure his condemnation of Ku Klux Klan terrorism. The picture shows seventeen members of the delegation, which included three women. Dunbar-Nelson can be seen slightly left of the photograph's center; the other two women can be seen on the right. "I have heard a dozen comments to the effect that I am alone in a bunch of men, and not in the vicinity of the other two women."[55]

The powerlessness and isolation that made Dunbar-Nelson's diary a rare outlet for expressing anger and other forbidden thoughts applied to the black elite, as well. The schism between uplift's public face of propriety and its potentially explosive private anger is evident from Dunbar-Nelson's lengthy account of the delegation to visit Harding. Harding stunned the group with his assertion that Klan attacks were not aimed at blacks. Afterward, Dunbar-Nelson recorded that Lincoln Johnson, the district recorder of deeds, and the poet Georgia's husband, called Harding "that lying nigger in the White House," an allusion to racist rumors spread during Harding's campaign by opponents that he had black ancestry. "Funny how the general disgust at the president among our folks in Washington has resulted in calling him nigger openly," Dunbar-Nelson mused, searching for some humor in an impossible situation.[56]

It somehow seems inadequate to claim that Dunbar-Nelson lived a double life within the black middle class. As a race woman who sometimes passed for white, who lived a life of genteel poverty, who chafed at the respect the world gave her only as Paul Laurence Dunbar's widow (especially when black audiences demanded that she recite his dialect poems, which she hated), and who secretly treasured her affairs with women as she "passed" for a heterosexual, the tensions of her inner life were many. Although Dunbar-Nelson's diary gathers increased personal and emotional immediacy as it proceeds (answering, as Gloria T. Hull has argued, a generally unfulfilled longing for personal truth and disclosure), this process of self-revelation itself against internalized forces of repression remained a struggle.

Dunbar-Nelson stoically bore her private doubts and fears. Her experience confirms the extent to which many blacks espoused middle-class values almost as a prayer for social mobility and the security of bourgeois status. In a segregated society that severely restricted black opportunities, assimilationist uplift ideals often brought only disappointment and alienation. Dunbar-Nelson often found herself materially no better off than those blacks she felt she was destined to serve in a spirit of noblesse oblige.

Booker T. Washington's famous appeal to industrialists in 1895 that they "cast down their bucket" to provide employment to black workers adrift in the stormy seas of the post-Reconstruction South is an apt, ironic image with which to conclude this chapter. Seeking to fill the void of black leadership left by Frederick Douglass's recent death, Washington implied that blacks had been thrown overboard by Douglass's proverbial sheltering ship—the Republican Party. But the titanic contradictions of the uplift ideology that accompanied Washington's rise to prominence as the acknowledged leader of the race proved a leaky vessel for black aspirations. By the 1920s, it had become painfully apparent to Alice Dunbar-Nelson that she could hardly be expected to uplift her race while struggling to keep her own head above water.

9

HUBERT H. HARRISON, NEW NEGRO MILITANCY,

AND THE LIMITS OF RACIALIZED LEADERSHIP, 1914–1954

> [Garvey's] claim to be recorded in history lies in the fact that
> he attracted a larger following than any Negro . . . in modern
> times. Negroes here and there have been hailed as leaders . . .
> but a thorough analysis of these famous Negro leaders will dis-
> close the fact that they owed their prominence mainly to
> white men who considered such spokesmen as those persons
> through whom they could work to keep the Negro in his place.
>
> CARTER G. WOODSON, 1940

❨ ❨ ❨

The manifold contradictions of uplift ideology, as lived by Alice Dunbar-
Nelson and others, were further accentuated by social developments and
popular awakenings that black leaders could not ignore, or resist as easily as
in the past. The triumph of Bolshevism in Russia, the democratic ideals of
World War I, and the anticolonial implications of Woodrow Wilson's Fourteen Points, along with the mass migration of African Americans cityward,
had all created the conditions for more militant "New Negro" intellectuals
and leadership. The spirit of the New Negro was enhanced considerably by
the arrival of black immigrants from the West Indies, including such intellectuals as Hubert H. Harrison. These intellectuals bypassed the barren
racialism of civilizationist ideology, bringing an international, diasporic, and
progressive socialist perspective on domestic race relations and the study of
African American culture and history.

Racial uplift ideology and its assumptions could not keep pace with whirlwind forces of change. Black soldiers' service in World War I itself did little
to improve the political status of African Americans, but the war provided the
stimulus for the mass migration that fashioned a socially ambitious and increasingly culturally diverse black industrial proletariat. Between 1914 and
1920 an estimated 400,000 to 1 million blacks left the South to work in
northern industries, filling a labor shortage created by the war's restriction of

immigration. Defense industries had recruited blacks, but another strong inducement to quit the South for the "promised land" came from the *Chicago Defender*, which was distributed throughout the region. The *Defender* printed letters such as this one from a migrant who had settled in Philadelphia. With the taste of freedom still sweet, he movingly described his escape from unpaid labor and the demeaning customs of Jim Crow. Still, he admitted to homesickness, and his sense of expanded horizons included a willingness to join the war effort:

> I do feel so fine . . . with the aid of God I am making very good I make $75 per month. . . . I don't have to work hard. [D]ont have to mister every little white boy comes along. I havent heard a white man call a colored a nigger . . . since I been in the state of Pa. I can ride in the electric street and steam cars any where I can get a seat. . . . I am not crazy about being with white folks, but if I have to pay the same fare I have learn[ed] to want the same accommodation. And if you are first in a place shopping you dont have to wait until the white folks get through tradeing. [Y]et amid all this I shall ever love the good old South and I am praying that God may give every well wisher a chance to be a man regardless of his color, and if my going to the front would bring about such conditions I am ready any day. . . . [T]he kids are in school every day.[1]

The magnitude of this social transformation and its effect on popular black aspirations cannot be overemphasized. Along with other conservative southern black elites, Sutton E. Griggs, the Baptist minister and novelist from Memphis, attempted to discourage the black exodus northward. Such a position was no doubt influenced by the spread of racial violence and a fear of further confrontations after riots in East St. Louis in 1917 and, two years later, in Washington, D.C., and Chicago, the latter two occasions notable for the organized self-defense waged by blacks. Black support for the war effort was unavailing as 1918 saw a continued onslaught of lynchings. The NAACP termed events in Georgia during that May a "lynching orgy," as mobs claimed eleven victims in the span of several days, including Mary Turner, who, according to Walter White, was in the eighth month of pregnancy. In the *Crisis*, White reported the "revolting" details of her death "with reluctance": Turner was hung upside-down from a tree, set afire, and "while she was yet alive," her abdomen was cut open, the unborn child falling from her womb to the ground. "The infant, prematurely born, gave two feeble cries and then," according to White, "its head was crushed by a member of the mob with his heel." According to grisly custom, hundreds of shots were then fired into Turner's lifeless body. The lynchings followed a dispute between a sharecropper and his landlord over wages that ended in the landlord's death. By

July, President Woodrow Wilson had condemned lynching, but made it clear that the federal government would do nothing to punish those responsible or to protect blacks in the future. After the armistice, returning black soldiers became targets of mob violence.[2]

The background for the violence was a rise in labor disputes with land-owners and employers and the federal government's campaign of repression against organized labor and radical activities. In 1919, a black organizer for the Industrial Workers of the World (IWW), Benjamin Fletcher, was arrested under the wartime Sedition Act and sentenced to ten years in jail. The *Messenger*, the black socialist magazine based in Harlem, reported that "one of the chief plutocratic mouthpieces of the country," the *Providence Journal*, warned its readers of a closer relationship between Negro workers and white unionists, which, if successful, "would dominate the politics and policies of the entire country." In this climate, conservative black leadership was at pains to make its class sympathies clear. But Fred Moore, editor of the New York *Age*, made more enemies than allies when he claimed that the "representative Negro does not approve of radical socialistic outbursts, such as calling upon the Negroes to defend themselves against the whites." The postwar violence and social discord led one Tuskegee appointee to wonder "why we, as a race, must lay down, and become submissive forever. . . . [E]ver since we have been chasing this will-o-wisp money, we have been losing rights and privileges in city after city." Black migrants, soldiers, and even college students were redefining uplift as agitation and were not to be so easily controlled or spoken for.[3]

Harrison and other black intellectuals, including A. Philip Randolph, Carter G. Woodson, Langston Hughes, Nella Larsen, and E. Franklin Frazier, were critical of accommodationist black leadership. They were the product of a new historical conjuncture heading into the Depression era, characterized by white violence and southern intransigence, certainly, but also several forms of interracial cooperation. These included the convergence of New Negro militancy and cultural radicalism, a growing alliance between blacks and organized labor during the Depression, and the mobilization of black and white left-wing activity from such crises as the Scottsboro case in Alabama.[4] This interracial cooperation, joining race and class struggles, produced a high pitch of contestation among black leadership.

Hubert H. Harrison was one of the more significant contributors to the progressive "New Negro" militancy of the years immediately following the war. Harrison contributed mightily to the increased diversity of black thought in the 1920s, especially its militancy. The wartime rhetoric of world democracy and national self-determination sparked the formation of nationalist organizations and pressure groups such as Harrison's short-lived Liberty League, founded in 1917; the African Blood Brotherhood, the socialist anti-Garveyite black nationalist organization founded by Cyril Briggs in 1918;

and the International League of Darker Peoples (which included the cosmetics tycoon Madame C. J. Walker and Rev. Adam Clayton Powell Sr., pastor of Harlem's Abyssinian Baptist Church) the next year. Along with Du Bois and the NAACP, these organizations sought a role for black Americans in the postwar negotiations that would determine the future of Germany's African colonies. Others criticized older, more staid black leadership, and fused economic and race issues. A. Philip Randolph, editor of the *Messenger*, provided a forum for such leading young intellectuals as E. Franklin Frazier, and was organizing the Brotherhood of Sleeping Car Porters, which, upon its recognition in 1925 by the American Federation of Labor (AFL), would make him among the more influential black leaders. The NAACP was compelled to respond to the wave of labor insurgency, often met with brutal repression, that swept the South in 1919. In Elaine, Arkansas, sharecroppers' attempts to organize left at least twenty-five black men murdered. That same year, a white professor published a survey of militant opinion culled from black newspapers. Many editors heralded the advent of the postwar New Negro. Others denounced the recent outbreaks of white violence in Chicago and Washington, D.C., and demanded "an eye for an eye" through armed self-defense.[5]

Race riots, lynching, and antilabor violence surely contributed to New Negro militant consciousness. But so did black social advances in higher education and the professions. Citing Carter Woodson's research, David Lewis estimated that the most privileged African American professionals numbered about 10,000, including 1,748 doctors, 1,230 lawyers, and 2,131 academics and administrators, the remainder to be found in business, banking, and commerce. In addition, college enrollment among blacks was on the rise. According to Lewis, in 1917 there were 2,132 African Americans in college; a decade later there were 13,580, with 200 to 300 in white institutions. The continued promotion by philanthropic bodies of vocational training meant chronic insolvency for such holdouts for liberal arts training as Atlanta and Lincoln Universities. By contrast, Hampton Institute boasted an endowment of $8.5 million, seventeenth among U.S. colleges in 1925. The paternalism of black college administrations and white philanthropic boards sparked campus protests at Fisk, Hampton, and Howard Universities. In the militant spirit of the "New Negro," angry students rejected the disciplinary, pietistic emphasis of black colleges, which to them came at the expense of quality education and professional training.[6]

A critical phase of black professionalization was the development of African American lawyers, a necessity in the struggle against the political and economic abuses of Jim Crow. In the post-Reconstruction South, the legal profession was effectively closed to blacks, with many of the few southern black attorneys, including John R. Lynch, Charles Chesnutt, D. A. Straker, and George White, joining the out-migration. In 1910, at the genesis of the

NAACP, of the nation's 114,000 lawyers, only 795, or .7 percent, were African American. The growth in the profession occurred largely in the North and West; after 1910, the number of black lawyers in the South declined for the next thirty years. Charles Houston, the Harvard-educated dean of the Howard Law School, found that of the few successful black lawyers practicing during the first quarter of the twentieth century, virtually none were involved in civil rights litigation, and few could claim expertise in constitutional law. Thus, the NAACP initially relied on such distinguished white attorneys as Moorfield Storey, Louis Marshall, and Clarence Darrow, although these men often worked in concert with black lawyers or followed in the wake of legal challenges against segregation initiated by such black attorneys as Baltimore's W. Ashbie Hawkins. Houston would be responsible for training at Howard a generation of black lawyers committed to the struggle for integration, including Thurgood Marshall.[7]

The training of black lawyers was solidly in the more group-oriented uplift tradition of socially responsible education. But new paths of struggle taken by black lawyers were made possible by more radical trends in black thought. Postwar radicalism in black thought owed much to Harrison, who was also known as the Black Socrates. Harrison, who was born on St. Croix, in the Danish Virgin Islands in 1883, taught school there before working his way to Europe as a ship's cabin boy with a group of science students, during 1899, pausing briefly to study at the University of Copenhagen. Largely self-taught, he slept little, reading widely on a variety of subjects. Orphaned and left penniless, Harrison migrated to the United States in 1900 and finished his secondary education at De Witt Clinton High School. Around 1906 he achieved a perfect score on his civil service examination, worked at the post office in New York City, and began working as a free-lance journalist. After he publicly criticized Booker T. Washington, Harrison, by now a contributor to the socialist organ, *Masses*, was dismissed from his post office job in 1911 after Charles Anderson pulled a few strings.[8] "The only outlet for his talent, ambition, sympathy and deep sense of justice," according to J. A. Rogers, who could have said the same of most black intellectuals, "seemed to lie in concentration on the problems affecting himself and his people."[9]

Harrison joined the Socialist Party and taught briefly at P.S. 89 in New York City before committing himself fully to black politics and journalism. Claude McKay referred to him as the black hope of the Socialists. Harrison had endorsed the syndicalism of the IWW. He worked with Elizabeth Gurley Flynn and William Haywood organizing strikes in New Jersey's silk mills. Harrison is credited with broad influence within interracial radical and reform circles in New York. At a pacifist mass meeting he shared the platform with, among others, an IWW representative and Alice Dunbar-Nelson, who uncharitably described him as a "polysyllabic monkey chaser," using the

African American epithet for West Indians. McKay and Harold Cruse note that Harrison moved among white Greenwich Village cultural radicals, including the Marxist scholar and editor V. F. Calverton. The novelist Henry Miller had lavish praise for Harrison's forensic abilities: "With a few well-directed words he had the ability to demolish any opponent . . . neatly and smoothly, too—'with kid gloves.'" Yet Harrison grew increasingly disillusioned with the Socialists' failure to address the race question. A volume of editorials from his magazine the *Voice*, published in 1917 as *The Negro and the Nation*, documents his alienation from the Socialists and his departure from the party. In subsequent writings, Harrison, unlike A. Philip Randolph and Chandler Owen, editors of the *Messenger*, emphasized "Race First" black nationalism over a doctrinaire, color-blind Marxism.[10]

Harrison staked out a middle ground between the *Messenger's* reductionist class analysis and the racialism of Marcus Garvey. In 1916, he created a public forum in Harlem for discussion on wide ranging topics, a space where the New Negro philosophy and politics might be refined. Harrison was the prototype of the Harlem soapbox street corner orator immortalized by Ralph Ellison in *Invisible Man*. A fixture at the corner of Lenox (now Malcolm X) Avenue and 135th Street, Harrison held forth along with Randolph and other outdoor lecturers. His contacts were wide, including figures such as John Bruce, Arthur Schomburg, William Ferris, and other members of the black intelligentsia in Harlem. Harrison had a hand in the founding of the New York Public Library's Schomburg collection in 1925. He was also a leading member of a circle of radical West Indian intellectuals, including Cyril Briggs, W. A. Domingo, J. A. Rogers, Lovett Fort-Whiteman, and Claude McKay. Rogers claimed that Harrison's modern views "brought him much opposition. . . . The Negro preachers, and sometimes their white colleagues, objected to his theories on evolution—which were darwinian—and would summon the police to break up his meetings." Harrison had been a vocal opponent of W. E. B. Du Bois and the interracial NAACP, and had joined the chorus of condemnation for Du Bois's prowar editorial in the *Crisis*.[11]

As a journalist and spokesman for the short-lived Liberty League, founded to rival the NAACP, with its slogan, the "New Negro Manhood Movement," Harrison provided Garvey with one of his first opportunities to address an audience in the United States. Almost immediately, Harrison was overshadowed by Garvey's charisma and organizational success. Unable to secure financial assistance from the Socialist Party for his own newspaper venture, Harrison signed on as a contributing editor for Garvey's *Negro World*. It is difficult to assess the impact of Harrison's cosmopolitan brand of black nationalism, partly modeled, among other influences, on Irish nationalism and Zionism and on Garveyism and the *Negro World*. Garvey owed many, though clearly not all, of his political ideas to Harrison. It seems a curious turn of events that the socialist Harrison served in the Garvey movement. In Portia James's account of the internecine rivalry between pro- and anti-UNIA factions of the New Negro leftists in Harlem, Harrison appeared to be a member of both factions. While on the staff of the Negro World, he organized independent political organizations amongst black socialists. Harrison quickly abandoned hope of influencing Garvey when the latter began to negotiate with white supremacists.[12]

Although on the one hand Garvey's organization helped launch a global anticolonial movement, affirmed blackness, and created an institutional space for radical critiques such as Harrison's, on the other hand, Garvey's racialized rhetoric made a fetish of civilizationism and embraced the trappings of empire and even white supremacy. The movement was ultimately bigger than Garvey, as his anticolonial rhetoric thrilled African nationalist elites, and as Tony Martin has shown, the cultural and literary wing of the Garvey movement was more influential than those literary historians who have narrowly defined the period as the Harlem Renaissance have led us to believe.

Garvey's appeals for racial purity were praised by members of the resurgent Ku Klux Klan and Anglo-Saxon clubs. In this society structured by white dominance, the alliance between white supremacists and black separatists is the sort of interracial cooperation that occurs most effortlessly. White supremacists thrilled to the "Back to Africa" image of the movement, just as others had done since the founding of the American Colonization Society in 1816. Roi Ottley has convincingly suggested that Garvey's resentment of the privileged mulatto caste in Jamaica led him, like many immigrants, to impose his own cultural background on an unfamiliar American social landscape. This may partly explain Garvey's stubborn insistence that the Klan was "a better friend of the race than all the groups of hypocritical whites put together." This was all the *Messenger* needed to launch its "Garvey Must Go" campaign. Its editor, Randolph, dismissed Garvey's plan of African redemption through business enterprise as futile: "The whole scheme of a black empire, in the raging sea of imperialism would make it impossible to maintain power; nor would it bring liberation to Africa, for Negro exploiters and tyrants are as bad as white ones." Taking advantage of the rising aspirations and wage income of those urban blacks who did not escape the speculation mania of the 1920s, Garvey sold stock certificates for the Black Star Line, the capstone of his black business empire, whose name echoed that of the British shipping concern. As Judith Stein has shown, Garvey's racial appeals were ultimately rejected by the ambitious followers whose involvement lasted only as long as the venture appeared to be viable. Garvey attracted the apprehension of European colonial powers and authorities in the United States. In the wake of the suppression of civil liberties during and after the war, federal surveillance on Garvey and his activities was extensive, as race-conscious militancy was equated with subversive activity. The Black Star Line was an ill-fated venture, as his managers paid excessive amounts for unseaworthy ships. A federal investigation, with which Harrison and other disgruntled black social-ists cooperated, produced an indictment on charges of mail fraud. Garvey was convicted in 1923. His assistant and second wife, Amy Jacques Garvey, esti-mated that the movement had taken in $10 million between 1919 and 1921, running a deficit of $700,000 and leaving no assets. Garvey was pardoned in 1925 by President Calvin Coolidge and exiled to Jamaica.[13]

Still, while Garveyites spoke the conservative language of uplift and uni-versal progress, Harrison's work as a literary gatekeeper with Garvey's paper was an extension of his streetcorner lecturing and teaching activities. Harri-son's writings reflected the increasingly diverse nature of black thought within the pages of the *Negro World* and the vibrancy of black intellectual life in the 1920s that existed before and after Garvey's meteoric appearance.

Harrison and other radical black intellectuals in and out of the Garvey movement debunked the universalist assumptions of Western civilization that had been so central within uplift ideology. Black nationalists such as Harrison and Robert L. Poston shared their postwar disenchantment with the idea of civilization with readers of the *Negro World*. Poston articulated a position approaching romantic racial primitivism in his attack on "civilization [which] to me is not something to seek, but something to shun. . . . I do not love it. I hate it. I have no wish to preserve it." Poston predicted, or hoped, that the "warlike" white man, "more a machine than a human being," would eliminate himself with technological instruments of destruction. For Poston, civilization was not even a good idea, its saving grace being that "it has at least taught me to hate it, and that is in the direction of complete recovery." Un-like many of his contemporaries, and no doubt many of those who walk among us, Poston had arrived at a critical stance toward civilization as an ideo-logical category, the West's racist theodicy, or justification, for the atrocities of the slave trade and colonialism. The teleological, evolutionary view of up-lift toward so-called civilization was an obscenity that left Poston, Harrison, and many others cold amidst accounts of the carnage of trench warfare, and of the naked aggression of colonial rule.[14]

Paralleling Poston's process of mental decolonization, Harrison's own cri-tique of "white civilization" stressed its unenunciated racial content, exposing the fallacious universalism that others, such as Crummell and Ferris, had be-lieved in so strongly. This insight appears in a collection of his editorials penned during the postwar period that appeared in book form in 1920 under the title *When Africa Awakes*. In that book, Harrison noted a similar depen-dence of black leaders on Republican Party patronage, and debunked the longstanding myth of Abraham Lincoln as the Great Emancipator. With the latter, he anticipated the massive shift in the 1930s of national black electoral support away from the GOP. Reviving a radical current of black leadership, Harrison recommended third-party politics as the only path toward political independence for African Americans, a plan he sought to enact with the short-lived Liberty League. Backing up political organization with militant self-help, Harrison called for armed self-defense after what he called "the East St. Louis pogrom." Since the 1890s, if not before, such arguments, as we have seen, were not uncommon among black journalists: "If white men are to kill unoffending Negroes, Negroes must kill white men in defense of their lives and property." Short of violence, he also urged, as had Ida B. Wells, an economic boycott by black residents of the town's banks.[15]

Once a Socialist, and always cosmopolitan in his outlook and associations, Harrison stressed race consciousness as the best means to mobilize the black population. Unlike those who perceived race and class as mutually exclusive categories, Harrison insisted that black radicalism was, or ought to be, diverse and international, encompassing "agnostics, atheists, I.W.W.'s, socialists and even Bolshevists." He denounced those black leaders—"intellectual pimps"—within establishment organizations like the Republican Party, the Episcopal church, the Urban League and the U.S. Justice Department and Civil Service, which presumed to represent and speak for the race. Harrison situated his analysis of domestic racial conflicts within international affairs. He called for federal antilynching legislation and saw the war as the catalyst for a world movement of the darker races: "By virtue of its great advertising campaign for democracy and the promises which were held out to all subject peoples, [the war] fertilized the Race Consciousness of the Negro people into the stage of conflict with the dominant white idea of the Color Line."[16]

Harrison anticipated much of the best and worst of contemporary black nationalism. He was prescient in promoting race pride through the mass communications media, and through businesses which catered to black consumers. Harrison made several entrepreneurial attempts at black newspaper ventures. Along similar lines, he encouraged "New Negro business men" to merge personal ambition and racial welfare by marketing Negro dolls at more affordable prices. The failure to do this made it easier for black mothers to select cheaper white dolls for their children, with disastrous results for black consciousness. Harrison's race pride reflected popular trends in the 1920s. Scornful of those who believed racial advancement would only result from amalgamation, Harrison celebrated dark-skinned blacks like Toussaint L'Ouverture, Phillis Wheatley, Dunbar, and others as sources of race pride: "It gives us a hope nobler than the hope of amalgamation, whereby in order to become men, we must lose our racial identity." But the quest for political and cultural authenticity to replace civilizationist ideals and the longtime political alliance with the GOP could, at times, unleash the longstanding antimulatto tendencies of black nationalists who associated light complexion with sycophantic leadership. That quest might thus become misguided, producing a knee-jerk veneration of the likes of Paul Laurence Dunbar at the expense of, for example, the Washington, D.C., Presbyterian theologian (and son of a slave owner) Francis Grimké, solely on the basis of skin color. Presumably this excused the worst of Dunbar's "black exploitation" distillations of racist stereotypes. Such assertions of racial conservation are best understood as defensive responses to a racist culture. Harrison's inversion of white supremacist hierarchies was clearly intended to boost black pride. But while many doubtless found this gratifying, it bordered on an irrational politics of pigmentation based on an illusory conception of racial purity. Although black nationalism was far more than a matter of skin color, racism might disable blacks, as well as whites, from thinking clearly on such matters, and letting a biological concept of race color its evaluation of black leadership. In this respect, black nationalism was American to its core.[17]

Although critical of civilizationist ideology, Harrison shared the sentimental association of race progress with Victorian gender roles that nationalists, black and white, subscribed to. In the absence of political struggles, nationalistic objectives often incorporated the rhetoric of domesticity as essential to the imperatives of the nation-state. This has never been more true than recently, illustrated by the frequent references to the family in presidential State of the Union messages under Republican administrations. Black nationalists were similar with a difference, echoing the veneration of the patriarchal black family which remains central to black middle-class ideology. Where white nationalists invoke images of family and community to conjure the implied whiteness and moral authority of small town ideals against racialized conceptions of pathological inner cities, blacks' discussion of the family symbolized freedom and stability, and like other forms of hegemonic ideology, might be appropriated as an authorizing discourse employed as a shield against racism, functioning much as Christianity, patriotism, Islam, or homophobia would in other contexts.

Although Harrison shared with such traditional black nationalists as Griggs, Crummell, and Bruce a concern for protecting, providing for, and praising black women, this particular ideal did not seem as central to Harrison's thought than for the others. Harrison, and other commentators, sought a new standard of feminine beauty as part of the New Negro cultural aesthetic. In *When Africa Awakes*, the chivalrous Harrison rhapsodized the beauty and physical symmetry of black women rather than asserting, in the older, late-Victorian manner, their maternal duty and function within racial uplift, or calling for their protection from sexual exploitation. The orthodox position on the woman question was represented by Bruce: "The Negro homes of this land

244 HUBERT H. HARRISON

with their intelligent mothers, wives, sisters, to give inspiration and encouragement and hope to the men who are to represent and defend this race must of necessity play an important part in the development of the character and manhood and womanhood of the race."[18] Although Harrison may have agreed with this, he emphasized black women's beauty. Black women of all walks of life were attractive because "they dress well," exhibiting the taste of the best dressed Parisian women. Resorting to the color categorizations of black women that prevailed within the black community, and more important, rejecting white standards of feminine beauty, Harrison averred that white women didn't compare with the "dark browns, light-browns, peach-browns, or gold and bronze" colors among black women. "What say you brothers! Shall we not love her while she is among us? Shall we not bend the knee in worship and thank high heaven for the great good fortune that has given us such sisters and sweethearts, mothers and wives?" Harrison was expanding the definition of feminine beauty to include women of all complexions. His efforts along these lines were similar to those of Theophilous Lewis, the theater critic for the *Messenger*, who, according to Theodore Kornweibel, crusaded against the preference for light-skinned women in the choruses of black musical revues, and, incidentally, as marriage partners. According to Kornweibel, Lewis perceived that the problem was in a psychology rooted in slavery. Apparently there were limits to this challenge to color caste. Thomas Cripps noted that some independent films made for segregated black audiences in the 1920s tried to distribute dark and light complexions across the ranks of good and evil characters, but he nonetheless discerned "a light-skin bias toward the good guys," reflecting the white bias affecting black life. Light complexioned black men and women continued to be offered up by independent black filmmakers as idealized objects of visual pleasure and desire for black audiences. This did not escape the notice of the Garveyites, who condemned white idolatry in films.[19]

The somewhat limited character of Harrison's reflections on black women was doubtless conditioned by his view of power politics and worldly affairs as a male-dominated realm. His discussion of the necessity of education as a weapon against the parochialism of black leadership had little to say about black women. In any case, Harrison, in addressing "the young men of my race," took for granted the militancy of the Negro masses, a situation that required merely "GUIDANCE! Guidance, shaping and direction." He found much of the present Negro leadership hopelessly backward in its ignorance of the modern world of international labor problems, political economy, wars, and diplomacy. Harrison distanced himself from racial uplift ideology's tendency toward condescending vanguardism. Elsewhere, he claimed that the leadership of the New Negro would be "based not upon the ignorance of the masses, but upon their intelligence," and sought a higher intellectual standard of leadership that would not undermine mass aspirations and sentiments. Following Arthur Schomburg, and the pan-Africanist group of intellectuals of the American Negro Academy, he demanded that "courses in Negro history and the culture of West African peoples . . . should be given in every college that claims to be an institution of learning for Negroes." With the pugnacious and heroic rhetoric of nationalism, Harrison urged that young men take an irreverent approach to getting an education, in their striving "to give the gift of manhood to this race of ours."[20]

Harrison's career and writings were committed to shifting the terms of public discussion away from essentialist understandings of race. Although he catered to various gendered aspects of black nationalist discourse, Harrison's fundamental concern was with clearing away the rubble of bourgeois humanism, civilizationism, and racism to make way for historical materialism as a mode of analysis. In a 1926 essay titled "The Real Negro Problem," Harrison pursued a materialist analysis of the phenomenon, stressing its economic origins against the usual racial explanations. With the African slave trade, "contact of white with black," Harrison insisted, "was . . . established on the basis of the economic subjection of one to the other." Europeans "did not buy black slaves because [they] had a special hatred or contempt for anything black," nor because they believed in black inferiority. Slavery was an economic system, whose ruling class later imposed its self-serving ethics on the nation in the form of contempt for blacks. Attempts to regain control of black labor after emancipation, the political violence of the Reconstruction period, and the suppression of black politics and suffrage, Jim Crow, and finally, the accommodation of certain Negro "leaders" to these conditions were only the later phases of a history shaped by three centuries of slavery. Before his untimely death, Harrison's thought was taking an interesting turn, advocating the establishment of a separate black homeland and promoting economic development.[21] Throughout, Harrison balanced a critical, historical understanding of the concept of race with an awareness of the importance of race as crucial means of political mobilization for African Americans.[22]

With his death in 1927, at age forty-four, from complications after surgery for appendicitis, Harrison became a legend for those who had observed him in action. Like William Ferris, his career and earnings were no match for his talents and education. When he died, leaving a wife and five children, he held the title of "special lecturer" in contemporary civilization at New York University. Despite his influence, and the indelible memory of his brilliance and erudition, Harrison was sufficiently controversial as to be neglected by establishmentarian black opinion makers. Though eulogized in the *Defender*, the *Amsterdam News*, the *Interstate Tattler*, and *Negro World*, the two leading black magazines, the *Crisis* and *Opportunity*, the organ of the Urban League, completely ignored his passing.

Harrison was one among a number of black intellectuals who were rethinking race and class. The tradition of internal dissension and criticism of black leadership was as old as racial uplift ideology itself. Indeed, the idea of racial uplift had emerged out of the need of a rising class of educated blacks, reformers, teachers, and professionals to constitute themselves as an elite group within a racist society against the exclusiveness of the Afro-American leisure class, the "aristocracy of color" from above, and yet also against the white supremacist fiction of subhuman blackness. With the urban migration of African Americans, black elites exchanged their normative vision of rural southern black folk, rooted in the dominant plantation legend, for a sociological concept of race progress measured by the status of black families in the urban setting. Conflict over political strategy and over the definition of rights, ranging from broader conceptions of social and economic rights to an attenuated vision of civil rights that restricted struggle to the toppling of formal racial barriers within the courts, characterized the postwar period, up until the dawn of the civil rights movement. Throughout, there were many polemics against black leadership grounded in the belief in uplift as a group phenomenon with an expanded progressive vision of social justice as its goal.

Harrison's critical approach was matched by the sociologist E. Franklin Frazier. Like Garvey, however, Frazier's legacy is ambiguous. Although Frazier, as we will see, posed imaginative challenges to racism, at times he did so within the confines of dominant racialized tropes of family disorganization and urban pathology. In any case, if intellectuals were questioning the conservative implications of uplift ideology, Frazier's analysis affirmed what uplift ideology had sought to convince whites—namely, that middle-class values and consciousness held sway in the black community. But although many of the Talented Tenth doubtless saw this as positive, Frazier was critical of the hegemony of bourgeois values. In a 1929 article entitled "La Bourgeoisie Noire," Frazier adopted the posture of the detached social observer. He addressed the question of why African Americans, despite their social subordination, seemed to lack working-class consciousness. Against the social determinism of the Left, Frazier argued, as uplift ideologues had been doing for years, that blacks were not homogenous but "highly differentiated, with about the same range of interests as whites." This was substantially the same argument that would inform his 1957 study *Black Bourgeoisie*. If white radicals viewed blacks as being in economic slavery, blacks themselves did not share this view. For Frazier, "the Negro reacts to the same illusions that feed the vanity of white men." In 1929, Frazier observed that the large number of blacks in domestic service instilled values that robbed blacks of self-respect and self-reliance. It was no surprise to Frazier that radical doctrines would have little appeal to blacks who were just beginning to enter industry, their proletarianization advancing them well beyond their former condition as agricultural peons.

Frazier found elites more susceptible to false consciousness than working-class blacks. He contrasted the New Negro cultural renaissance negatively with the economic independence of the rising class of black businessmen. Unlike the "black Babbitts" they disparaged, black artists and writers, and mainstream race organizations such as the NAACP and the Urban League, were dependent on white patronage and philanthropy, and thus remained indifferent to cultivating an economic base within segregated black communities. Frazier concluded, "The New Negro Movement functions in the third dimension of culture, but so far it knows nothing of the other two dimensions—Work and Wealth." Frazier's criticism of the Harlem intelligentsia would be echoed by others, including Du Bois, Claude McKay, and later, Harold Cruse. These critics questioned the integrationist strategy of the NAACP, as well as that of black Communists, which they regarded as detrimental to the economic and cultural independence and advancement of the group. Toward the end of his life, Frazier criticized the more superficial, ideological aspects of black middle-class identity, which were often a mere imitation of the values of more wealthy and powerful whites.[23]

Carter Woodson found much to criticize in the undemocratic character of black leadership, particularly in the assumption that a single spokesman might effectively represent, or speak for, the entire race. Over the years, the indefatigable and combative Woodson, who rose from the coal mines of West Virginia to a Harvard Ph.D. in history, could be relied upon to issue a rebuttal to each new volume of antiblack historiography, or to eulogize the passing of a notable black pioneer in politics or letters. During a period in which African scholars, including such future nationalist leaders and heads of state as Kwame Nkrumah of Ghana and Nnamdi Azikiwe of Nigeria, studied at black colleges in the United States, Woodson's activities, particularly his editorship of the *Journal of Negro History*, not only expanded the study of African American history but also encouraged a broader, diasporic, and pan-African, intellectual approach. Too many educated blacks were engaged in wasteful squabbling over meaningless patronage spoils, and over command of black institutions. Indeed, leadership, as practiced by most black elites, meant the relentless pursuit of hegemony over black political affairs. Such a perspective was the outcome of oppression: "The oppressor must have some dealing with the despised group, and rather than have contact with individuals he approaches the masses through his own spokesman." The true measure of black advancement, for Woodson, was African Americans' rejection of those leaders chosen by powerful whites for the purpose of "directing the course of the ostracized group along sane lines." Woodson cautioned, however, that the blame did not rest solely with those leaders who catered to dominant interests. Blacks would waste energy abusing such charlatans, those wolves in race men's clothing, if they failed to realize the extent to which African Americans, despite their best intentions, shared the blame with their exploiters by supporting those who would betray the race. Yet true to uplift ideals, Woodson called for an ethic of service over the singleminded pursuit of leadership. Woodson bitterly denounced those black elites who accepted segregation, and faulted elite whites as well for discouraging professional education among blacks. The closing of law schools was especially insidious, occurring precisely when blacks required such expertise to safeguard their civil and political rights. "This one act . . . [was] an outstanding monument to the stupidity or malevolence of those in charge of Negro schools," serving as a striking example of Woodson's general theme, "the mis-education of the race."[24]

Besides those of Harrison, Woodson, and Frazier, there would be a variety of challenges to the middle-class orientation of black intellectuals and leadership. Many would have taken issue with James Weldon Johnson's claim, in 1932, that the status of blacks in America "is more a question of national mental attitude toward the race than of actual conditions." Nothing would improve the status of blacks as much as "a demonstration of intellectual parity by the Negro through the production of literature and art." Johnson, a lawyer, a former beneficiary of Tuskegee patronage, and, after Washington's death, the executive secretary of the NAACP throughout the 1920s, was reiterating the older generation's middle-class agenda of racial vindication and interracial cooperation in a manner that casts doubt on whether the so-called renaissance was really that after all. Confining racial conflict to interpersonal relations, disregarding lawlessness and violence, and seemingly stressing the need for black Americans to prove their humanity, Johnson's prescription came to represent liberal orthodoxy on race during the civil rights era that sought change in the character and behavior of black Americans rather than in the society that kept them down.[25]

Johnson believed that a recognition of the cultural contribution of blacks to American civilization would be liberatory. But earlier, Langston Hughes had challenged the assimilationist cultural aesthetic of uplift ideology, noting that the black artist was caught between the misunderstanding of black elites and the "unintentional bribes" of white patrons. " 'O be respectable, write about nice people, show how good we are,' say the Negroes. 'Be stereotyped . . . , don't shatter our illusions about you . . . , we will pay you,' say the whites." Hughes lamented, as others had before him, that the decorous standards of elite blacks prevented them from appreciating literary and cultural innovations such as Jean Toomer's modern masterpiece, *Cane*, or popular musical forms such as jazz and blues. Hughes told of a Philadelphia clubwoman (participating in the discursive feminization of racial disloyalty as William Ferris and others have done) who abhorred the music—as he saw it, "the old subconscious 'white is best' runs through her mind." Hughes sought to exorcise "the Nordicized Negro intelligentsia's" aversion toward "racial" cultural expression. He boldly sought to elevate the complaint of "too Negro" into a virtue. "Let the blare of Negro jazz bands and the bellowing voice of Bessie Smith penetrate the closed ears of the colored near-intellectuals until they listen and perhaps understand. . . . We younger Negro artists . . . intend to express our individual dark skinned selves without fear or shame."[26] Although Hughes recognized all too well the dangers of the underwriting of black artists by those whites who were enslaved by preconceptions of racial primitivism, he and other New Negro artists, particularly in the sphere of popular music, were moving black cultural production away from the ambiguous terrain of minstrelsy toward innovation and autonomous expression.

Hughes's manifesto was representative of a younger generation of black artists whose bold foray into racial expression was not without problematic baggage of authenticity and primitivism. Still, the decade of Depression would vindicate their perspective. As editor of the *Journal of Negro History*, founded in Washington, D.C., in 1915, Carter Woodson commented on most events of intellectual and cultural significance to African Americans. Woodson had generous praise for Hughes's autobiography, *The Big Sea*, which appeared in 1940. Woodson felt that Hughes "easily excelled" most contemporary black poets, and noted that until the rise of Richard Wright, Hughes was the only writer "who visioned the entire race as a mass of suffering humanity represented by the impoverished Negro." While his contemporaries "have been concerned solely with the humiliation and social proscription suffered by the talented tenth of the race," Hughes was truly the poet of the race and did not "drift toward clownishness as often Dunbar did." For Woodson, Hughes's writings about "the lowly" made him more representative of the race than the "indignant memorialist."[27]

Motion pictures provided another cultural arena in which class attitudes among African Americans were being renegotiated before mass audiences. Thomas Cripps finds in the independent black movies of the 1920s further evidence of ideological constructions of social class among African Americans. These films, unlike the literary productions of Hughes and his fellow Negro artists, "retailed a black bourgeois success myth" to their northern audiences of working-class migrants, serving as "a manual for those on the make, and a caution to the weak-willed who might be diverted from success by urban temptations." The heroes of these movies stumbled onto sudden success, a plot convention that, according to Cripps, would be more plausible to their audiences: "In a racist society, luck always seemed to matter more than pluck." Cripps locates the origins of black independent cinema within a black bourgeois sensibility. After *Birth of a Nation* caused a sensation in 1915, with its prosouthern attack on Reconstruction (which included white actors in blackface), Emmett J. Scott, Booker T. Washington's private secretary, attempted to film Washington's *Up From Slavery* as "The Birth of the Race," which would celebrate "not only Dr. Washington's personal strivings" but also those of a rising race. As the derivative title attests, the uplift imperatives of racial vindication could be as detrimental to formal innovation in film as they were in language and literature. Other black entrepreneurs entered the picture, and the black press championed their fledgling productions. But class and cultural tensions played themselves out in the debate between producers, audiences, and critics over the content of these films. Cripps describes an "aesthetic guerilla war . . . between the respectables who demanded 'uplift' and the less demanding moviegoers who demanded 'action.'"

A glimpse of this tension between black intellectuals and cultural entrepreneurs is evident in the negotiation between Oscar Micheaux, the most prolific independent black filmmaker, and Charles Chesnutt, who sold Micheaux the rights to his novel *The House Behind the Cedars*. Early in their collaboration, Micheaux complained to Chesnutt that black audiences disapproved of "the use of the word nigger, coon, darky, etc.," an irksome situation that, to him, detracted from the realism and originality of his work. Despite his grave reservations with Micheaux's standards, Chesnutt resigned himself to the filmmaker's demand for total license in adapting his novel. Of course, matters were far worse regarding black representations in nonblack productions. The multitalented singer, actor, and activist Paul Robeson, who made several films for Hollywood and British studios throughout the 1930s, commented wistfully, "I thought I could do something for the Negro race in the films: show the truth about them." His satisfaction with his own performances could not withstand the experience of seeing the films, in which black images were inevitably distorted. "That made me think things out. It made me more conscious politically," Robeson recalled. Denouncing the racist content in films as integral to the corporate studio system, Robeson concluded, "So no more films for me," as if movie acting were akin to the auction block.[28]

If Robeson had shared the sort of optimism that animated uplift ideology's view that exceptional individuals might conquer race prejudice, he and other younger intellectuals and activists were self-consciously departing from the older construction of black bourgeois identity rooted in the idea of "the Negro problem." Black intellectuals' willingness to represent the masses, instead of dissociating themselves from them, if not condemning them out of hand, was a development that paralleled the Depression 1930s, when left-wing intellectuals celebrated folk and urban mass cultures as stepping stones to interracial democracy. For younger black intellectuals, the Depression and the progressive popular front politics of wartime returned a working-class inflection to black politics and uplift ideology.

Ella Baker, a labor organizer and longtime civil rights activist who was instrumental in the founding of the Student Nonviolent Coordinating Committee (SNCC), which conducted a voter education program in the Deep South in the early 1960s, recalled that the Depression altered her perception of success. Baker's goal became "to succeed in doing with people some of the things I thought would raise the level of the masses of people, rather than . . . the individual being accepted by the establishment." Robeson's reflections on race and class led him to reject the view equating individual success with racial uplift, and its attendant achievement ideology: "Where is the benefit when a small class of Negroes makes money and can live well?" Such success may be encouraging to some, but to Robeson, it held no deeper significance. Noting that he had relatives who could neither read nor write, Robeson explained, "I have had a chance. They have not. That is the difference." For him, class distinctions among blacks were produced not by differences in character or moral fiber, as many others believed, but by the inequitable distribution of social opportunities for education.[29]

As Baker's example indicated, the Depression of the 1930s saw a resurgence in radicalism at the national level, reflected within the black intelligentsia as well. Black writers, including Langston Hughes, Ralph Ellison, and the self-exiled Mississippians Margaret Walker and Richard Wright, were associated with the Communist Party, as was Robeson. With Garveyism in eclipse, the Communist Party would, for a time, come to challenge the NAACP as the preeminent organization advocating the cause of African Americans. Toward the liberal end of the political spectrum, more than one hundred blacks served in the Roosevelt administration during the 1930s, but primarily in an advisory and public relations capacity. Although the image of political visibility was celebrated in the black press, this "black brain trust" held little accountability for policy, and throughout the decade was unable to obtain the president's support for federal antilynching legislation, or the desegregation of the armed forces.[30] These progressive demands collided with the establishmentarian views of older black institutions. Two cases from the 1930s, the Scottsboro case, and the Tuskegee syphilis experiment, illustrate, albeit in significantly different respects, the ideological and class tensions within black leadership and organizations. If middle-class civil rights organizations such as the NAACP might face internal and external challenges over the need to protect the interests of poor and working-class blacks, black institutions such as Tuskegee Institute might find themselves deeply implicated as bureaucratic instruments of segregationist state power.

Since its inception the NAACP had waged its fight for racial justice on several fronts. In addition to its campaign for a federal antilynching law, the association pursued a middle-class agenda against residential segregation and sought in the 1930s to integrate professional schools. But during the labor insurgency of 1919, the organization had come to the assistance of black workers in Arkansas who faced violent retribution for organizing to improve their wages. Moreover, it had pursued legal challenges to peonage. Its most significant victory was the Supreme Court decision in 1927 that weakened the southern electoral practice of the white-only primary, which effectively disfranchised blacks. Generally, the association's arguments in the courts against residential segregation privileged the interests of middle-class blacks over those of the poor, and drew on class-bound arguments claiming the plaintiffs' legal standing by virtue of the singular injustice of discrimination against industrious, thrifty, and well-educated blacks.

In 1931, at Scottsboro, Alabama, nine black youths were arrested, charged with raping two white women on a train. Almost immediately, they were sentenced to death. The NAACP was hesitant to take up their defense. Class considerations played a significant role. Walter White initially voiced skepticism regarding the defendants' innocence. He feared that the youths, who were illiterate and whose "reputations were not particularly good," would reflect badly on the organization. The NAACP's hesitation left a vacuum that was filled by the Communist Party. The International Labor Defense (ILD), the party's legal wing, helped make the case a national cause célèbre by calling attention to the difficulties of securing legal counsel and the denial of the constitutional right to due process. White, the association's new executive secretary, opposed the party's involvement and condemned the ILD. As James Siegal has written of the case, "White's initial presumption of guilt, based on a direct link between economic status and moral character, narrowed his conception of racial justice."[31]

As a glaring instance of legal racism in the South, the Scottsboro case galvanized opposition among blacks; some black editors praised the ILD for its antiracist efforts, putting the NAACP on the defensive. Eventually the association forged an alliance with the ILD through which the two organizations cooperated on the Scottsboro defense. Although the defendants were saved from execution, this was a hollow victory, for most of them remained incarcerated for years before they were released, the last one leaving jail in 1950.

The Scottsboro case also heightened tensions within the NAACP between national leadership and local branches on matters of tactics and strategy. Some members of the association contended that confining its strategy to the pursuit of racial justice in the courts was a limited, if not flawed, course. For a time, militant younger leaders sought to engage the NAACP in extralegal protests, involvement in working-class issues, and pressure politics. The association was rife with ideological conflict in the 1930s, as local branch leaders in the South pressured the national office for strategies that would meet the urgent needs of harassed, desperate black tenant farmers and sharecroppers. In short, the tension pitted the NAACP's middle-class, integrationist vision of racial justice against strategies pursuing a broader, working-class program of social justice. After World War II, anticommunism, antilabor sentiment, and Cold War liberalism influenced White's stewardship of the association, whose top priority remained the gradual assault on segregation under the leadership of Thurgood Marshall and the NAACP Legal Defense fund, culminating in the unanimous *Brown v. Topeka Board of Education* Supreme Court decision in 1954. Throughout the Cold War, accusations of communist ties by liberals and southern conservatives alike had a chilling effect on civil rights groups and on such anticolonial activists as Du Bois and Robeson.[32]

Scottsboro brought the injustice of southern courts to national attention, but it almost pales before the horror of the Tuskegee syphilis experiment, a case that epitomizes the extent to which blacks of all social strata were reduced by the unchecked will of the state in the era of Jim Crow. From 1932 to 1972, more than four hundred African American sharecroppers and manual laborers were subjects in a medical study sponsored by the U.S. Public Health Service that examined the effects of untreated syphilis. The federally subsidized experiment had the cooperation of local black and white physicians, nurses, medical technicians, and the officials of Tuskegee Institute, including its principal, Robert R. Moton (the successor of Booker T. Washington). The objective of the experiment was to track the progress of the disease until death, which participants in the experiment described as "bringing the cases to autopsy." Besides syphilis, the rural subjects of the study contended with poverty, malnutrition, illiteracy, and an absence of medical care. Under the circumstances, their participation in the study carried the appearance of receiving care, or treatment, for what they were told was "bad blood." As historian James Jones observed of the study, "Nothing more illustrated the dilemma of black middle-class professionals who wanted to succeed in a society dominated by whites." It is conceivable that the black employees and professionals involved did not have the luxury or the inclination to make a moral choice in the matter.[33]

The largely uneducated subjects of the experiment received periodic examinations by doctors, with the assistance of Nurse Eunice Rivers, who facilitated the study by serving as a liaison, maintaining contact with subjects and encouraging them in the belief that they were receiving treatment. Jones notes that the study was not clandestine but had actually been the subject of numerous medical journal articles. Furthermore, it had been publicly discussed at professional meetings and conferences. Thus, many others—a wide network of medical and public health professionals—were aware of the project. In 1943, the availability of penicillin as a widely used treatment for syphilis became, ironically, a further justification for withholding treatment. The combined forces of the civil rights movement and pressures to regulate medical experimentation in the 1960s led to attacks on the experiment from within the medical profession. These controversies subsided as supervisors continued to secure the participation of physicians and participants in the study. Finally, the experiment was exposed in the national press in 1972. The federal government assumed costs of medical treatment for surviving subjects and their relatives. Although the experiment violated state health laws passed in 1927, 1943, 1957, and 1969, no legal action was taken. Montgomery attorney Fred Gray filed a $1.8 billion class action civil suit on behalf of survivors and heirs of the deceased subjects (Jones provided his historical materials and assisted in preparation of the suit). The case was settled by the government in 1974 for $10 million. According to Jones, Gray found the heirs' lack of social and economic mobility distressing. Many impoverished, poorly educated descendants were just as vulnerable to ill treatment as the victims of the study had been.[34]

As it pertains to issues of power, class, and black leadership, the Tuskegee syphilis experiment is a tragic illustration of a how hunger for status combined with economic dependence can result in a suspension of moral agency. As a violation of medical ethics tantamount to the human experiments conducted under the Third Reich, the Tuskegee case raises profound moral questions that, one hopes, the present study has begun to address. In one sense, the syphilis experiment was nothing new, as African Americans had been enlisted to supervise and enforce systems of racial dominance since slavery. It is difficult to determine, from the perspective of Nurse Rivers and the black doctors with knowledge of the experiment, whether it represents a perversion of racial uplift ideals of altruistic service and caring, or, more broadly, a logical outcome of the construction of intraracial class differences founded on racist bourgeois morality. Those supervising the experiment no doubt regarded its subjects, an already despised class afflicted with a venereal disease, as beyond moral consideration, and valuable to authorities only as instruments of medical and scientific curiosity. Sexual racism, combined with the moral stigma of disease and the poverty of the sharecroppers, may have enabled all those involved at some level in the experiment to justify their role in the mistreatment of the participants. And as Jones and others have suggested, the racist abuse and poverty the men were subjected to permitted Nurse Rivers to regard herself as their guardian angel, their only ally. While the question of consent is more ambiguous in this instance, as economic coercion seems to have played some part in blacks' participation, the Tuskegee syphilis experiment was an extreme manifestation of a particular characteristic of black leadership, namely, its functional, instrumental character. One might view this as either an extreme, rapacious individualism or the repression of one's group identity in the service of some presumably larger interest, for example, a patriotic support of the nation-state, or, otherwise, of one's employer. Reflecting the desperation of their plight, many African Americans have idealistically based their appeal for rights or inclusion by speaking for or serving the powers that be, believing that their own betterment might ensue.

Scottsboro and the Tuskegee syphilis experiment reveal the dire human costs of segregation as well as the flawed intellectual challenge to racism that resorted to claims of class differentiation, bourgeois respectability, and assumptions that moral and material uplift and the behavioral status of patriarchal families were preconditions for fundamental human rights. The tendency to locate the problem in the bodies and behavior of African Americans, rather than in their lack of citizenship, political rights, and ultimately, in social inequities, persisted, as one can see in the continuing work of E. Franklin Frazier.

For Frazier, the lack of material progress among blacks despite significant socioeconomic changes in class structure, was attributable to an absence of cultural identity. Rapid social mobility led blacks to sacrifice their folk traditions and social heritage. Black institutions replaced these traditions with materialistic values of conspicuous consumption, anti-intellectualism, political apathy, and a vapid spiritualism. These values were the product of segregation, leading Frazier to conclude that "the Negro community may be regarded as a pathological phenomenon." Frazier inverted his family disorganization thesis, borrowing the title of a contemporary social study to claim that the middle-class Negro "shows the mark of oppression more than the lower-class Negro who finds a shelter from the contempt of the white world" in his culture "and in his freedom from a gnawing desire to be recognized and accepted." Beset by insecurity and self-hatred, middle-class blacks erected a world of make believe in their social organizations and institutions, a world of inflated prestige narcissistically reflected back to them in the black press. Frazier noted the deep ambivalence of black elites toward integration. They vociferously demanded the end of segregation, but at the same time feared the competition and demands of the larger community. For too many, integration was merely a matter of shedding their "racial identification." Frazier suggested that African Americans should accept their cultural identity and work for the economic betterment of black communities.[35]

Despite the occasional broadside against black elites, and criticism of racial uplift ideology, the notion of pathology as a sign of racial discrimination enjoyed considerable popularity among Frazier and other social researchers, including Gunnar Myrdal and Kenneth Clark. These racial liberals relied on a hypothesis of pathology, whereby racial discrimination could be proven to have damaged its victims. Thus, the intellectual and legal basis for desegregation relied less on the constitutional principle of equal protection or inalienable human rights than it did on arguments claiming psychic injury, low self-esteem, or family disorganization. At the same time, this liberal social science discourse on race spoke somewhat dubiously of African Americans' social marginality as a matter of personal choice, manifested by their failure to adopt values that might facilitate their integration into American society. According to one such expert, segregation had produced "atypical institutional patterns which are viewed as dysfunctional. . . . Doubtless the foremost of these institutions is the Negro family which, because of historical circumstances connected with slavery and the isolated conditions under which Negroes have lived in both urban and rural areas, is characterized by rather significant variations from the dominant American family pattern." Here were vestiges of the old, developmental uplift ideology, specifically, a racialized image of pathology, neutralized by a seemingly benign sociological language representing black life. The locus of discussion imperceptibly shifts from segregation and racial discrimination to a notion of cultural, or behavioral, deficiency that ultimately settles on psychocultural notions of damage to the black personality. Family disorganization and its attendant psychopathologies become sociological markers of victimization.[36]

This liberal social science discourse equating cultural difference and black matriarchy with pathology was by no means antiblack in intent. It sought integration throughout the dark ages of Jim Crow, attacking not only the segregationists' assertions of "separate but equal" but also the legacy of the plantation legend that insisted that blacks were hardly oppressed, but in fact, content with their lot in the South. Scholars of this persuasion held that African Americans remained culturally different, deviant, and thus were hindered from assimilating into the American economy and political culture as other immigrant groups had done. It took Kenneth Clark's experiments finding psychological damage in southern black children's preference for white dolls over dolls that looked more like themselves to convince the Court that segregation was in fact, unequal, leading to the 1954 *Brown* decision desegregating public schools. By this logic, the failure to adapt to the urban environment and to assimilate, as had other, nonblack ethnic groups, into a U.S. society theorized as nondiscriminatory, or color blind, implied an aberrant, deficient black culture. As Moynihan and Glazer described it, "An open society prevails for individuals and groups," each of which "participates sufficiently in the goods and values of social life of a common society so that all can accept the common society as good and fair. . . . Individual choice, not law or rigid custom, determines the degree to which any individual participates, if at all, in the life of an ethnic group, and assimilation and acculturation proceed at a rate determined in large measure by individuals." This mainstream view of assimilation, founded on pluralistic ideals, was extended to African Americans following the civil rights reforms outlawing formal discrimination. Disregarding the history of antiblack racism and the continuing social effects of residential segregation, this normative view of ethnic assimilation explained away, and in the wake of northern urban rebellions, discredited the grievances of impoverished blacks (and poor whites) whose failure to choose assimilation in an open society, so to speak, cast over them the shadow of pathology.[37]

Interestingly enough, this normative view of assimilation, with its implicit hostility to cultural difference, had been challenged years before by a diverse group of scholars. Noting his approval of a study of Haitian folklore, Carter Woodson concluded that the distinctiveness of black diaspora cultures "shows how absurd it is for Dr. Robert E. Park and the innocent Negroes who have been trained under him to contend that the Negro who was brought from Africa to America has retained nothing but his temperament." Writing in 1939, the white anthropologist Hortense Powdermaker noted the relatively loose, elastic, and matriarchal family structure among African Americans in the Deep South. Powdermaker saw little evidence that fatherless households created the psychological complications among black children that social and clinical workers had associated with fatherless white families. In an unpublished review of Gunnar Myrdal's universally praised social study *An American Dilemma*, Ralph Ellison faulted Myrdal for regarding black culture and personality as a "social pathology" and argued that black culture (which he insisted was, at bottom, American culture) not only possessed value and richness but also constituted a rejection of the pathological U.S. culture of lynching, exclusion, and white racial sentimentalism.

Thus, long before the war of words over the supposed culture of poverty among black Americans unleashed by the Moynihan report, however, the liberal, social science orthodoxy calling for African Americans' assimilation and acquisition of the traits valued by white Americans was hotly contested. Despite these critical perspectives, the discourse of psychic damage, matriarchy, and family disorganization gained the upper hand within postwar liberal social science discourse. This reformist consensus, uniting black and white racial liberals, represented the mainstreaming of the sociological component of racial uplift ideology, perpetuating the equation of patriarchal authority with race progress.[38]

The mainstreaming of racial uplift ideology, that is, its incorporation into a dominant racial liberalism, has replicated and reinforced the construction of both race progress, and its lack, in ideological terms of class differentiation and patriarchal gender hierarchy. At the same time, there remains a constant and continuing tension between racialized visions of uplift and more critical

:iohistorical analyses of the condition of African Americans and of Ameri-
.n politics and society.

This chapter has described both the opening of a Pandora's box of critical
perspectives on racial uplift and black leadership and its subsequent closing.
The impact of power on knowledge and political strategy is strikingly apparent in black intellectuals' struggles with the dissemblance and double-
consciousness imposed by violent segregationist repression, academic social
science, and Cold War liberalism. For many black intellectuals, a conscious or
unconscious desire to overcome invisibility by speaking the language of racial
uplift's master narratives closed off other intellectual and political paths. Ostensibly divergent dominant and oppositional languages of race joined to per-
petuate racialized and patriarchal notions of class differences, progress, and
poverty. Although this neoracism relies less on outright violence than its
turn-of-the-century antecedents, it continues racial and sexual scapegoating,
rendering the black middle class invisible and denying many African Americans political and economic rights.

Well before the middle-class agenda of racial justice ran up against the economic and political crises of the Depression era, the post-Reconstruction
racial uplift ethos that had emphasized class differentiation and the leadership
of the Talented Tenth and had internalized notions of urban pathology at the
expense of black citizenship rights had come under attack, questioned by
those espousing more internationalist and radical views such as those embodied by Harrison. In any case, since Harrison, black intellectual life, always dis-
putatious, had further fragmented, reflecting the ideological conflicts within
American political culture.

Subsequent generations of politically assertive African Americans throughout the civil rights era would continue to challenge liberal orthodoxies on
race that would restrict black struggles to those of formal equality or integration. Some African American intellectuals brought an alternative perspective
informed by African national liberation struggles to domestic social issues. In
his classic account of African American history at the turn of the century,
Rayford Logan attributed the failure of Reconstruction in part to the fact that
conceptions of social and economic rights were practically nonexistent. As a
contemporary example of such resistance to social and economic rights, Logan cited the United States government's opposition during the early 1950s
to the United Nations' Universal Declaration of Human Rights and the
Draft Covenants on Human Rights, for fear that its inclusion of economic
rights might be binding on the United States government.[39]

But in Logan's time, segregationists and so-called moderates remained
steadfastly opposed to even the narrower claim by blacks for civil and political rights. Logan's interpretation of the post-Reconstruction assault on black

citizenship placed in historical perspective the struggles of Martin Luther King and the civil rights movement against the establishment view that blacks were pushing too fast and had to wait for white society to recognize and grant their full citizenship rights. Later, as the civil rights movement and its calls for "freedom, now!" (sometimes alternated with its Swahili counterpart, "Uhuru!") gave way to the war on poverty, King, Fannie Lou Hamer, Malcolm X, and numerous others employed more comprehensive claims of human rights that rejected the old civilizationist logic that held citizenship to be a privilege, not a basic, inalienable right.

Yet this would hardly prove to be a dominant or everlasting trend in black leadership, as uplift ideology and its claims of class differentiation, which left intact the racist logic of black pathology, became post–civil rights orthodoxy. The civil rights reforms, called by some commentators the second Reconstruction, and aided by postwar economic affluence, have expanded the black middle class, consolidating the goals of class differentiation that advocates of racial uplift ideology at the turn of the century had so desperately sought to achieve and maintain. And yet the expansion of the black middle class has failed, as so often promised, to undermine racist logic and practice. Within public policy and media debates, black progress remains inseparable from black pathology. With economic decline, discussions of race in the mainstream mass media continue to engage in dissemblance in their faulty construction of social reality, as if the spectacle of race will make a deepening economic crisis disappear. Articulations of racism, sexism, and contempt for the poor still serve to scapegoat and exclude large segments of the population from the rights, protections, and entitlements of citizenship. Rights are increasingly defined as the exclusive privilege of those with power and property, as opponents of the welfare state seek to dilute the power of the federal government, save to safeguard the interests of the wealthiest citizens and corporations. The legacy of race as a driving force in our political culture thus endures alongside professions of color-blind ideals.

African American elites' faith that their attempts to distinguish themselves from racist constructions of black depravity might save them from prejudice, discrimination, and antiblack policies remains illusory. This is instructive for aspiring and middle-class members of racialized immigrant populations who believe that the plague of reactionary racial scapegoating will pass, leaving their respectable homes and citizenship rights unscathed and intact. And those whites who succumb to such racial and gendered distractions in supporting attacks on the welfare state invite upon themselves the social chaos and impoverishment they presently identify solely with African Americans. What the future holds for African Americans, and for the nation, depends on how clearly we can resist the deep-seated temptation to racialize poverty, and refuse to submit to complacent myths of a classless, color-blind society. The nation, and the health of its political institutions, stand only to benefit from assimilating the best, and most truly democratic, of African Americans' uplift ideals—compassion, service, education, and a commitment to social and economic justice for all citizens.

NOTES

❨ ❨ ❨

Preface

1. Quoted in Breitman, ed., *Malcolm X Speaks*, pp. 34–35.

2. Franklin, *Color Line*, pp. 31–51; Fraser and Gordon, "Genealogy of Dependency," pp. 309–36.

3. Plessy v. Ferguson, 163 US 537 (1896), in Joseph Tussman, ed., *The Supreme Court on Racial Discrimination* (New York: Oxford University Press, 1963), p. 80.

4. Moss, *American Negro Academy*.

5. Lott, "Love and Theft," pp. 23–50; Lubiano, "Black Ladies, Welfare Queens," pp. 323–63.

6. Cornel West, "The Dilemma of the Black Intellectual," in West, *Keeping Faith*, p. 85.

7. The contributions include Hall, "Notes on Deconstructing 'The Popular,'" pp. 227–39; Carby, *Reconstructing Womanhood*; Bell, *Faces at the Bottom*; Morrison, ed., *Race-ing Justice, En-gendering Power*; Gates, ed., *"Race," Writing, and Difference*; Wallace, *Invisibility Blues*.

8. Morrison, *Playing in the Dark*; Baldwin, *Price of the Ticket*.

Introduction

1. Frazier, *Black Bourgeoisie*.

2. Hine, "Rape and the Inner Lives of Black Women," pp. 292–97.

3. Redding, *No Day of Triumph*, pp. 30–31.

4. Ibid., pp. 31–39.

5. Gwaltney, *Drylongso*, pp. 84–86.

6. Du Bois, *Souls of Black Folk*.

7. Ibid.

8. Ibid., p. 5.

9. Annotation of Du Bois's text is quoted in Pemberton, *Hottest Water*, pp. 74–77.

10. Du Bois, *Autobiography of W. E. B. Du Bois*, p. 122.

11. Williams, *Marxism and Literature*, pp. 55–71; Jewell, *From Mammy to Miss America*, pp. 4–5.

12. Santino, *Miles of Smiles*, pp. 6–31.

13. Joel A. Rogers, *From Superman to Man* (Plainview, N.Y.: Books for Libraries Press, 1976).

14. Santino, *Miles of Smiles*, pp. 17–18.

15. "More Slavery at the South," by a Negro Nurse, *Independent*, 72, no. 3295 (January 25, 1912): 196–200, reprinted in Lerner, ed., *Black Women in White America*, pp. 227–29. See also Tucker, ed., *Telling Memories*; Jaynes, *Branches Without Roots*, p. 275.

16. The self-help, inspirational literature of racial uplift is voluminous; for several examples, see Pipken, *Story of a Rising Race*; Northrop, *College of Life*; and Penn, *United Negro*.

Chapter One

1. Meier, *Negro Thought in America*, pp. 210–11; Bardolph, *Negro Vanguard*, p. 172; Baker, *Following the Color Line*, p. 92. See James G. Spady, "Richard Robert Wright, Sr.," *Dictionary of Negro Biography*, ed. Rayford Logan and Michael Winston (New York: Norton, 1982), pp. 674–75. This notion of uplift endured in the minds of progressive reformers. In 1892, at a Sunset Club discussion, the temperance leader Frances Willard cited the "little fellow['s]" response to "General Fisk" as evidence that "the masses are sending us word that they are rising, and I do not believe that the question 'How would you uplift the masses?' will be germane to any program ten years from now, for they will be up and at it themselves." Willard is quoted in "How Would You Uplift the Masses?" *The Sunset Club, Forty-Second Meeting*, February 4, 1892.

2. See George W. Reid, "George Henry White," *Dictionary of Negro Biography*, pp. 645–46; and Krislov, *Negro in Federal Employment*, p. 17.

3. Logan, *Betrayal of the Negro*.

4. Although such attempts at periodization are useful, they also risk distortion. As will be seen, the idea of uplift was not confined to the post-Reconstruction era. F. E. W. Harper, "An Address Delivered at the Centennial Anniversary of the Pennsylvania Society for Promoting the Abolition of Slavery," Philadelphia, April 14, 1875, in Dunbar, ed., *Masterpieces of Negro Eloquence*, pp. 104–6.

5. Anderson, *Education of Blacks in the South*, pp. 4–32.

6. Berry, *Black Resistance*, pp. 61–78.

7. Jaynes, *Branches Without Roots*, pp. 264–65.

8. Ibid., pp. 269–72.

9. Rachleff, *Black Labor*, pp. 86–91; Berry, *Black Resistance*, pp. 103–21; Harris, *Harder We Run*, pp. 9–14; Painter, *Exodusters*, pp. 93–94.

10. Fortune, *Black and White*, pp. 95, 105–6.

11. Straker, *New South Investigated*, pp. 84–91.

12. Berry, *Black Resistance*, p. 116; Stein, "Of Mr. Booker T. Washington and Others," pp. 422–63; Krislov, *Negro in Federal Employment*, pp. 7–27.

13. On Frances Willard and her public feud with Ida B. Wells in England over lynching, see Giddings, *When and Where I Enter*, pp. 90–91, and Gossett, *Race*, pp. 269–71.

14. Gossett, *Race*, p. 236; Kovel, *White Racism*, pp. 211–13; Jackson, "From Our Friends in the Far East," pp. 145–49; Fletcher, *Black Soldier*; Eduardo Galleano, *Century of the Wind* (New York: Pantheon, 1988); Bessie L. Pierce, *Public Opinion and the*

Teaching of History in the United States (New York: Knopf, 1926), pp. 281–82.

15. A good example of textual and visual representations of racial ideology involving black soldiers can be found in *The Race Crisis* (n.p., 1904), pp. 10–11.

16. Langford and Vardamann quoted in Henri, *Black Migration*, pp. 22–23. See Marks, ed., *Black Press*, p. 109.

17. Henri, *Black Migration*, p. 22.

18. The Atlanta Exposition Address is reprinted in Washington, *Up From Slavery*, pp. 217–37. Berry, *Black Resistance*, pp. 118–19; Harper, *Iola Leroy*; Cooper, *Voice from the South*.

19. Bardolph, *Civil Rights Record*, pp. 149–52.

20. *Plessy v. Ferguson*, 163 US 537 (1896).

21. Herd, "Prohibition, Racism and Class Politics," pp. 85–86; Woodward, *Origins of the New South*, pp. 327–49.

22. Rev. J. P. Campbell, editor of the *A.M.E. Christian Recorder*, insisted that blacks "have to wait for nothing. The right [to freedom] is a natural one." To Frederick Douglass, religious, egalitarian claims of human rights rendered racist scientific theories based on anatomical differences irrelevant. Douglass insisted that claims to liberty and freedom were not based on so-called natural differences or similarities, but on a higher law, "registered in the Courts of Heaven, . . . enforced by the eloquence of the God of all the earth." Campbell quoted in Sernett, *Black Religion and American Evangelicalism*, pp. 140–41. Douglass quoted in Stepan and Gilman, "Appropriating the Idioms of Science," p. 81. Equal rights antislavery discourse is discussed in Quarles, *Black Mosaic*, pp. 92–108; and McPherson, *Struggle for Equality*. See Garnet's "Address to the Slaves," in Stuckey, ed., *Ideological Origins of Black Nationalism*.

23. Berry and Blassingame, *Long Memory*, pp. 57–69; Moss, *American Negro Academy*, pp. 9–17; Quarles, *Black Abolitionists*; George, *Segregated Sabbaths*, pp. 135–59; Stuckey, *Ideological Origins of Black Nationalism*; Franklin, *George Washington Williams*, pp. 100–133; Cromwell, *Negro in American History*; Meier, *Negro Thought in America*, pp. 260–64.

24. Julia De Cora, "My People," *Southern Workman*, 26, no. 6 (June 1897): 115–16.

25. For letters to Armstrong from "Chinese, Japanese, Indian and Colored students," see "Letters from Hampton Graduates and Ex-Students," *Southern Workman*, 21, no. 1 (January 1892): 7; Harlan, *Booker T. Washington: Making of a Black Leader*, pp. 102–8. Quotations from Benjamin Brave, "The Old and The New," *Southern Workman*, 26, no. 4 (April 1897): 72.

26. Anderson, *Education of Blacks in the South*, pp. 28–30; Wells, quoted in Duster, ed., *Crusader for Justice*, p. 22; "A Message to the Race," *Voice of the Negro* 2, no. 1 (January 1905): 696.

27. Anderson, *Education of Blacks in the South*, pp. 33–40; Bardolph, *Negro Vanguard*, pp. 99–101; Kelly Miller, "Howard University," in *From Servitude to Service: Being the Old South Lectures on the History and Work of Southern Institutions for the Education of the Negro* (New York: Negro Universities Press, 1969), pp. 24–26. Du Bois, "Hampton Idea," pp. 632–35.

28. Hovenkamp, "Social Science and Segregation," p. 648; Ida B. Wells, "'Iola' on Discrimination," *New York Freeman* (January 15, 1887): 4; Wells, *Crusader for Justice*, pp. 18–20.

29. Harper, *Iola Leroy*, p. 116.

30. Buck, *Road to Reunion*; John L. Thomas, "Romantic Reform in America, 1815–1865," in Davis, ed., *Antebellum Reform*, pp. 153–76; Gossett, *Race*, pp. 146–47; Washington, "Storm Before the Calm," pp. 199–213.

31. See the review of W. E. B. Du Bois's "The Souls of Black Folk" in *Southern Workman* 32, no. 6 (June 1903): 263. Washington, *Up From Slavery*, pp. 16, 80, 111.

32. Harlan, *Booker T. Washington: The Wizard of Tuskegee*, pp. 3–31.

33. Williams, *Black Americans and Evangelization*; Bowen, ed., *Africa and the American Negro*. On Crummell, see Moses, *Alexander Crummell*. Source quoted is William T. Alexander, *History of the Colored Race in America* (Kansas City, Mo.: Palmetto Publishing, 1888), pp. 530–31, quoted in Williams, *Black Americans and Evangelization*, p. 96.

34. Washington, *Up From Slavery*, pp. 94–97.

35. Washington, "Industrial Education," pp. 87–92; Washington, *Up From Slavery*, pp. 80–83. Quoted in Woodward, *Origins of the New South*, p. 95. Governor James Vardamann of Mississippi spoke more directly to the risks inherent in educating blacks: "What the North is sending South is not money, but dynamite; this education is ruining our Negroes. They're demanding equality." Quoted in Baker, *Following the Color Line*, p. 247.

36. Proceedings, *Hampton Negro Conference* (Hampton, Va.: Hampton Institute, 1901), p. 34.

37. Luker, *Social Gospel*.

38. Meier, *Negro Thought in America*, pp. 161–70. John E. Bruce to John W. Cromwell, December 1, 1902, Alain Locke Papers. Griggs, *Imperium in Imperio*; Cooper, *Voice from the South*, p. 35.

39. E. W. Blyden to Rev. Edward Cooke, March 7, 1910, John E. Bruce Collection. Du Bois, "St. Francis of Assisi"; Du Bois, *Souls of Black Folk*, pp. 68–69.

40. On Washington, D.C., black intellectuals, see Moses, "Lost World of the New Negro," pp. 61–84. Crummell, "Civilization, The Primal Need of the Race."

41. Cooper, *Voice from the South*, pp. 25–28, 192.

42. Fannie Williams, in *Women's Era* (March 24, 1894): 4, cited in Giddings, *When and Where I Enter*, p. 83. Cooper, *Voice from the South*. See Williams, "Work Attempted and Missed," pp. 281–85. Ida B. Wells also denounced petty ambition among clubwomen, referring specifically to her feud with Mary Church Terrell. See Duster, ed., *Crusade for Justice*, p. 260.

43. Krislov, *Negro in Federal Employment*, pp. 18–19. Examples of the reform efforts of black women abound; see, for example, R. Antoine Rogers, "Mrs. Frances A. Joseph: President of the Frances Willard W.C.T.U. and Superintendent of Prison Mission," *Colored American Magazine* 6, no. 3 (January 1903): 218–21. Harper and Wells's remarks on temperance are recorded in "Symposium—Temperance," *A.M.E. Church Review* 7, no. 4 (April 1891): 372–81.

44. Stemons, "Unmentionable Crime," pp. 636–41. Washington arranged a dinner with Boston opponents in an unsuccessful attempt to negotiate a reconciliation in 1898. Fox, *Guardian of Boston*, pp. 25–30, 49–58. For an example of northern opposition to Washington, see "An Editorial" in the Cleveland Gazette, July 20, 1901, reprinted in Harlan, ed., *Booker T. Washington Papers* 6: 178–79; Meier, *Negro Thought in America*, pp. 163–64, 171–89.

45. Hopkins, *Contending Forces*, pp. 127–29. For more information on the occupational and social status of northern blacks, see Nielson, *Black Ethos*, pp. 56–60; Woodward, *Strange Career*, pp. 18–21; Kusmer, *Ghetto Takes Shape*, pp. 66–90; *New York Times* editorial cited in Osofsky, *Harlem*, p. 40.

46. "The Niagara Movement," *Colored American Magazine* 13, no. 4 (October 1907): 247–48. On student teachers in the rural South, see Johnson, *Along This Way*, pp. 104–12.

47. *Colored American Magazine* 13, no. 4 (October 1907): 247. By this time, the magazine was edited by Fred Moore, and subsidized by Washington. The black American poet and critic William Stanley Braithwaite had attempted to buy a controlling interest in the magazine in 1903. See Butcher, ed., *William Stanley Braithwaite Reader*, p. 240.

Chapter Two

1. Du Bois, *Souls of Black Folk*, p. 4; Terrell, *Colored Woman*, pp. 22–23; Garvey, "The Negro's Greatest Enemy," in Wagstaff, ed., *Black Power*, pp. 77–78.

2. White, *Man Called White*, pp. 3–5.

3. Quoted in ibid., p. 8.

4. Ibid., p. 9. Harlan, *Booker T. Washington: The Wizard of Tuskegee*, p. 299.

5. Harlan, *Booker T. Washington: The Wizard of Tuskegee*, pp. 8–13.

6. *Outlook* (September 29, 1906): 241–42, reprinted in Joseph Boskin, ed., *Urban Racial Violence in the Twentieth Century* (Beverly Hills, Calif.: 1969), pp. 6–8.

7. My discussion of social equality is indebted to Nell Irvin Painter, "'Social Equality,' Miscegenation, Labor and Power," in Numan V. Bartley, ed., *The Evolution of Southern Culture* (Athens: University of Georgia Press, 1988), pp. 47–67.

8. White, *Man Called White*, pp. 135–38. The controversy surrounding Bessie Smith's death from an automobile accident, and her son's insistence that she died from medical neglect, is discussed in Chris Albertson, *Bessie* (New York: Stein and Day, 1972), pp. 216–26. On blacks' abhorrence of hospitalization, see Hine, *Black Women in White*, pp. 70–71. Platt, *E. Franklin Frazier Reconsidered*, p. 100.

9. Arna Bontemps, "Why I Returned," in *Black Voices: An Anthology of Afro-American Literature*, ed. Abraham Chapman (New York: New American Library, 1968), pp. 322–23.

10. "The Student Strike at Talladega," *Voice of the Negro* 3, no. 3 (March 1906): 166–67.

11. Griggs, *Imperium in Imperio*, pp. 129–31. Middle-class black women preferred the independence they enjoyed as teachers or seamstresses to the more common urban occupation of domestic labor. W. E. B. Du Bois noted that women outnumbered men in the Philadelphia black community because "the industrial opportunities of Negro women in cities have been far greater than those of men." Du Bois, *Philadelphia Negro*, pp. 54–55. Jacqueline Jones discusses the occupational status of black women and the relation of their material condition to the threat of "white men's persistent violation of black women that served as a backdrop for periodic lynchings . . . during the years 1890 to 1910." Jones, *Labor of Love, Labor of Sorrow*, pp. 134–51. Alexander

Crummell denounced the persecution of black women in the South, who, regardless of status, fell prey to "the ruffianly element in Southern society, who think that black men have no rights which white men should regard, and black women no virtue which white men should respect." Quoted in Shapiro, *White Violence*, pp. 59–60. Dittmer, *Black Georgia*, p. 137, also addresses the sexual harassment of black women and its relation to lynching, as black men who themselves resorted to violence to defend their female relatives from such assaults often faced immediate mob retribution.

12. Du Bois, *College-Bred Negro*, pp. 62–63; Du Bois, "The Talented Tenth," in *The Negro Problem: A Series of Articles by Representative American Negroes of To-Day* (Miami: Mnemosyne, 1969), p. 51. Benjamin Brawley to James Weldon Johnson, October 17, 1933, ser. 1, folder 57, James Weldon Johnson Collection.

13. Lightfoot, *Balm in Gilead*, pp. 164–66.

14. Ibid., p. 166. Southern white newspapers were given to referring to black women by such generic names as Jane, Annie, Matilda, and the like. See "What is a Good Negro?" *Voice of the Negro* 1, no. 12 (December 1904): 618–19.

15. Alda Marion Johnson, "Atlanta Beautiful," *Voice of the Negro* 3, no. 7 (July 1906): 508–9.

16. Powdermaker, *After Freedom*, pp. 150–51, 191.

17. Ibid., p. 151; John D. Swain, "A Warning to the South," *Voice of the Negro* 3, no. 6 (June 1906): 427–28; Wells, *Crusade for Justice*, pp. 42–45.

18. Du Bois, "Conservation of Races," (1897) in Wagstaff, ed., *Black Power*, p. 70. Cooper, *Voice from the South*, pp. 24–25. Cooper's use of the phrase "fatally beautiful" refers to the vulnerability of black women to the attacks of white men. For examples of racist slanders of the morals of black women in the mainstream press, and on the black clubwomen's movement response, see Giddings, *When and Where I Enter*, pp. 82, 75–131. For primary source documents on black clubwomen, see Davis, ed., *Lifting as They Climb*.

19. Page, "The Negro," pp. 548–54. For brief reviews of negrophobic literature, see Fullenwider, *Mind and Mood of Black America*, pp. 3–4; Woodward, *Origins of the New South*, p. 352; and Meier, *Negro Thought in America*, pp. 161–62. A valuable survey of antiblack opinion in Progressive Era journalism is provided in Shapiro, "Muckrakers and Negroes," pp. 76–88.

20. Williamson, *New People*, pp. 61–109.

21. Frederick Douglass, "The Future of the Colored Race," *North American Review* 142 (May 1886): 437–40, reprinted in Moses Rischin, ed., *The American Gospel of Success: Individualism and Beyond* (Chicago: Quadrangle Books, 1965): 254–57; Fortune, "Race Absorption," pp. 54–66; Daniel Murray's views are discussed in Gatewood, *Aristocracy of Color*, pp. 174–75.

22. Page is quoted in Gossett, *Race*, p. 273. See Thomas Nelson Page, *The Negro: The Southerner's Problem* (New York: Young People's Missionary Movement of the United States and Canada, 1904). For an accommodationist black position on social equality, see W. H. Councill, *Address to the White People of Alabama* (Normal, Ala.: n.p. 1901); Kelly Miller, "The Attitude of the Intelligent Negro Toward Lynching," *Voice of the Negro* (May 1905): 307–12; and William Pickens, "Social Equality," *Voice of the Negro* 3, no. 1 (January 1906): 25–27.

23. Dittmer, *Black Georgia*, pp. 127–28.

24. Luker, *Social Gospel*, pp. 184–85.

25. A representative example of uplift success literature was "The Progress of a Race," which promised up to date "race statistics" measuring business and professional activity, "The Colored Woman and Her Social Standing," and "The Negro in War." For typical advertisements, see *Voice of the Negro* 1, no. 2 (December 1904); "Render Unto Caesar that Which is Caesar's," *Voice of the Negro* 1, no. 9 (October 1904): 410–11.

26. John E. Bruce, "The Necessity for Business Leagues," *Voice of the Negro* 1, no. 8 (August 1904): 338–39; W. P. Burrell, "History of the Business of Colored Richmond," ibid., pp. 317–22; J. R. E. Lee, "The Negro National Business League," ibid., p. 327; William P. Moore, "Progressive Business Men of Brooklyn," *Voice of the Negro* 1, no. 7 (July 1904): 304–8; Daniel Murray, "The Industrial Problem of the United States and the Negro's Relation to It," *Voice of the Negro* 1, no. 9 (September 1904): 403–8.

27. Archibald A. Grimke, "An Education and Property Basis," *Voice of the Negro* 1, no. 9 (September 1904): 384–85.

28. John H. Adams, "Rough Sketches: A Study of the Features of the New Negro Woman," *Voice of the Negro* 1, no. 8 (August 1904): 323–26; John Henry Adams, "Rough Sketches: The New Negro Man," *Voice of the Negro* 1, no. 10 (October 1904): 447–52.

29. "The Louisiana Purchase Exposition," *Voice of the Negro* 1, no. 8 (August 1904): 342. On imperialism, see Harry H. Pace, "The Philippine Islands and the American Negro," *Voice of the Negro* 1, no. 10 (October 1904): 482–85, W. S. Scarborough, "Roosevelt: The Man, The Patriot, The Statesman," *Voice of the Negro* 1, no. 9 (September 1904): 391–93.

30. Addie Hunton, "Negro Womanhood Defended," *Voice of the Negro* 1, no. 7 (July 1904): 280–82; Josephine Silone Yates, "The National Association of Colored Women," ibid., pp. 283–87; Josephine B. Bruce, "The Afterglow of the Women's Convention," *Voice of the Negro* 1, no. 11 (November 1904): 540–43; Fannie Barrier Williams, "The Woman's Part in a Man's Business," ibid., pp. 543–47; and Gussie Mims Logan, "The Carrie Steele Orphanage," ibid., pp. 538–40.

31. On lynching, see the editorials "Oh Lord! How Long?" *Voice of the Negro* 1, no. 9 (September 1904): 411–13; "The Southern Campaign Against Lynching," *Voice of the Negro* 1, no. 11 (November 1904): 564–65; and L. J. Brown, "Philosophy of Lynching," ibid., pp. 554–59.

32. "John Mitchell at the Banker's Convention," *Voice of the Negro* 1, no. 11 (November 1904): 514–16.

33. "What Is a Good Negro?" *Voice of the Negro* 1, no. 12 (December 1904): 618–19; "The Frederick Douglass Centre," ibid., pp. 586–87; "The Menace of Vagrants," *Voice of the Negro* 3, no. 7 (July 1906): 475–76; "Three Significant Lynchings," ibid., p. 468; Fannie Barrier Williams, "The Frederick Douglass Centre; A Question of Social Betterment, and Not of Social Equality," ibid., pp. 601–4; "What Is an Insolent Negro," ibid., pp. 619–21; J. Max Barber, "The Niagara Movement at Harper's Ferry," *Voice of the Negro* 3, no. 10 (October 1906): 402–11; and Harlan, *Booker T. Washington: The Wizard of Tuskegee*, pp. 85–86.

34. "The South and Free Speech," *Voice of the Negro* 1, no. 11 (November 1904): 510–11. On interracial cooperation in Atlanta, see Luker, *Social Gospel*, pp. 178–90; Harlan, *Booker T. Washington: The Wizard of Tuskegee*, pp. 297–98.

35. Berry, *Black Resistance*, pp. 128–29; "The Colored Soldiers Again," *Voice of the Negro* 3, no. 12 (December 1906): 542–43; W. E. B. Du Bois, "The President and the Soldiers," ibid., pp. 552–53; Mary Church Terrell, "The Disbanding of the Colored Soldiers," ibid., pp. 554–58. Roosevelt's message is quoted in Harlan, *Booker T. Washington: The Wizard of Tuskegee*, 318–20. See "The Negro in the Message," *Voice of the Negro* 3, no. 12 (December 1906): 536–37.

36. J. Max Barber, "The Atlanta Tragedy," *Voice of the Negro* 3, no. 11 (November 1906): 473–79.

37. Ida B. Wells described the phenomenon of white criminals blackening their faces in her antilynching writings. See Wells, *On Lynchings*, p. 24. In the 1930s, the Commission on Interracial Cooperation, based in Atlanta, published a pamphlet collecting news dispatches from throughout the South and including Detroit, detailing incidents in which white criminals attempted to frame blacks by wearing blackface disguises. See "Burnt Cork and Crime: Stories Summarized from Press Reports," *Commission on Interracial Cooperation, Inc. Miscellaneous Publications*, n.d.

38. Barber, "Why Mr. Barber Left Atlanta," *Voice of the Negro* 3, no. 11 (November 1906): 470–72.

39. "The Scarcity of Farm Labor," *Voice of the Negro* 3, no. 9 (September 1906): 620–21.

40. Penelope Bullock, "Jesse Max Barber," *Dictionary of Negro Biography*, ed. Rayford Logan and Michael Winston (New York: 1982), pp. 27–28. See *Proceedings of the National Negro Conference* (New York, n.p., 1909), pp. 115–16.

41. Harlan, *Booker T. Washington: The Wizard of Tuskegee*, p. 300.

Chapter Three

1. On minstrelsy, see Toll, *Blacking Up*; and Lott, "Love and Theft," pp. 23–50. Mainstream journals such as *Century Magazine* were crucial in promoting racial stereotypes in dialect stories for white consumption. For blacks' deviation from gender conventions, see Harry Stillwell Edwards, "Tom's Strategy," *Century Magazine* 16 (May 1889): 84–89. Books and ephemera containing minstrel stereotypes were abundant well into the twentieth century; see, for example, Harry L. Newton, *A Bundle of Burnt Cork Comedy* (Chicago: T. S. Denison, 1905); and Walter Ben Hare, *The Minstrel Encyclopedia* (Boston: Walter M. Baker, 1921).

2. For a discussion of the complex responses of desire and aversion minstrelsy evoked in its audiences, see Lott, "Love and Theft."

3. The pioneering work on this phenomenon is Logan, *Negro in American Life*. See also Shapiro, "Muckrakers and Negroes," pp. 76–86.

4. Gates, "Trope of a New Negro," pp. 129–55, provides examples of racist postcards and ephemera. For an analysis of representations of race in photographs taken to promote the Hampton Institute, see Wexler, "Black and White in Color," pp. 341–90.

5. Gatewood, *Black Americans*, pp. 241–43. Shaler is quoted in Jones, "Proving Blacks Inferior," p. 126. Parkhurst is quoted in Luker, *Social Gospel*, p. 209.

6. Virginia B. Sherrard, "Recollections of my Mammy," *Southern Workman* 30, no. 2 (February 1901): 86–87. On the desexualized image of the mammy, which de-

nied that black women were raped by white men, see Jewell, *From Mammy to Miss America*, p. 37.

7. Mrs. L. H. Harris, "A Southern Woman's View," *Independent* 57, no. 2633 (May 18, 1899): 1354–55.

8. On Milton's bill, see Logan, *Betrayal of the Negro*, 363–64.

9. Hovenkamp, "Social Science and Segregation," p. 657.

10. Logan, *Betrayal of the Negro*; Litwack, "Trouble in Mind," pp. 315–37; and Jones, *Labor of Love, Labor of Sorrow*, p. 147. For useful analyses of the Progressive Era, see Burnham, Buenker, and Crunden, *Progressivism*, pp. 3–29.

11. Booker T. Washington, preface to "Twenty-Four Negro Melodies Transcribed for the Piano by S. Coleridge-Taylor, Op. 59" (Boston: n.p. 1904), ix. See the discussion of minstrelsy in Washington's speeches and writings in Baker, *Modernism and the Harlem Renaissance*, pp. 25–36.

12. Booker T. Washington, "Interesting People—Bert Williams," *American Magazine* 70 (September 1910): 600, 603.

13. Wexler, "Black and White in Color."

14. Du Bois, "The College-Bred Negro," p. 57; Howard, *Social History of American Family Sociology*, pp. 11–62. In an address before the American Negro Academy, the Wilberforce University classicist W. S. Scarborough reminded his audience that "home is the social center for a race, the real center of race improvement." Scarborough, "Educated Negro and His Mission," p. 8. On the significance of marriage and race progress, see the discussion of the novel *Iola Leroy* (1892), by Frances E. W. Harper, in Carby, *Reconstructing Womanhood*, pp. 79–80.

15. Duster, ed., *Crusader for Justice*, p. 255.

16. Cooper, *Voice from the South*, pp. 68–69.

17. Morrissey, "Hereditary Influences and Medical Progress," pp. 283–92. The role of black motherhood is stressed in Tucker, "Formation of Child Character," pp. 258–61. Logan, "Prenatal and Hereditary Influences," pp. 37–40; Cooper, *Voice from the South*, p. 235.

18. Johnson, "Penal Sentence," pp. 180–82. Baker, "The Ethical Significance of the Connection Between Mind and Body." References to phrenology include Minott, "Phrenology and Child Culture," pp. 387–89; and Shadrach, "Furnace Blasts: Black or White," pp. 348–52. Shadrach cites as an "indispensable" authority George Combe, *The Constitution of Man* (Boston, 1830), which, for a time, was the standard text in phrenology.

19. Hackley, *Colored Girl Beautiful*, pp. 34, 44. A concern with neutralizing deterministic hereditary traits through morally upright behavior is seen in Stewart, "Heredity in Character," pp. 22–33. Mrs. A. E. Pride is quoted in proceedings of *Hampton Negro Conference* (Hampton, Va.: Hampton Institute, 1901), p. 31.

20. Harris, "Physical Condition of the Race," pp. 20–28. *Hampton Negro Conference*, pp. 22–24. For similar official moralistic approaches to "Negro problems," see contributions to Penn, ed., *United Negro*.

21. Higginbotham, *Righteous Discontent*, pp. 185–229.

22. Jones, *Recreation and Amusement Among Negroes*, pp. 45–50, 55–63. On uplift and moral purity, see also Shadrach, "Furnace Blasts: The Growth of the Social Evil," pp. 259–63.

23. Lewis, "Young American Negro," pp. 273–75; Du Bois, ed., "College-Bred

Negro," pp. 91–95. Charles Chesnutt, "The Disfranchisement of the Negro," in *The Negro Problem: A Series of Articles by Representative American Negroes of To-Day* (1903; reprint, New York: Arno Press, 1969), p. 97. Harper, *Iola Leroy*, p. 259.

24. For emigrationist movements such as that promoted by Turner, see Redkey, *Black Exodus*.

25. Du Bois, "College-Bred Negro," pp. 91–95.

26. Shapiro, *White Violence*, pp. 34–36.

27. Duster, ed., *Crusade for Justice*, pp. 69–72; Wells, "A Red Record," in Wells, *On Lynchings*, pp. 22–23.

28. Woodward, *Origins of the New South*, p. 351; Shapiro, *White Violence*, pp. 37–38, 41–44.

29. For a condemnation of lynching, see *Nation* 68, no. 1765 (April 27, 1899): 303.

30. Mitchell, "Shall the Wheels," pp. 386–91. On Mitchell, see Rabinowitz, *Race Relations*, p. 234.

31. Carole Marks, "The Social and Economic Life of Southern Blacks during the Migration," in *Black Exodus: The Great Migration from the American South*, ed. Alfredteen Harrison (Jackson: University Press of Mississippi, 1991), pp. 36–50.

32. Osofsky, *Harlem*, pp. 18–34.

33. Scarborough, "Educated Negro and His Mission," pp. 6–7; Dunbar, *Sport of the Gods*. On minstrelsy, see Dormon, "Shaping the Popular Image," pp. 450–71. On the debate in the South on black labor and migration, and on legislative action taken throughout the region from the late 1880s to the first decade of the twentieth century, see Osofsky, *Harlem*, 25–26. For a discussion of opposition to migration and racist stereotypes in Progressive Era journalism, see Logan, *Negro in the United States*, pp. 54–55.

34. Downs, "Educated Fools," p. 463. On black minstrels who entered blackface minstrelsy after emancipation and exploited plantation nostalgia, see Toll, *Blacking Up*, 195–263.

35. Pickens, "Educational Condition," pp. 427–30.

36. Washington, "Storm Before the Calm," pp. 199–213. Meier, *Negro Thought in America*, p. 105; Harlan, *Separate and Equal*, p. 83; Du Bois, *College-Bred Negro*, p. 114. In this connection, C. Vann Woodward notes the "deeply pessimistic . . . view of the Negro" held by "public-spirited professional people of a humanitarian bent." Such pessimism was usually focused on the urban black community. The frequent injunctions against urban migration for rural blacks indicate the resistance black leaders and New South industrialists waged against the influx of black labor into New South industries. Washington's alarmist comments on urbanization as an outcome of black education reflected the probusiness view of Professor Paul B. Barringer, presumably a white man, who told the Southern Education Association in 1900 that "the negro race is essentially a race of peasant farmers and laborers. . . . As a source of cheap labor for a warm climate he is beyond competition; everywhere else he is a foreordained failure, and as he knows this he despises his own color." Quoted in Woodward, *Strange Career of Jim Crow*, pp. 94–95. At the time, agriculture was the dominant occupation for black workers, and the eventual demand for blacks as a reserve unskilled labor force at harvest time and the increasing incidence of tenancy among black farmers reduced their educational and economic opportunities for social advancement. Confinement

to farm labor was enhanced as black employment in several industries declined through the 1890s and blacks were excluded from craft unions. In this context, leaders like Washington thought it prudent to stress the virtues of farming, thus participating in the commodification of black workers. Meier, *Negro Thought in America*, p. 105; Harris, *Harder We Run*, pp. 14–18, 29–50. Bowers's impressions of Washington are reprinted in Harlan, ed., *Booker T. Washington Papers* 4: 330–32.

37. Baker, *Following the Color Line*, pp. 56–59, 178.

38. Baldwin is quoted in Harlan, *Separate and Unequal*, pp. 76–78. Miller, *Radicals and Conservatives*, pp. 143–44. *Hampton Negro Conference*, p. 8.

39. On Turner and Elliott, see Jaynes, *Branches Without Roots*, pp. 276–77. Morin, "Change, Destructive of Character-Growth," pp. 182–87.

40. Howe, "Symposium—Temperance," p. 376.

41. Jaynes, *Branches Without Roots*. For praise of the Negro Business League, see editorial "Remarkable Progress of the Negro Race as Told at Topeka," *Colored American Magazine* 13, no. 4 (October 1907): 257–64. Meier, *Negro Thought in America*, pp. 124–27; and Weinstein, *Corporate Ideal in the Liberal State*, pp. 3–39. Washington is quoted in Meier, *Negro Thought in America*, p. 104.

42. Dorkins, "Results of Some Hard Experiences," pp. 271–72; Andrew F. Hilyer, "Report on Committee on Business and Labor," *Hampton Negro Conference* 5 (July 1901): pp. 17–19; Woodson, *Negro Professional Man*, p. xii; Woodson, *Negro as a Business Man*, pp. 14–16. See also Harris, *Negro as a Capitalist*, pp. 14–16.

43. Foner, *Antonio Maceo*.

44. Editorial, *Iowa State Bystander*, May 6, 1898, reprinted in Marks, ed., *Black Press Views American Imperialism*, p. 52.

45. Putnam, "Negro's Part in New National Problems," pp. 69–76; R. C. Ransom, "The Negro and Socialism," *A.M.E. Church Review* 13, no. 2 (October 1896); Hall, "Old or the New Faith," pp. 173–79. See also Foner, ed., *Black Socialist Preacher*, which collects the writings of black socialists Rev. George Washington Woodbey, Ransom, and Rev. James Theodore Holly.

46. Marks, ed., *Black Press Views American Imperialism*; Gatewood, *Black Americans and the White Man's Burden*.

Chapter Four

1. "The education of the Negroes, then, the most important thing in the uplift of the Negroes, is almost entirely in the hands of those who have enslaved them and now segregate them." See Woodson, *Mis-education of the Negro*, p. 22. For details on his life and career, see the entry on Ferris in Rayford L. Logan and Michael Winston, eds., *Dictionary of Negro Biography* (New York: Norton, 1982), pp. 221–22.

2. See the obituary, "William Henry Ferris," *Journal of Negro History* 26 (1941): 549–50. Much autobiographical material is also contained in Ferris, *African Abroad*. Wilson Moses has challenged those literary historians who have represented the Harlem Renaissance of the 1920s as a radical departure from the literary and intellectual community based in black Washington, D.C., and the American Negro Academy. See Moses, "Lost World of the New Negro," pp. 71–72, which situates Ferris within the black intelligentsia centered in Washington, D.C., at the turn of the century.

Not all black nationalists shared Ferris's antimodern world view. Hubert H. Harrison, a journalist, public school teacher, and socialist, believed that black intellectuals should be more attentive to modern ideas. "I look at Mr. Ferris's two volumes," he confided to James Weldon Johnson, "and as a man of the 20th century, I feel thoroughly disgusted at [his] seventeenth century mode of translating ideas." Harrison to Johnson, May 12, 1915, ser. 1, folder 197, James Weldon Johnson Collection.

3. "Negroes Who Protect American Rights Abroad Must Be Protected at Home," *Congressional Record*, U.S. Senate, 55th Cong., 2d sess., pp. 2404–5, March 3, 1898, reprinted in Marks, ed., *Black Press Views American Imperialism*, pp. 199–200.

4. Ferris, *African Abroad*, p. 131.

5. Harper, "Nationalism and Social Division," pp. 234–55. On the range of black intellectuals and organizations in the 1920s, see Cruse, *Crisis of the Negro Intellectual*.

6. Taylor, "Will He Survive?" pp. 242–50.

7. *Negro World*, October 4, 1919, cited in Stein, *World of Marcus Garvey*, p. 81. Ferris, "Marcus Garvey Was Genius," p. 1.

8. Meier, *Negro Thought in America*, pp. 262–63. Records of the association between Ferris, Bruce, Cromwell, Locke, Grimké, Blyden, and Schomburg are contained in the Bruce/Cromwell corrspondence in the Alain Locke Papers. I am indebted to Esmé Bhan for calling this corrspondence to my attention. For Locke's trip to Egypt, see John E. Bruce to Alain L. Locke, October 22, 1923, Alain Locke Papers. See also "The American Negro Academy," *African Times and Orient Review* (November–December 1913): 243–44, probably written by Alí, which contains a comprehensive list of members. Fortune served as editor of Garvey's *Negro World* from 1923 until his death in 1928. See Thornbrough, *T. Thomas Fortune*, pp. 356–57. Ida B. Wells addressed a Garveyite convention, and although she objected to his Black Star line steamship venture and Garvey's megalomania, she considered his movement "wonderful." See Duster, ed., *Crusader for Justice*, pp. 380–82. Rayford Logan noted that Ferris contributed valuable information, including a history of the Negro Society for Historical Research, in *African Abroad*, pp. 863–66.

9. See Theodore Vincent, "The Garveyite Parents of Malcolm X," *Black Scholar* (March/April 1989): 10–13. For an antecedent to current Afrocentric perspectives, see "Magazines and Reviews," *A.M.E. Church Review* 13, no. 2 (October 1896): 252, for a favorable mention of an article by a white scholar that notes, "The blacks were a fundamental element in the origin not only of the primitive races of Southern Europe, but of the civilized races of antiquity as well."

10. See Moses, *The Wings of Ethiopia*, p. 101.

11. On the civilizationist, assimilationist character of black nationalism at the turn of the century, see Moses, *Golden Age of Black Nationalism*.

12. Ibid., pp. 748, 760.

13. Ferris, *African Abroad*, pp. 101–2, 198–99.

14. Horton, "Freedom's Yoke," pp. 51–76.

15. Hortense Spillers, "Moving on Down the Line: Variations on the African-American Sermon," in *The Bounds of Race: Perspectives on Hegemony and Resistance*, ed. Dominick LaCapra, pp. 59–60 (Ithaca, N.Y.: Cornell University Press, 1991).

16. J. Max Barber, *The Negro of the Earlier World: An Excursion into Ancient Negro History* (Philadelphia, n.d.); Ferris, *African Abroad*, p. 32.

17. On Ethiopianism, see Moses, *Golden Age of Black Nationalism*, p. 74. Hopkins is quoted in *Voice of the Negro* 2, no. 3 (March 1905): 189–91.

18. Carby, ed., *Of One Blood*, pp. 562–63, 621. On the aryanization of ancient history, see Diop, *African Origin of Civilization*; and Bernal, *Black Athena*. See Martin R. Delany, *Principia of Ethnology: The Origin of Races and Color, with an Archaeological Compendium of Ethiopian and Egyptian Civilization from Years of Careful Examination and Enquiry* (Philadelphia: Harper and Brother, 1879). Hopkins, *Primer of Facts*; Barber, *Negro of the Earlier World*.

19. On Kipling, see Gossett, *Race*, pp. 332–33. On Roosevelt and "The Strenuous Life," see Filene, *Him/Her/Self*, pp. 71–72. Roosevelt's speech is found in its entirety in Theodore Roosevelt, *The Strenuous Life: Essays and Addresses* (New York: Century, 1902; New York: Scholarly Press, 1970), pp. 1–21. "A Nation's Manhood," *Independent*, p. 621.

20. Ferris, *African Abroad*, pp. 304, 587–88. Ferris cited approvingly the work of Prof. Wilson S. Naylor, who was optimistic concerning "the native African's capacity to absorb and assimilate civilization. . . . The African is precocious when young, imitative and teachable always. Right example and incentive influence him as perhaps no other race of men." On Naylor, see Brantlinger, "Victorians and Africans," pp. 166–203.

21. For Anglo-American concerns over racial purity in the context of debates over imperialism, and the Dos Passos quotation, see Gossett, *Race*, p. 326, and pp. 145–75, 310–38.

22. For a discussion of "hegemonic masculinity," see Connell, *Gender and Power*, pp. 183–88.

23. Ferris, *African Abroad*, pp. 631–51, 653, 653–70, 707, 721.

24. Griggs, *Imperium in Imperio*, pp. 132–35, 145.

25. Ibid., p. 57.

26. Ferris, "Alexander Crummell: An Apostle of Negro Culture (1920)," *American Negro Academy, Occasional Papers*, 1–22, No. 20. See also Ferris, *African Abroad*, pp. 117, 206, 228–29.

27. Ferris, *African Abroad*, pp. 264, 70.

28. Ferris to Booker T. Washington, January 1902, in Harlan, ed., *Booker T. Washington Papers* 6: 384–85. Washington's opinion of Ferris is clear from a letter to Julius Rosenwald, marked "confidential." Enclosing Ferris's prior correspondence with him, Washington advised that "Mr. Ferris represents a very pathetic case. . . . [H]e has tried to do several kinds of work since he graduated, but has proved a failure in everything . . . I have tried several times to find a place he could fill, but have not been successful." Washington to Rosenwald, August 29, 1912, in Harlan, ed., *Booker T. Washington Papers* 12: 586. Despite Washington's statement to the contrary, it is likely that Ferris's difficulties resulted in part from Washington's influence.

29. See Washington to William Colfax Graves, December 18, 1913, in Harlan, ed., *Booker T. Washington Papers* 12: 375; Graves to Washington, December 23, 1913, in ibid., p. 380.

30. Showing irritation and a lack of sensitivity, particularly since Ferris's father had recently died, Du Bois wrote to Ferris, bluntly attributing Ferris's difficulties to character flaws. Du Bois went on to suggest that Ferris attend to his financial problems by

performing manual labor. Du Bois to Ferris, March 23, 1912, in the W. E. B. Du Bois Papers. For Ferris's feud with Trotter, see Fox, *Guardian of Boston*, pp. 108–9; and Ferris to Washington, December 16, 1907, in Harlan, ed., *Booker T. Washington Papers* 9: 423.

31. Ferris, *African Abroad*, p. 132.

32. Ibid., pp. 330–31.

33. Ferris, *African Abroad*, pp. 125–26. A photograph of Ferris is reproduced in the frontispiece of *African Abroad*.

34. Ferris, *African Abroad*, pp. 120–24. Ferris to Schomburg, February 19, 1925, in Arthur A. Schomburg Correspondence. Quoted in Stein, *World of Marcus Garvey*, pp. 80–81. Ferris goes on to state, "I have sent out a few letters to some of my caucasian friends and colored debtors saying in substance, 'There is a lightening [*sic*] rod in New Haven waiting and praying to be struck by financial lightening.'" There is no evidence that Ferris ever married.

35. Gatewood, *Aristocrats of Color*; Bardolph, *Negro Vanguard*, pp. 131–273; Reuter, *Race Mixture*, pp. 167–80; John E. Bruce to John W. Cromwell, November 10, 1899, Alain Locke Papers; Crummell to Bruce, April 7, 1896, John Bruce Collection. The desire of a lighter-hued Afro-American elite to maintain a separate identity from the black population is indicated by a letter reprinted in the *Colored American Magazine* in which the correspondent objected to the use of the term "Negro" to refer to "the colored population of the South" and noted the "impropriety of classing as 'Negroes' many men and women who are practically more closely allied with the Anglo-Saxon race." "Colored people," the correspondent argued, was far preferable to "Negro, with its opprobrious popular corruption of 'nigger.'" Henry Blackwell, "Colored People Not Negroes," *Colored American Magazine* 15, no. 2 (February 1909): 110–11. Among the new black middle-class the term "Negro" carried nationalistic connotations of race pride, serving as a repudiation of an older generation's desire to preserve a patriotic sense of dual identity (as well as a reference to mixed racial heritage) with the term "colored American."

36. Ralph W. Tyler, "Real Society," *Colored American Magazine* 13, no. 5 (November 1907): 391–92. On Tyler and the Negro Business League, see Harlan, *Booker T. Washington: The Wizard of Tuskegee*, p. 420. Robert Terrell, "The Negro in Domestic Service," *Colored American Magazine* 9, no. 5 (November 1905): 631–32.

37. Hovenkamp, "Social Science and Segregation," pp. 655–56.

38. Ibid., p. 32. W. E. B. Du Bois, "The Conservation of Races," *American Negro Academy, Occasional Papers*, No. 2, p. 12. Fortune's charge was overdrawn, as several members of the academy were flexible on the question of race mixing. See the discussion of Du Bois's paper in Moses, *Alexander Crummell*, pp. 264–65. Durham is quoted in Bruce, *Black American Writing*, p. 135; Young, "A Race Without an Ideal," p. 609.

39. Lynch, "Race Assimilation," pp. 211–13.

40. Alexander, "Appeal for Race Integrity," pp. 16–17; Baker, "Ideals, Part 1."

41. See the short story by Hopkins, "Talma Gordon," pp. 271–90, which favorably portrays the marriage of a black woman to a wealthy northern white man.

42. Roberts, *Papa Jack*.

43. A Harvard anthropological study of biracial families published in 1932 challenged the social science view of mulatto degeneracy. See Day, *Study of Negro-White Families*, p. 106.

44. Shadrach, "Furnace Blasts: Black or White?" p. 349; Hopkins, *Contending Forces*, pp. 220–22, 321. Griggs, *Imperium in Imperio*, pp. 171–76.

45. Fortune is quoted in "Question of Intermarriage," pp. 228–29.

46. Hovenkamp, "Social Science and Segregation," pp. 656–57. On Ransom, see Luker, *Social Gospel*, p. 174. On the Manassah Society, see Gatewood, *Aristocrats of Color*, p. 177. Duster, ed., *Crusader for Justice*, pp. 72–75. Fortune, "Question of Intermarriage."

47. Burroughs, "Not Color But Character," p. 277.

48. Du Bois, *Philadelphia Negro*, p. 71; Baker, "Negro Woman," p. 77.

49. Ferris, *African Abroad*, pp. 267–68.

Chapter Five

1. Cooper, "American Negro Academy," pp. 35–36. On the history of the academy, see Moss, *American Negro Academy*.

2. An important exception is Giddings, *When and Where I Enter*.

3. Gabel, *From Slavery to the Sorbonne*; Giddings, *When and Where I Enter*, Carby, *Reconstructing Womanhood*, pp. 95–107; Mary Helen Washington, introduction to Anna Julia Cooper, *Voice from the South*, pp. xxxiii–xxxvi.

4. Chateauvert, "The Third Step," p. 7.

5. Cooper wrote, "It seems to me that the *Tragic Era* should be answered—adequately, fully, ably, . . . *Thou* art the Man!" Anna Julia Cooper to W. E. B. Du Bois, December 31, 1929, in Aptheker, ed., *Correspondence of W. E. B. Du Bois* 1: 411.

6. On the writings and activities of Cooper, Ida B. Wells, Frances Harper, Gertrude Mossell, Pauline Hopkins, and others, along with the organizational efforts of the National Association of Colored Women, see Carby, *Reconstructing Womanhood*.

7. See "A Voice From the South, By a Black Woman of the South," *A.M.E. Church Review* 9, no. 4 (1892): 416; Tillman, "Afro-American Women," p. 495; Painter, *Standing at Armageddon*, pp. 47–50, 110–14; Berry, *Black Resistance*, p. 112.

8. Anna J. Cooper, "Colored Women as Wage-Earners," *Southern Workman* 28 (August 1899): 295.

9. On the matter of protecting black women in the South, Cooper cited approvingly Alexander Crummell's earlier discussion: "I would beg, however, with the Doctor's permission, to add my plea for the *Colored Girls* of the South." Cooper, *Voice from the South*, p. 24. Crummell had declared in 1883 that black women emerged from slavery in a more degraded condition than black men: "From her childhood she was the doomed victim of the grossest passions. . . . When she reached maturity all the tender instincts of her womanhood were ruthlessly violated." Even after slavery, educated black women working as school teachers, "as well as their more ignorant sisters in rude huts, are followed and tempted and insulted by the ruffianly element of Southern society, who think that black *men* have no rights which white men should regard, and black *women* no virtue which white men should respect!" See Crummell, "The Black Woman of the South: Her neglects and her needs," in Crumwell, *Africa and America*, pp. 59–82.

10. Cooper, *Voice from the South*, pp. 134–35, i–ii.

11. Ibid., p. 25. For documentation of the sexual persecution of black women in the post-Reconstruction era, see Sterling, ed., *We Are Your Sisters*, pp. 344–55; and Davis, *Women, Race and Class*, pp. 175–76.

12. Cooper, *Voice from the South*, pp. 24–31. See also Carby, *Reconstructing Womanhood*, pp. 103–5.

13. George Henry Murray, "Educated Colored Men and White Women," *Colored American Magazine* 8, no. 2 (February 1905): 94. James H. A. Johnson, "Woman's Exalted Station," *A.M.E. Church Review* 8, no. 4 (April 1892): 402. On Amanda Smith, see the biographical sketch in Shockley, ed., *Afro-American Women Writers*, pp. 225–27. On the history of black women's efforts to preach in the AME church, see the introduction by Jualynne E. Dodson to the reprint edition of Smith, *Autobiography*, pp. xxvii–xlii.

14. Cooper, *Voice from the South*, p. 44.

15. See Tillman, "Afro-American Women"; L. A. Scruggs, "Inflence of Negro Women in the Home," in Scruggs, ed., *Women of Distinction*, pp. 372–82; Brown, *Homespun Heroines*; Majors, *Notable Negro Women*; and Lee, "The Home-Maker," pp. 63–66 for arguments for women's natural place as mothers and homemakers. Interestingly, both sources also make explicit claims in support of sexual equality and extravagantly praise the nobility and sacrifice of motherhood. For a somewhat more varied treatment of black women's public activities that nonetheless endorses dominant assumptions of motherhood and domesticity, see Mossell, *Work of the Afro-American Woman*, pp. 9–47. While Mossell departs from convention by discussing black women's work in a variety of male-dominated occupations and politics, her use of her husband's married name and the authenticating introduction of AME church bishop Benjamin E. Lee were strategic acts in conformity with the ideology of "true womanhood." The *Women's Era* is quoted in Giddings, *When and Where I Enter*, p. 108.

16. Cooper, *Voice from the South*, pp. 134–35. For examples of anthologies of representative black women with biographical sketches and illustrations, see Majors, *Noted Negro Women*; and Scruggs, ed., *Women of Distinction*. The quotation is from the introduction, written by Mrs. Josephine Turpin Washington, to *Women of Distinction*, p. xi. Anna Julia Cooper to Francis J. Grimké, January 1, 1934, in Woodson, ed., *Works of Francis Grimke*, pp. 497–98.

17. For misogynist arguments against woman suffrage in the 1890s, see Aileen Kraditor, *Ideas of the Woman Suffrage Movement*, pp. 12–26.

18. Cooper, "Colored Women as Wage-Earners," pp. 295–98.

19. Cotson is quoted in Majors, *Notable Negro Women*, p. 253. Wells's recollection is in Duster, ed., *Crusader for Justice*, pp. 221–22. See "Iola's Southern Field," *New York Age* (November 19, 1892): 2.

20. Anderson, *Education of Blacks in the South*, pp. 33–109. Kelly Miller, "Surplus Negro Women," in Miller, *Radicals and Conservatives*, p. 189. For general arguments against higher education for women, see Newman, ed., *Men's Ideas/Women's Realities*, pp. 54–104.

21. Newman, ed., *Men's Ideas/Women's Realities*. Baker is quoted in Noble, *Negro Woman's College Education*, p. 157.

22. Miller saw the presence of single women in the cities, with diminished prospects for marriage, as a vulnerable, morally suspect group: "These left-over, or to-be-left-

over, Negro women, falling as they do in the lower stratum of society, miss the inhib-
itive restraint of culture and social pride, and, especially if they be comely of appearance, become the easy prey of the evil designs of both races." Miller, "Surplus Negro
Women," pp. 184–85. Du Bois also notes this phenomenon in *Philadelphia Negro*. S. B.
Stevens, "The Development of Stronger Womanhood," paper read at the Hampton
Negro Conference No. 2, July 1898, pp. 69–75, quoted in Noble, *Negro Woman's College Education*, 156–58. Davis is quoted in Bruce, *Black American Writing*, p. 117.

23. "Colored Women's Influence," *Southern Workman* 27, no. 11 (November 1898):
217; Higginbotham, *Righteous Discontent*, pp. 97–101.

24. Cooper, "Colored Women as Wage-Earners," p. 62.

25. Ibid., 127–31.

26. Ibid., pp. 51–53. See Higham, *Strangers in the Land*, p. 113. Examples of black
comment on the subject are "Immigration and the Negro," *Alexander's Magazine* 2,
no. 2 (June 1906): 16–17; and Kent, "Afro-American Problem," pp. 724–26.

27. Cooper, "Colored Women as Wage Earners," pp. 80, 101. On racial divisions
within the woman suffrage movement, see Kraditor, *Ideas of the Woman Suffrage Movement*, pp. 138–71.

28. Cooper, "Colored Women as Wage Earners," pp. 53–54.

29. Ibid., pp. 54, 123, 125.

30. Ibid., p. 173.

31. Ibid., pp. 252–56. In a survey of black college graduates distributed in 1930 by
Charles S. Johnson, Cooper described herself as a member of the "National N[egro]
Association for Suppression of Atheism and Communism among colored youth." In
Anna Julia Cooper Papers. See also Johnson, *Negro College Graduate*.

32. Charles Flynn, *White Land, Black Labor: Caste and Class in Nineteenth Century
Georgia* (Baton Rouge: Louisiana State University Press, 1983), pp. 84–114, 152–54.

33. Anna Julia Cooper, "Do Two and Two Make Four?" *Independent* 46 (July 26,
1894): 7.

34. For Crummell's position on democracy, see Moses, *Alexander Crummell*,
pp. 59–82.

35. Ibid., pp. 172–73.

36. Cooper, *Voice from the South*, pp. 208–9, 179–80, 185–86. See also Cooper's
letter praising Hampton Institute's project of collecting Negro folklore: "The black
man is readily assimilated to his suroundings and the original simple or distinct type is
in danger of being lost or outgrown." *Southern Workman* 23, no. 1 (January 1894): 5.

37. Cooper, *Voice from the South*, pp. 211–19.

38. An accommodationist attitude toward whites' sexual conduct was expressed in a
curious statement by the journalist and publisher Charles Alexander. "Nothing makes
us prouder of our race than the doggedness with which it refuses to lose its common
sense and spirit of fair play, and brand the white race as a race of rapists, because some
white men have raped, and do rape black women." It might be argued, however, that
Alexander was "signifying," saying one thing while meaning its opposite. See "Marks
of True Greatness," *Alexander's Magazine* 3, no. 2 (December 15, 1903): 59–60.

39. Cooper, *Voice from the South*, pp. 217–21.

40. Ibid., 287, 295–300, 303–4.

41. Ibid., pp. ii.

Chapter Six

1. Du Bois, *Autobiography of W. E. B. Du Bois*, pp. 159, 162, 170–71, 197, 183. For a groundbreaking psychological analysis of the significance of his background and early childhood, see Davis, *Leadership, Love and Aggression*, pp. 105–52.

2. Du Bois, *Autobiography of W. E. B. Du Bois*, 195, 198, 194, 198–99. On the sponsorship of the study, see Rampersad, *Art and Imagination of W. E. B. Du Bois*, pp. 50–51. Eaton contributed a study of domestic service in Philadelphia that appeared in an appendix to *Philadelphia Negro*. See Isabel Eaton, "Special Report on Negro Domestic Service In the Seventh Ward, Philadelphia" in Du Bois, *Philadelphia Negro*, pp. 437–509.

3. Du Bois, "The Negro and Crime," *Independent* 57, no. 2633 (May 18, 1899): 1355–56.

4. Rampersad, *Art and Imagination of W. E. B. Du Bois*, pp. 53, 299.

5. Lewis, *W. E. B. Du Bois*. Du Bois is quoted in Michael Goldstein, "Preface to the Rise of Booker T. Washington: A View from New York City of the Demise of Independent Black Politics, 1889–1902," *Journal of Negro History* 62, no. 1 (January 1977): 89.

6. See "The Souls of Black Folk," *Southern Workman* 32, no. 6 (June 1903): 262–63.

7. Du Bois, *Autobiography of W. E. B. Du Bois*, pp. 142–43.

8. W. E. B. Du Bois, "The Conservation of Races," in Wagstaff, ed., *Black Power*, p. 69.

9. Du Bois, *Autobiography of W. E. B. Du Bois*, pp. 205–6.

10. Du Bois, *Philadelphia Negro*, p. 1.

11. See the reviews "The Philadelphia Negro," *Southern Workman* 29, no. 2 (February 1900): 121; and "The Negro Problem in the North," *Nation* 69, no. 1791 (October 26, 1899): 310. See E. Franklin Frazier, *The Negro Family in the United States* (Chicago: University of Chicago Press, 1966). The Moynihan report and contemporary commentaries on it are collected in Lee Rainwater and William Yancey, eds., *The Moynihan Report and the Politics of Controversy* (Cambridge, Mass.: MIT Press, 1967). On the culture of poverty thesis, see Charles Valentine, *Culture and Poverty: Critique and Counter-Proposals* (Chicago: University of Chicago Press, 1968).

12. For background information of urban politics and the black community in Philadelphia in the nineteenth century, see Lane, *Roots of Violence*, esp. pp. 45–81. For the association of "pathological forms of recreation" with urban life, see Jones, *Recreation and Amusement Among Negroes*, pp. 87–189.

13. Hoffman quoted in Bardolph, ed., *The Civil Rights Record*, p. 105.

14. Brief reviews of popular negrophobic writings can be found in Fullenwider, *Mind and Mood of Black America*, pp. 3–4, and Rampersad, *Art and Imagination of W. E. B. Du Bois*, p. 60.

15. Du Bois, *Philadelphia Negro*, pp. 21–22.

16. Ibid., pp. 25–30.

17. Ibid., pp. 43–44.

18. Ibid., p. 98.

19. Ibid., p. 8.

20. Ibid., pp. 120–22.

21. Ibid., pp. 7, 310.

22. Ibid., p. 92. See Mary White Ovington, *The Walls Came Tumbling Down* (New York: Harcourt, 1947), pp. 37–38.

23. Hine, *Black Women in White*, pp. 34–35.

24. Du Bois, *Philadelphia Negro*, pp. 113–14, 147–63. On urban mortality in antebellum times, see Curry, *Free Black in Urban America*, pp. 136–46.

25. Du Bois, *Philadelphia Negro*, pp. 192–93.

26. Ibid., pp. 58–61.

27. Bryan S. Green, *Knowing the Poor: A Case Study in Textual Reality Construction* (London: Routledge and Kegan Paul, 1983).

28. Du Bois was well aware that "the best available methods of sociological research" were "liable to inaccuracies." Indeed, he was deeply sensitive to the inevitable intrusions of personal bias, but this "bias" pertained more to his antiracist intentions. Du Bois, *Philadelphia Negro*, pp. 2–3.

29. Du Bois, *Souls of Black Folk*, pp. 96–108.

30. As we have seen, among certain exponents of uplift, black migration to cities was feared as a departure from the evolutionary plan of uplift. Compared with the stresses of urban life, some spokesmen invoked nostalgic myths of rural freedom and innocence, however dubious their relevance for oppressed southern blacks. Following Booker T. Washington's peculiar notion of enslavement as an industrial school for black workers, black writers like Kelly Miller romanticized the "discipline of slavery" compared with the city, which "indisposes [the Negro] to hard work," and which fostered black disease, immorality, and pathology. For examples of racist representations of urban blacks, see Takaki, *Iron Cages*, pp. 207–8; Rabinowitz, *Race Relations*, p. 243. For a representative view of anxiety over black urban migration, see Miller, *Radicals and Conservatives*, pp. 107–8, 146.

31. Du Bois, *Philadelphia Negro*, pp. 309–16. Joseph DeMarco, *The Social Thought of W. E. B. Du Bois* (Lanham, Md.: University Press of America, 1983), pp. 48–53.

32. Du Bois, *Philadelphia Negro*, pp. 316–17, 11.

33. Arnold Rampersad has observed that, unlike *The Souls of Black Folk*, it was impossible to tell in the work under present consideration that its author was "flesh of the flesh" of his subject. See Rampersad, *Art and Imagination of W. E. B. Du Bois*, p. 53.

34. W. E. B. Du Bois, "A Program of Social Reform," *College Settlement News* 3, no. 3 (March 1897): 4, reprinted in Aptheker, ed., *Writings by W. E. B. Du Bois*, p. 31.

35. Du Bois, *Philadelphia Negro*, pp. 69–72, 164–68, 269–309, 322–58.

36. Ibid., pp. 58–59.

37. Ibid., pp. 108–11.

38. Ibid., pp. 66–67, 136–41.

39. Symanski, *Immoral Landscape*, pp. 5, 99–106, 125–47. For Du Bois's discussion of prostitution, see *Philadelphia Negro*, pp. 313–14.

40. In a study of black residential districts along the Philadelphia "Main Line," it was found that more than half the men were laborers and that "the practice is general for the woman of the household to work outside of the home." See Marvin E. Porch, "The Philadelphia Main Line Negro: A Social, Economic and Educational Survey" (Ph.D. diss., Temple University, 1938).

41. Du Bois, *Philadelphia Negro*, p. 72.

42. "Why the Men Don't Marry," *Colored American Magazine* 13, no. 5 (November 1907): 328–29.

43. "How to Keep Women at Home," *Colored American Magazine* 14, no. 1 (January 1908): 7–8.

44. These angry words were spoken by Douglass's master, Hugh Auld, when he discovered that his wife, Sophia, was defying southern law and custom by teaching the young Douglass to read. See Douglass, *My Bondage*, pp. 145–46.

45. For a treatment of the tensions created by changing sex roles, or more accurately, shifting social relations between the sexes, see Filene, *Him/Her/Self*.

46. Du Bois, *Philadelphia Negro*, pp. 383–84.

47. Ibid., p. 61.

48. Ibid., pp. 112, 195, 205–7.

49. Ibid., pp. 220, 229.

50. Ibid., pp. 127–29.

51. Ibid., pp. 322–53.

52. Ibid., pp. 119–26, 129.

53. Ibid., pp. 388–93.

54. Ibid., p. 350.

55. Du Bois, *Souls of Black Folk*, pp. 111–32.

56. For an example of the mainstreaming of uplift ideology in social science discourse on urban blacks and family disorganization, and its reliance on minstrelsy and the plantation legend, see Corinne Sherman, "Racial Factors in Desertion," *Family* (January 1923): 221–25. For a rebuttal to Sherman by a black social worker, see Helen B. Pendleton, "Case Work and Racial Traits," *Family* (February 1923): 252–54.

57. C. Wright Mills, "The Professional Ideology of Social Pathologists," *American Journal of Sociology* 47, no. 2 (September 1943): 165–80.

58. Rampersad, *Art and Imagination of W. E. B. Du Bois*, pp. 54–58.

59. Du Bois, "Two Negro Conventions," p. 2425. Shapiro, *White Violence*, p. 63.

60. Du Bois, *Philadelphia Negro*, p. 351.

Chapter Seven

1. Alexander Crummell, "The Need of New Ideas and New Aims," in Crummell, *Africa and America*, 22–24.

2. Osofsky, *Harlem*, pp. 13–16, 45–46; Spear, *Black Chicago*, pp. 11–27; Williams, "Social Bonds in the Black Belt of Chicago," *Charities* 15 (October 7, 1905): 40–41, cited in Spear, *Black Chicago*, p. 25.

3. The concept "cultural capital" as formulated by the sociologist Pierre Bordieu broadly describes the matrix of middle-class values and habits inherited by young people in the course of their education. See Bordieu, "Cultural Reproduction and Social Reproduction," in *Power and Ideology in Education*, ed. Jerome Karabel and A. H. Halsey (New York: Oxford University Press, 1971).

4. Faduma, "Defects of the Negro Church," pp. 4–5. On minstrelsy, see Dormon, "Shaping the Popular Image," pp. 450–71.

5. Paul Laurence Dunbar, "The Negroes of the Tenderloin," *New York Sun*, n.d., clipping in the Paul Laurence Dunbar Collection, box 16, reel 4.

6. Johnson, *Along This Way*, pp. 152, 159–62. "Paul Laurence Dunbar," *Southern Workman* 35, no. 3, pp. 136–37.

7. Review of "Lyrics of the Hearthside," *Independent* 51, no. 2640 (July 6, 1899): 1829.

8. James Weldon Johnson, the intellectual and activist, faced a similar dilemma. For a discussion of his early career as a composer of vaudeville songs for the Broadway stage based on racial stereotypes, and of his subsequent attempts to distinguish these activities from that which trafficked in demeaning minstrel stereotypes, see James Robert Saunders, "The Dilemma of Double Identity: James Weldon Johnson's Artistic Acknowledgment," *Langston Hughes Review* 8, nos. 1 and 2 (Spring/Fall 1989): 68–75.

9. Du Bois, *Souls of Black Folk*, pp. 204–15.

10. Johnson, *Book of American Negro Spirituals*, pp. 13–14.

11. Osofsky, *Harlem*, p. 50.

12. My reading of Dunbar and Corrothers in the context of American social realism was greatly assisted by Kaplan, *Social Construction of American Realism*.

13. Dunbar, *Sport of the Gods*. Subsequent page number references are noted in parentheses. An exception to the general apprehension surrounding black migration to cities is Pickens, *New Negro*; Bruce, *Black American Writing*, p. 93.

14. Dunbar, *Sport of the Gods*, pp. 13, 29, 45. Alice Moore Dunbar voiced dismay over her husband's reputation as "prince of the coon song writers." Their marriage ended in separation in 1902. See Jean Wagner, *Black Poets of the United States from Paul Laurence Dunbar to Langston Hughes*, trans. Kenneth Douglas (Urbana: University of Illinois Press, 1973), p. 78, cited in Bruce, *Black American Writing*, p. 67.

15. In poems and stories from this period, Dunbar angrily attacked lynching, the consolidation of wage slavery among black farmers, and the convict-lease system. See Bruce, *Black American Writing*, pp. 81–88.

16. Dunbar, *Sport of the Gods*, pp. 49–50.

17. Ibid., pp. 53–54.

18. Ibid., pp. 77, 84.

19. Ibid., pp. 98–103, 203. James Dornon notes that black composers composed some of the most popular coon songs. Unfortunately, this point seems to have little bearing on his analysis of coon songs. See Dormon, "Shaping the Popular Image," pp. 454, 458–59.

20. Dunbar, *Sport of the Gods*, p. 98.

21. Ibid., p. 113.

22. Ibid., pp. 198–200.

23. Ibid., pp. 237, 255.

24. Washington, *Up From Slavery*; Corrothers, *In Spite of the Handicap*. Recent scholarly surveys of black autobiography include Andrews, *To Tell a Free Story*; and Braxton, *Black Women Writing Autobiography*. On the subject of autobiography in the Progressive Era, see Stinson, "S. S. McClure's My Autobiography," pp. 203–12.

25. James D. Corrothers, "At the End of the Controversy," *American Magazine* 77 (March 1914): 36. Corrothers, *In Spite of the Handicap*, p. 37.

26. Cassandra Smith-Parker, "James D. Corrothers," in *Dictionary of Negro Biography*, ed. Rayford Logan and Michael Winston (New York: Norton, 1982), pp. 135–36.

27. Bruce, *Black American Writing*, discusses literary experiments with Negro dialect.

On black migration and intraracial class conflicts over urban popular amusements and black women's sexuality, see Hazel Carby, "Policing the Black Woman's Body in an Urban Context," *Critical Inquiry* 18 (Summer 1992): 738–55.

28. Corrothers, *In Spite of the Handicap*, 22, 26–27.

29. On racist stereotypes, see Logan, *Betrayal of the Negro* ,242–75; Corrothers, *In Spite of the Handicap*, 85; James D. Corrothers, "A Man They Didn't Know," *Crisis* 7 (December 1913–January 1914): 85–87, 135–38; Corrothers, "At the End of the Controversy."

30. Corrothers, *Black Cat Club*, 20, 137. The black poet and critic William Stanley Braithwaite and the black journalist Charles Alexander reviewed *The Black Cat Club* favorably. See Bruce, *Black American Writing*, 121; Corrothers, *In Spite of the Handicap*, 137–38, 189, 193.

31. George McClellan, "The Negro as a Writer," in *Twentieth Century Negro Literature*, ed. D. W. Culp (Naperville, Ill.: J. L. Nichols, 1902), p. 280.

32. In Charles Chesnutt's *Conjure Woman* (1899), the reminiscences of slavery in Negro dialect by the shrewd and venerable servant "Uncle" Julius McAdoo enable their teller to subtly negotiate power relations with his employers, a northern white couple who have invested in the New South economic order. As Frances Ellen Watkins Harper used it in her 1892 novel *Iola Leroy*, dialect signaled the oppositional folk consciousness of Harper's former slave characters. See Charles Chesnutt, *The Conjure Woman* (Ridgewood, N.J.: Gregg Press, 1968); Harper, *Iola Leroy*. For dialect humor in black periodicals, see, for example, "Young Men's Congressional Club Mock Trial," *Colored American Magazine* 1 (August 1900): 144–45. In 1931, James Weldon Johnson pronounced Negro dialect dead as a literary form in the introduction to his *Book of American Negro Poetry*. Johnson's collection includes seven poems by James Corrothers.

33. For Douglass's account of Jenkins within a general discussion of conjuring, see Levine, *Black Culture and Black Consciousness*, pp. 67–69.

34. Corrothers, *Black Cat Club*, 65–77, 23–25. On coon song "razor" stereotypes, see Dormon, "Shaping the Popular Image," 455.

35. Corrothers, *Black Cat Club*, 58–59.

36. On the complex racial "structures of feeling" in nineteenth-century minstrelsy and the extent to which the threatening image of the black male body, subjected to control, could also effect in white audiences a return of the repressed, see Eric Lott, "'The Seeming Counterfeit': Racial Politics and Early Blackface Minstrelsy," *American Quarterly* 43 (June 1991): 223–54.

37. Corrothers, *In Spite of the Handicap*, 8.

38. Ibid., 29–30, 83–86.

39. Ibid., 93–98. For Wells's antilynching position, see Gail Bederman, "'Civilization,' the Decline of Middle-Class Manliness, and Ida B. Wells' Antilynching Campaign (1892–1894)," *Radical History Review* 52 (Fall 1992): 5–30. For the dispute between Wells and Frances Willard over the latter's justification for lynching, see Vron Ware, *Beyond the Pale: White Women, Racism, and History* (London: Verso, 1992), 198–209.

40. Corrothers, *In Spite of the Handicap*, 109.

41. Michael Denning, *Mechanic Accents: Dime Novels and Working Class Culture in America* (London: Verso, 1987), 167–84. Of the "quadroon girl," Corrothers wrote

that after an unescorted evening with him she complained to her girlfriends, "He walked to church with me . . . through the rain, under an umbrella, in the night; *and never kissed me!*" Corrothers, *In Spite of the Handicap*, 114–15.

42. Corrothers, *In Spite of the Handicap,* 120.

43. Ibid., 92.

44. Ibid., 101, 107–8, 112.

45. Ibid., pp. 105, 163.

46. Ibid., p. 20.

47. Ibid., pp. 69–71.

48. Ibid., p. 38.

49. Ibid., 60–61.

50. Ibid., 229.

51. "An Indignation Dinner," *Century Magazine* 91 (December 1915): 320. Corrothers also published poems in standard English in the *Century Magazine*, *Crisis*, and *Voice of the Negro*. See "At the Closed Gate of Justice," *Century Magazine* 86 (June 1913): 272; "Lincoln," *Voice of the Negro* 2 (January 1905): 686.

52. "In the Matter of Two Men," *Crisis* 9 (January 1915): 138; Corrothers, *In Spite of the Handicap*, 176.

53. Corrothers, "At the End of the Controversy."

54. "A Man They Didn't Know," *Crisis* 7 (December 1913–January 1914): 85–87, 136–38.

55. "At the Closed Gate of Justice," p. 272.

Chapter Eight

1. Hull, ed., *Give Us Each Day*.

2. Ibid., p. 41.

3. For Dunbar-Nelson's secret marriage to Callis, see Hull, ibid., p. 144. Callis, a graduate of Cornell who later became a prominent Washington, D.C., physician, helped found the black college fraternity Alpha Phi Alpha. See Charles H. Wesley, *Henry Arthur Callis: Life and Legacy* (Chicago: Foundation Publishers, 1977). Apparently such marriages were common enough to merit public notice; see "The Evils of Secret Marriages," *Negro World*, December 27, 1924.

4. Biograhical details are from Hull, ed., *Give Us Each Day*, pp. 13–32.

5. "I know," she wrote to the black bibliophile Arthur A. Schomburg in 1918, "yea verily do Mr. Nelson and I [?] about $2000 worth of know—how apathetic is this race of ours . . . on matters literary." Alice Dunbar-Nelson to Arthur A. Schomburg, May 29, 1918, in the Arthur A. Schomburg Correspondence. Dunbar-Nelson's entrepreneurial publications were not unlike those of the historian Carter G. Woodson, who brought out his *Negro Orators and Their Orations* in 1925. Dunbar-Nelson and Woodson, it seems, collaborated on several projects during the 1920s, none of which seem to have been completed. See Hull, ed., *Give Us Each Day*, p. 425.

6. Hull, ed., *Give Us Each Day*, 57–58, 75–77, 95. On Micheaux, see Cripps, "Race Movies," pp. 39–55.

7. Cripps, "Race Movies," pp. 67, 93.

8. Jackson, *Ku Klux Klan in the City*; "From the South" *Crisis* (August 1911):

166–67, reprinted in Aptheker, ed., *Documentary History of the Negro People*, pp. 30–32. For an account of Washington's assault and the ensuing trial, see Harlan, *Booker T. Washington: The Wizard of Tuskegee*, pp. 379–404.

9. Fox, *Guardian of Boston*, pp. 179–82. Trotter is quoted in Aptheker, ed., *Documentary History of the Negro People*, p. 76.

10. Fox, *Guardian of Boston*, pp. 183–87.

11. Rudwick, *Race Riot in East St. Louis*; Berry, *Black Resistance*, pp. 139–54.

12. The account of the lynching of Henry Lowery is taken from a Memphis newspaper and is reprinted in Johnson, *Along This Way*, p. 361.

13. For an account of the trial, see "A Celebrated Case," *Washington Evening Star*, ca. 1902, n.p., clipping in Paul Laurence Dunbar Collection, reel 6, nos. 899–900.

14. See Hull, ed., *Works of Alice Dunbar-Nelson* 2: 110, 123, 140, 241. Another expression of the particular dilemmas of educated black women is Bonner, "On Being Young—a Woman—and Colored," pp. 63–65.

15. Hull, ed., *Give Us Each Day*, pp. 29, 373–382.

16. Hull, ed., *Works of Alice Dunbar-Nelson* 2: 194. Elsewhere, she criticized the GOP, comparing its abandonment of blacks with that of the fair-skinned black who "passes for white" (ibid., 2: 238–39).

17. Ibid., pp. 183–84.

18. Green, *Secret City*, pp. 171–73.

19. Julianne Malveaux demonstrates the irrelevance of "feminization of poverty" thesis for black women whose poverty is often the result of the institutional racism that bars black men from employment. See Malveaux, "The Political Economy of Black Women," in *The Year Left 2: Toward a Rainbow Socialism*, ed. Mike Davis, Manning Marable, Fred Pfeil, and Michael Sprinker (London: Verso, 1987), pp. 52–73.

20. In a satirical vein, Wallace Thurman observed that "people who are moral in every other respect, church going folk, who damn drinking, dancing or gambling in any other form, will play the numbers. . . . I guess I will play fifty cents on the number I found stamped inside the band of my last year's straw hat." Thurman, *Negro Life in New York's Harlem* (Girard, Kans.: Haldeman-Julius, 1928), 47.

21. See Hull, ed., *Give Us Each Day*, pp. 270–71, 304, for marital tensions; on Dunbar-Nelson's attitude toward the Industrial School, p. 234; on playing the numbers, see pp. 188–89, 252, 257, 323. For her views on her husband's prospects for a political appointment, see pp. 119–20.

22. Hull, ed., *Works of Alice Dunbar-Nelson* 2: 227, 430.

23. "Our Book List," *A.M.E. Church Review* 9, no. 4 (1892): 416–17.

24. Nannie H. Burroughs, "Not Color but Character," *Voice of the Negro* 1, no. 7 (July 1904): 277–79.

25. Edwina Kruse to Alice Moore Dunbar, March 31, 1908, roll 6, no. 138, Paul Laurence Dunbar Collection.

26. Hull, ed., *Give Us Each Day*, pp. 250, 283, 313.

27. Hull, ed., *Works of Alice Dunbar-Nelson* 2: 141.

28. See Rampersad, *Art and Imagination of W. E. B. Du Bois*, pp. 146–47, on Du Bois's support for the war. See Du Bois, "Close Ranks," *Crisis* 16 (July 1918): 111.

29. Hull, ed., *Works of Alice Dunbar-Nelson* 2: 212, 207–8. Dunbar-Nelson's view of war and imperialism as a struggle between the capitalist Western nations and colo-

nized African peoples essentially followed an earlier critique made by Du Bois. See Du Bois, *Darkwater*, pp. 56–74.

30. Lester A. Walton, "Art is Helping in Obliterating the Color Line," in Aptheker, ed., *Documentary History*, p. 485.

31. Langston Hughes, "The Negro Artist and the Racial Mountain," *Nation* 122 (June 23, 1926): 692–94.

32. Lewis, *When Harlem Was in Vogue*.

33. Hull, ed., *Give Us Each Day*, p. 54.

34. Hull, ed., *Works of Alice Dunbar-Nelson* 2: 221, 197.

35. Hull, ed., *Give Us Each Day*, pp. 143, 167, 252.

36. Ibid., p. 460.

37. Ibid., p. 22.

38. See, for example, the diary entry for March 20, 1930, in Hull, ed., *Give Us Each Day*, pp. 360, 363.

39. See the entry for March 18, 1931, for Dunbar-Nelson's feelings of separation from her lover, in ibid., pp. 421–22. See Shadrach, "Furnace Blasts: The Growth," p. 261 for a statement attributing prostitution to lesbianism practiced within the female house of refuge in Baltimore. In a discussion of Dunbar-Nelson within the context of lesbian historiography, Bettina Aptheker notes that her "lesbian connections were forged in secrecy and through a labyrinth of personal and political hazard." See Aptheker, *Tapestries of Life*, pp. 98–100. See also Rich, "Compulsory Heterosexuality and Lesbian Existence," *Signs* 5 (Summer 1980): 4.

40. Hull, ed., *Give Us Each Day*, pp. 282, 264. Dunbar-Nelson's assessment of the interracial conference of church women is also reprinted in Hull, ed. *Works of Alice Dunbar-Nelson* 2: 232.

41. Hull, ed., *Give Us Each Day*, pp. 23, 305, 314, 311, 327, 330, 371–72.

42. For Dunbar-Nelson's estimate of the number of blacks who pass, see ibid., p. 248. For examples of black activists who were white in appearance, but chose a black identity, see Theophilus Gould Steward, "Robert Purvis, Last Survivor of the American Anti-Slavery Society," *A.M.E. Church Review* 13, no. 2 (October 1896): 214–18; White, *Man Called White*, pp. 3–12. For general discussions of passing, see Gatewood, *Aristocrats of Color*, pp. 175–77; Green, *Secret City*, pp. 207–8. For literary treatments, see Larsen, *Passing*. Dunbar-Nelson's review of *Passing* is reprinted in Hull, ed., *Works of Alice Dunbar-Nelson* 2: 261–63.

43. Williamson, *New People*, pp. 100–109.

44. On Dunbar-Nelson's occasional passing, see Hull, ed., *Give Us Each Day*, pp. 113–14. See also White, *Man Called White*, pp. 39–43. Terrell, *Colored Woman*, p. 378. The Chicago black clubwoman Fannie Barrier Williams admitted to passing to avoid Jim Crow facilities. See Gatewood, *Aristocrats of Color*, pp. 176–77.

45. Terrell, pp. 375–76.

46. Hull, ed., *Works of Alice Dunbar-Nelson* 2: 238–39, 247–50.

47. See the editorials "Rhinelander" in *Crisis* (January 1926): 112–13; "Rhinelander-Jones Romance Goes to Smash on the Color Bar," *Negro World*, December 6, 1926.

48. Rodrigue, "The Black Community and the Birth Control Movement," in *Passion and Power: Sexuality in History*, ed. Kathy Peiss and Christina Simmons, with

Robert A. Padgug (Philadelphia: Temple University Press, 1989), pp. 138–54. See Miller, "Educated Negroes."

49. Alice Dunbar-Nelson, "Woman's Most Serious Problem," pp. 287–92.

50. Hazel Carby, "Policing the Black Woman's Body in an Urban Context," *Critical Inquiry* 18 (Summer 1992): 738–55.

51. Hine, "Rape and the Inner Lives of Black Women," pp. 292–97.

52. Hull, ed., *Give Us Each Day*, pp. 330–31.

53. Dunbar-Nelson's application to return to teaching at Howard High School (after her public marriage to Nelson) was rejected on the grounds that married women were ineligible. Upon receiving this blow, she wrote in her diary, "I wished I was dead and buried." She had lost the job years before after a dispute with the school's black male principal, who had taken over the job when her mentor, Edwina Kruse, a black woman who had founded the school, was forced into retirement. In 1926, she had undergone a protracted, humiliating application for a teaching appointment with the Washington, D.C., school district only to be rejected for health reasons after submitting to several health examinations and tests and having her case endlessly juggled by a bureaucratic huddle of male doctors, administrators, and politicians. Hull, ed., *Give Us Each Day*, pp. 439, 163–68.

54. Harley, "For the Good of Family and Race," pp. 159–72. Hine, *Black Women in White*, pp. 26–46, 187–93.

55. Hull, ed., *Give Us Each Day*, pp. 224, 86.

56. Ibid., p. 87.

Chapter Nine

1. Letter reprinted in Richard B. Sherman, ed., *The Negro and the City* (Englewood Cliffs, N.J.: Prentice-Hall, 1970), pp. 12–13.

2. Walter White, "The Work of a Mob," in Aptheker, ed., *Documentary History of the Negro People* 3: 229–30; Shapiro, *White Violence*, pp. 145–46.

3. Born, "Memphis Negro Workingmen," pp. 90–107. For the Fletcher case and the quote from the *Messenger* see Aptheker, ed., *Documentary History of the Negro People* 3: 252–53, 265. Stein, *World of Marcus Garvey*, pp. 38–60. Moore is quoted in Stein, *World of Marcus Garvey*, p. 42. Ralph Tyler to Emmett Scott, March 29, 1919, in the Emmett P. Scott Papers, quoted in Stein, *World of Marcus Garvey*, pp. 57–58.

4. Kelley, *Hammer and Hoe*.

5. Stein, *World of Marcus Garvey*; Born, "Memphis Negro Workingmen"; Kerlin, ed., *Voice of the Negro: 1919*.

6. Lewis, *When Harlem Was in Vogue*, pp. 157–59; Wolters, *New Negro on Campus*.

7. August Meier and Elliott Rudwick, "Attorneys Black and White: A Case Study of Race Relations Within the NAACP," *Journal of American History* 62 (1976): 913–46; Rabinowitz, *Race Relations*, pp. 36–37.

8. Osofsky, *Harlem*, p. 164.

9. J. A. Rogers, *World's Great Men of Color* (New York: Collier Books, 1972), 2: 433.

10. Hull, ed., *Give Us Each Day*, p. 150. Henry Miller is quoted in Foner, ed., *Voice of Black America* 2: 82–83.

11. Rogers, *World's Great Men of Color* 2: 435; Mark Ellis, "'Closing Ranks' and 'Seeking Honors': W. E. B. Du Bois in World War I," *Journal of American History* (June 1992): 115–17. On Harrison's West Indian intellectual protégés, see Cruse, *Crisis of the Negro Intellectual*; McKay, *Long Way From Home*, p. 41.

12. Stein, *World of Marcus Garvey*, pp. 43–46. See the chapter on Harrison in Wilfred D. Samuels, *Five Afro-Caribbean Voices in American Culture, 1917–1929* (Boulder, Colo.: Belmont Books, 1977), pp. 27–41. See also Ottley and Weatherby, eds., *Negro in New York*, p. 223. Lewis, *When Harlem Was in Vogue*.

13. James, "Hubert H. Harrison," pp. 82–91; Roi Ottley, *New World A Coming* (New York: 1943), pp. 74–81.

14. Martin, *Literary Garveyism*; Robert L. Poston, "Why I Refuse to be 'Civilized,'" *Negro World*, November 10, 1923.

15. Harrison, *When Africa Awakes*, pp. 15–16.

16. Ibid., pp. 49–53, 55–60.

17. Ibid., pp. 87–89, 63–66.

18. Ibid., 89–91. John E. Bruce, "The Influence of Woman on the Advancement of a Race," n.d. (ca. early 1920s), manuscript in the John E. Bruce Collection.

19. Cripps, "'Race Movies,'" p. 50; Kornweibel, *No Crystal Stair*, p. 111.

20. Kornweibel, *No Crystal Stair*, pp. 91–95, 124, 130–31.

21. James, "Hubert H. Harrison," pp. 38–39.

22. Harrison, "The Real Negro Problem," *Modern Quarterly* 3, no. 4 (September–December 1926): 314–21.

23. E. Franklin Frazier, "La Bourgeoisie Noire," *Modern Quarterly* 5, no. 1 (November 1928–February 1929), pp. 78–84.

24. Woodson, *Mis-education of the Negro*.

25. Johnson, *Book of American Negro Poetry*, p. 9.

26. Langston Hughes, "The Negro Artist and the Racial Mountain," reprinted in Sochen, ed., *Black Americans and the American Dream*, pp. 117–22.

27. Carter G. Woodson, review of "The Big Sea, an Autobiography," in *Journal of Negro History* 25, no. 4 (October 1940): pp. 567–68.

28. Cripps, "Race Movies," pp. 44–53, Oscar Micheaux to Charles W. Chesnutt, January 18, 1921, in the Charles Chesnutt Papers, Western Reserve Historical Society, Cleveland, Ohio. Robeson is quoted in Susan Robeson, ed., *The Whole World in His Hands: A Pictorial Biography of Paul Robeson* (Secaucus, N.J.: 1981), p. 92.

29. Baker is quoted in John Britton, ed., Transcript of Recorded Interview with Ella Baker, in Ella Baker Papers, June 19, 1968, Moorland-Spingarn Research Center, Howard University. Robeson is quoted in Robeson, ed., *Whole World in His Hands*, p. 121.

30. Kirby, *Black Americans in the Roosevelt Era* (Knoxville: University of Tennessee Press, 1980), pp. 106–10.

31. White is quoted in Siegal, "NAACP at the Crossroads," p. 35.

32. Duberman, *Paul Robeson*.

33. Jones, *Bad Blood*, p. 138.

34. Ibid. On Nurse Rivers, see also Hine, *Black Women in White*, pp. 154–56.

35. E. Franklin Frazier, "The New Negro Middle Class," in *The New Negro Thirty Years Afterward, Papers Contributed to the Sixteenth Annual Spring Conference of the*

Division of the Social Sciences (Washington, D.C.: Howard Univrsity Press, 1955), pp. 26–32.

36. Quotation is from G. Franklin Edwards, "Community and Class Realities: The Ordeal of Change," *Daedalus* (Winter 1966): 8. See the special issues of *Daedalus, the Journal of the American Academy of Arts and Sciences*, on "The Negro American," collecting articles by leading liberal sociologists, historians, and social psychologists.

37. E. Franklin Frazier, "Problems and Needs of Negro Children and Youth Resulting from Family Disorganization," *Journal of Negro Education* (Summer 1950): 269–77; Nathan Glazer and Daniel Patrick Moynihan, *Beyond the Melting Pot: The Negroes, Puerto Ricans, Jews, Italians and Irish of New York City* (Cambridge, Mass.: MIT Press, 1970), xxiii–xxiv.

38. Carter G. Woodson, review of *Haiti Singing*, by Harold Courlander, *Journal of Negro History* 25, no. 2 (April 1940): 241–42; Powdermaker, *After Freedom*, pp. 197–98; Ralph Ellison, "An American Dilemma: A Review," in Ladner, ed., *Death of White Sociology*, pp. 93–95. For an interesting critique of black social science perspectives stressing class differentiation and environmentalism, see Fontaine, "Social Determination," pp. 302–13, with a rejoinder by E. Franklin Frazier.

39. Logan, *Betrayal of the Negro*, p. 17.

SELECTED BIBLIOGRAPHY

《 《 《

Manuscript Collections

John E. Bruce Collection, Schomburg Center for the Study of Black Culture, New
 York Public Library
Anna Julia Cooper Papers, Moorland-Spingarn Research Center, Howard University
Paul Laurence Dunbar Collection, Western Reserve Historical Society, Cleveland,
 Ohio
W. E. B. Du Bois Papers, University of Massachusetts at Amherst
Alexander Gumby Collection, Butler Library, Columbia University
James Weldon Johnson Collection, Beineke Rare Book Library, Yale University
Alain Locke Papers, Moorland-Spingarn Research Center, Howard University
Arthur A. Schomburg Correspondence, Schomburg Center for Research in Black
 Culture, New York Public Library

Newspapers and Magazines

African Times and Orient Review
A.M.E. Church Review
Alexander's Magazine
Arena
Colored American Magazine
Crisis
Negro World
New York Age
Southern Workman
Voice of the Negro

Published Sources

Alexander, Charles. "An Appeal for Race Integrity." *Alexander's Magazine* 2, no. 5
 (September 15, 1906): 16–17.
American Negro Academy, Occasional Papers, Nos. 1–22. New York: Arno Press, 1969.
"The American Negro Academy." *African Times and Orient Review* (November–
 December 1913): 243–44.
Anderson, James D. *The Education of Blacks in the South, 1860–1935.* Chapel Hill:
 University of North Carolina Press, 1988.

Anderson, Stuart. *Race and Rapprochment*. Rutherford, N.J.: Associated University Presses, 1981.

Andrews, William. *To Tell a Free Story: The First Century of Afro-American Autobiography, 1760–1865*. Urbana: University of Illinois Press, 1986.

Angelou, Maya. *All God's Children Need Traveling Shoes*. New York: Random House, 1986.

Appiah, Anthony. "The Uncompleted Argument: Du Bois and the Illusion of Race." In *Race, Writing and Difference*, edited by Henry Louis Gates, pp. 21–37. Chicago: University of Chicago Press, 1985.

Aptheker, Bettina. *Tapestries of Life: Women's Work, Women's Consciousness and the Meaning of Daily Experience*. Amherst: University of Massachusetts Press, 1989.

Aptheker, Herbert. *American Negro Slave Revolts*. New York: International Publishers, 1987.

Aptheker, Herbert, ed. *The Correspondence of W. E. B. Du Bois. Vol. 1, 1877–1934*. Amherst: University of Massachusetts Press, 1973.

———. *A Documentary History of the Negro People in the United States*. Vol. 3. New York: Carol Publishing, 1973.

———. *Writings by W. E. B. Du Bois in Periodicals Edited by Others*. Millwood, N.Y.: Kraus-Thompson Organization, 1982.

Arnold, Matthew. *Culture and Anarchy*. Cambridge: Cambridge University Press, 1963.

Baker, Houston. *Modernism and the Harlem Renaissance*. Chicago: University of Chicago Press, 1987.

Baker, Ray Stannard. *Following the Color Line*. 1908. Reprint, New York: Harper Torchbooks, 1964.

Baker, Thomas. "Ideals, Part 1." *Alexander's Magazine* 2 (September 1906): 23–29.

———. "The Negro Woman." *Alexander's Magazine* 3 (December 15, 1906): 77.

Baldwin, James. *The Price of the Ticket: Collected Nonfiction, 1948–1985*. New York: St. Martin's/Marek, 1985.

Barber, J. Max. *The Negro of the Earlier World: An Excursion Into Ancient Negro History*. Philadelphia: A.M.E. Book Concern, n.d.

Bardolph, Richard. *The Negro Vanguard*. New York: Vintage Books, 1959.

Bardolph, Richard, ed. *The Civil Rights Record: Black Americans and the Law, 1849–1970*. New York: Thomas Crowell, 1970.

Beale, Frances. "Double Jeopardy: To Be Black and Female." In *The Black Woman: An Anthology*, edited by Toni Cade, pp. 90–100. New York: New American Library, 1970.

Bell, Derrick. *Faces at the Bottom of the Well*. New York: Basic Books, 1992.

Bell, Howard H. *A Survey of the Negro Convention Movement*. New York: Arno Press, 1970.

Bernal, Martin. *Black Athena: The Afroasiatic Roots of Classical Civilization. Vol. 1, The Fabrication of Ancient Greece*. New Brunswick, N.J.: Rutgers University Press, 1987.

Berry, Mary Frances. *Black Resistance, White Law: A History of Constitutional Racism in America*. New York: Appleton-Century-Crofts, 1971.

Berry, Mary Frances, and John Blassingame. *Long Memory: The Black Experience in America*. New York: Oxford University Press, 1982.

Berwick-Sayers, W. C. *Samuel Coleridge-Taylor, Musician: His Life and Letters.* 1915. Reprint, Chicago: Afro-Am Books, 1969.

Blackett, R. J. M. *Beating Against the Barriers: The Lives of Six Nineteenth-Century Afro-Americans.* Ithaca, N.Y.: Cornell University Press, 1986.

Bonner, Marita O. "On Being Young—a Woman—and Colored." *Crisis* (December 1925): 63–65.

Born, Kate. "Memphis Negro Workingmen and the NAACP." *West Tennessee Historical Society Papers* 28 (1974): 90–107.

Bowen, J. W. E., ed. *Africa and the American Negro.* Miami: Mnemosyne Publishing, 1969.

Bracey, John, August Meier, and Elliott Rudwick, eds. *Black Nationalism in America.* New York: Bobbs-Merrill, 1970.

Brantlinger, Patrick. "Victorians and Africans: The Genealogy of the Myth of the Dark Continent." *Critical Inquiry* 12 (Autumn 1985): 166–203.

Braxton, Joanne M. *Black Women Writing Autobiography: A Tradition Within a Tradition.* Philadelphia: Temple University Press, 1989.

Breitman, George, ed. *Malcolm X Speaks: Selected Speeches and Statements.* New York: Grove Weidenfeld, 1990.

Brown, Hallie Q. *Homespun Heroines and Other Women of Distinction.* New York: Oxford University Press, 1988.

Bruce, D. D. *Black American Writing from the Nadir: The Evolution of a Literary Tradition, 1877–1915.* Baton Rouge: Louisiana State University Press, 1989.

Buck, Paul H. *The Road to Reunion, 1865–1900.* New York: Vintage Books, 1959.

Burnham, John C., John D. Buenker, and Robert M. Crunden. *Progressivism.* Cambridge, Mass.: Schenkman, 1977.

Burroughs, Nannie. "Not Color But Character." *Voice of the Negro* 1, No. 7 (July 1904): 277–79.

Butcher, Philip, ed. *The William Stanley Braithwaite Reader.* Ann Arbor: University of Michigan Press, 1972.

Calloway, Thomas J. "The American Negro at the Paris Exposition." *Hampton Negro Conference Proceedings,* no. 5 (July 1901): 74–80.

Carby, Hazel. *Reconstructing Womanhood: The Emergence of the Afro-American Woman Novelist.* New York: Oxford University Press, 1987.

Chateauvert, Melinda. "The Third Step: Anna Julia Cooper and Black Education in the District of Columbia, 1910–1960." *SAGE* (Student Supplement 1988): 7–13.

Connell, R. W. *Gender and Power.* Stanford, Calif.: Stanford University Press, 1987.

Cooper, Anna Julia. "The American Negro Academy." *Southern Workman* (February 1898): 35–36.

———. *A Voice from the South.* New York: Oxford University Press, 1988.

Corrothers, James D. *The Black Cat Club: Negro Humor and Folklore.* New York: Funk and Wagnalls, 1902.

———. *In Spite of the Handicap.* Freeport, N.Y.: Books for Libraries Press, 1971.

Cott, Nancy. *The Bonds of Womanhood.* New Haven, Conn.: Yale University Press, 1977.

Cripps, Thomas. "'Race Movies' as Voices of the Black Bourgeoisie: The Scar of Shame (1927)." In *American History/American Film: Interpreting the Hollywood Im-*

age, edited by John E. O'Connor and Martin A. Jackson, 39–55. New York: Ungar, 1987.

Cromwell, John Wesley. *The Negro in American History*. Washington, D.C.: American Negro Academy, 1914.

Crummell, Alexander. *Africa and America: Addresses and Discourses*. 1891. Reprint, New York: Negro Universities Press, 1969.

———. "Civilization, The Primal Need of the Race." *American Negro Academy Occasional Papers, No. 3*. Washington, D.C.: American Negro Academy, 1898.

Cruse, Harold. *The Crisis of the Negro Intellectual*. New York: Quill Publishers, 1984.

Curry, Leonard P. *The Free Black in Urban America, 1900–1850*. Chicago: University of Chicago Press, 1981.

Curtin, Philip D. *The Image of Africa: British Ideas and Action, 1780–1850*. London: Macmillan, 1965.

Davis, Allison. *Leadership, Love and Aggression*. New York: Harcourt Brace Jovanovich, 1983.

Davis, Angela. *Women, Race and Class*. New York: Vintage Books, 1983.

Davis, David Brion. *Slavery and Human Progress*. New York: Oxford University Press, 1984.

Davis, David Brion, ed. *Antebellum Reform*. New York: Harper and Row, 1967.

Davis, Elizabeth Lindsay. *The Story of the Illinois Federation of Colored Women's Clubs, 1900–1922*. Chicago: 1922.

———, ed. *Lifting as They Climb*. Washington, D.C.: National Association of Colored J.W. Women, n.d.

Davis, Thadious M. *Nella Larsen, Novelist of the Harlem Renaissance: A Woman's Life Unveiled*. Baton Rouge: Louisiana State University Press, 1994.

Day, Caroline. *A Study of Negro-White Families in the United States*. Cambridge: Peabody Museum of Harvard University, 1932.

Diop, Cheikh Anta. *The African Origin of Civilization: Myth or Reality*. Chicago: Lawrence Hill Books, 1974.

Dittmer, John. *Black Georgia in the Progressive Era, 1900–1920*. Urbana: University of Illinois Press, 1977.

Dorkins, William H. "Results of Some Hard Experiences. A Practical Talk to Young Men." *Colored American Magazine* 5, no. 4 (August 1902): 271–72.

Dormon, James H. "Shaping the Popular Image of Post-Reconstruction American Blacks: The 'Coon Song' Phenomenon of the Gilded Age." *American Quarterly* 40 (December 1988): 450–71.

Douglass, Frederick. *My Bondage and My Freedom*. New York: Dover Publications, 1969.

———. "Lessons of the Hour." *A.M.E. Church Review* 11, no. 3 (July 1895): 139.

Downs, R. R. "Educated Fools." *A.M.E. Church Review* 11 (April 1895): 463.

Duberman, Martin. *Paul Robeson*. London: Pan Books, 1991.

Du Bois, W. E. B. *The Autobiography of W. E. B. Du Bois: A Soliloquy on Viewing My Life from the Last Decade of Its First Century*. New York: International Publishers, 1983.

———. *Darkwater: Voices from Within the Veil*. New York: Schocken Books, 1969.

———. "The Hampton Idea." *Voice of the Negro* 3, no. 9 (September 1906): 632–35.

———. *The Philadelphia Negro*. New York: Schocken Books, 1967.

———. "The Problem of Amusement." *Southern Workman* 26 (September 1897): 181–84.

———. "St. Francis of Assisi." *Voice of the Negro* 3, no. 10 (October 1906): 419–26.

———. *The Souls of Black Folk*. New York: Penguin, 1989.

———, ed. *Atlanta University Publications, Vols. 1–6, 1896–1901*. New York, Octagon Books, 1968.

———. "The College-Bred Negro." *Atlanta University Publications Numbers 1–6–1896–1901*. No. 5. New York: Octagon Books, 1968.

Dunbar, Alice M., ed. *Masterpieces of Negro Eloquence*. New York: Bookery Publishing, 1914.

Dunbar, Paul Laurence. *The Sport of the Gods*. 1902. Salem, N.H.: Ayer Publishers, 1984.

Dunbar-Nelson, Alice. "Woman's Most Serious Problem." In *Works of Alice Dunbar-Nelson*. Vol. 2, edited by Gloria T. Hull, pp. 287–92. New York: Oxford University Press, 1987.

Duster, Alfreda, ed. *Crusader for Justice: The Autobiography of Ida B. Wells*. Chicago: University of Chicago Press, 1970.

"Emancipation." *A.M.E. Church Review* 15, no. 2 (October 1898): pp. 605–17.

Faduma, Orishatukeh. "The Defects of the Negro Church." *American Negro Academy, Occasional Papers, No. 10*. Washington, D.C.: American Negro Academy, 1904.

———. "Thoughts for the Times; Or, the New Theology." *A.M.E. Church Review* 7, no. 2 (October 1890): 139–45.

Fanon, Frantz. *Black Skin, White Masks*. New York: Grove Press, 1967.

Ferris, William H. *The African Abroad, or His Evolution in Western Civilization, Tracing His Development under Caucasian Milieu*. 2 vols. New Haven, Conn.: Tuttle, Morehouse and Taylor Press, 1913.

———. "Marcus Garvey Was Genius, But Could Not Spend Money." *Philadelphia Tribune*, June, 27, 1940, p. 1.

Filene, Peter G. *Him/Her/Self: Sex Roles in Modern America*. Baltimore: Johns Hopkins University Press, 1986.

———. "An Obituary for 'The Progressive Movement.'" *American Quarterly* 22 (1970): 20–34.

Fletcher, Peter. *The Black Soldier and Officer in the United States Army, 1891–1917*. Columbia: University of Missouri Press, 1974.

Foner, Eric. *Free Soil, Free Labor, Free Men*. New York: Oxford University Press, 1970.

Foner, Philip S. *Antonio Maceo: The Bronze Titan of Cuba's Struggle for Independence*. New York: Monthly Review Press, 1977.

———, ed. *Black Socialist Preacher*. San Francisco: Synthesis Publications, 1983.

———. *The Voice of Black America*. Vol. 2. New York: Capricorn Books, 1975.

Fontaine, William T. "'Social Determination' in the Writings of Negro Scholars." *American Journal of Sociology* 49, no. 1 (1943): 302–13.

Fortune, T. Thomas. *Black and White: Land, Labor, and Politics in the South*. 1884. Reprint, Chicago: Johnson Publishing, 1970.

———. "The Question of Intermarriage." *Alexander's Magazine* 3, no. 5 (February 15, 1907): 228–29.

———. "Race Absorption." *A.M.E. Church Review* 18, no. 1 (July 1901): 54–66.

Fox, Stephen R. *The Guardian of Boston: William Monroe Trotter*. New York: Atheneum, 1970.

Franklin, John Hope. *The Color Line: Legacy for the Twenty-First Century*. Columbia: University of Missouri Press, 1993.

———. *George Washington Williams: A Biography*. Chicago: University of Chicago Press, 1985.

———. *Race and History: Selected Essays, 1938–1988*. Baton Rouge: Louisiana State University Press, 1989.

Fraser, Nancy, and Linda Gordon. "A Genealogy of Dependency: Tracing a Keyword of the U.S. Welfare State." *Signs* 19, no. 2 (Winter 1994): 309–36.

Frazier, E. Franklin. *Black Bourgeoisie*. New York: Free Press, 1957.

Fredrickson, George. *The Black Image in the White Mind*. New York: Harper Torchbooks, 1971.

Fullenwider, S. P. *The Mind and Mood of Black America*. Homewood, Ill.: Dorsey Press, 1969.

Gabel, Leona C. *From Slavery to the Sorbonne and Beyond: The Life and Writings of Anna J. Cooper*. Northampton, Mass.: Smith College, 1982.

Gates, Henry Louis. "The Trope of a New Negro and the Reconstruction of the Image of the Black." *Representations* 24 (Fall 1988): 129–55.

Gates, Henry Louis, ed. *"Race," Writing, and Difference*. Chicago: University of Chicago Press, 1985.

Gatewood, Willard B. *Aristocrats of Color: The Black Elite, 1880–1920*. Bloomington: Indiana University Press, 1990.

———. *Black Americans and the White Man's Burden, 1898–1903*. Urbana: University of Illinois Press, 1975.

Gay, Joseph R. *Progress and Achievements of the 20th Century Negro*. Chicago: Howard, Chandler, 1913.

George, Carol V. R. *Segregated Sabbaths: Richard Allen and the Rise of Independent Black Churches, 1760–1840*. New York: Oxford University Press, 1973.

Giddings, Paula. *When and Where I Enter: The Impact of Black Women on Race and Sex in America*. New York: Bantam Books, 1984.

Gordon, Linda. *Heroes of Their Own Lives: The Politics and History of Family Violence*. New York: Penguin Books, 1988.

Gordon, Milton. "Assimilation in America: Theory and Reality." In *The Shaping of Twentieth Century America*, edited by Richard M. Abrams and Lawrence W. Levine, pp. 296–316. Boston: Little, Brown, 1965.

Gorn, Elliott J. *The Manly Art: Bare Knuckle Prize Fighting in America*. Ithaca, N.Y.: Cornell University Press, 1986.

Gossett, Thomas. *Race: The History of an Idea in America*. New York: Schocken Books, 1969.

Green, Constance McLaughlin. *The Secret City: A History of Race Relations in the Nation's Capital*. Princeton, N.J.: Princeton University Press, 1967.

Griggs, Sutton E. *Imperium in Imperio*. New York: AMS Press, 1975.

Gwaltney, John Langston. *Drylongso: A Self-Portrait of Black America*. New York: Vintage Books, 1980.

Hackley, Emma Azalia. *The Colored Girl Beautiful*. Kansas City:·Burton Publishing, 1916.

Hall, Charles Winslow. "The Old or the New Faith, Which?" *Colored American Magazine* 1, no. 3 (August 1900): 173–79.

Hall, Stuart. "Notes on Deconstructing 'The Popular.'" In *Peoples' History and Socialist Theory*, edited by R. Samuel, pp. 227–39. London: Routledge and Kegan Paul, 1981.

———. "Race, Articulation and Societies Structured in Dominance." In *Sociological Theories: Race and Colonization*, edited by UNESCO, pp. 32–50. Paris: UNESCO, 1980.

Harding, Vincent. *There is a River: The Black Struggle for Freedom in America*. New York: Vintage Books, 1983.

Harlan, Louis. *Booker T. Washington: The Making of a Black Leader*. New York: Oxford University Press, 1972.

———. *Separate and Unequal*. Chapel Hill: University of North Carolina Press, 1958.

———, ed. *The Booker T. Washington Papers*. Urbana: University of Illinois Press, 1975.

———. *Booker T. Washington: The Wizard of Tuskegee, 1901–1915*. New York: Oxford University Press, 1983.

Harley, Sharon. "For the Good of Family and Race: Gender, Work, and Domestic Roles in the Black Community, 1880–1930." In *Black Women in America: Social Science Perspectives*, edited by Micheline R. Malson, Elisabeth Mudimbe-Boyi, Jean F. O'Barr, and Mary Wyer, pp. 159–72. Chicago: University of Chicago Press, 1990.

Harper, Frances E. W. "An Address Delivered at the Centennial Anniversary of the Pennsylvania Society for Promoting the Abolition of Slavery." In *Masterpieces of Negro Eloquence*, edited by Alice Moore Dunbar, pp. 104–6. New York: Bookery Publishing, 1914.

———. *Iola Leroy, or Shadows Uplifted*. Boston: Beacon Press, 1987.

Harper, Philip Brian. "Nationalism and Social Division in Black Arts Poetry of the 1960s," *Critical Inquiry* 19 (Winter 1993): 234–55.

Harris, Abram. *The Negro as Capitalist: A Study of Banking and Business Among American Negroes*. 1936. Reprint, Gloucester, Mass.: P. Smith, 1968.

Harris, Eugene. "The Physical Condition of the Race; Whether Dependent on Social Conditions or Environment." In *Mortality Among Negroes in Cities, no. 1*. Reprinted in *Atlanta University Publications*. New York: Octagon Books, 1968.

Harris, William H. *The Harder We Run: Black Workers Since the Civil War*. New York: Oxford University Press, 1982.

Harrison, Hubert H. *When Africa Awakes: The "Inside Story" of the Stirrings and Strivings of the New Negro of the Western World*. New York: Porro Press, 1920.

Haskins, James, with Kathleen Benson. *Scott Joplin: The Man Who Made Ragtime*. Garden City, N.Y.: Doubleday, 1978.

Henderson, Rev. John M. "The Afro-American Press and School Subordinate to the Pulpit." *A.M.E. Church Review* 8, no. 1 (July, 1891): 51–54.

Henri, Florette. *Black Migration: Movement North, 1900–1920*. Garden City, N.Y.: Doubleday, 1975.

Herd, Denise A. "Prohibition, Racism and Class Politics in the Post-Reconstruction South." *Journal of Drug Issues* (Winter 1983): 85–86.

Higginbotham, Evelyn Brooks. *Righteous Discontent: The Women's Movement in the Black Baptist Church, 1880–1920*. Cambridge: Harvard University Press, 1993.

Higham, John. *Strangers in the Land: Patterns of American Nativism, 1860–1925*. New York: Atheneum, 1970.

Hill, Robert, ed. *The Marcus Garvey and Universal Negro Improvement Association Papers*. Vol. 1. Berkeley and Los Angeles: University of California Press, 1983.

Hine, Darlene Clark. *Black Women in White: Racial Conflict and Cooperation in the Nursing Profession, 1890–1950*. Bloomington: Indiana University Press, 1989.

———. "Rape and the Inner Lives of Black Women in the Middle West: Preliminary Thoughts on the Culture of Dissemblance." In *Unequal Sisters: A Multicultural Reader in U.S. Women's History*, edited by Ellen Du Bois and Vicki L. Ruiz, 292–97. New York: Routledge, 1990.

Hobsbawm, Eric. *The Age of Empire, 1875–1914*. New York: Vintage, 1989.

Hopkins, Pauline. *Contending Forces, A Romance Illustrative of Negro Life North and South*. New York: Oxford University Press, 1988.

———. *A Primer of Facts Pertaining to the Early Greatness of the African Race and the Possibility of Restoration by Its Descendants*. Cambridge, Mass.: P. E. Hopkins, 1905.

———. "Talma Gordon." *Colored American Magazine* 1, no. 5 (October 1900): 271–90.

Horton, James Oliver. "Freedom's Yoke: Gender Conventions Among Antebellum Free Blacks." *Feminist Studies* 12, no. 1 (Spring 1986): 51–76.

Hovenkamp, Herbert. "Social Science and Segregation Before *Brown*." *Duke Law Journal* (June–September 1985): 624–72.

Howard, Ronald L. *A Social History of American Family Sociology, 1865–1940*. Westport, Conn.: Greenwood Press, 1981.

Howe, Mary W. "Symposium—Temperance," *A.M.E. Church Review* 7, no. 4 (April 1891): 372–81.

"How to Keep Women at Home." *Colored American Magazine* 14, no. 1 (January 1908): 7–8.

Hull, Gloria T., ed. *Give Us Each Day: The Diary of Alice Dunbar-Nelson*. New York: Norton, 1984.

———. *The Works of Alice Dunbar-Nelson*. Vol. 2. New York: Oxford University Press, 1988.

Hutchinson, Louise D. *Anna Julia Cooper: A Voice from the South*. Washington, D.C.: Smithsonian Institution Press, 1981.

"Immigration and the Negro." *Alexander's Magazine* 2, no. 2 (June 1906): 16–17.

Jackson, Capt. W. H. "From Our Friends in the Far East." *Colored American Magazine* 1, no. 3 (August 1900): 145–49.

Jackson, Kenneth T. *The Ku Klux Klan in the City, 1915–1930*. New York: Oxford University Press, 1967.

James, Portia. "Hubert H. Harrison and the New Negro Movement." *Western Journal of Black Studies* 13, no. 2 (1989): 82–91.

Jaynes, Gerald. *Branches Without Roots: Genesis of the Black Working Class in the American South, 1862–1882*. New York: Oxford University Press, 1986.

Jewell, K. Sue. *From Mammy to Miss America and Beyond*. London: Routledge, 1993.

Johnson, Charles S. *The Negro College Graduate*. New York: Negro Universities Press, 1969.

Johnson, James H. A. "Woman's Exalted Station," *A.M.E. Church Review* 8, no. 4 (April 1892): 402.

Johnson, James Weldon. *Along This Way*. New York: 1937.

———, ed. *Book of American Negro Poetry*. New York: Harcourt, Brace and World, 1959.

Johnson, James Weldon, ed. *The Book of American Negro Spirituals*. New York: Viking Press, 1925.

Johnson, T. H., M.D. "Penal Sentence." *Colored American Magazine* 1, no. 4 (September 1900): 180–82.

Jones, Jacqueline. *Soldiers of Light and Love: Northern Teachers and Georgia Blacks, 1865–1873*. Chapel Hill: University of North Carolina Press, 1980.

———. *Labor of Love, Labor of Sorrow: Black Women, Work and the Family from Slavery to the Present*. New York: Vintage Books, 1986.

Jones, James. *Bad Blood: The Tuskegee Syphillis Experiment, A Tragedy of Race and Medicine*. New York: Free Press, 1981.

Jones, Rhett. "Proving Blacks Inferior: The Sociology of Knowledge." In *The Death of White Sociology*, edited by Joyce Ladner. New York: Vintage Books, 1973.

Jones, William H. *Recreation and Amusement Among Negroes in Washington, D.C.* Westport, Conn.: Negro Universities Press, 1970.

Jordan, David Starr. *The Blood of the Nation: A Study of the Decay of Races through the Survival of the Unfit*. Boston: American Unitarian Association, 1902.

Kaplan, Amy. *The Social Construction of American Realism*. Chicago: University of Chicago Press, 1988.

Kelley, Robin D. G. *Hammer and Hoe: Alabama Communists During the Great Depression*. Chapel Hill: University of North Carolina Press, 1990.

Kennedy, Ellen Conroy, ed. *The Negritude Poets: An Anthology*. New York: Viking Press, 1975.

Kent, J. Mariner. "The Afro-American Problem." *Colored American Magazine* 6, no. 10 (October 1903): 724–26.

Kerlin, Robert T., ed. *The Voice of the Negro: 1919*. New York: E. P. Dutton, 1920.

Kornweibel, Theodore. *No Crystal Stair: Black Life and the Messenger, 1917–1928*. Westport, Conn.: Greenwood Press, 1975.

Kovel, Joel. *White Racism: A Psychohistory*. New York: Vintage Books, 1971.

Kraditor, Aileen. *The Ideas of the Woman Suffrage Movement, 1890–1920*. Garden City, N.Y.: Doubleday, 1971.

Krislov, Samuel. *The Negro in Federal Employment*. Minneapolis: University of Minnesota Press, 1967.

Kusmer, Kenneth. *A Ghetto Takes Shape: Black Cleveland, 1870–1930*. Urbana: University of Illinois Press, 1976.

Ladner, Joyce A., ed. *The Death of White Sociology*. New York: Random House, 1973.

Lane, Roger. *Roots of Violence in Black Philadelphia, 1860–1900*. Cambridge: Harvard University Press, 1986.

Larsen, Nella. "Passing." In *Quicksand and Passing*, edited by Deborah McDowell. New Brunswick, N.J.: Rutgers University Press, 1988.

Lears, T. J. Jackson. *No Place of Grace: Antimodernism and the Transformation of American Culture, 1880–1920.* New York: Pantheon Books, 1981.

Lee, Mrs. M. E. "The Home-Maker." *A.M.E. Church Review* 8 (July 1891): 63–66.

Lerner, Gerda, ed. *Black Women in White America: A Documentary History.* New York: Vintage Books, 1972.

Levine, Lawrence. *Black Culture and Black Consciousness.* New York: Oxford University Press, 1977.

Lewis, David. *W. E. B. Du Bois.* New York: Henry Holt, 1993.

———. *When Harlem Was in Vogue.* New York: Vintage Books, 1982.

Lewis, W. A. "The Young American Negro; His Opportunities in Life and the Goal He Should Strive to Reach." *Colored American Magazine* 13, no. 4 (October 1907): 273–75.

Lightfoot, Sara Lawrence. *Balm in Gilead: Journey of a Healer.* Reading, Mass.: Addison-Wesley, 1988.

Litwak, Leon F. *Been in the Storm So Long.* New York: Vintage Books, 1979.

———. "Trouble in Mind: The Bicentennial and the Afro-American Experience." *Journal of American History* 74, no. 2 (September 1987): 315–37.

Logan, Mrs. Adela Hunt. "Prenatal and Hereditary Influences." In *Social and Physical Condition of Negroes in Cities, no. 2.* Reprinted in *Atlanta University Publications.* New York: Octagon Books, 1968.

Logan, Rayford W. *The Betrayal of the Negro: From Rutherford B. Hayes to Woodrow Wilson.* New York: Collier, 1965.

———. *The Negro in American Life and Thought: The Nadir, 1877–1901.* New York: Dial Press, 1954.

———. *The Negro in the United States.* New York: Van Nostrand Reinhold, 1957.

Lorimer, Douglas A. *Colour, Class and the Victorians.* Leicester, England: Leicester University Press, 1978.

Lott, Eric. "Love and Theft: The Racial Unconscious." *Representations* 39 (Summer 1992): 23–50.

Lubiano, Wahneema. "Black Ladies, Welfare Queens, and State Minstrels: Ideological War by Narrative Means." In *Race-ing Justice, En-gendering Power: Essays on Anita Hill, Clarence Thomas, and the Construction of Social Reality*, edited by Toni Morrison, 323–63. New York: Pantheon, 1992.

Lubove, Roy. *The Professional Altruist: The Emergence of Social Work as a Career, 1880–1930.* New York: Atheneum, 1983.

Luker, Ralph E. *The Social Gospel in Black and White: American Racial Reform, 1885–1912.* Chapel Hill: University of North Carolina Press, 1991.

Lynch, William A. "Race Assimilation." *A.M.E. Church Review* 8, no. 2 (October 1891): 211–13.

Majors, Monroe. *Notable Negro Women: Their Triumphs and Activities.* Chicago: Donohue and Henneberry, 1893. Ann Arbor, Mich.: University Microfilm, 1970.

Malcolm X. *The Autobiography of Malcolm X.* New York: Grove Press, 1965.

McCloskey, Robert G. *American Conservatism in the Age of Enterprise, 1865–1910.* New York: Harper Torchbooks, 1951.

McKay, Claude. *A Long Way from Home.* New York: Harvest/Harcourt Brace Jovanovich, 1970.

McPherson, James. *The Struggle for Equality*. Princeton, N.J.: Princeton University Press, 1964.

Malveaux, Julianne. "The Political Economy of Black Women." In *The Year Left 2: Toward a Rainbow Socialism*, edited by Mike Davis, et al., pp. 52–73. London: Verso, 1987.

Marks, George, ed. *The Black Press Views American Imperialism, 1898–1900*. New York: Arno Press, 1971.

"Marks of True Greatness." *Alexander's Magazine* 3, no. 2 (December 15, 1903): 59–60.

Martin, Tony. *Literary Garveyism: Garvey, Black Arts and the Harlem Renaissance*. Dover, Mass.: Majority Press, 1983.

Meier, August. *Negro Thought in America, 1880–1915*. Ann Arbor: University of Michigan Press, 1971.

Miller, Kelly. "Educated Negroes Said Not to Marry and Raise Large Families." *Negro World*, February 7, 1925.

———. "Review of W. Hannibal Thomas' 'The American Negro'" *Hampton Negro Conference* 5 (July 1901): 64–74. Hampton, Va.: Hampton Institute Press, 1901.

———. *Radicals and Conservatives*. New York: Schocken Books, 1970.

Mills, C. Wright. "The Professional Ideology of Social Pathologists." *American Journal of Sociology* 49, no. 2 (1943): 165–80.

Minott, Adena C. E. "Phrenology and Child Culture." *Colored American Magazine* 8, no. 5 (November 1907): 387–89.

Mitchell, John, Jr. "Shall the Wheels of Race Agitation be Stopped?" *Colored American Magazine* 5, no. 5 (September 1902): 386–91.

Morin, M. Arnold. "Change, Destructive of Character-Growth." *A.M.E. Church Review* 7, no. 2 (August 1890): 182–87.

Morrison, Toni. *Playing in the Dark: Whiteness and the Literary Imagination*. Cambridge: Harvard University Press, 1992.

———, ed. *Race-ing Justice, En-gendering Power: Essays on Anita Hill, Clarence Thomas, and the Construction of Social Reality*. New York: Pantheon, 1992.

Morrissey, J. J., M.D. "Hereditary Influences and Medical Progress." *Arena* 76 (January 1897): 283–92.

Moses, Wilson J. *Alexander Crummell: A Study of Civilization and Discontent*. New York: Oxford University Press, 1989.

———. *The Golden Age of Black Nationalism, 1850–1925*. New York: Oxford University Press, 1989.

———. "The Lost World of the New Negro, 1895–1919: Black Literary and Intellectual Life before the 'Renaissance.'" *Black American Literature Forum* 21, nos. 1–2 (Spring–Summer 1987): 61–84.

———. "Sexual Anxieties of the Black Bourgeoisie in Victorian America: The Cultural Context of W. E. B. Du Bois' First Novel." *Western Journal of Black Studies* 6, no. 4 (1982): 202–11.

———. *The Wings of Ethiopia: Studies in African-American Life and Letters*. Ames: Iowa State University Press, 1990.

Moss, Alfred A. *The American Negro Academy: Voice of the Talented Tenth*. Baton Rouge: Louisiana State University Press, 1981.

Mosse, George L. *Nationalism and Sexuality: Respectability and Abnormal Sexuality in Modern Europe*. New York: Howard Fertig, 1985.

Mossell, Mrs. N. F. *The Work of the Afro-American Woman*. New York: Oxford University Press, 1988.

Newman, Louise Michele, ed. *Men's Ideas/Women's Realities, Popular Science, 1870–1915*. New York: Pergamon Press, 1984.

Ngugi wa Thiong'o. *Decolonizing the Mind: The Politics of Language in African Literature*. London: James Currey, 1987.

Nichols, J. L., and William H. Crogman. *Progress of a Race, or the Remarkable Advancement of the American Negro*. Chicago: Wilmore Book and Bible, 1925.

Nielson, David Gordon. *Black Ethos: Northern Urban Negro Life and Thought, 1890–1930*. Westport, Conn.: Greenwood Press, 1977.

Noble, Jeanne L. *The Negro Woman's College Education*. New York: Bureau of Publications, Teachers College, Columbia University, 1956.

Northrop, Henry Davenport. *The College of Life, or Practical Self-Educator: A Manual of Self-Improvement for the Colored Race, Forming an Educational Emancipator and a Guide to Success*. 1895. Reprint, Miami: Mnemosyne Publishing, 1969.

Osofsky, Gilbert. *Harlem: The Making of a Ghetto: Negro New York, 1890–1930*. New York: Harper Torchbooks, 1968.

Ottley, Roi, and William J. Weatherby. *The Negro in New York: An Informal Social History, 1626–1940*. New York: Praeger, 1969.

Page, Thomas Nelson. "The Negro, The Southerner's Problem." *McClure's* 22 (March–May 1904): 548–54, 619–26, 96–102.

Painter, Nell Irvin. *Exodusters*. New York: Norton, 1992.

———. *Standing at Armageddon: The United States, 1877–1919*. New York: Norton, 1987.

Pemberton, Gayle. *The Hottest Water in Chicago*. Boston: Faber and Faber, 1992.

Penn, I. Garland, ed. *The United Negro: His Problems and His Progress*. 1902. Reprint, New York: Negro Universities Press, 1969.

Pickens, William. "The Educational Condition of the Negro in Cities." *Voice of the Negro* 3, no. 10 (October 1906): 427–30.

———. *The New Negro*. 1916. Reprint, New York: Negro Universities Press, 1969.

Pipken, Rev. J. J. *The Story of a Rising Race: The Negro in Revelation, in History and in Citizenship*. 1902. Reprint, Freeport, N.Y.: Books for Libraries Press, 1971.

Platt, Anthony. *E. Franklin Frazier Reconsidered*. New Brunswick, N.J.: Rutgers University Press, 1991.

Powdermaker, Hortense. *After Freedom: A Cultural Study in the Deep South*. New York: Atheneum, 1968.

Proctor, Rev. H. H. "The Need of Friendly Visitation." In *Social and Physical Conditions of Negroes in Cities, no. 2*. Reprinted in *Atlanta University Publications*. New York: Octagon Books, 1968.

Putnam, Frank. "The Negro's Part in New National Problems." *Colored American Magazine* 1, no. 2 (June 1900): 69–76.

Quarles, Benjamin. *Black Abolitionists*. New York: Oxford University Press, 1969.

———. *Black Mosaic: Essays in Afro-American History and Historiography*. Amherst: University of Massachusetts Press, 1988.

Rabinowitz, Howard. *Race Relations in the Urban South, 1865–1890*. Urbana: University of Illinois Press, 1980.

Rachleff, Peter. *Black Labor in Richmond, 1865–1890*. Urbana: University of Illinois Press, 1989.

Rafter, Nicole Hahn. *White Trash: The Eugenic Family Studies, 1877–1919*. Boston: Northeastern University Press, 1989.

Rampersad, Arnold. *The Art and Imagination of W. E. B. Du Bois*. Cambridge: Harvard University Press, 1989.

Redding, Jay Saunders. *No Day of Triumph*. New York: Harper and Brothers, 1942.

Redkey, Edwin S. *Black Exodus: Black Nationalist and Back-to-Africa Movements, 1890–1910*. New Haven, Conn.: Yale University Press, 1969.

"Report of First Universal Races Congress." *African Times and Orient Review* (July 1912): 27–30.

Reuter, Edward B. *Race Mixture*. New York: McGraw-Hill, 1931.

"Rhinelander." *Crisis* (January 1926): 112–13.

"Rhinelander-Jones Romance Goes to Smash on the Color Bar." *Negro World*, December 6, 1926.

Rich, Adrienne. "Compulsory Heterosexuality and Lesbian Existence." In *Blood, Bread, and Poetry: Selected Prose, 1979–1985*, pp. 23–75. New York: Norton, 1986.

Richards, Leonard L. *Gentlemen of Property and Standing: Anti-Abolition Mobs in Jacksonian America*. New York: Oxford University Press, 1970.

Roberts, Randy. *Papa Jack: Jack Johnson and the Era of White Hopes*. New York: Free Press, 1983.

Rodrigue, Jessie. "The Black Community and the Birth Control Movement." In *Passion and Power: Sexuality in History*, edited by Kathy Peiss and Christina Simmons, 138–54. Philadelphia: Temple University Press, 1989.

Roosevelt, Theodore. *The Strenuous Life: Essays and Addresses*. 1902. Reprint, New York: Scholarly Press, 1970.

Rudwick, Elliott M. *Race Riot in East St. Louis: July 2, 1917*. Cleveland: Meridian Books, 1966.

Santino, Jack. *Miles of Smiles, Years of Struggle: Stories of Black Pullman Porters*. Urbana: University of Illinois Press, 1989.

Saunders, James Robert. "The Dilemma of Double Identity: James Weldon Johnson's Artistic Acknowledgment." *Langston Hughes Review* 8, nos. 1 and 2 (Spring/Fall 1989): 68–75.

Scarborough, William S. "The Educated Negro and His Mission." *American Negro Academy, Occasional Papers, No. 8*. Washington, D.C.: American Negro Academy, 1903.

Scruggs, L. A., ed. *Women of Distinction: Remarkable in Works and Invincible in Character*. Raleigh, N.C.: L. A. Scruggs, 1893.

Sernett, Milton C. *Black Religion and American Evangelicalism*. Metuchen, N.J.: Scarecrow Press, 1975.

Shadrach, J. Shirley. "Furnace Blasts: Black or White—Which Should be the Young Afro-American's Choice in Marriage." *Colored American Magazine* 6, no. 5 (March 1903): 348–52.

———. "Furnace Blasts: The Growth of the Social Evil Among All Classes and Races in America." *Colored American Magazine* 6, no. 4 (February 1903): 259–63.

Shapiro, Herbert. "The Muckrakers and Negroes." *Phylon* 31, no. 1 (1970): 76–88.

———. *White Violence and Black Response*. Amherst: University of Massachusetts Press, 1988.

Shockley, Ann Allen, ed. *Afro-American Women Writers, 1746–1933: An Anthology and Critical Guide*. New York: New American Library, 1989.

Smith, Amanda. *An Autobiography: The Story of the Lord's Dealings with Mrs. Amanda Smith the Colored Evangelist*. New York: Oxford University Press, 1988.

Smith, Timothy L. *Revivalism and Social Reform: American Protestantism on the Eve of the Civil War*. New York: Harper Torchbooks, 1965.

Smith-Rosenberg, Carroll. *Disorderly Conduct: Visions of Gender in Victorian America*. New York: Oxford University Press, 1985.

Sochen, June, ed. *The Black Man and the American Dream: Negro Aspirations in America, 1900–1930*. Chicago: Quadrangle Books, 1971.

Sollors, Werner, Thomas A. Underwood, and Caldwell Titcomb, eds. *Varieties of Black Experience at Harvard*. Cambridge: Harvard University Department of Afro-American Studies, 1986.

Spear, Allan. *Black Chicago: The Making of a Negro Ghetto, 1890–1920*. Chicago: University of Chicago Press, 1967.

———. *Slave Culture*. New York: Oxford University Press, 1987.

Stein, Judith. "'Of Mr. Booker T. Washington and Others': The Political Economy of Racism in the United States." *Science and Society* 38 (Winter 1974–75): 422–63.

———. *The World of Marcus Garvey: Race and Class in Modern Society*. Baton Rouge: Louisiana State University Press, 1986.

Stemons, James Samuel. "The Unmentionable Crime." *Colored American Magazine* 6, no. 9 (September 1903): 636–41.

Stepan, Nancy L., and Sander Gilman. "Appropriating the Idioms of Science: The Rejection of Scientific Racism." In *The Bounds of Race: Perspectives on Hegemony and Resistance*, edited by Dominick LaCapra. Ithaca, N.Y.: Cornell University Press, 1991.

Sterling, Dorothy, ed. *We Are Your Sisters: Black Women in the Nineteenth Century*. New York: Norton, 1984.

Steward, Theophilus Gould. "Robert Purvis, Last Survivor of the American Anti-Slavery Society." *A.M.E. Church Review* 13, no. 2 (October 1896): 214–18.

Stewart, T. McCants. "Heredity In Character." *A.M.E. Church Review* 7, no. 1 (July 1890): 22–33.

Stidum, A. B. "Originality in Individual and Race Development." *A.M.E. Church Review* 7, no. 4 (April 1891): 408–12.

Stinson, Robert. "S. S. McClure's My Autobiography: The Progressive as Self-Made Man." *American Quarterly* 22 (Summer 1970): 203–12.

Straker, D. A. *The New South Investigated*. Detroit, 1888.

Stuckey, Sterling, ed. *The Ideological Origins of Black Nationalism*. Boston: Beacon Press, 1970.

Symanski, Richard. *The Immoral Landscape: Female Prostitution in Western Societies*. Toronto: Butterworths, 1981.

Takaki, Ronald. *Iron Cages: Race and Culture in 19th-Century America*. New York: Alfred A. Knopf, 1979.

Taylor, C. H. J. "Will He Survive?" *A.M.E. Church Review* 14, no. 2 (October 1897): 242–50.

Terrell, Mary Church. *A Colored Woman in a White World*. Washington, D.C.: Ransdell, 1940.

Terrell, Robert. "The Negro in Domestic Service," *Colored American Magazine* 9, no. 5 (November 1905): 631–33.

Thomas, William Hannibal. *The American Negro: What He Was, What He Is, and What He May Become*. New York: Macmillan, 1901.

Thornbrough, Emma Lou. *T. Thomas Fortune: Militant Journalist*. Chicago: University of Chicago Press, 1972.

Toll, Robert. *Blacking Up: The Minstrel Show in Nineteenth-Century America*. New York: Oxford University Press, 1974.

Trachtenberg, Alan. *The Incorporation of America: Culture and Society in the Gilded Age*. New York: Hill and Wang, 1982.

Tucker, Annie E. "Formation of Child Character." *Colored American Magazine* 2, no. 4 (February 1901): 258–61.

Tucker, Susan. *Telling Memories Among Southern Women: Domestic Workers and Their Employers in the Segregated South*. New York: Schocken Books, 1988.

Tyler, Ralph W. "Real Society." *Colored American Magazine* 13, no. 5 (November 1907): 391–92.

Vincent, Theodore G. *Voices of a Black Nation*. Trenton, N.J.: Africa World Press, 1973.

Wagstaff, Thomas, ed. *Black Power: The Radical Response to White America*. Beverly Hills, Calif.: Glencoe Press, 1969.

Walker, David. *Appeal to the Colored Citizens of the World*. New York: Hill and Wang, 1982.

Walker, Walter F. "The Young Man and the Church." *Alexander's Magazine* 2, no. 5 (September 1906): 37–41.

Wallace, Michele. *Invisibility Blues: From Pop to Theory*. London: Verso, 1990.

Washington, Booker T. "Industrial Education, Will it Solve the Negro Problem." *Colored American Magazine* 7, no. 2 (February 1904): 87–92.

———. "The Storm Before the Calm." *Colored American Magazine* 1, no. 2 (September 1900): 199–213.

———. *Up From Slavery*. New York: Penguin, 1986.

Washington, Mary Helen, ed. *Invented Lives: Narratives of Black Women, 1860–1960*. Garden City, N.Y.: Doubleday, 1987.

Weinstein, James. *The Corporate Ideal in the Liberal State*. Boston: Beacon Press, 1968.

Wells, Ida B. *On Lynchings*. Salem, N.H.: Ayer, 1987.

West, Cornel. *Keeping Faith: Philosophy and Race in America*. New York: Routledge, 1993.

Wexler, Laura. "Black and White in Color: American Photographs at the Turn of the Century." *Prospects* 13 (1988): 341–90.

White, Walter. *A Man Called White*. New York: Viking Press, 1948.

"Why the Men Don't Marry." *Colored American Magazine* 13, no. 5 (November 1907): 328–29.

Wiebe, Robert. *The Search for Order, 1877–1920*. New York: Hill and Wang, 1967.

Williams, F. B. "The Club Movement among the Colored Women." *Voice of the Negro* 1, no. 3 (1904): 99–100.

———. "Work Attempted and Missed in Organized Club Work." *Colored American Magazine* 14, no. 5 (May 1908): 281–85.

Williams, Raymond. *Culture and Society, 1780–1950.* New York: Doubleday, 1960.

———. *Marxism and Literature.* New York: Oxford University Press, 1978.

Williams, Walter L. *Black Americans and the Evangelization of Africa, 1877–1900.* Madison: University of Wisconsin Press, 1982.

Williamson, Joel. *New People: Miscegenation and Mulattoes in the United States.* New York: New York University Press, 1984.

Wolters, Raymond. *The New Negro on Campus: Black College Rebellions of the 1920s.* Princeton, N.J.: Princeton University Press, 1975.

Woodson, Carter G. *Mis-education of the Negro.* Washington, D.C.: Associated Publishers, 1987.

———. *The Negro as a Business Man.* 1921. Reprint, College Park, Md.: McGrath, 1969.

———. *The Negro Professional Man and the Community.* Washington, D.C.: Association for the Study of Negro Life and History, 1934.

———, ed. *Works of Francis Grimké.* Washington, D.C.: Associated Publishers, 1942.

Woodward, C. Vann. *Origins of the New South, 1877–1913.* Baton Rouge: Louisiana State University Press, 1951.

———. *The Strange Career of Jim Crow.* New York: Oxford University Press, 1966.

Young, Nathan B. "A Race Without an Ideal: What Must It Do to Be Saved? Or, The Negro's Third Emancipation." *A.M.E. Church Review* 15, no. 2 (October 1898): 605–17.

Unpublished Sources

Baker, Thomas N. "The Ethical Significance of the Connection Between Mind and Body." Ph.D. diss., Yale University, 1903. In the Sterling Library, Yale University.

Newman, Louise. "Ideologies of Womanhood at the Turn of the Century: A Re-Examination of Anna Julia Cooper's *A Voice From the South* (1892)." Paper given at the American Studies Association, New Orleans, Louisiana, November 2, 1990.

Siegal, James. "NAACP at the Crossroads: The Scottsboro Case and the Crisis of Black Leadership." B.A. thesis, Princeton University, 1992.

Terborg-Penn, Rosalyn, "Afro-Americans in the Struggle for Woman Suffrage." Ph.D. diss., Howard University, 1977.

INDEX

❨ ❨ ❨

Define uplift ideology , 67, 75
Defensive ~ oppressed - 41
nontool 52
assimilationist aesthetic 76

heuristic theodicy
Jim McAdams - Pol. Sci.
- American policy towards Africa
- Minority coalition formation
- urban

1:30 - Friday 103 Heshyh
12:30 Thursday (Kent.)

[Alvin Tillery]